7 day loan

Cou Poly
Cou Oni

Power, Strategy, and Security

Written under the auspices of the Center of International Studies, Princeton University. A list of other Center publications appears at the back of this book.

A *WORLD POLITICS* READER

Power, Strategy, and Security

EDITED BY

KLAUS KNORR

PRINCETON UNIVERSITY PRESS

Published by
Princeton University Press,
41 William Street,
Princeton, New Jersey 08540
In the United Kingdom:
Princeton University Press,
Guildford, Surrey
First Princeton Paperback
Printing, 1983
First Hardcover Printing, 1983
LCC 82-48561
ISBN 0-691-05665-X
ISBN 0-691-01071-4 pbk.

Clothbound editions of
Princeton University Press books
are printed on acid-free paper,
and binding materials are chosen
for strength and durability.
Paperbacks, while
satisfactory for personal
collections, are not usually
suitable for library rebinding.

Printed in
the United States of America
by Princeton University Press
Princeton, New Jersey

CONTENTS

THE CONTRIBUTORS

KLAUS KNORR is William Stewart Tod Professor of Public Affairs, Emeritus, at Princeton University. He has served as an editor of *World Politics* since its inception, and is at present Chairman of the Board of Editors.

DAVID A. BALDWIN is Professor of Government at Dartmouth College.

LOWELL DITTMER is Chairman of the Center for Chinese Studies, and Associate Professor of Political Science, at the University of California, Berkeley.

HEDLEY BULL is Professor of International Relations at Balliol College, Oxford.

LOUIS RENÉ BERES is Professor of Political Science at Purdue University.

JOHN STEINBRUNER is Director of Foreign Policy Studies at the Brookings Institution.

ANDREW J. R. MACK is a Research Fellow at the Richardson Institute for Conflict and Peace Research in London.

ROBERT JERVIS is Professor of Political Science and a member of the Research Institute on International Change at Columbia University.

AVI SHLAIM is a Lecturer in Politics at the University of Reading (England).

RICHARD K. BETTS is a Senior Fellow in the Foreign Policy Studies Program at the Brookings Institution.

I. M. DESTLER is a Senior Associate at the Carnegie Endowment for International Peace.

PREFACE

Judged by the frequency with which they have been used and quoted in the social science literature, the articles in this volume are among the best that *World Politics* has published over some years. Now offered as a *Reader*, they address a number of interconnected analytical problems on the role of national power in interstate relations, strategic configurations between powerful states, strategic theory and doctrine concerning nuclear arms, the effect of national commitment on the outcome of war, the fundamental difficulty of estimating the intentions of opponents and the roots of strategic surprise and, finally, some institutional aspects of national decision making in matters of foreign and military policy.

During the 1960s and 1970s, the majority of theorists doing research on international relations turned away from the phenomenon of power—especially military power—as a major determinant of such relationships. These specialists asserted that the usability of military power had drastically diminished, in part because of the emergence of nuclear arms. They developed and favored other concepts—such as international interdependence, non-power influences, and transnational configurations—in order to advance our understanding of global complexities and international linkages. This shift of analytical focus unquestionably added to our knowledge, but it unduly neglected the power variable in teaching and research. Whether we like it or not, national power and its uses—including military power—continue to engender significant and sometimes decisive impacts in the real world. Global military expenditures have gone up, not down. No recent year has been free from a number of armed conflicts raging somewhere in the world. On the other hand, sizable peace movements have sprung up in Europe, the United States, and Japan. It is important, therefore, that power phenomena and related problems be restored to their proper place in teaching and research. The articles in this volume should make a useful contribution toward this end.

David A. Baldwin's article is a masterly survey of theories regarding the recently neglected factor of power analysis. He presents a rich typology of international power and critically reviews the merits and demerits of key hypotheses. Lowell Dittmer, using both game theory and historical analysis, explores the logical choices of reciprocal behavior open to three major powers: the United States, the Soviet Union, and China. He demonstrates how they lead to modifications in the pattern of their relations.

The next three papers deal with various aspects of nuclear military strategy. Hedley Bull incisively examines the work of civilian strategists, a new and impressive development, and the criticisms to which it has been subjected because of the authors' neglect of nonrational behavior in decision making, moral considerations, and factors other than military force for purposes of deterring war. Louis René Beres turns to the recent shift in American nuclear doctrine from reliance on the deterrent threat of massive retaliation to a "countervailing" strategy of waging nuclear war if deterrence fails. He identifies and challenges several major assumptions on which the new strategy is based. John Steinbruner further probes one of these assumptions—i.e., that of rational decision makers. He shows it to be shaky in the real world of choosing the design, deployment, control, and use of nuclear weapons, and points to two intractable problems: controlling the nuclear arms race, and the way in which states should react in the event deterrence breaks down.

Andrew Mack convincingly explains the not infrequent defeat of a great power by a small one—as in the case of the United States' war in Vietnam—when the conflict is a limited one for the former and a total one for the latter. He shows that the outcome is likely if, on the one hand, the great power fighting for limited stakes is incapable of inducing the public to make sacrifices essential to success, while on the other hand, the war has absolute priority for the small country that is prepared to absorb enormous casualties and other costs in order to prevail.

Three articles deal with the crucial problem of perceiving external threats correctly and of escaping the blow of strategic surprise. Robert Jervis's essay presents an abbreviated version of the seminal work that gave us the first systematic treatment of international perception and the main conditions that tend to produce erroneous assessments of foreign intentions. Avi Shlaim addresses the question of why Israel was unable to foresee the Arab surprise attack in 1973 despite the fact that ample and accurate information was available in time. He traces several roots of the failure of Israeli intelligence, adding appreciably to our knowledge of the problems inherent in threat perception. Richard Betts explores the same problem in terms of organizational and procedural resources; he demonstrates that faults of perception cannot be prevented by institutional solutions because such mistakes result less from bad analysis than from ineradicable psychological predispositions. Finally, I. M. Destler discusses some major institutional problems in making decisions in foreign and military policy by scrutinizing the role of the National Security Council in the United States. He describes the impact of each President's personal abilities and needs, and by taking bureaucratic behavior into proper account, he clarifies the difficulties of institutional design for assistance in the making and execution of policy decisions.

Together, the ten papers are highly instructive in introducing the reader to a sophisticated understanding of a number of interrelated phenomena and the ways in which social scientists go about analyzing them.

KLAUS KNORR

Power, Strategy, and Security

POWER ANALYSIS AND WORLD POLITICS:
New Trends versus Old Tendencies

By DAVID A. BALDWIN*

FROM Niccolò Machiavelli and David Hume to E. H. Carr and Hans Morgenthau, power has been an important (some would say too important) variable in international political theorizing. Although some may regard power analysis as old-fashioned and outdated, recent refinements in social science thinking about power suggest the possibility of revitalizing this approach to understanding international relations.

Exact turning points in intellectual history are difficult to identify, but many would regard the publication of *Power and Society* by Harold Lasswell and Abraham Kaplan as the watershed between the older, intuitive and ambiguous treatments of power and the clarity and precision of more recent discussions.[1] Since then, Herbert Simon, James March, Robert Dahl, Jack Nagel, and others have developed the idea of power as a type of causation.[2] This causal conception of power, according to Nagel, has proved attractive for three reasons: First, there are compelling similarities between intuitive notions of power and

* An earlier version of this paper was presented at the Fourth Annual Conference of the British International Studies Association, University of Durham, December 15-17, 1977. The author would like to express his appreciation for the helpful comments provided by Conference participants and by Jeffrey Hart, Robert O. Keohane, and James P. Sewell.

[1] Harold D. Lasswell and Abraham Kaplan, *Power and Society* (New Haven: Yale University Press 1950). In an early and influential article, Herbert A. Simon described his discussion as "a series of footnotes on the analysis of influence and power by Lasswell and Kaplan." "Notes on the Observation and Measurement of Political Power," *Journal of Politics*, xv (November 1953), 501. See also Jack H. Nagel, "Some Questions About the Concept of Power," *Behavioral Science*, xiii (March 1968), 129.

[2] Simon (fn. 1), and *Models of Man* (New York: Wiley 1957); James G. March, "An Introduction to the Theory and Measurement of Influence," *American Political Science Review*, xlix (June 1955), 431-51; Robert A. Dahl, "The Concept of Power," *Behavioral Science*, ii (July 1957), 201-15, and "Power," *International Encyclopedia of the Social Sciences*, XII (New York: Free Press 1968), 405-15; Jack H. Nagel, *The Descriptive Analysis of Power* (New Haven: Yale University Press 1975); and Felix E. Oppenheim, "Power and Causation," in Brian Barry, ed., *Power and Political Theory: Some European Perspectives* (London: John Wiley 1976), 103-16.

Excellent reviews of the literature on power, reflecting both consensus and healthy intellectual dispute, are the following: Dorwin Cartwright, "Influence, Leadership, Control," in James March, ed., *Handbook of Organizations* (Chicago: Rand McNally 1965), 1-47; Dahl, "Power"; James T. Tedeschi and Thomas V. Bonoma, "Power and Influence: An Introduction," in Tedeschi, ed., *The Social Influence Processes* (Chicago: Aldine-Atherton 1972), 1-49; and Nagel, *The Descriptive Analysis of Power*.

causation. Second, causal conceptions of power are less likely to lead to tautologies. And third, "treatment of power as causation enables power researchers to employ methods developed for more general applications."[3]

Despite the ancient origins of the study of power, Dahl maintains that "the systematic empirical study of power relations is remarkably new."[4] He attributes the "vast improvement in the clarity" of power concepts to the fact that "the last several decades probably have witnessed more systematic efforts to tie down these concepts than have the previous millennia of political thought."[5] Even those who would dispute such assertions could agree that international political theorists might find it useful to rethink their views of power in terms of the recent literature on that subject.[6] The purpose of this article is to review some recent scholarship in international relations with special reference to the literature on social power.[7] Topics for discussion include potential power, interdependence, military power, positive sanctions, the zero-sum concept of power, and the distinction between compellence and deterrence.

Before the discussion begins, however, one *caveat* is in order. The increased precision in recent concepts of power has threatened to overwhelm the analyst. Even those most familiar with this literature have complained of interminable theoretical distinctions that make a broad overview difficult to achieve.[8] For purposes of this discussion, therefore, the term "power" will be used in a broad generic sense that is interchangeable with such terms as "influence" and "control." This usage is not intended to deny the validity or the utility of distinguishing among such terms for other purposes; it is intended to imply the relevance of the following discussion for all situations in which A gets B to do

[3] Nagel (fn. 2), 9-10.   [4] Dahl, "Power" (fn. 2), 414.
[5] Robert A. Dahl, *Modern Political Analysis* (3rd ed.; Englewood Cliffs, N.J.: Prentice-Hall 1976), 26.

[6] Two important recent works in international relations use Hans Morgenthau's textbook published in 1948 as their basic reference on power: Charles P. Kindleberger, *Power and Money* (New York: Basic Books 1970), and Robert Gilpin, *U.S. Power and the Multinational Corporation* (New York: Basic Books 1975).

[7] For a review of a different set of international relations works with regard to a different set of topics, see Baldwin, "Inter-Nation Influence Revisited," *Journal of Conflict Resolution*, xv (December 1971), 471-86. For a suggestion that current "academic practitioners of international relations analysis and theory" have neglected the study of power, see Colin S. Gray, *The Geopolitics of the Nuclear Era* (New York: Crane, Russak 1977), 1-5. Gray's contention that power analysis is the only approach that "enables students to appreciate the essence of the field" of international relations, however, goes considerably beyond the argument I am presenting here.

[8] Cartwright (fn. 2), 4; and Robert A. Dahl, *Modern Political Analysis* (2d ed., Englewood Cliffs, N.J.: Prentice-Hall 1970), 16.

something he would not otherwise do, regardless of how such situations are labeled.[9] The primary focus will be on basic distinctions *essential* to thinking about power rather than on distinctions that are useful in some contexts but irrelevant in others. In discussing power as a type of causation, it is *essential* to specify or at least imply who is influencing whom with respect to what; in short, both scope and domain must be specified or implied.[10] Such distinctions may seem obvious and trivial at first, but I will argue that insistence on them would orient discussions of international power less toward general theories of power and more toward contextual analysis.

POWER: POTENTIAL, PROBABLE, AND ACTUAL

The frequent failure of power predictions has been noted so often by scholars, journalists, statesmen, and the "man in the street" that it deserves a label—something like "the paradox of unrealized power." How is it that "weak powers" influence the "strong"? How is it that the "greatest power in the world" could suffer defeat at the hands of a "band of night-riders in black pajamas"?[11] How do we explain the "cruel and ridiculous paradox" of the "big influence of small allies"? How can the Arabs get away with defying the United States? How can tiny Israel exercise so much influence on U.S. foreign policy? I shall consider two alternative explanations of this so-called paradox.

First, failure to translate alleged "potential power" (or power "resources") into actual power may be explained in terms of malfunctioning conversion processes. The would-be wielder of power is described as lacking in skill and/or the "will" to use his power resources effectively: "The Arabs had the tanks but didn't know how to use them."

---

[9] For useful arguments in favor of the validity and desirability of distinguishing power from influence, see David V. J. Bell, *Power, Influence, and Authority* (New York: Oxford University Press 1975); and Klaus Knorr, *The Power of Nations: The Political Economy of International Relations* (New York: Basic Books 1975).

[10] On the importance of this point, see Lasswell and Kaplan (fn. 1), 76; Dahl, "Power" (fn. 2), 408; Dahl (fn. 5), 33; and Nagel (fn. 2), 14, 115. Among students of international politics, the strongest proponents of this view have been Harold and Margaret Sprout. See their *Man-Milieu Relationship Hypotheses in the Context of International Politics*, Center of International Studies, Princeton University, Research Monograph (Princeton 1956), 39-49; "Environmental Factors in the Study of International Politics," *Journal of Conflict Resolution*, I (December 1957), 309-28; *The Ecological Perspective on Human Affairs: With Special Reference to International Politics* (Princeton: Princeton University Press 1965), 83-98, 214-16; and *Toward a Politics of the Planet Earth* (New York: Van Nostrand 1971), 163-78.

[11] "I still believe he [President Johnson] found it viscerally inconceivable that what Walt Rostow kept telling him was 'the greatest power in the world' could not dispose of a collection of night-riders in black pajamas." Arthur Schlesinger, Jr., "The Quagmire Papers," *New York Review of Books* (December 16, 1971), 41.

"The Americans had the bombs but lacked the will to use them." "The large states controlled the money but lacked organizational unity." And so forth.[12] Bad luck, incompetence, and pusillanimity are the most common elements in such explanations. "He had the cards but played them poorly" is the theme.

A second explanation for the failure of power predictions focuses on variations in the scope, weight, and domain of power. As Harold and Margaret Sprout have reminded us many times, the capabilities (or potential power) of an actor must be set in the context of a "policy-contingency framework" specifying who is trying (or might try) to get whom to do what.[13] From this perspective, the failure of power predictions is likely to be attributed to faulty predictive techniques rather than to the actors themselves. The so-called "paradox of unrealized power" results from the mistaken belief that power resources useful in one policy-contingency framework will be equally useful in a different one. So-called "weak powers" influence so-called "strong powers" because of the power analyst's failure to account for the possibility that a country may be weak in one situation but strong in another. Planes loaded with nuclear weapons may strengthen a state's ability to deter nuclear attacks but may be irrelevant to rescuing the *Pueblo* on short notice. The ability to get other countries to refrain from attacking one's homeland is not the same as the ability to "win the hearts and minds of the people" in a faraway land. The theme of such explanations is not "he had the cards but played them poorly," but rather "he had a great bridge hand but happened to be playing poker."

In order to evaluate these alternative explanations of the "paradox of unrealized power," a closer examination of the concept of "power resources" is in order. What distinguishes power resources from other things? How fungible are power resources? What is the range of variation in the value of power resources? And what working assumptions about power resources are most suitable for international political analysis?

---

[12] For examples of this type of explanation, see Knorr (fn. 9), 9-14; 17-18; Robert O. Keohane and Joseph S. Nye, *Power and Interdependence: World Politics in Transition* (Boston: Little, Brown 1977), 11, 18-19, 53, 225; Dahl (fn. 5), 37; and Ray S. Cline, *World Power Assessment: A Calculus of Strategic Drift* (Boulder, Colo.: Westview Press 1975). The inclusion of Dahl in this list is somewhat anomalous since Dahl stresses variations in the scope and domain of power.

[13] Sprout and Sprout (fn. 10). Actually the Sprouts' concept of a "policy-contingency framework" goes beyond specification of scope and domain to include the time, place, and means of an influence attempt. For purposes of this article, however, the Sprouts' insistence that "policy-contingency frameworks" be specified will be treated as roughly equivalent to Dahl's insistence that scope and domain be specified.

How are we to recognize power resources when we see them? Implicitly or explicitly, almost everyone conceives of such resources as the "means by which one person [actor] can influence the behavior of other persons [actors]."[14] One problem is that it is difficult to imagine what is excluded, since almost anything could be used to influence someone to do something in some situation or another. Another problem is that the means by which one actor can influence the behavior of another depends on who is trying to get whom to do what. A pleasant smile may suffice as a means to get the boss's attention, but a threat to quit may be required to get a raise. Diplomatic pressure may suffice to gain support on a relatively unimportant vote in the U.N. General Assembly, but force may be necessary to get a country to relinquish land claims. What functions as a power resource in one policy-contingency framework may be irrelevant in another. The only way to determine whether something is a power resource or not is to place it in the context of a real or hypothetical policy-contingency framework.[15] Prior to the 19th century, neither oil nor uranium were power resources, since no one had any use for them. Only within the policy-contingency framework of the last hundred years or so have they become resources.

Although it might seem that the predictive value of power resource inventories is impaired by insistence on prior specification of scope and domain (or policy-contingency framework), the opposite is true. The accuracy of our estimate of whether an architect has "adequate" raw materials to complete his project is likely to improve if we first ascertain whether he plans to build a birdhouse or a cathedral.

If there were some generalized means of exercising political power —just as money is a generalized means of exercising purchasing power —the problem of conceiving and measuring political power would be much simpler.[16] Political power resources, however, tend to be much less liquid than economic resources. The owner of an economic resource, such as a petroleum field, has little trouble converting it into another economic resource, such as a factory; but the owner of a political power resource, such as the means to deter atomic attack, is likely to have difficulty converting this resource into another resource

[14] Dahl (fn. 5), 37.
[15] "It seems that what we call a 'resource' is such, not on its own account, but solely because of the uses to which it can be put, and its quantitative aspect, how much resource there is, is still more evidently determinable only in terms of the use." Frank H. Knight, Risk, Uncertainty, and Profit (New York: Harper & Row 1921), 65-66.
[16] For a comparison of political power and purchasing power which emphasizes the absence of a political counterpart to money, see Baldwin, "Money and Power," Journal of Politics, xxxiii (August 1971), 578-614.

that would, for instance, allow his country to become the leader of the Third World. Whereas money facilitates the exchange of one economic resource for another, there is no standardized measure of value that serves as a medium of exchange for political power resources.

That is not to say that some political power resources are not more fungible than others. One could rank-order power resources according to fungibility; that is, those most likely to be effective in most situations with regard to most people over the most scopes would rank high. Although agreement on the rank-ordering would be far from complete, one would expect money, time, information, and a reputation for making credible threats or promises to rank generally high; while two-headed goats, smog, hula hoops, and asses' jawbones would rank generally low. Despite such variation in the fungibility of political power resources, it is important to recognize that *no political power resource begins to approach the degree of fungibility of money.*[17] As a group, political power resources are relatively low in fungibility; that is precisely why specification of scope and domain is so essential in analyzing political power.

If the range of variation in the effectiveness of power resources were relatively narrow, explaining the failure of power predictions in terms of A's inability or unwillingness to convert his resources into actual power would be less objectionable. As it is, however, even a *caveat* to the effect that power resources in one issue-area may lose some of their effectiveness when applied to another does not suffice. Power resources (or assets) in one policy-contingency framework may not only lose their effectiveness in another context; they may actually become liabilities rather than assets. Threatening voters with nuclear attack is not merely one of the less effective ways to win a mayoral election in New Haven; it is a guarantee of defeat. Possession of nuclear weapons is not just irrelevant to securing the election of a U.S. citizen as U.N. Secretary-General; it is a hindrance. "First-strike weapons" may not only decline in effectiveness in deterrent situations; they may actually impair one's ability to deter.[18]

The source of this problem is the failure to insist that scope and

[17] See Joseph S. Nye, Jr., and Robert O. Keohane, "Transnational Relations and World Politics," *International Organization,* xxv (Summer 1971), 736; Robert O. Keohane and Joseph S. Nye, "World Politics and the International Economic System," in C. Fred Bergsten, ed., *The Future of the International Economic Order: An Agenda for Research* (Lexington, Mass.: Lexington Books 1973), 121; Keohane and Nye (fn. 12), 146. For an extended critique of the analogy between power and money, see Baldwin, "Money and Power" (fn. 16).

[18] See Thomas C. Schelling, *The Strategy of Conflict* (Cambridge, Mass.: Harvard University Press 1960), 205-54.

domain be specified with regard to power resources as well as to power relationships. Money, tanks, bombs, information, and allies are often called "power resources"; but one can easily imagine plausible policy-contingency frameworks within which each of these becomes a liability rather than an asset. To insist that the scope and domain of power resources be specified would probably inhibit (but not prevent) the development of general theories of international power relationships and promote the development of contextual analyses of power. Such contextual power analysis is precisely what Lasswell and Kaplan were calling for:

> Failure to recognize that power may rest on various bases, each with a varying scope, has confused and distorted the conception of power itself, and retarded inquiry into the conditions and consequences of its exercise in various ways. . . .
>
> In particular, it is of crucial importance to recognize that power may rest on various bases, differing not only from culture to culture, but also within a culture from one power structure to another. . . .
>
> What is common to all power and influence relations is only effect on policy. What is affected and on what basis are variables whose specific content in a given situation can be determined only by inquiry into the actual practices of the actors in that situation. . . .
>
> Political analysis must be contextual, and take account of the power practices actually manifested in the concrete political situation.[19]

Although a contextual approach to power analysis would undoubtedly reduce the parsimony of theorizing about power, this disadvantage is less serious than it seems. Specification of scope and domain need not imply atheoretical empiricism. Policy-contingency frameworks can be defined more or less specifically to suit the purpose of the analyst. As the Sprouts put it:

> Estimates of capabilities covering all members of the society of nations in all imaginable contingencies would run to millions of combinations and permutations. No government, even more emphatically no university or private individual, could conceivably carry out so massive a research and analysis. Nor is any such undertaking contemplated or needed by anyone. A great many contingencies—for example, Canadian-U.S. military confrontation—are too remote to justify any consideration. By a process of elimination, one comes eventually to a hard core of contingencies that seem more or less likely to set the major patterns of international politics in the years to come, and with regard to which the relative capabilities of interacting nations are not self-evident.[20]

[19] Lasswell and Kaplan (fn. 1), 85, 92, 94.

[20] Sprout and Sprout, *Toward a Politics of the Planet Earth* (fn. 10), 178. Dahl makes a similar point regarding the possibility of comparing policy-contingency frame-

Emphasis on policy-contingency frameworks could improve theorizing about international politics by encouraging the development of "middle-level" theories and by forcing the acknowledgment of assumptions that are often left implicit; e.g., the assumption of war-winning capacity that is implicit in much balance-of-power theorizing.[21]

The question of whether to emphasize the fungibility or lack of fungibility of power resources is not a black-and-white issue. The fruitful way to pose the question is: "What working assumption about the fungibility of power resources is most useful for international political analysis during the next decade?" How one answers this question will depend partly on the extent to which one believes power resources to be fungible, and partly on the particular distortions in current thinking about international power relationships that one regards as most in need of correction. The demonstrations by Schelling[22] that even slight changes in the context of an influence attempt can convert a power asset into a power liability, the recent painful demonstration that the "most powerful state the world has ever known" could not achieve its goals in Southeast Asia, and the effect of the 1973 Arab oil embargo on U.S. foreign policy suggest that political power resources are much less fungible than has often been implied. Among students of international politics there is a tendency to exaggerate the fungibility of power resources, often to the point of ignoring scope and domain; but there is hardly any example of international power analysis that exaggerates the importance of contextual variables, i.e., the policy-contingency framework. In the absence of contrary evidence, I would

---

works: "Power comparability will have to be interpreted in the light of the specific requirements of research and theory, in the same way that the decision as to whether to regard any two objects—animals, plants, atoms, or whatnot—as comparable depends upon general considerations of classification and theoretical import. To this extent, and to this extent only, the decision is 'arbitrary'; but it is not more 'arbitrary' than other decisions that establish the criteria for a class of objects." "The Concept of Power" (fn. 2), 209. Nagel also notes that "domain and scope need not be particularistic or unique. Depending on one's purpose and the limits imposed by reality, the outcome class may contain a few similar members or many diverse elements." (Fn. 2), 14.

[21] Two excellent yet quite different examples of power theorizing based on explicit recognition that power configurations vary from one policy-contingency framework to another are Keohane and Nye (fn. 12), and Hayward Alker, "On Political Capabilities in a Schedule Sense: Measuring Power, Integration, and Development," in Hayward Alker, Karl W. Deutsch, and Antoine Stoetzel, eds., *Mathematical Approaches to Politics* (San Francisco: Jossey-Bass 1973), 307-73. The former work illustrates the value of "middle-level" empirical theorizing about power; the latter work demonstrates that abstract model-building is not precluded by the assumption that power is multi-dimensional.

[22] Schelling (fn. 18).

propose that the international political analyst start with the assumption that power resources are situationally specific. As evidence of fungibility is discovered, appropriate modifications in this working assumption can be made.

Although Keohane and Nye are clearly skeptical about the fungibility of power resources, they appear unwilling to place the burden of proof on those who maintain that power resources are highly fungible. They note that "one of our most important analytical tasks is . . . to understand the exceptions and limitations to basic structural hypotheses that rest on assumptions about the fungibility of power."[23] Whereas they place the burden of proof on those who purport to find exceptions to assumptions of *highly* fungible power, the approach advocated here would place the burden of proof on those who purport to find evidence of exceptions to assumptions that power resources tend to be *low* in fungibility. Whereas the Sprouts and Dahl[24] reject as practically meaningless any statement about influence that does not clearly indicate scope, Keohane and Nye confine themselves to the suggestion that "we may need to reevaluate the usefulness of the homogeneous conception of power."[25]

The "paradox of unrealized power," then, can be explained either in terms of inadequate conversion processes or in terms of mistaken judgments regarding the fungibility of power resources. The latter explanation is preferable for two reasons. First, the emphasis on A's inability and/or unwillingness to convert his alleged power resources into actual power encourages sloppy power analysis. No matter how inept the power analyst has been at estimating A's power resources, the failure of A to influence B can always be attributed to A's lack of commitment, or incompetent execution of the influence attempt. To take it to an absurd but illuminating extreme, one can imagine a power analyst saying, "I just don't understand how a country with so many two-headed goats, so much smog, and so many asses' jawbones could have lost World War III. It must have been due to a lack of skill or commitment on the part of the leaders." To take it to an equally illuminating, more painful, but less absurd point, one frequently hears the following: "I just don't understand how a country with so many nuclear weapons and so many soldiers could have failed to accomplish

[23] Keohane and Nye (fn. 12), 146-47.
[24] Dahl, "Power" (fn. 2), 408; Sprout and Sprout, "Environmental Factors . . ." (fn. 10), 325.
[25] Keohane and Nye, "World Politics and the International System" (fn. 17), 163.

its goals in Vietnam. It must have been caused by clumsy and spineless national leadership." Emphasis on skill and will in conversion processes makes it all too easy for the power analyst to avoid facing up to his mistakes. In estimating the *capabilities* of states, the probability of successful conversion should be included in the estimate. In estimating *probable* power, the likelihood of sufficient commitment should also be included.

A second reason for rejecting the conversion-process explanation in favor of the relative-infungibility explanation is that the latter is more likely to focus attention on the contextual nature of power. Whereas the former approach draws attention to the skill of the would-be power wielder, the latter treats such skill as just another resource and focuses attention on the actual or postulated policy-contingency framework within which capabilities are being estimated. Thus, the conversion-process analyst is more likely to attribute the failure of A's threatened beating of B to get B to do X to A's clumsy execution of the threat, but the relative-infungibility analyst is more likely to point out that since B is a masochist, A's threat was doomed to fail from the beginning.[26]

Let us examine some recent examples of international power analysis from the perspective of a relative-infungibility analyst.[27] Knorr, in *The Power of Nations*, emphasizes the importance of the distinction between putative and actualized power; he notes that the frequent failure to convert the former into the latter is a source of puzzlement to many. The distinction, according to Knorr, is between power as a "means" and power as an "effect." Power as a "means" is something that nations "have and can accumulate."[28]

At this point, the relative-infungibility analyst is likely to ask two questions: First, why is the distinction not made in terms of potential and actual effects? That would be straightforward and would retain the basic relational quality of the concept of power.[29] The distinction between an actual and a postulated relation between A and B should

---

[26] The idea that power resources or "power bases" could be identified without reference to the value system of the person or group to be influenced is not found in Lasswell and Kaplan. They make it clear that power relations presuppose B's value system. (Fn. 1), 76-77, 83-84.

[27] Generally speaking, I consider this to be the perspective of all those who emphasize the importance of scope specification, policy-contingency frameworks, and/or contextual analysis, including Lasswell and Kaplan (fn. 1), the Sprouts (fn. 10), and Dahl (fn. 2).

[28] Knorr (fn. 9), 9.

[29] Cf. Nagel (fn. 2), 172-73.

be easy enough for most readers to grasp. In describing putative power as a means that can be possessed and accumulated, Knorr risks obscuring the relational nature of power and returning to the earlier concept of power as an undifferentiated quantifiable mass. A similar risk is incurred when Knorr describes putative power as "inherent in the things of value" that A is ready to give.[30] A relational concept of power assumes that actual or potential power is never inherent in properties of A, but rather inheres in the actual or potential relationship between A's properties and B's value system. Knorr views putative power as "capabilities that permit the power wielder to make effective threats."[31] These capabilities may be transformed into actual power through a conversion process in which the crucial variables are B's perceptions, values, and propensities. The problem is that such variables must be considered in determining whether A has putative power in the first place, since the effectiveness or potential effectiveness of a threat depends partially on B's perceptions of it and on B's value system. *Before* one postulates whether he is dealing with a coward or a masochist, one can say nothing whatever about the potential effectiveness of a threat. *Before* one can attribute putative power to A, one must postulate a scenario or set of scenarios which specify whom A might try to influence and in what respects. Consideration of B's perceptions, values, and skills cannot be delayed until it is time to discuss A's ability to convert his putative power into actual power. If B's perceptions, values, and skills are such as to make it impossible for A to influence him, then putative power should never have been attributed to A in the first place.

A second question that might be asked is whether Knorr makes it sufficiently clear that there are no generalized means of exercising political power. The means that work in one policy-contingency framework may be counterproductive or irrelevant in another. Although Knorr notes that actualized power differs in weight, scope, and domain,[32] he fails to apply these distinctions to putative power. There is no reason to believe, however, that statements about potential power are less subject to the requirement to specify scope and domain than are statements about actual power relationships.

Cline's *World Power Assessment* represents the polar opposite of the type of contextual analysis advocated by the Sprouts and Lasswell and

[30] Knorr (fn. 9), 313.
[31] *Ibid.*, 9.
[32] *Ibid.*, 18.

Kaplan. Cline's basic conceptual framework is a formula for measuring national power:

$$Pp = (C + E + M) \times (S + W)$$

where:

Pp = perceived power
C = critical mass = population + territory
E = economic capability
M = military capability
S = strategic purpose
W = will to pursue national strategy.[33]

This formula is applied to forty nations, each receiving a number representing "total weighted units of perceived power."[34] The United States is assigned 35 such units; the Soviet Union gets 67.5.

For the most part, Cline's analysis ignores questions of scope and domain. Although he defines power as the ability of one government to cause another government to do something it would not otherwise do, there is little or no indication that power resources useful in causing one government to do X may be useless or counterproductive in causing another government to do Y.[35]

Whereas the Sprouts insist that strategies (actual or postulated) be treated as *givens* in capability analysis, Cline treats strategy as a variable to be discussed *after* weights have already been assigned to the other variables. Whereas Cline assigns power weights to territory and population, the Sprouts maintain that "such data acquire political relevance only when viewed in some frame of assumptions as to what is to be attempted, by whom, when and where, vis-à-vis what adversaries, allies, and unaligned onlookers."[36]

In allocating weights for national strategy, Cline assigns high values to countries with "clearcut strategic plans for international aggrandizement" and low values to those without such plans. American strategy is given 0.3, while Russian strategy receives 0.8. Toward the end of

---

[33] Cline (fn. 12), 11. Cline's book is especially interesting as an indication of how power analysis is performed by high-level government officials. He has served as Deputy Director for Intelligence in the CIA and as Director of Intelligence and Research in the Department of State.

[34] *Ibid.*, 130.

[35] Cline describes power as "a subjective factor" (*ibid.*, 8) and uses the term "perceived power" in his formula. In a puzzling footnote, however, he indicates that "real power" is something different from "perceived power" (p. 12n). The distinction is not developed, thus leaving one wondering about the significance of the formula.

[36] Sprout and Sprout, *Toward a Politics of the Planet Earth* (fn. 10), 177.

. the book, Cline describes his preferred strategy for the United States and admits that this strategy has been "implicit in the situation described in preceding pages of this book."[37] A relative-infungibility analyst might point out that it would have been helpful if Cline had made such policy assumptions explicit earlier in the book.

Despite the fact that one can eventually ferret out the vague and implicit policy-contingency framework underlying Cline's *World Power Assessment*, the wisdom of treating power at such an abstract general level may be questioned. If one wanted to promote the idea of power as monolithic, homogeneous, unidimensional and highly fungible, it would be difficult to improve on Cline's approach.

In *Power and Money*, Kindleberger differentiates between "strength" and "power" along lines similar to the distinction between potential and actual power. He treats strength as a means which "exists independently of whether it is used to assert or achieve control over policies of other countries" and power as strength capable of being used effectively.[38] This definition of power, he claims, "does not imply a purpose." But power divorced from purpose begins to sound like generalized or highly fungible power. In context, however, it is clear that Kindleberger intends the statement to differentiate probable from potential power in the sense that a state may have the potential power to influence the policies of another state, but may have neither the intention nor the desire to actually exercise such power. The weakness in Kindleberger's concept of power is that he implies that power can be divorced completely from goals or purposes. Although it is true that potential power does not imply actual purposes, it does imply at least a hypothetical purpose in the sense of a postulated policy-contingency framework.

In considering the "paradox of unrealized power," it has been argued that the most useful way to resolve the paradox is by tying power analysis more closely to specific contexts. I have suggested that one of the most crucial weaknesses in current thinking about international power relationships is the failure to specify scope and domain, and the consequent tendency to exaggerate the fungibility of power resources. In order to demonstrate the usefulness of contextual power analysis, I shall conclude with an examination of the problem of "worst-case" analysis from the perspective of the above discussion.

[37] Cline (fn. 12), 134-35.
[38] Kindleberger (fn. 6), 56. He defines power in terms of ability to use strength "efficiently" at one point (p. 56) and in terms of ability to use strength "effectively" at another point (p. 65). In the context of power analysis the difference is not trivial.

In worst-case analysis, the assumption is that preparing for the worst is wise and prudent policy. This assumption, often espoused by military thinkers, is usually associated with the idea that policymakers should concentrate on assessing the *capability* of other actors more than (or rather than) on the *intentions* of other actors. "Why not prepare for the worst?" is a superficially appealing slogan that must be refuted each year when military appropriations are being considered. Recognition of the multidimensional nature of power and the low fungibility of power resources is vital in showing why worst-case analysis is not a wise and prudent basis for policy. The reason may be demonstrated by comparing political power with purchasing power.

Storing up purchasing power in order to be able to deal with unforeseen financial catastrophies is an ancient, honorable, and prudent undertaking. The existence of a common denominator of economic value that also serves as a medium of exchange (i.e., money) enables us to treat economic resources *as if* they were unidimensional, thereby allowing us to prepare *simultaneously* for small, medium, and large financial difficulties. The fact that I am indebted to druggists, farmers, the government, bankers, and insurance companies for a wide variety of goods and services hardly matters, since I can use the same purchasing power resource—money—to pay them all. This is why we say that money is highly fungible. In dealing with problems of purchasing power, more money is almost always better than less. Aside from tax problems, it is difficult (but not impossible) to imagine a situation in which too much money prevents one from exercising one's purchasing power.

Political power is quite different from purchasing power. There is no common denominator of political value corresponding to money in terms of which political debts can be discharged. The lack of fungibility of political power resources means that preparing to deal with the worst contingencies may hinder one's ability to deal with less severe ones. ("The worst may be the enemy of the bad!") Thus, preparing for a nuclear first strike may weaken a country's deterrent capability; preparing for nuclear war may weaken a country's ability to get one of its citizens elected Secretary General of the U.N.; preparing for a seven-year famine may weaken a nation's ability to resist the demands of poor countries for food aid; preparing for military domination of the world may make it hard to win the hearts and minds of the people; and preparing for autarky may hurt a country's bargaining ability in international trade negotiations. Because political power is multidimensional and political power resources are low in fungibility, more power in one policy-contingency framework may mean less in another. Although in terms of purchasing power, more is almost always better than less, the same cannot be said of any particular kind of political power. Since not all contingencies are equally probable, policy makers who prepare for the worst and ignore the intentions of other nations may wind up preparing for a very costly but unlikely contingency at the expense of preparing for a less devastating but more likely contingency. Such policy makers are neither wise nor prudent.

POWER AND INTERDEPENDENCE

Everyone seems to agree that "interdependence" is important; but not everyone agrees on how it should be defined, or on whether it is increasing or decreasing.[39] Although many would agree that interdependence refers to a situation in which states are "significantly" affected by their interaction, there is less agreement as to how to differentiate "significant" effects from "insignificant" ones. Three possibilities may be considered. First, interaction can be equated with interdependence. It is sometimes suggested that this denotes mere interconnectedness rather than interdependence.[40] Second, interdependence can be defined in terms of interactions (or transactions) that have reciprocal costly effects.[41] The difficulty with this definition is that many forms of international interaction, such as trade, involve reciprocal costly effects but not mutual dependency. Such a conception does not seem to capture the notion of dependence underlying the use of that term in common parlance. Buying what is easy to buy elsewhere (e.g., sand) or buying what is easy to do without (e.g., caviar) are not usually considered to create dependency, although both kinds of transactions involve costs for each trading partner.[42] In conceiving of dependence or interdepend-

---

[39] See Oran R. Young, "Interdependencies in World Politics," *International Journal*, XXIV (Autumn 1969), 726-50; Richard Rosecrance and Arthur Stein, "Interdependence: Myth or Reality?" *World Politics*, XXVI (October 1973), 1-27; Kenneth Waltz, "The Myth of Interdependence," in Charles Kindleberger, ed., *The International Corporation* (Cambridge, Mass.: The MIT Press 1970), 205-23; Robert O. Keohane and Joseph S. Nye, "International Interdependence and Integration," in Nelson W. Polsby and Fred I. Greenstein, eds., *Handbook of Political Science*, VIII, *International Politics* (Reading, Mass.: Addison-Wesley 1975), 363-414.

[40] Alex Inkeles, "The Emerging Social Structure of the World," *World Politics*, XXVII (July 1975), 467-95, esp. 477-86.

[41] This definition seems to be the basic concept of interdependence espoused by Keohane and Nye (fn. 12), 8-9. There is some ambiguity about this point, however, since their concept of "vulnerability interdependence" corresponds more closely with the idea of interdependence as transactions that are mutually costly to forego.

[42] The pioneering work by Albert O. Hirschman, *National Power and the Structure of Foreign Trade* (Berkeley: University of California 1945) is still the best statement

ence, the relevant costs are not those involved in *carrying out* the transaction, but rather those involved in *foregoing* it. Not everyone who drinks is an alcoholic; not everyone who smokes is an addict; and not every international trading relationship involves dependency. The true measure of our dependency on imported oil is not what we have to give up in order to get it, but rather what we would have to give up in order to go without it. The smoker who can quit whenever he wants to is not an addict; the drinker who can take it or leave it is not an alcoholic; and the country that can easily forego imported oil is not dependent on it. This basic insight of the Stoics deserves reiteration in the context of discussions of interdependence.

A third way to conceive of interdependence, then, is in terms of relationships that are costly for each party to forego.[43] This conception of interdependence has three advantages over most others. First, it captures the intuitive notion of dependency underlying most common parlance. Second, it is consistent with the theoretical treatments of dependency by Thibaut and Kelley, Emerson, and Blau.[44] Although these works are well known in the literature on social power, they are rarely cited in discussions of international interdependence.[45] Cross-fertilization between the social power literature and the international relations literature is more likely if our fundamental concepts of de-

---

of the relationship between trade and dependency. "The influence which country A acquires in country B by foreign trade depends in the first place upon the total gain which B derives from that trade; the total gain from trade for any country is indeed nothing but another expression for the total impoverishment which would be inflicted upon it by a stoppage of trade. In this sense, the classical concept, gain from trade, and the power concept, dependence on trade, now being studied are seen to be merely two aspects of the same phenomenon" (p. 18). See also Jean-Jacques Rousseau, *The First and Second Discourses*, trans. Roger D. Masters and Judith R. Masters (New York: St. Martin's Press 1964), 36n, and *On the Social Contract*, trans. Judith R. Masters; ed. Roger D. Masters (New York: St. Martin's Press 1978), 74n.

[43] See Waltz (fn. 39); also Inkeles (fn. 40), 483-88; Stephen D. Krasner, "State Power and the Structure of International Trade," *World Politics*, xxviii (April 1976), 317-47, at 320. Note that the concept of interdependence as entailing relations that would be mutually costly to break need not imply that such relations are "positive" or "beneficial" for the participants. It merely implies that those involved have a choice, and that in choosing to maintain the relationship they forego some other alternative.

[44] John W. Thibaut and Harold H. Kelley, *The Social Psychology of Groups* (New York: Wiley 1959), 100-125; Richard M. Emerson, "Power-Dependence Relations," *American Sociological Review*, xxvii (February 1962), 31-41; Peter M. Blau, *Exchange and Power in Social Life* (New York: Wiley 1964), 118-25, 133, 197. If a graduate student were to ask me where to begin the study of international interdependence, I should direct attention to these writers and to Hirschman (fn. 42) rather than to more recent treatments of this topic in the international relations literature.

[45] The extensive bibliography on interdependence compiled by Keohane and Nye for the *Handbook of Political Science* (fn. 39) contains no entry for any of the authors cited in the preceding footnote—including Hirschman.

pendency are compatible. A third advantage of this conception of interdependence is that it facilitates thinking about the links between dependency and power. In order to study dependency, one must look at opportunity costs of alternative relationships as well as at actual relationships. Likewise, in order to study power, one must look not only at what B does, but at what B would otherwise do.

Interdependence interests international theorists primarily because of its relationship to power. If A and B are mutually dependent on one another, then each could inflict costs on the other by severing the relationship. And the ability to inflict costs on other actors is one measure of influence.[46] Thus, to say that A and B are interdependent implies that they possess the ability to influence one another in some respect. (Note that this approach does not involve the difficulty of describing a gun as a power resource only to discover that one is trying to influence someone who wants to be shot. Both the value systems and the available alternatives for each actor must be considered in determining whether severance of the relationship would entail costs.) In this sense, interdependence *always* implies mutual potential power of some kind. Whether either actor will be able to influence the other to a satisfactory degree, soon enough, with respect to the desired scopes, or at acceptable cost to itself, is quite another matter. As Young has pointed out, a rising level of interdependence increases both the opportunities and the costs of exercising power.[47]

If dependency and power are closely linked concepts, some of the distinctions useful in studying one may be useful in studying the other. Knorr has outlined a number of such distinctions in his discussion of interdependence.[48] Just as power relationships vary in scope, weight, domain, and symmetry, so do relationships of interdependency: contextual analysis may be as appropriate for the study of interdependence as it is for the study of power.

Keohane and Nye suggest that in order to understand the role of power in interdependence, we must distinguish between "sensitivity" and "vulnerability."[49] "Sensitivity interdependence" refers to the liability to incur costly effects within a given policy framework; "vulnerability interdependence" refers to the liability to incur costly effects even after the policy framework has been altered. For example, "sensitivity

---

[46] Cf. John C. Harsanyi, "Measurement of Social Power, Opportunity Costs, and the Theory of Two-Person Bargaining Games," *Behavioral Science*, VII (January 1962), 67-80; and Nagel (fn. 1).

[47] Young (fn. 39), 746-47. [48] Knorr (fn. 9), 207-10.

[49] Keohane and Nye (fn. 12), 11-12.

interdependence" could be used to refer to the costs of working within the framework of the Bretton Woods monetary regime during the late 1960's; "vulnerability interdependence" could be used to refer to the costs associated with changing to a different international monetary regime. The distinction between the two types of interdependence indicates that dependence, like power, varies from one policy-contingency framework to another. Sensitivity interdependence and vulnerability interdependence are simply labels applied to particular kinds of policy-contingency frameworks. Although Keohane and Nye use these distinctions imaginatively to generate important observations about world politics, the distinctions themselves represent no new theoretical insights. Lasswell and Kaplan, Dahl, and the Sprouts have previously pointed out that power relationships in one policy-contingency framework are likely to differ from those in another.

Instead of treating the distinction between sensitivity interdependence and vulnerability interdependence as one of many ways to differentiate among policy-contingency frameworks, Keohane and Nye maintain that the distinction is essential to understanding the "role of power in interdependence."[50] In answer to the question of how this distinction helps us to understand the relationship between interdependence and power, they reply: "Clearly, it indicates that sensitivity interdependence will be less important than vulnerability interdependence in providing power resources to actors."[51] As an empirical proposition, this answer is debatable; as a logical deduction, it is a *non sequitur*. Consider the example of a marriage. Sensitivity interdependence could be used to refer to the costs associated with working nonviolently within the framework of the marriage, of "making the marriage work." Vulnerability interdependence could be used to refer to the costs associated with violent divorce. Although the husband might have the advantage in terms of brute force and economic ability to survive a divorce, it is not clear that this power resource would be more important than the power resources provided by sensitivity interdependence. If both husband and wife were strongly committed to nonviolent resolution of conflict within the framework of the marriage, the power resources associated with asymmetrical vulnerability interdependence might be of little or no importance compared to those associated with sensitivity interdependence. Likewise, if nation-states have a strong commitment to making a given international regime work, the power resources associated with sensitivity interdependence may be more im-

[50] *Ibid.*   [51] *Ibid.*, 15.

portant than those associated with vulnerability interdependence.[52] If revolution is "unthinkable," the ability to foment a revolution is not a particularly useful power resource. In the absence of information or assumptions about the degree of commitment to maintaining a given policy framework, one can say *nothing* about the relative importance of the power resources provided by sensitivity interdependence and vulnerability interdependence. Although Keohane and Nye have formulated a useful distinction, they have overestimated its importance for understanding the relation between power and interdependence.

It has recently been suggested that Dahl's concept of power is incapable of dealing with interdependence.[53] Since Dahl is close to the "mainstream" of contemporary thinking about social power, some consideration of this viewpoint is in order. It will be argued that Dahl's concept is capable of dealing with interdependence and that the contrary claim is based on a distorted view of Dahl's position. Hart's argument is based on a distinction among three conceptions of power: (1) as control over resources, (2) as control over actors, and (3) as control over events and outcomes. Dahl's concept of power as the ability of A to get B to do what he would otherwise not do is classified as (2): control over actors.[54] Such a classification seriously distorts Dahl's idea, since his concept of power includes *both* actors and outcomes as necessary components. Dahl's insistence that statements about power that fail to specify scope verge on meaninglessness underscores the fact that his concept of power concerns the ability of one actor to influence another actor *with respect to certain outcomes*. In the literature on social power, Dahl's position is often referred to in terms of control over outcomes and is sometimes even classified as an "outcome definition."[55] As Nagel points out, anyone who employs a causal concept of power, such as Dahl's, must state the outcome caused.[56]

Hart's suggestion that Dahl's concept of power cannot account for the possibility of interdependence among actors is puzzling.[57] In the mutual nuclear deterrence between the Soviet Union and the United

[52] The distinction between "sensitivity" interdependence and "vulnerability" interdependence bears some resemblance to that between limited war and "total" (or not-so-limited) war. The policy constraints are obviously fewer in one situation than in the other. For a demonstration that ability to fight a "total" war may be of little help in fighting a limited war, see Charles Wolf, Jr., "The Logic of Failure: A Vietnam 'Lesson,'" *Journal of Conflict Resolution*, xvi (September 1972), 397-401.
[53] Jeffrey Hart, "Three Approaches to the Measurement of Power in International Relations," *International Organization*, xxx (Spring 1976), 297, 303.
[54] *Ibid.*, 291. A similar line of reasoning, drawing on Hart's article, is found in Keohane and Nye (fn. 12), 11.
[55] Nagel (fn. 2), 9-10, 14, 29, 114-22, 175-76.
[56] *Ibid.*, 14.   [57] Hart (fn. 53), 303.

States, the security of each depends on the other. This is typically regarded as an example of interdependence and can be described in terms of simultaneous attempts by each nation to get the other one to do what it might not otherwise do—i.e., refrain from attack. In the third edition of *Modern Political Analysis*, the system of mutual deterrence is even cited by Dahl as an example of a situation of reciprocal influence.[58] The contention that Dahl's concept of power can neither account for nor deal with interdependence is unconvincing.

MILITARY POWER

Two of the most important weaknesses in traditional theorizing about international politics have been the tendency to exaggerate the effectiveness of military power resources and the tendency to treat military power as the ultimate measuring rod to which other forms of power should be compared. Both tendencies are anathema to the approach advocated by Lasswell and Kaplan. Although these authors give "special consideration to the role of violence," they repeatedly assert that power does not rest "always, or even generally, on violence"; that "power may rest on various bases"; that "none of the forms of power is basic to all the others"; and that "political phenomena are only obscured by the pseudosimplification attained with any unitary conception of power as being always and everywhere the same."[59] Despite the vigorous efforts of Lasswell and Kaplan and the tradition of contextual power analysis they spawned, the contemporary literature on international relations often exhibits the same tendencies to exaggerate the effectiveness of military power bases as did the earlier works.

Cline's *World Power Assessment* notes the existence of various forms of power, but describes war as the "true end game" in international "chess." "A study of power," according to Cline, "in the last analysis, is a study of the capacity to wage war."[60] In a similar vein, Gilpin acknowledges that power may take many forms, "though, in the final analysis, force is the ultimate form of power." Gilpin even makes the more extreme contention that "ultimately, the determination of the distribution of power can be made *only* in retrospect as a consequence of war."[61] Phrases describing force as the "ultimate" form of power imply that all forms of power are arrayed on a single continuum of

[58] Dahl, *Modern Political Analysis* (fn. 5), 50. See also Nagel (fn. 2), 142-43; Baldwin (fn. 16), 606.
[59] Lasswell and Kaplan (fn. 1), ix, 76, 85, 94, 92.
[60] Cline (fn. 12), 8.
[61] Gilpin (fn. 6), 24; emphasis added.

effectiveness or importance. If power is conceived of as a multidimensional phenomenon, it is harder to think in terms of such a continuum. If one thinks of power as situationally specific rather than generalized, the idea of an "ultimate" form of power does not make much sense. It may well be that there are some very important policy-contingency scenarios in which force is a critically important power resource, but it would be more helpful to identify such situations than to assert that force is the "ultimate" form of power. Most states, after all, resolve most international disputes most of the time without the actual or threatened use of force.

Although Keohane and Nye continually criticize the traditional emphasis on military force, even they sometimes seem to exaggerate the effectiveness of military force as a power resource. While noting the increasing costs associated with military force and the inapplicability of force to many situations, they contend that force "dominates" other means of power.[62]

The proposition that military force is more effective than other power resources is both ambiguous and debatable. In the absence of clearly specified or implied policy-contingency frameworks, the proposition that force is more effective than other power bases has little, if any, meaning. As I argued earlier, all generalizations about power should be set in a context specifying (as a minimum) who is trying to get whom to do what. In some situations, force works very well, but in others it is actually counterproductive. Underlying the analysis of Keohane and Nye there seems to be a set of implicit assumptions as to the number of policy-contingency frameworks in which force is effective, and as to the relative importance of such frameworks. It would be helpful if the authors would spell out such assumptions, including the criteria used in assigning weights to such frameworks.

As an empirical proposition, the idea that force dominates other means of power could be formulated as a hypothesis to be tested, but it does not deserve the status of an assumption. According to Keohane and Nye, "*if* there are no constraints on one's choice of instruments"— i.e., if cost considerations are ignored—"the state with superior military force will prevail."[63] Despite the fact that *Power and Interdependence* describes several situations in which force would *not* be effective, and

---

[62] See Keohane and Nye (fn. 12), 8, 11-18, 27-29, 228. Although the authors use the term "dominates," the context indicates that they are referring to the relative "effectiveness" of force. Credence is lent to this interpretation by their use of the term "effectiveness" instead of "dominance" in an earlier similar discussion. Cf. Keohane and Nye, "World Politics and the International Economic System" (fn. 17), 125-26.

[63] Keohane and Nye (fn. 12), 27; emphasis in original.

despite the easily demonstrable counterproductivity of military power resources in many policy-contingency frameworks, Keohane and Nye imply that military force will prevail if costs can be ignored.

Let us examine three situations referred to in *Power and Interdependence*. First, Keohane and Nye contend that "military power dominates economic power in the sense that economic means alone are likely to be ineffective against the serious use of military force."[64] Although this is a rather special situation that can hardly serve as the basis for sweeping generalizations about the relative effectiveness of economic and military power, it is not self-evident or manifestly true. Opinions differ, of course, but it is not obvious to me that in 1973 the American threat to use force worked better than the Arab oil embargo. Second, they indicate that "in the worst situations, force is ultimately necessary to guarantee survival."[65] That may have been a useful assumption for students of international politics prior to the atomic age—although I doubt it—but at a time of rapidly multiplying (military and non-military) threats of planetary disaster, it should be treated as a hypothesis to be scrutinized carefully.[66] In today's world, the effectiveness of military force in guaranteeing survival may be steadily and rapidly declining. Third, Keohane and Nye state that "military power helps the Soviet Union to dominate Eastern Europe economically as well as politically."[67] That hypothesis may be plausible, but it also sounds plausible when stated backwards—i.e., "military power *hinders* the Soviet attempt to dominate Eastern Europe, at least in some respects." *A priori*, I have no reason to believe that the 1968 invasion of Czechoslovakia bolstered the long-run prospects for communism in Eastern Europe. *A priori*, it seems reasonable to suspect that this invasion may have generated (intensified?) some anti-Russian resentment that will not disappear quickly. Although Nye and Keohane may be right, one wishes that students of international politics would consider the possibility that the Soviet use of force in Eastern Europe was counterproductive in at least some respects.[68]

---

[64] *Ibid.*, 16.   [65] *Ibid.*, 27.

[66] For a review of some of these threats, see Harold Sprout and Margaret Sprout, *Multiple Vulnerabilities: The Context of Environmental Repair and Protection*, Center of International Studies, Princeton University, Research Monograph No. 40 (Princeton 1974).

[67] Keohane and Nye (fn. 12), 28.

[68] I do not want to push this argument too far. Jacob Viner was fond of quoting William Stanley Jevons as follows: "It is always to be remembered that the failure of an argument in favor of a proposition does not, generally speaking, add much, if any probability, to the contradictory proposition." For a discussion of Soviet domination of Eastern Europe that identifies several drawbacks to the Soviet use of force, see Chris-

Even within the military sphere, power discussions could be fruitfully considered in a more contextual manner. The idea of "maximizing the military might" of a state does not make much sense unless military power resources are relatively fungible. In a world of widely differing military policy-contingency frameworks—nuclear war, conventional war, limited war, guerrilla war, and so forth—it might be more useful to speak about different kinds of military power.[69] This approach is especially appealing to the extent that military power assets in one policy-contingency framework become liabilities in another. Schelling's demonstration that first-strike weapons can be liabilities in certain kinds of deterrent situations is a case in point.[70]

Positive Sanctions

Positive sanctions (rewards and promised rewards) have long been important as a means by which some states get other states to do things they would not otherwise do. Whether such relationships should be labeled "power," "influence," or "nonpower influence," need not concern us here, since we are using the term "power" in the generic sense that includes all such labels. The important thing is recognition that positive sanctions are significant resources by which international actors affect the behavior, beliefs, attitudes, or policies of other actors. Knorr has rightly pointed out the paucity of academic literature concerning the role of positive sanctions in world politics.[71] In a world in which destructive power seems to grow exponentially, improved understanding of the actual and potential role of positive sanctions is highly desirable.

The increased attention being focused on economic power in world politics reinforces the need for more research on positive sanctions, since economic power often takes such a form.[72] It is interesting—but not encouraging—to note that the *International Encyclopedia of the Social Sciences* (1968) includes an index entry for "threat" but none for "promise"; an article on "punishment" but none on "reward"; and an article on "military power potential" but none on "economic power potential." Knorr's recent consideration of military power, economic

---

topher D. Jones, "Soviet Hegemony in Eastern Europe: The Dynamics of Political Autonomy and Military Intervention," *World Politics*, xxix (January 1977), 216-41.

[69] On this point, see Knorr (fn. 9), 46.

[70] Schelling (fn. 18), 207-54.

[71] Knorr (fn. 9), ix, 310-11. See also Baldwin, "The Power of Positive Sanctions," *World Politics*, xxiv (October 1971), 19-38.

[72] See Baldwin, "Economic Power," in James T. Tedeschi, ed., *Perspectives on Social Power* (Chicago: Aldine 1974), 395-413.

power, interdependence, negative sanctions, and positive sanctions in
The Power of Nations, however, provides some hope that the next
International Encyclopedia may fill such lacunae.

One of the most difficult conceptual problems in thinking about
positive sanctions is the relationship between exchange and power.
Despite the fact that ordinary economic exchange relations can be described in terms of Dahl's broad intuitive notion of power, many scholars resist the use of power terminology in analyzing such relations.[73]
Knorr acknowledges positive sanctions as important, but his attempt
to distinguish such "nonpower influence" from exchange relations adds
little to the discussion.[74] On the one hand, "power influence" is described as "harmful" to B because it restricts his choices. On the other
hand, "nonpower influence" is described as "beneficial" to B because
it enriches his choices. Although it is useful to define positive and negative sanctions in terms of whether B *perceives* them as rewards or
punishments, it seems unwise to assume that B always knows what is
best for him. It is not necessarily harmful to restrict the choices available to children, drug addicts, or nation-states. Children can be rewarded with too much candy; drug addicts can be rewarded with too
much heroin; and countries can be given more foreign aid than is
good for them. The question of whether rewards are actually beneficial to the recipient is an important one, but it seems more useful to
treat it as an empirical rather than a definitional question.

Within the category of mutually "beneficial" interaction, Knorr distinguishes between "exchange" and "nonpower influence" as follows:

> What distinguishes nonpower influence flows from . . . exchanges is
> that one actor gives something of value to another without condition,
> without any stipulated payment, now or later. For instance, A may
> extend economic assistance to B, exclusively in order to enable the lat-
> ter to accelerate his economic development. A expects to receive nothing
> in return from B, and B understands this.[75]

Such a distinction seems almost impossible for researchers to apply to
relations among nation-states. Stipulations regarding repayment may be
unstated and may be only vaguely perceived by the actors involved.
The social exchange theorists have demonstrated that exchange can
be a subtle process and that feelings of indebtedness on the part of the

---

[73] On this point, see Baldwin, "Power and Social Exchange," *American Political
Science Review* (forthcoming). In the literature on international relations, Hirschman's
National Power and the Structure of Foreign Trade (fn. 42) is of fundamental importance. His treatment demonstrates that power potentially inheres in all international
trade relations.

[74] Knorr (fn. 9), 7-8, 310-19.   [75] *Ibid.*, 311.

reward recipient may be created *regardless* of the stipulations or intentions of the reward giver.[76] Furthermore, even the most altruistic benefactor may change his mind and remind the aid recipient that he owes him a favor. In strictly economic exchanges such attempts to make retroactive stipulations regarding payment are unlikely to succeed, because the original recipient can point out that the terms of the transaction were clearly specified at the time it occurred. But social and political exchange are distinguished from economic exchange partly by the vagueness of the obligations involved.[77] Even the example cited by Knorr could be regarded as a type of social exchange. State A could be viewed as exchanging economic assistance for state B's promise to use the money to accelerate economic development (rather than to buy weapons or swell the Swiss bank accounts of the leaders). People and countries exchange money for promises all the time; so there is nothing particularly unusual about such an interpretation of Knorr's example. As long as A places any strings at all on the use of his aid, he may be viewed as making a stipulation as to payment. After all, if the behavior (attitude, policy, or whatever) stipulated by A had no value to him, he would not make the stipulation in the first place. I have never encountered a real-world example of totally stringless aid, and I never expect to. The United States has dispersed billions of dollars to promote economic development in other countries, but it is clear that American policy makers—rightly or wrongly—believed that faster economic development in those countries would enhance the long-run welfare and security of the United States.[78] In sum, although distinctions between power and exchange can be made, I suspect that students of international relations would find it as profitable to focus on the similarities as on the differences.

The fact that the mutual exchange of rewards is so prevalent in international relations may partly explain why the subject lacks excitement; that, in turn, may partly explain why students of international relations have focused their attention on the rarer but presumably more exciting instances in which countries have exchanged threats and/or punishments. However, the role of positive sanctions in world politics has begun to attract scholarly attention. Roger Fisher, Klaus

[76] See Blau (fn. 44); Alvin W. Gouldner, "The Norm of Reciprocity," *American Sociological Review*, xxv (April 1960), 161-78.
[77] "Social exchange differs in important ways from strictly economic exchange. The basic and most crucial distinction is that social exchange entails *unspecified* obligations." Blau (fn. 44), 93; emphasis in original.
[78] See Baldwin, *Economic Development and American Foreign Policy* (Chicago: University of Chicago Press 1966).

Knorr, Johan Galtung, Richard Rosecrance, Alexander George, Richard Smoke,[79] and a few others have contributed to this discussion, but much work remains to be done. I suggest that further research on this topic could be built on the earlier work of Hirschman and the social exchange theorists. Eckstein's suggestion that exchange theory has much to offer students of international politics deserves to be taken seriously.[80]

Power as a Zero-Sum Game

Traditionally, scholars of international relations have distinguished between conflict and cooperation. Power, it has often been argued, has to do with conflict but not with cooperation. The implied assumption was that we needed less conflict and more cooperation. Thomas Schelling, in *The Strategy of Conflict*, called into question the usefulness of this dichotomy by showing that most, if not all, interesting international political situations involved mixtures of both conflictual and cooperative elements. Although zero-sum games and games of pure cooperation might be useful ways to define the ends of a continuum, neither was likely to describe a real-world situation. Even war—traditionally regarded as the epitome of intense conflict—was shown by Schelling to involve significant cooperative dimensions. Although Schelling relied primarily on limited war to make his point, his logic can easily be extended to include so-called "total war." Nuclear war may not be unthinkable, but a war in which the participants would be *indifferent* to the prospects of planetary destruction is difficult to imagine. Even poker—that prototypical example of a zero-sum game—is hardly ever a zero-sum game in real life. Such values as the enjoyment of the game, concern about the player who is in over his head, and worries about whether the other players will be willing to play again in the future, almost always intrude on what is supposed to be a zero-sum game.

Despite Schelling, nuclear weapons, and ever-increasing awareness of the fragility of the earth's ecosystem, one still finds references to international politics as a zero-sum game in some or all respects. Stan-

---

[79] Roger Fisher, *International Conflict for Beginners* (New York: Harper and Row 1969); Knorr (fn. 9); Johan Galtung, "On the Effects of International Economic Sanctions, With Examples from the Case of Rhodesia," *World Politics*, xix (April 1967), 378-416; Richard Rosecrance, ed., *The Future of the International Strategic System* (San Francisco: Chandler 1972); Alexander George and Richard Smoke, *Deterrence in American Foreign Policy* (New York: Columbia University Press 1974).

[80] Harry Eckstein, "Authority Patterns: A Structural Basis for Political Inquiry," *American Political Science Review*, Vol. 67 (December 1973), 1157-59.

ley Hoffmann, for example, has recently argued that the model of a zero-sum game is "a valid account for considerable portions of world politics."[81] His citation of the Arab-Israeli dispute as a case in point is instructive. Although conflict may be the dominant mode of Arab-Israeli interaction, conceiving of the situation as a zero-sum game virtually assures that cooperative dimensions will be overlooked. Even Hoffmann's *caveat*—that he is using the zero-sum model as an "ideal-type" in order to "reveal the essence of the game"—fails to balance the perspective. In zero-sum games, the absence of cooperative elements is not merely one characteristic among many; it is the essential defining characteristic. A portrayal of the Arab-Israeli dispute as a zero-sum game strengthens neither our understanding of the situation nor the prospects of peace.[82]

Robert Gilpin argues that international politics *always* takes the form of a zero-sum game. After noting that "politics is the realm of power," he states that "the essential fact of politics is that power is always relative; one state's gain in power is by necessity another's loss." "From this *political* perspective," he adds, "the mercantilists are correct in emphasizing that in power terms, international relations is a zero-sum game."[83] Regardless of what one thinks of Gilpin's concept of power, it is important to realize that the Dahl-Lasswell-Kaplan conception of power is not a zero-sum view. Their conception permits us to describe situations in which A's ability to get B to do X increases *simultaneously* with B's ability to get A to do X.[84]

The model of the zero-sum game may be a potentially useful conceptual tool for the student of international politics. However, given traditional propensities to exaggerate the importance of negative sanctions while ignoring positive ones and to concentrate on conflictive dimensions of world politics while neglecting cooperative ones, theorists would do well to leave this particular conceptual tool on the shelf for a few years. Mixed-motive game models almost always provide a more accurate description of real-world situations than do zero-sum models.

[81] Hoffmann, "Notes on the Elusiveness of Modern Power," *International Journal*, xxx (Spring 1975), 191.

[82] It is interesting to note that one could neither predict nor advocate Sadat's dramatic visit to Israel on the basis of zero-sum game assumptions. The players in a zero-sum game have no common interests—by definition. Therefore, they never have a reason to negotiate (unless they think their opponent is stupid and can be outwitted).

[83] Gilpin (fn. 6), 22-25, 34; emphasis in original.

[84] For further discussion of this point, see Baldwin (fn. 16), 605-6.

Compellence and Deterrence

The distinction between compellence and deterrence is frequently noted by scholars in international relations—usually with reference to Schelling.[85] No instance of a challenge to the validity or the usefulness of this distinction has come to my attention. I will argue that an implicit assumption about the probability of a successful influence attempt underlies Schelling's discussion of compellence and deterrence, and that this assumption calls into question both the validity and the usefulness of the distinction.[86] There are, according to Schelling, typical differences between threats intended to make an adversary do something and threats intended to keep him from starting something. These differences concern the probability of success, the clarity of the threat, timing, and the difficulty of compliance.[87]

There is a difference between trying to discourage the Russians from launching a nuclear attack and trying to encourage the South Africans to change their form of government, but describing that difference as the difference between keeping someone from doing something and getting someone to do something is not very helpful. From a purely semantic standpoint, any deterrent threat can be stated in compellent terms, and any compellent threat can be stated in deterrent terms. Thus, we could talk about compelling the Russians to do X (when X is anything except launching a nuclear attack) and about deterring South Africans from doing X (when X is continued white dominance). When we describe an influence attempt as deterrence, we usually have

[85] At times such references become rather confusing. Keohane and Nye, for example, usually use the terms "positive" and "negative" power to refer to the compellence/deterrence distinction ("World Politics and the International Economic System" [fn. 17], 119, 134; *Power and Interdependence* [fn. 12], 44). But elsewhere they refer to the ability to resist influence attempts as "the negative dimension of power." ("World Politics and the International Economic System" [fn. 17], 134.) It seems desirable to maintain a clear distinction between deterring influence attempts and resisting them. The difference between deterring a nuclear attack and resisting one is a difference that matters.

[86] Parts of the argument that follows are drawn from Baldwin, "Bargaining with Airline Hijackers," in I. William Zartman, ed., *The 50% Solution* (Garden City, N.Y.: Doubleday 1976), 416-21. One example of the extent to which students of international relations have accepted the compellence/deterrence arguments of Schelling is provided by the following passage: "Enough has already been said to indicate the disparities between American and Soviet strategic doctrines in the nuclear age. These differences may be most pithily summarized by stating that whereas we view nuclear weapons as a deterrent, the Russians see them as a 'compellant' [sic]—with all the consequences that follow." Richard Pipes, "Why the Soviet Union Thinks It Could Fight and Win a Nuclear War," *Commentary*, Vol. 64 (July 1977), 34. It will be argued here that the consequences that follow are by no means obvious.

[87] Schelling (fn. 18), 195-99; and Schelling, *Arms and Influence* (New Haven: Yale University Press 1966), 69-91.

in mind a threat that is intended to *reduce* the probability of occurrence of an event that was not very likely to occur in the first place—e.g., nuclear attack, murder, or airline hijacking. When we describe an influence attempt as compellence, however, we usually have in mind a threat intended to *increase* the probability of occurrence of an event that was not very likely to occur anyway. Schelling is quite right in observing that "it is easier to *deter* than to *compel*,"[88] but that is more of a truism than an empirical observation. The person who tries to prevent unlikely things from happening will probably succeed; while the person who tries to cause unlikely things to happen will probably fail.

There are nontrivial differences between trying to do hard things (like changing South Africa's policy of white supremacy), and trying to do easy things (like preventing the Russians from launching a nuclear attack). Almost all of the differences between compellent and deterrent threats suggested by Schelling can be accounted for by the difference in the autonomous probability of the outcome one is trying to influence.[89] The observation that deterrent threats are more likely to succeed than compellent threats seems less profound when one lays bare the implicit assumption that deterrent threats are used for easy tasks while compellent threats are used for hard tasks.

Most of the discussion of the different requirements in timing of deterrence and compellence can be reduced to the truisms that considerable effort will be required to accomplish hard things, while one can accomplish easy things with much less effort. Why do compellent threats have to be "put in motion to be credible"?[90] Because they need

---

[88] *Ibid.*, 100; emphasis in original.

[89] The autonomous probability of the outcome X is defined as the probability that X would have occurred in the absence of any attempt by A to make it occur. Thus, the autonomous probability of X in a situation in which A is trying to influence B to do X is the probability that B would have done X anyway. See Karl W. Deutsch, *The Analysis of International Relations* (2d ed.; Englewood Cliffs, N.J.: Prentice-Hall 1978), 29-31, 159. Strictly speaking, the autonomous probability of B's performance of X is not the same as the probability of success of A's attempt to get B to do X. A high autonomous probability need not indicate a high probability of success for A, and a low autonomous probability does not necessarily mean that it will be hard for A to get B to do X. B's strong dislike of A may make him reluctant to do X if he knows A wants him to; likewise, B's respect for A may make him eager to do X after he learns of A's desire. Other things being equal, however, it is generally harder to make unlikely events occur than it is to make likely events occur. For purposes of this article, therefore, it will be arbitrarily assumed that influence attempts aimed at bringing about outcomes of low autonomous probability have a low probability of success; while influence attempts aimed at bringing about outcomes of high autonomous probability have a high probability of success.

[90] Schelling (fn. 87), 72.

a lot of credibility. Why do they need so much credibility? Because they are so unlikely to succeed in the first place!

Schelling also argues that it is likely to be especially difficult to comply with a compellent threat:

> There is another characteristic of compellent threats, arising in the need for affirmative action, that often distinguishes them from deterrent threats. It is that the very act of compliance—of doing what is demanded—is more conspicuously compliant, more recognizable as submission under duress, than when an act is merely withheld in the face of a deterrent threat. Compliance is likely to be less casual, less capable of being rationalized as something that one was going to do anyhow.[91]

Since Schelling uses the term "compellent threat" to refer to situations in which A is trying to get B to do something he is very unlikely to do, and the term "deterrent" threat to refer to situations in which A is trying to get B to do something he was likely to do anyway, the above passage is not surprising. Of course it is harder to rationalize compliance with compellent threats as something one intended to do anyhow, especially since compliance was something one had no intention of doing. It is much easier to give the appearance of doing what comes naturally if one really *is* doing what comes naturally. All of Schelling's comments about ease of compliance must be reversed if one compares the compellent threat—"Breathe or I'll shoot"—with the deterrent threat—"Don't breathe or I'll shoot." It is virtually tautological to say that the higher the autonomous probability of B's performance of X, the harder it will be to detect whether B's performance of X resulted from A's influence attempt. Schelling is quite right in saying that compliance is difficult in what he calls compellence situations. This difficulty, however, is not a characteristic of compellent threats; it is a characteristic of the particular type of influence situations that are being labeled "compellent." The difficulty of compliance with a compellent threat disappears if we change the situation from "Stand on your head and whistle Yankee Doodle or I'll shoot" to "Breathe or I'll shoot."[92] Compliance is conspicuous in some compellent threat situations; in others it is not.

Another difference between compellent and deterrent threats, according to Schelling, is that the former tend to be more ambiguous

---

[91] *Ibid.*, 82.

[92] "Breathe or I'll shoot" is actually just a variation of "act normally or I'll shoot" —a compellent threat often found in TV dramas depicting the criminal hiding in the closet while the prisoner answers the doorbell.

than the latter. Once again, particular kinds of situations seem to be implied:

> In addition to the question of "when," compellence usually involves questions of where, what, and how much. "Do nothing" is simple; "Do something" ambiguous. "Stop where you are" is simple; "Go back" leads to "How far?" "Leave me alone" is simple; "Cooperate" is inexact and open-ended.[93]

"Do nothing," however, is not that simple. It leads to "What do you mean; I have to do something, don't I?" or "I can't just do nothing!" "Do nothing that will upset me" is more ambiguous than "Get the hell out of here!" "Stop where you are" is not so simple when said by a hijacker to the pilot of a plane at 30,000 feet. "Leave me alone" is not so simple when said by a tired father to a small child. It invariably leads to "Does that mean I must leave the room or merely that I must stop talking to you?" "Is it all right if I talk to myself?" "How about if I just listen to records?" In such a situation, "Leave me alone" is ambiguous; "Go play in the yard" is simple. Even if one accepts the distinction between deterrent and compellent threats, there is no reason to believe that one type of threat is intrinsically clearer than the other.

The alleged greater clarity of deterrent threats carries over to assurances.[94] Because the assurances associated with compellent threats tend to be ambiguous, they tend to lack credibility. Blackmailers, as Schelling says, "find the 'assurances' troublesome when their threats are compellent"; but blackmailers also find assurances troublesome *even when their threats are not compellent*. The credibility of assurances is not a function of the kind of threat being made; it is a function of the same sorts of things that determine the credibility of threats and promises. The credibility of one's assurance that he will not explode a nuclear bomb if his demands are met grows out of the obvious unpleasantness of such an act, not out of the nature of the threat being made. Sadists, kidnappers, blackmailers, extortionists, and airline hijackers find that the credibility of their assurances is undermined by the obvious opportunities and incentives they have to renege on their assurance commitments, regardless of whether they have made deterrent or compellent threats.

Although the distinction between deterrence and compellence at first appears to be very helpful in analyzing world politics, further scrutiny raises serious questions about the utility of the distinction. The failure to provide a precise definition of compellence makes it hard to

---

[93] Schelling (fn. 87), 72-73.   [94] *Ibid.*, 74.

be sure, but a low probability of success seems to be inextricably bound up with the implied definition of this term. It is worthwhile to distinguish between threats and promises and between influence attempts with a high probability of success and those with a low probability of success. Until more precise definitions and more persuasive arguments are produced, however, students of international relations should be wary of the distinction between compellence and deterrence.[95]

CONCLUSION

A review of selected works in recent scholarship in international relations reveals the continued existence of a number of traditional tendencies in the treatment of power. First, the tendency to exaggerate the fungibility of power resources and the related tendency to neglect considerations of scope are still with us. Despite twenty years of exhortation by the Sprouts, discussions of national capabilities without reference to explicitly stated or clearly implied policy-contingency frameworks are common. Second, the propensity to treat military power resources as the "ultimate" power base, and the related propensity to overestimate the effectiveness of military force, have not disappeared. And third, emphasis on conflict and negative sanctions at the expense of emphasis on cooperation and positive sanctions is not uncommon.

It was suggested that the contextual analysis of power advocated by Lasswell and Kaplan, Dahl, the Sprouts, and others would provide a useful corrective for traditional weaknesses in treatments of power by students of international relations. Such contextual analysis would have a number of implications for the way scholars of international relations talk about their subject. First, the division of the world into "great powers," "small powers," and "middle powers" would be called into question, since such terms usually connote generalized rather than situationally specific power. At the very least, users of such terms would be required to specify the issue-area they have in mind. Second, the idea of a single monolithic international "power structure" would be called into question, since such a concept implies either highly fungible power resources or a single dominant issue-area. Students of world politics must recognize, as students of American politics have recognized, "that the notion of 'the power structure' of a social unit is a

---

[95] The closest Schelling comes to a precise definition of compellence is in *Arms and Influence* (fn. 87), 70-71. I suspect that psychologists may have some persuasive arguments as to why it is useful to distinguish between deterrence and compellence. Schelling does not present such arguments, however.

dangerously misleading siren. There are as many power structures as there are issues fruitfully distinguished."[96] Keohane and Nye take two steps forward when they demonstrate that international power structures vary from one issue-area to another; but they slip one step backward when they imply that an overall structural approach that fails to distinguish among issue-areas and that is based on the assumption that power, like money, is highly fungible, can provide even a partial explanation of world politics.[97] It is time to recognize that the notion of a single overall international power structure unrelated to any particular issue-area is based on a concept of power that is virtually meaningless.[98] It is difficult to see how a model based on a virtually meaningless concept of power can provide even a partial explanation of international political relations. Instead of talking about *the* distribution of power resources underlying *the* international power structure, students of world politics could more profitably focus on the multiple distributional patterns of a wide variety of resources related to a number of significant issue-areas.

The point here is not to deny either the possibility or the desirability of generalizations about power patterns within very broadly—perhaps even vaguely—defined issue-areas. It is to suggest that healthy skepticism and scholarly caution should be proportionate to the broadness and vagueness of the specification of the issue-area. Rough indicators of power hierarchies in given issue-areas can be useful, but only if the limitations and pitfalls of such an approach are clearly understood and acknowledged.[99] The important thing is recognition that the absence of a common denominator of political value in terms of which different scopes of power could be compared is not so much a methodological problem to be solved as it is a real-world constraint to be lived with.[100] Economists, after all, did not invent money in order to solve the conceptual problem of aggregating economic values; they just hap-

---

[96] Frederick W. Frey, "Comment: On Issues and Nonissues in the Study of Power," *American Political Science Review*, Vol. 65 (December 1971), 1086. See also Raymond E. Wolfinger, "Nondecisions and the Study of Local Politics," and "Rejoinder to Frey's 'Comment,'" both in *American Political Science Review*, Vol. 65 (December 1971), 1063-80 and 1102-04, respectively.

[97] Keohane and Nye (fn. 12), 43-54, 222-25.

[98] Dahl (fn. 5), 33: "Any statement about influence that does not clearly indicate the domain and scope it refers to verges on being meaningless." For a similar comment, see Sprout and Sprout, "Environmental Factors . . ." (fn. 10), 325.

[99] For an impressive demonstration of generalizaton at a high level of abstraction based on explicit acknowledgment of the importance of scope and domain and the resulting multidimensional nature of power, see Alker (fn. 21).

[100] Cf. Dahl (fn. 5), 32-36; Baldwin (fn. 16).

pen to be luckier than political scientists. If the real world has not chosen to provide political analysts with a political counterpart to money, it would be folly to pretend that it has.

Although power analysis is probably the oldest approach to the study of world politics, it is also one of the most promising for the years ahead. Refinements in the causal notion of power since 1950 have not yet been fully integrated into the literature on international relations, but there is no reason why this should not happen. Both social power literature and social exchange theory have much to offer the student of world politics. As Hayward Alker has recently observed, "Far from being nearly dead, weak, or inadequate as some critics have implied, power measurement has just begun."[101]

[101] Alker (fn. 21), 370-71.

THE STRATEGIC TRIANGLE:
An Elementary Game-Theoretical Analysis

By LOWELL DITTMER*

T HE notion of a "strategic triangle" has been widely used in recent discussions of the relationship between the United States, the Soviet Union, and the People's Republic of China, particularly since the Sino-American rapprochement began in the early 1970s.[1] Yet it is generally used in a loose, offhand way, as if its meaning were self-evident. The purpose of this paper is to posit a more explicit definition of the concept, to explore its inner logic and dynamic propensities, and finally to apply this conceptual framework to the evolving pattern of relationships within the triangle over the past three decades in order to see whether it can help illuminate past developments and make future prospects somewhat more comprehensible. If we succeed in bringing clarity to this pattern of relationships, it may be worthwhile to apply the same mode of analysis to other triangular situations (or even to more complex arrangements); eventually, we may accumulate convincing empirical generalizations.

A "strategic triangle" may be understood as a sort of transactional game among three players. Of course, as Wittgenstein noted, there is a great variety of games: some are essentially cooperative, such as "catch"; some are hierarchical, such as "Mother, may I?"; some competitive, such as football and poker; and some based on a logic of ostracism and redemption, such as touch-tag or hide-and-seek. The following reconstruction does not incorporate the sort of formal game theory used so effectively by Thomas Schelling or Anatol Rapoport; it is an exploratory venture designed to generate hypotheses and perhaps to stimulate more systematic strategic thinking.

* I wish to thank Avery Goldstein for his criticisms of an earlier draft of this article.

[1] Among the best of these are Michel Tatu, *The Great Power Triangle: Washington-Moscow-Peking* (Paris: Atlantic Institute, 1970); Thomas M. Gottlieb, *Chinese Foreign Policy Factionalism and the Origins of the Strategic Triangle* (Santa Monica: RAND R-1902-NA, November 1977); Roger Glenn Brown, "Chinese Politics and American Policy: A New Look at the Triangle," *Foreign Policy*, No. 23 (Summer 1976), 3-24; Michael Pillsbury, "U.S.-Chinese Military Ties?" *Foreign Policy*, No. 20 (Autumn 1975), and "Future Sino-American Security Ties: The View from Tokyo, Moscow and Peking," *International Security*, 1 (Spring 1977), 142; John W. Garver, "China's Rapprochement with the United States, 1969-1971," unpub. (Ann Arbor, Mich., 1979); and Banning Garrett, "China Policy and the Strategic Triangle," in Kenneth A. Oye, Donald Rothchild, and Robert Lieber, eds., *Eagle Entangled: U.S. Foreign Policy in a Complex World* (London and New York: Longman, 1979), 228-64.

Any international game is highly complex but not highly formalized; indeed, the players may not even be conscious that they are playing a game, and may choose to adhere to or disregard its rules (such as they are) almost at will. Yet, for as long as they remain *in the situation described by the game*, their foreign policy options will to some degree be circumscribed by its constraints and opportunities.

RULES OF THE GAME

Before taking a closer look at the strategic triangle in particular, it may prove useful, as a way of making my premises clear, to pose the more general question: Why do states fall into patterned relationships with one another in the first place, and of what do such relationships consist? My (hardly novel) answer to this question is that states (representing their constituent members, of course)[2] experience needs that cannot be adequately satisfied at the domestic level, leading them to enter into contact with those countries that dispose of the pertinent values. These contacts normally consist of transactions, or *exchanges*.[3] Thus, there may be exchanges of goods and services, as in international trade; exchanges of population, as in migration; or exchanges of information, as in mail flows, propaganda, or espionage. These exchanges may be legally regulated through treaties, tariffs, censorship, and other forms of legislation. It seems analytically convenient to adopt a general distinction between exchanges of *benefits* (for example, trade) and exchanges of *sanctions* (for example, warfare). *Exchanges are in the normal course of things reciprocal* (a benefit elicits a benefit, a sanction elicits a sanction), but *they may or may not be symmetrical*. Thus, we may speak of positive or negative, symmetrical or asymmetrical exchanges, as depicted in Figure 1:

[2] I am taking what Graham Allison would call a "rational actor" approach, ignoring all but international payoffs. A country's foreign (or domestic) policy may be analyzed in terms of its constituent pressure groups, bureaucratic interests, resource constraints, and other internal determinants, just as an individual decision maker may be psychoanalyzed in terms of constituent drives and complexes. But the focus of this analysis is on *the inherent logic of specific patterns of relationships among nation-states*; the *reasons* motivating a particular nation-state to adhere to (or deviate from) any particular pattern is irrelevant to the validity of that logic.

[3] The classic studies of exchange theory are: George C. Homans, *Social Behavior: Its Elementary Forms* (New York: Harcourt, Brace & World, 1961), and Peter Blau, *Exchange and Power in Social Life* (New York: Wiley, 1964). For an application to politics, see Warren F. Ilchman and Norman T. Uphoff, *The Political Economy of Change* (Berkeley: University of California Press, 1971). I am not aware of any explicit attempts to apply the theory to international relations, though it would seem particularly suitable to that context in view of the relative lack of institutionalization.

Balance

		symmetrical	asymmetrical
	positive	1	3
Value			
	negative	2	4

FIGURE I

Type 1 would involve a mutually beneficial exchange of equal values, as in balanced trade; type 2 might involve deterrence or military stalemate; type 3 would include economic dependency, population brain drain, and other such unequal trades; type 4 might involve blackmail or conquest.

Which of these four logically possible "pure" types of exchange relationship are most stable and durable? Assuming that all parties to the transaction have access to the same information, it will always be easier to sustain a symmetrical than an asymmetrical exchange, and it will normally be easier to sustain a positive than a negative exchange. Symmetrical exchanges have greater stability because they are balanced and do not arrive at an outcome that sorts out winners and losers; positive exchanges are more durable because they cater to the interests of both participants. A negative symmetrical exchange may be self-sustaining if it is passive (as in mutual nuclear deterrence), but otherwise it incurs unacceptable costs with inadequate benefits to sustain it. An asymmetrical positive exchange may be prolonged, but only if the chief beneficiary is capable of deluding or coercing the lesser beneficiary, who is otherwise apt to rebel against it. Negative asymmetrical exchanges are costly and of brief duration, normally resulting in the exacerbation of a symmetry between the strong and the weak.

Three variables may affect the type of exchange selected. First, the *value* (positive/negative) of an exchange is determined chiefly by the behavior of the two players in the bilateral relationship vis-à-vis one another. Second, the *symmetry* of a relationship is strongly influenced by the power ratio (strong/weak) between the two players. Third, both value and symmetry of any bilateral relationship are marginally affected by each player's relationship with the third player.

Ceteris paribus, any player will prefer a positively valued relationship (hereafter abbreviated "amity") with other players to a negative one ("enmity"). The reason is that exchanges tend to reciprocate in kind: an amity begets benefits—trade and information flows, national security, even an affirmative mirror-image—whereas an enmity incurs sanctions—bombs, tariff barriers, and so forth. It would seem to follow that it is in each player's interest to behave ingratiatingly toward other players. The problem is that an *asymmetrical* amity provides more immediate benefits than a symmetrical one, and that a negative-positive relationship (wherein *A* imposes sanctions on *B*, *B* confers benefits on *A*) nets an even greater short-term payoff. Because of the paucity of strong norms in the international arena and the domestic source of most positive reinforcements for the actors, there is an ever-present temptation to cheat or double-cross—to reciprocate with less than equal value in positive exchanges, or to return evil for good. However, the fact that the three players in the triangle have nuclear second-strike capabilities reduces the appeal of a sudden and decisive double-cross (a Pearl Harbor); moreover, self-limiting efforts to "win" negative exchanges are apt to prove inconclusive (for example, the bombing of North Vietnam did not long forestall "liberation" of the South, and the Cuban missile crisis stimulated heavier Soviet investment in naval and strategic arms).[4] Visible cheating may also be counterproductive, eliciting retaliation from the victim or at least a public outcry; even Hitler, announcing his unilateral invasion of Poland in September 1939, sought to convey the impression that Germany was responding to a Polish attack. Thus, *at the present stage of weapons development, symmetrical amity is normative among members of the triangle, and undetectable cheating the preferred form of deviation.* In the absence of international enforcement mechanisms, each player must constantly and scrupulously monitor all transactions—for, aside from the danger of cheaters, the perception of symmetry in such dealings is notoriously subjective, and the data are nearly always equivocal. If confronted by evidence of cheating, a player must either check such behavior or permit the relationship to deteriorate from a positive to a negative one; otherwise that player submits willy-nilly to a losing negative-positive exchange.

The power ratio between two players is the objective factor most likely to affect the *symmetry* of their relationship. This is not an "analytic" truth, nor is the relationship fully deterministic: there may be symmetrical relationships between players of unequal power, such as the ideal-typical patron-client relationship, in which each player accepts a different (but equally necessary) role in a shared division of labor. In a world of capital- and technology-intensive megaweapons, whose

---

[4] For an analysis of the failure of limited coercion in the Vietnamese case, see Wallace J. Thies, *When Governments Collide: Coercion and Diplomacy in the Vietnam Conflict, 1964-1968* (Berkeley: University of California Press, 1980).

unit cost decreases with large-scale production, a great power is better equipped to provide a security blanket than a small one, for example; but the latter may compensate by deferring to the former's leadership in strategic policy making (*vide* Japan's postwar relationship with the United States, or the Cuban relationship with the Soviet Union). Thus a great power may acquire a number of clients by dint of its dominance in certain crucial power dimensions, creating a wheel-shaped cluster of bilateral relationships (as in NATO or the Warsaw Pact). The presumption is strong, however, that the great power will take advantage of its dominance to transform the relationship into an asymmetrical one. The smaller state, should it prefer not to suffer such relegation, may try to negotiate more favorable terms with another great power, or to play the two off against each other.

The relationship of each player in a bilateral relationship to a third player—the distinctively triangular variable in the equation—may affect either the value or the symmetry of the first relationship. If player A adds an amity with player C to an existing amity with player B, the power ratio of both A and C vis-à-vis B is improved, creating the preconditions for asymmetry. If the relationship between A and B is negative, it poses an actual threat; if it is positive, it poses a potential threat. Thus, both sides in a potentially negative relationship (particularly the weaker side, if it is an asymmetrical relationship) have an interest in securing the support of the third, or at least in preventing collusion between the other two. Collusion between the other two players would be acceptable only if one had amities with both and trusted each of them implicitly.

Three different systemic *patterns* of exchange relationships are conceivable: the "*ménage à trois*," consisting of symmetrical amities among all three players; the "romantic triangle," consisting of amity between one "pivot" player and two "wing" players, but enmity between each of the latter; and the "stable marriage," consisting of amity between two of the players and enmity between each and the third.

If the desideratum lay in optimizing the interests of all players of the game, the most desirable pattern would be the *ménage à trois*. It would preserve balance and provide incentives to all three for continued cooperation at minimal cost. But from the point of view of the individual player, the *ménage à trois* is not maximally secure. Such insecurity is perhaps inherent in the bilateral conventions of international diplomacy: I may be able to ascertain the motives and goals of my immediate negotiating partner, but I can never be sure whether the relationship between second and third parties is in my interest—unless it is visibly negative. Thus, from my perspective the most desirable arrangement is the "romantic triangle," in which I have an amity with two other players and they have an enmity with each other. I am Queen Guinevere (or Isolde), and my favor is ardently pursued by both Arthur and Lancelot (or Marke and Tristan). I may choose to maintain this delicate balance quite cold-bloodedly, deriving maximum benefits from both suitors in their rivalry to outbid one another, or I may be genuinely torn between them and unable to make up my mind; whatever my motives, the relationship can be sustained only as long as I treat each suitor "fairly." Although this arrangement maximizes the benefits of the player in the pivotal position, fictional precedents suggest that it has serious drawbacks from the viewpoint of both other players. Each of the "wing" players is placed in a position of considerable uncertainty: unable to form an amity with the rival wing player, and dependent exclusively on amity with the pivot, each may feel vulnerable to being excluded from a hostile bilateral coalition. This uncertainty, so favorable to the pivot player, is apt sooner or later to prove intolerably ambiguous to one of the competing "suitors"—at least that has been the case in the legendary precedents, where such a relationship normally leads to marriage to one of the suitors and exile or death to the other. Yet we should not reify our analogy, for the norm of monogamy need not apply to international relations.

The third and most elementary form of triangle is of least cumulative benefit to the three players and yet perhaps the most durable: it is the "stable marriage," consisting of symmetrical amity between two players and enmity between these two and the third (which may or not be symmetrical). In such a triangular pattern it is clearly in the interest of the excluded player to form an amity with one (or both) of the others and thereby escape further ostracism. But it may not be easy to establish such links, inasmuch as both of the other players may have acquired a vested interest in the existing pattern, which is premised upon mutual hostility to the ostracized third party. If the positive relationship between the two alliance partners is asymmetrical, the third may be able to persuade the lesser beneficiary to defect, and thereby establish a new and more favorable balance.

ORIGINS OF THE STRATEGIC TRIANGLE: 1949–1971

Although the participants need not be aware they are playing a game in order for us to conclude that a game is being played, two objective conditions must be met for a strategic triangle. First, *all participants must recognize the strategic salience of the three principals.* Each player may concurrently engage in various side-games, but these must be subordinated to the central game with other members of the triangle. Second, although the three players need not be of equal strategic weight, each must be accepted by the other two as a legitimate autonomous player. Thus, the *relationship between any two participants will be influenced by each player's relationship to the third.* These two conditions were obviously not applicable to the entire period under review, so it may be of interest to see how they came to apply (and why they failed to apply previously). We will then be able to analyze the pattern of play once the game was joined in 1971.

During roughly the first decade of the P.R.C.'s existence, the pattern of interaction between China and the Soviet Union was that of "stable marriage": they were joined in a positive relationship by formal treaty as well as by ideological affinity, and both had enmities with the United States, as depicted in the following diagram:

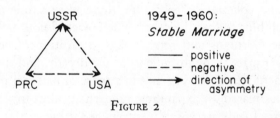

USSR   1949–1960:
Stable Marriage

—————— positive
— — — negative
⟶ direction of asymmetry

PRC   USA

FIGURE 2

Indeed, so tight was the bloc alignment between the U.S.S.R. and the P.R.C. that Western politicians did not even recognize the latter's autonomy. Subsequently, students of this period found that the alliance was not as seamless as had previously been assumed, and that Chinese leaders had attempted to signal their interest in some form of independent contact with the United States; these early harbingers were dispelled by the invasion of South Korea in June 1950 and by the concurrent rise of McCarthyism in the U.S.[5]

Hence, the conditions for a strategic triangle did not, strictly speaking, apply at this stage. The autonomy of the three players was not recognized, nor was the existence of a triad of essential players. Rather, it was a period of tight bipolarity in which only two autonomous decision-making centers were acknowledged, each of which disposed of a

[5] Two recent such "revisionist" interpretations of this period are James Reardon-Anderson, *Yenan and the Great Powers* (New York: Columbia University Press, 1980), and Kenneth Chern, *Dilemma in China: America's Policy Debate, 1945* (Hamden, Conn.: Shoe String Press, 1980).

cluster of bilateral positive relationships with weaker client states. The rigidity of the bipolar structure was enhanced by two factors: the novelty and awesome power of nuclear weapons, which the two bloc leaders monopolized at that time; and the motivational efficacy attributed to ideology. Each bloc became integrated around mutually antagonistic idea systems; the logical antithesis between proletarian dictatorship and bourgeois democracy was conceived to be so stark and compelling that all honorable alternatives were foreclosed. A certain amount of triangularity was introduced to the system with the advent of the nonaligned bloc in the mid-1950s. Yet, although the nonaligned countries were not part of the two nuclear deterrence systems and sought to formulate independent ideological positions, weakness made their claims to full autonomy somewhat unconvincing: they were of no more than regional military significance, and usually remained enmeshed in the "free world's" economic network.

Tight bipolarity tended to enhance the status and power of Moscow and Washington as bloc leaders: inter-bloc tension fostered intra-bloc allegiance and cohesion.[6] To be sure, there were ample objective reasons for each bloc to fear the other. The Soviet Union had been devastated by the Germans and remained in a position of economic and strategic inferiority through the end of the decade, and the U.S. policy of containment lent some credence to a sense of national paranoia. The United States feared an expanding juggernaut akin to the Nazis; the U.S.S.R. was already irrevocably entrenched athwart the heartland of the Eurasian landmass and in a strong geopolitical position to dominate its rimland and to threaten Africa, Oceania, and ultimately the Americas. It was a logically orderly but rigid and volatile system. The Manichaean perspective each side had adopted tended to exacerbate local incidents by translating them into an ideological context that gave them global meaning, sometimes threatening nuclear confrontation. The "loss" of China was considered particularly perilous for the future of democracy, not only because of China's enormous size, population, and potential, but also because the Chinese soon proved to be more attractive exponents of Marxist-Leninist ideology in the Third World than their Soviet mentors. Their peasant-guerrilla form of revolution with its premium on mobilized nationalism, and their claim to having discovered a self-reliant, labor-intensive route to modernity that

---

[6] Cf. Coral Bell, *The Diplomacy of Detente: The Kissinger Era* (New York: St. Martin's Press, 1977), 138.

preserved indigenous cultural values, made the Chinese model relevant to the problems faced by the developing countries.[7]

The following decade (1960–1969) was an ambiguous, transitional one, during which none of the three triangular patterns applied fully. The relationship between China and the United States remained negative, despite the first exploratory contacts between the two sides since Panmunjom. The relationship between China and the Soviet Union was transformed into an increasingly bitter enmity. At the same time, détente assuaged the negative relationship between the Soviet Union and the United States: each continued to consider the other the most likely adversary in a nuclear exchange, but an attempt was made to regulate the arms race and to cultivate various compensatory positive relationships (e.g., trade, cultural exchanges). It would be going too far to call this competitive-collusive relationship a stable marriage; at best it might be termed an "affair."

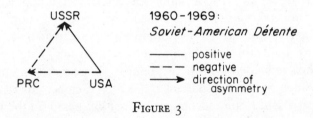

USSR 1960-1969:
Soviet-American Détente

—— positive
– – – negative
PRC USA ——▶ direction of
 asymmetry

FIGURE 3

The two most decisive changes in the triangular pattern during this decade—Soviet-American détente and the Sino-Soviet dispute—were, I would argue, causally linked. The most important single factor contributing to the dispute was the disintegration of the rigid structure of bipolarity at the end of the 1950s, which was a precondition for the first phase of Soviet-American détente. China had been chafing at the asymmetry of the relationship with the U.S.S.R. for some time, but once the Soviet Union began basking in the spirit of Camp David, further sacrifices for the sake of the anti-imperialist alliance seemed unjustifiable. The P.R.C. had premised its future foreign policy objectives (including plans for nuclear armament and the recovery of Taiwan) on the assumption of continued confrontation between the two camps, and found no way to adapt them to this milder climate. The

[7] For a clear exegesis of the Maoist developmental model in all its pristine cogency, see John G. Gurley, *China's Economy and the Maoist Strategy* (New York: Monthly Review Press, 1976).

Chinese vulnerability to American nuclear blackmail was increased as well, for Soviet-American détente did not entail Sino-American détente, and may have even focused American anti-Communist impulses on the containment of China. In cases such as the Sino-Indian border dispute or the Taiwan Straits embroilment with the Seventh Fleet, the Soviets seem to have neglected to take Chinese interests into account—or else they dismissed them under the assumption that China had "nowhere to go" and would subordinate its national interest to the interests of international communism (as perceived by the Soviet Union). But China responded with an increasingly comprehensive critique of the Soviet system. Détente with capitalism necessitated a general diminution of the role of ideology, and resulted in specific doctrinal adjustments that exposed the Soviet Union to telling Chinese polemics against "revisionism," "goulash communism," and so forth.[8]

And yet, because the principal Chinese grievance against the U.S.S.R. had to do with the Soviet Union's defection from its role responsibilities as bloc leader in an international ideological crusade, China was inhibited from taking the dispute outside the bloc—let alone forming any sort of coalition with non-Communist states, which would have undermined the Chinese ideological position entirely. The Sino-Soviet dispute thus remained within the family; it consisted mainly of attempts to mobilize the support of other bloc members to censure the apostate party and restore ideological consensus, based on the model of intra-Party rectification. Both China and the Soviet Union, as *de facto* competitors for bloc leadership, were thus driven to advocate more militantly "revolutionary" positions than they might otherwise have considered prudent. Domestically, both undertook sweeping organizational and programmatic innovations designed to bring their countries nearer to the Communist Utopia. (In China, these included the Hundred Flowers, the commune, and the Great Leap Forward; in the Soviet Union, the Third Party Program of the 22nd Congress of the CPSU with its accompanying Twenty-Year Plan, the movement from *kolkhozy* to *sovkhozy*, and the proclaimed advent of a state and party of the "whole people.") In foreign affairs, while the Soviet Union continued (in rather fitful and defensive fashion) to pursue détente with the United States, the Sino-Soviet dispute emerged in the form of an intensely competitive suit for the hearts of the newly emerging countries of the Third World, since both the U.S.S.R. and China evaluated their future international potential more highly than their current strategic

[8] See Alfred D. Low, *The Sino-Soviet Dispute: An Analysis of the Polemics* (Cranbury, N.J.: Associated University Presses, 1976).

significance. In this competition, China tended to espouse the efficacy of national liberation by disestablished parties or movements, whereas the Soviet Union more easily accommodated itself to conventional alliances with governments, replete with trade, aid, advisors, and cultural exchanges.[9] But, although the Soviet and Chinese Communist Parties vigorously denounced one another on all fronts, they remained ostensibly dedicated to the same doctrinal objectives and opposed to capitalism and imperialism; this underlying accord seemed to contain their dispute for a time. There is even some indication that the P.R.C. continued to rely on the Soviet nuclear umbrella.

Nor did the United States deem it in its interest during this period to take advantage of the widening cleavage between the two powers, though the possibility was raised from time to time.[10] Exploratory negotiations were initiated on an unofficial level through the Polish embassy in Warsaw in 1955; roughly speaking, the Chinese seemed more forthcoming in these talks between 1955 and the launching of the Great Leap Forward (1958), the Americans more conciliatory in the ensuing years.[11] The Sino-Soviet connection was not really brought into these talks, though one of the assumptions behind them was undoubtedly that China might be brought to exercise at least as much flexibility in its foreign policy behavior as had the Soviet Union.[12] But the early 1960s happened to be a period when the Chinese were unduly sensitive to ideological deviation, not merely because they were challenging the CPSU for leadership of the international communist movement from a position very nearly bereft of all but ideological resources, but also because they had only recently suffered a serious setback in their efforts to realize ideological prophecies, and tended to compensate by overstating their own orthodoxy and shunning any prospect of reconciliation. For their part, American policy makers were put off by the radical phase in Chinese foreign policy in the early

[9] Cf. Charles Neuhauser, *Third World Politics: China and the Afro-Asian People's Solidarity Organization*, Harvard East Asia Monograph No. 27 (Cambridge: Harvard University Press, 1968); Alvin Rubinstein, ed., *Soviet and Chinese Influence in the Third World* (New York: Praeger, 1975).

[10] Foster Rhea Dulles, *American Policy Towards Communist China, 1949–1969* (New York: Crowell, 1972); Warren Cohen, "American Perceptions of China," in Michael Oksenberg and Robert Oxnam, eds., *Dragon and Eagle: United States-China Relations, Past and Future* (New York: Basic Books, 1978), 77-79.

[11] Kenneth T. Young, *Negotiating with the Chinese Communists: The United States Experience, 1953–1967* (New York: McGraw Hill, 1968); see also Arthur Lall, *How Communist China Negotiates* (New York: Columbia University Press, 1968).

[12] Young (fn. 11), 44-47, 58-59; see also Robert G. Sutter, *China-Watch: Toward Sino-American Reconciliation* (Baltimore: The Johns Hopkins University Press, 1978), 31-62.

1960s; moreover, Sino-Soviet "united action" in support of North Vietnam tended to corroborate the image of monolithic communism. China's acquisition of nuclear weapons in 1964 presented the United States with the prospect of a two-front war (thus helping to mobilize support for the ABM), and the Great Proletarian Cultural Revolution produced fear of Chinese xenophobia and apparent irrationality.[13] By the late 1960s, Chinese foreign policy seemed to have demonstrated its "autonomy": it had simultaneously disaffected both of the world's major powers without deriving any national benefit from it at all (aside from the allegiance of the Albanians and a handful of other far-left ideologues).

By the end of the decade, Chinese foreign policy had moved from an autonomy based on ideological principle to one based on national interest. Ironically, the primary stimulus for this secularization of Chinese policy was provided by the player who stood to benefit least: the Soviet Union. In moving aggressively in 1968 to prevent further Czech liberalization (of which the Chinese also disapproved), the Soviets demonstrated—in much more blatant fashion than had been the case either in Berlin in 1953 or in Poland and Hungary in 1956—their disdain for the concept of national sovereignty.[14] Having endured a series of imperialist humiliations extending from the first Opium War in 1839 to the Japanese invasion of 1931–1945, China was deeply committed to national sovereignty—indeed, the Communist Revolution had succeeded principally by emphasizing this commitment.[15] The Brezhnev doctrine, enunciated *post hoc* to justify the invasion, in effect asserted the Soviet Union's right to alter or replace the regime of any other state socialist system at its discretion. The implications of this doctrine were underlined the following spring, when violent clashes erupted over disputed sections of the Sino-Soviet border. Fortification of this border had begun in 1965, at Soviet initiative, and it now accel-

---

[13] See Franz Schurmann, *The Logic of World Power* (New York: Pantheon Books, 1974); also Morton Halperin, *China and the Bomb* (New York: Praeger, 1965).

[14] Linda D. Dillon, Bruce Burton, and Walter C. Soderland, in "Who Was the Principal Enemy? Shifts in the Official Chinese Perceptions of the Superpowers, 1968–1969," *Asian Survey*, XVII (May 1977), 456-74, detect a significant shift in Chinese perception of the superpowers between late 1968 and early 1969, illustrating the traumatic impact of the Soviet invasion of Czechoslovakia in August 1968 and the Sino-Soviet border clashes of spring 1969. They conclude that fear of attack from the Soviet Union was the most important factor underlying a "new" post-Cultural Revolution foreign policy. For a qualification of these conclusions, however, see Garver (fn. 1).

[15] The best-known advocate of this position is, of course, Chalmers Johnson, *Peasant Nationalism and Communist Power: The Emergence of Revolutionary China, 1937–1945* (Stanford, Calif.: Stanford University Press, 1962).

erated apace: the Soviets increased their strength at the border from 13 "thin" divisions in 1965 to 25 "thick" divisions by the spring of 1969, and to more than 40 divisions by 1972; infantry troops were reinforced by tanks, artillery, and missiles.[16] In the summer and fall of 1969, China mobilized its own border defenses, placed its economy on a war footing, launched a campaign to "store grain and dig tunnels deep," and evacuated unessential civilians from exposed northern cities.[17]

It was in this context that the Sino-Soviet conflict was transformed from an intra-bloc dispute to an international altercation.[18] The Soviets began to float rumors to the effect that they were considering a preemptive strike against the P.R.C.'s nascent nuclear facilities, leading to speculation that they were tacitly proposing Soviet-American collusion.[19] Moscow also established ties with Taiwan, improved relations with India and Japan, increased aid to North Vietnam, and (in June 1969) proposed an Asian collective security pact, evincing a desire to assume America's former role in the "containment" of the P.R.C. Beginning in late 1970, China launched a vigorous and ideologically promiscuous courtship of allies in the Third and Second Worlds, which facilitated its entry into the United Nations in the summer of 1971. Since the U.S.S.R. and the P.R.C. could now trade epithets before a global forum, the dispute was further internationalized. Internationalization had a secularizing effect, as both sides shifted from a debate over Marxist doctrine to a less specialized vocabulary (hegemony, imperialism, etc.) capable of mobilizing ideologically heterodox Third-World support.

[16] Robert C. Horn, "The Soviet Union and Asian Security," in Sudershan Chawla and D. R. Sardesai, eds., *Changing Patterns of Security and Stability in Asia* (New York: Praeger, 1980), 63-99.

[17] See An Sung Tai, *The Sino-Soviet Territorial Dispute* (Philadelphia: Westminster Press, 1973).

[18] Chalmers Johnson, "The Achievements of Chinese Foreign Policy," unpub. paper presented at the Third Joint Soviet-American Conference on Asia, Santa Barbara, Calif., December 10-15, 1979.

[19] Marvin Kalb and Bernard Kalb, *Kissinger* (New York: Dell, 1975), 259-60; Bell (fn. 6), 15-16. According to Bell,

> The Soviet signals that they were contemplating a preventive war, perhaps including nuclear strikes, were so deliberate, clumsy and obvious that it is difficult not to believe that they were intended to be heard by the Chinese, who should be cowed into a more submissive attitude. They included, for instance, letters to Communist parties in the West that seemed to be asking for advance approval of a strike against China. . . . The Russians apparently offered, via the military attachés in Washington and Moscow, a clear hint if not an actual bid for American acquiescence in such a strike. They were snubbed by the U.S. policy makers concerned, and knowledge of the bid and the snub were conveyed to the Chinese government.

The strategic triangle thus came into being in response to China's attempts to break out of an impending Soviet encirclement and to launch its own counterencirclement of the U.S.S.R. The P.R.C. saw itself confronting an ambiguous liaison between the United States and the Soviet Union which, if it became more collusive, could be extremely dangerous; but it was judged still to be sufficiently competitive that a wedge could be driven between the two. Both the U.S. and the U.S.S.R. had enmities with China at that time, obviously entailing the need to transform one of them. Interestingly enough, China's first option may have been an attempt at rapprochement with the Soviet Union.[20] The Soviets seem not to have reciprocated with what the P.R.C. considered acceptable terms, however; they would certainly have been delighted to welcome the Chinese back into "stable marriage," but they seem to have envisaged essentially a return to the *status quo ante*, placing China in an asymmetrical position.[21] The P.R.C. was thus open to consider an American offer. With the proclamation of the "Nixon Doctrine" (1969) and the initiation of phased withdrawal from Vietnam and Taiwan, the United States no longer posed an immediate threat to Chinese security. Kissinger and "the new Nixon" brought a cool and innovative spirit to the conduct of foreign affairs, attempting to isolate it from the passions of domestic politics and to analyze national interests essentially in terms of power rather than ideology. They were probably the first explicitly to adopt a "triangular" view of world strategy, according to which there were perhaps five major economic power centers, but only three powers of global strategic significance: the United States, the Soviet Union, and China. Though unwilling to betray the Taiwan lobby completely, Washington devised a formula that placed the Taiwan question—which had so long inhibited any rapprochement between the two countries—in abeyance, thus facilitating the establishment of unofficial but extensive contacts between the two countries.[22] The United States was very careful to emphasize that the budding Sino-American friendship was not directed against any "other" country, and even contended that it took no sides in the Sino-Soviet dispute. Thus a romantic triangle was born, with the United States at the pivot:

[20] Garver (fn. 1) offers evidence to this effect gleaned from content analysis of official statements and shifts in trade flows, as well as "Kremlinological" inferences.

[21] For a perceptive analysis of post-Cultural Revolution Sino-Soviet relations, see Kenneth Lieberthal, *Sino-Soviet Conflict in the 1970s: Its Evolution and Implications for the Strategic Triangle* (Santa Monica, Calif.: RAND Report, July 1978).

[22] Tang Tsou, "Statesmanship and Scholarship," *World Politics*, XXVI (April 1974), 428-51.

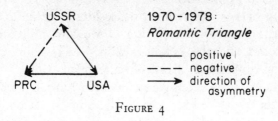

FIGURE 4

The logic of the new relationship was stated most explicitly by Kissinger: "Our relationships to possible opponents should be such . . . that our options toward both of them are always greater than their options toward each other."[23] Thus the two positive sides of the triangle seemed to be premised on a negative relationship between the Soviet Union and the P.R.C.—but the United States was nevertheless cautious not to aggravate that relationship: "Triangular diplomacy must avoid the impression that it is 'using' either of the contenders against the other; otherwise one becomes vulnerable to retaliation or blackmail. The hostility between China and the Soviet Union served our purposes best if we maintained closer relations with each side than they did with each other."[24]

China and the United States derived immediate political benefits from the triangle. China had previously not had an amity with either power, and it now did with at least one, which might be able to provide protection against the other. Indeed, although tension and occasional violence persisted along the Amur-Ussuri, once the United States declared its opposition to a pre-emptive strike and escalation of border hostilities, rumors of war began to evaporate. Though the Vietnamese conflict turned out to be far less dependent upon Chinese support than Washington had anticipated, the U.S. succeeded in perceptibly moderating Peking's support for Hanoi (to the latter's lasting chagrin); in fact, China changed its general posture toward the Third World, abandoning talk of people's war and invoking détente and peaceful coexistence.[25] The Soviet Union, like the jilted wife who still hopes to save her marriage, redoubled efforts "to demonstrate that the U.S.-Soviet relationship was more important than the U.S.-China relationship," with the result that "the tone in all our dealings changed

---

[23] Henry Kissinger, *White House Years* (Boston: Little, Brown, 1979), 165.
[24] *Ibid.*, 712.
[25] Peter Van Ness, *Revolution and China's Foreign Relations: Peking's Support for Wars of National Liberation* (Berkeley: University of California Press, 1971); Low (fn. 8).

dramatically."[26] Two months earlier, American planes had been bombing Haiphong harbor even while Soviet ships were docked there, but when Nixon proceeded from Peking to Moscow, he received a most cordial welcome, and the Nixon-Brezhnev talks culminated in the signing of an impressive array of agreements. The U.S.S.R. also launched a major peace offensive in Western Europe after shifting its forces from the Warsaw Pact area to the Sino-Soviet border.[27] Faced with a choice between construing Sino-American rapprochement as an anti-Soviet coalition and accepting American assurances that the relative value of the Soviet-American relationship would not be thereby devalued, the Soviets had for the time being chosen the more optimistic interpretation.

We would conclude from this review that the origins of the strategic triangle lay in the demise of polarity between the two camps. This polarity had served not only to define the relationship between the leaders of the two blocs, but also to order and rationalize the patron-client relationships between the bloc leaders and the weaker members of the bloc (including the "stable marriage" between the U.S.S.R. and the P.R.C.). We may generalize, then, that there is a functional correlation between positive and negative relationships: during a period of détente, or the relaxation of enmity, old friendships also lose some of their *raison d'être* and tend to wane; during periods of heightened cold war, on the other hand, solidarity among allies will thrive.

PLAYING THE GAME

We must now establish what would be a rational game plan from the perspective of the individual player, and evaluate each player's performance since 1971 to see whether "winners" and "losers" begin to sort themselves out. This is an analytical rather than a prescriptive task and is meant to be objective in the sense that value judgments not implicit in the definitions of terms and premises are to be avoided.

The U.S.S.R. was placed at an initial disadvantage by the way in which the triangle was introduced; although China's opening to the West certainly did not eliminate a coalition partner (inasmuch as Sino-Soviet relations had already soured so badly), it introduced the novel and unpleasant prospect of collusion between the world's most populous and most technologically advanced nations. The Soviet response

[26] Richard Nixon, *RN: The Memoirs of Richard Nixon* (New York: Grosset & Dunlap, 1978), 878; Kissinger (fn. 23), 838.
[27] Roger E. Kanet, "The Soviet Union and China," *Current History*, LXV (October 1973), 145-50.

was, on the one hand, to pursue reconciliation with China, and on the other, to try to thwart further Sino-American collusion. Yet both policies were either fraught with such ambivalence or implemented so maladroitly that they fell short.

The Soviet Union seems to have held an unrealistically optimistic view of what it would take to win reconciliation with China; it attributed the dispute essentially to the megalomania of Mao Zedong and thus expected his death to remove all impediments to renewed amity. That the Soviet post-Mao peace offensive was met by temporary suspension of anti-Soviet polemics but not by a settlement (beyond a 1977 agreement on border river navigation) indicates that, although the Chinese were receptive to Soviet proposals, Moscow was unwilling to make meaningful concessions.[28] Even when negotiations resumed late in 1979, the U.S.S.R. firmly rejected China's demands to reduce aid to Vietnam, draw border troop strength down to 1964 levels, and withdraw troops from Outer Mongolia; in fact, in the course of the year troop strength on the Chinese border was increased from 46 to 54 divisions. The Soviet Union was happy to signal its willingness to make peace with the Chinese and let bygones be bygones, but unwilling to do much more than that.

What concessions would the P.R.C. have required? It would probably have acceded to rapprochement if the Soviet Union had repudiated tsarist "unequal treaties" and perhaps agreed to minor territorial adjustments (signifying acceptance of China as a sovereign equal), reduced border troop strength (there is no realistic prospect of a Chinese infantry invasion of the Soviet Union, and in any case Soviet defensive capabilities are more than adequate), and disclaimed any right to intervene in China's domestic affairs. Yet the U.S.S.R. would have some difficulty making these concessions. The territorial issue is sensitive because the Soviets (and their tsarist predecessors) had also annexed territory from Japan and various East European countries, and any cession might set a precedent leading to further claims. The Soviet Union would have a hard time accepting full equality between Moscow and Peking: not only is the Soviet domestic political system hierarchical, but Soviet relations with all foreign communist parties in its orbit have remained hierarchical as well, premised on the "Caesaro-papist" principle legitimating its leadership.[29] For the U.S.S.R. to reduce bor-

---

[28] Lieberthal (fn. 21); Thomas Gottlieb, "The Hundred-Day Thaw in China's Soviet Policy," *Contemporary China*, III (Summer 1979), 3-15.

[29] Richard Lowenthal, *World Communism: The Disintegration of a Secular Faith* (New York: Oxford University Press, 1964).

der fortifications and negotiate from a position of formal equality would militate against deeply ingrained assumptions concerning the relationship between power and truth. Finally, to disclaim any right to intervene in China's domestic politics would undermine the Brezhnev doctrine and pave the way to the disintegration of COMECON.

Perhaps even more important than the paltry offer the Soviet Union tendered to China was the ambivalent stance it took toward rapprochement. A Soviet peace initiative would be accompanied by continued fortification of the U.S.S.R.'s side of the border and by attempts to promote alliances with China's opponents, such as the friendship treaties with India in 1971 and with Vietnam in 1978. Such treaties might be followed by the provision of sophisticated armaments (often more advanced than those that had been supplied to China), or even by the establishment of basing facilities for the Soviet Navy (as seems to have been the case in Vietnam). In this context, the P.R.C. perceived Soviet proposals for an Asian collective security pact as part of an overall containment strategy, and tended to greet overtures for normalization of Sino-Soviet relations with considerable skepticism. Whatever the success of the Soviet containment strategy, it seems to have foreclosed any possibility of Sino-Soviet rapprochement for the foreseeable future, and should be weighed against that opportunity cost.

In the West, Soviet warnings against arms sales and other forms of Sino-American collusion have been vitiated by a vigorous Soviet-Cuban offensive in support of various client states in the Third World, culminating in the Soviet invasion of Afghanistan in 1979. Again, whatever the U.S.S.R.'s gains in this arena (and however lasting they prove to be), such ventures were the surest way of provoking Sino-American collusion.

In sum, whereas the Soviet Union began the 1970s at the height of détente—with realistic options of propitiating China and gaining the pivot, or even converting the Soviet-American link into a stable marriage—by the end of the decade it had gravitated to the position of odd-man-out.

While the Soviet Union has been the net loser in the triangle, the P.R.C. has clearly been the winner—partly because it started the game from a relatively weak position. From a position of estrangement from both other players, China became the second side in a two-sided triangle that swung around an American pivot, thereby increasing its amities from zero to one. Beyond a desire to counter the Soviet threat, China's objectives in opening relations with the United States were to facilitate the "liberation" of Taiwan and to expedite modernization by means of Western technology. Though the Taiwan question has remained unresolved, the other two objectives were pursued with some success. Although the U.S. has not been as vigorous in countering Soviet global initiatives as the Chinese would prefer, the Soviet strategic threat to the P.R.C. has been allayed (which is undoubtedly China's top priority). China has entered Western capital and technology markets with great éclat, taking an active role in world commerce within a very short time.[30]

China has at times considered rapprochement with the Soviet Union —a move that would be rational in terms of the game logic because it would reduce the cost of maintaining negative symmetry with the U.S.S.R. and open the way to a two-sided triangle pivoting around Peking (with the U.S. not taking umbrage at a Sino-Soviet rapprochement provided it was assured that Sino-American relations would not be jeopardized). But in view of the Soviet Union's military superiority, the long and heavily fortified border, and the historical proximity of their clash of arms, China has been unable to overcome its profound suspicion of the U.S.S.R.; secure opposition still seems preferable to the dangers of manipulation or subversion by a mistrusted partner. In attempting to secure the Sino-American relationship, it is also in China's interest to discourage Soviet-American collusion (as already noted, the potential danger of such collusion was a major factor in motivating China's entry into the triangle). Thus, in the bilateral talks leading to normalization, the Chinese structured the negotiations so that those negotiators (such as Brzezinski) and those sessions (such as his May 1978 visit) that produced the harshest denunciations of Soviet international misbehavior were rewarded with the most impressive "breakthroughs" toward normalization. Immediately after the establishment of ambassadorial relations, Deng Xiaoping arranged his January 1979 visit to the United States to create the impression of Sino-American collusion in China's punitive attack on Vietnam on February 17. The Chinese have thus shown considerable skill in "playing the American card" to bluff the Soviets.

Since 1978, the Sino-American relationship has gradually come to approximate a stable marriage. With most-favored-nation status and entry into the International Monetary Fund and World Bank, the P.R.C. acquired clear economic preferment over the U.S.S.R., and since

---

[30] See Japan External Trade Organization, *China: A Business Guide—The Japanese Perspective on China's Opening Economy* (Tokyo: Japan External Trade Organization and Press International, Ltd., 1979), 67-103.

Defense Secretary Harold Brown's visit to China in January 1980 and the return visit of his counterpart, Geng Biao, five months later, there has been increasing public reference to a quasi-military alliance. Thus far, this seems to imply the sale of sophisticated civilian and nonlethal military technology, the withdrawal of an American veto to the European sale of actual military equipment, and some coordination of joint strategies to counter Soviet expansion.[31] As the weaker partner, China may seek to promote bloc unity and militancy as a shield behind which it can pursue limited offensive maneuvers (e.g., Vietnam in 1978), much as it attempted to play the "Soviet card" in the Taiwan Straits imbroglio of 1958.

The most important shift for the United States since 1971 has been from pivot position in a romantic triangle to senior partner in a stable marriage. It would follow from the premises of the game that the latter is a less advantageous position than the former, and that a rational player would avoid such a shift unless the attrition of either wing renders the pivot position untenable. So why did it occur?

We have already noted that the Sino-American rapprochement was stage-managed to suggest anti-Soviet collusion between the two countries. To the degree that this factor precipitated the deterioration in Soviet-American relations, the P.R.C. may be said to have "outplayed" the U.S., making strategic gains at American expense: junior partnership in a stable marriage is a more secure position for the Chinese to be in than wing position in a romantic triangle. But the deterioration in Soviet-American relations *preceded* the normalization of Sino-American relations, having taken a perceptible turn for the worse in the period between 1975 and 1977. It therefore seems reasonable to attribute the decline more to bilateral difficulties than to China's admittedly provocative behavior.

According to the logic of the game, both the Soviet Union and the United States have suffered from the deterioration of their bilateral relationship—the U.S.S.R. by dropping from a wing position in a romantic triangle to a pariah position facing a stable marriage, and the U.S. by shifting from the pivot in the former to senior partnership in the latter. So the question of responsibility for that deterioration is an unusually sensitive and controversial one. One may also wonder

---

[31] A Chinese military official told a visiting Senate delegation that Beijing favored a countervailing U.S. naval buildup in the Pacific and would welcome port calls by the U.S. Seventh Fleet. When the Iranian revolution deprived the United States of its intelligence-gathering ground stations near the Caspian Sea, Deng Xiaoping suggested that the U.S. could set up facilities in the P.R.C. to monitor Soviet missile test launches in Central Asia. Strobe Talbott, "U.S.-Soviet Relations: From Bad to Worse," *Foreign Affairs*, Vol. 58 (No. 3, 1980), 15-39.

whether either side has made compensatory gains, but it is difficult to supply precise or objective answers. From the American perspective, Soviet-Cuban military collaboration in support of various leftist regimes in Africa and the Middle East was *prima facie* evidence of Soviet cheating—part of a grand strategy designed to overthrow the international status quo.[32] The invasion of Afghanistan in 1979 was another significant step in the escalation of tactics employed, involving Soviet troops in military combat beyond bloc borders for the first time since World War II. The rules of the game regulating superpower competition in the Third World under détente were never very clearly formulated, but, in view of the American performance in Vietnam, the Soviet Union might perhaps be forgiven for inferring that it is permissible to intervene militarily on behalf of client states. True—the U.S. intended merely to maintain the international status quo, whereas the U.S.S.R. meant to upset it; but it is also true that since Vietnam, the Soviet Union has been intervening far more actively in Third-World conflicts than has the United States. In any event, the original understanding had indicated that such peripheral issues should not be allowed to interfere with the central concerns of détente (e.g., strategic arms control). Here it was the United States, increasingly perturbed by perceived Soviet gains in the Third World and yet inhibited by domestic public opinion from intervening effectively, that seems to have first violated the understanding by making SALT II ratification contingent upon quiescent Soviet behavior in Africa. Such "linkage" tends to reduce progress in all other areas of détente to the pace attained in the most problematic ones.[33] If the Soviet gains in the Third World—however fairly won in terms of the original rules of the game—were considered so disequilibrating that countermeasures were deemed necessary to redress the power balance, it would have been preferable from the perspective of salvaging a positive Soviet-American relationship to confine the dispute to the Third World. Various solutions might be found there—perhaps by coming to an understanding over global spheres of influence (at present the United States tends to define all areas in the world outside the Soviet bloc as being within its sphere of influence), or by devising some more effective local or regional strategy (such as covert arms aid to guerrillas, or use of "proxy" forces) to counter Cuban-Soviet military intervention.

Détente also presupposes some diminution of the role of ideology

[32] Donald Zagoria, "Into the Breach: New Soviet Alliances in the Third World," *Foreign Affairs*, Vol. 57 (No. 4, 1979), 733-54.
[33] Lawrence Caldwell and Alexander Dallin, "U.S. Policy Toward the Soviet Union," in Oye and others (fn. 1), 199-228.

(which would otherwise dictate implacable enmity between the two systems), and the cultivation of various (apolitical) ties designed to foster understanding and friendship between the two countries. There was a perceptible diminution of ideological rhetoric on the American side during the Nixon-Ford years, as well as a proliferation of cultural exchanges, business transactions, and other forms of social interchange; it is difficult to detect any corresponding decrease in the Soviet propaganda offensive, although Brezhnev's approval of the Helsinki agreement at the 1975 Conference on Security and Cooperation in Europe represented a significant concession, with attendant risks. By initiating a global crusade against human rights violations in 1976, the Carter administration unleashed great mischief within the Soviet dissident community, encouraging activities Washington was in no way prepared to support consequentially. The United States could also not forbear taking advantage of the Soviet Union's vulnerability to cultural and social exchange (because of lower living standards and heavier reliance on repression) to cultivate critical and even anti-Communist intellectuals (offering them asylum, fame, and publication outlets) and to demand, quite successfully, a high rate of emigration for certain national minorities (Jews, Volga Germans, Armenians). There is little doubt that the U.S. considers internal liberalization and possibly eventual regime transformation one of the long-term desiderata of détente, but such goals must be pursued with a certain amount of subtlety and patience if they are not to elicit a counterproductive response from Soviet leaders. The latter no doubt prefer their regime to remain the way it is and regard any attempt to encourage domestic groups to oppose it as an insidious misuse of purported channels of mutual understanding and friendship. That is not to say that the West should refrain from calling for more liberal emigration or censorship policies, or stifle its indignation when these are rescinded; but it should also positively reinforce the Soviet leadership on whatever progress is made, rather than exploit each concession to demonstrate the barbarity of the Soviet system and make further demands. Admittedly, the Soviet Union also uses cultural and social contacts to advance its national interests—primarily to try to overcome certain areas of scientific and technological inferiority—but it does not necessarily do so in order to undermine the legitimacy of the U.S. government. Since Afghanistan, all these areas of social interchange have seriously deteriorated—as most visibly symbolized, of course, by cancellation of American participation in the Moscow Olympics. Again, if the U.S. considers a positive Soviet-American relationship more important than the "loss" of Afghanistan,

Ethiopia, or South Yemen, that relationship should be insulated as much as possible from such disturbances; more effective tactics to counter violations in peripheral arenas should be sought.

In view of the vast destructiveness of the combined nuclear arsenals, it is not surprising that strategic arms control and disarmament has always held pride of place in détente. Although SALT I heralded the advent of strategic parity, and both signatories have gone on record in support of this concept and the general need to cooperate to limit the arms race,[34] there are powerful political groupings on both sides who have not accepted this idea. In a delicate balance of terror, marked by technological volatility and unpredictable shifts in the advantage that innovations bestow to offense and defense, parity seems less secure to both than superiority; so both sides struggle for asymmetry even while attempting to regulate the competition. Although regulation is considered preferable to a war that would inflict intolerable losses upon victor as well as vanquished, competition is sustained by the prospect that some technological breakthrough will lend its host the requisite edge to make war (or its threat) a rational instrument of national policy once again. It is this intense but aim-inhibited competition for primacy that makes détente so unstable and tends to infiltrate every other channel, no matter how well-intentioned.

In sum, the Soviet-American relationship deteriorated because, in the wake of a general American withdrawal, the Soviet Union appeared for a time to be "winning" détente; even though its gains could plausibly be construed as having been legitimately achieved, the resulting shift in the international balance of power was considered disequilibrating and unacceptable to the United States. Rather than take effective steps to counter Soviet advances in those arenas in which they had been won, the U.S. allowed the entire relationship to worsen. China certainly supported and abetted this shift, which reduced its insecurity and increased its leverage without committing it in the way that an alliance would. (Dependency is more reciprocal in a stable marriage than in a romantic triangle.) But ultimate responsibility rests with Moscow and Washington.

[34] In internal debate lasting from 1974 to 1977, Soviet civilian politicians clearly laid down the line of superpower equality and the unthinkability of nuclear war. Brezhnev first went public with the new doctrine at the 1971 Congress of the CPSU, when he discarded earlier calls to "preserve the superiority" of Soviet weapons and defined the Soviet goal in the SALT negotiations as "the security of the parties considered equally." He reaffirmed this statement in January 1977. In 1974, he termed the world's nuclear stockpiles excessive, asserting that "there is an immeasurably greater risk in continuing to accumulate weapons without restraint" than in reducing arsenals, as stockpiles were already "sufficient to destroy everything living on earth several times." Soviet military

Conclusions

The purpose of this paper has been to conceive of the interests and situational constraints acting upon the three leading participants in an ongoing international relationship as logically consistent "rules" in a coherent transactional "game," which each player must adhere to if it wishes to "win." It is assumed that each player will seek to maximize benefits and minimize risks or losses, and will pursue its objectives rationally. The game's logic has implications both for *policy* issues (that is, which "moves" are of greatest advantage to the individual player under various conceivable contingencies), and broader *systemic* issues (that is, what causes the game as a whole to sustain or change its pattern dynamics).

POLICY IMPLICATIONS

In the foreseeable future, the United States seems most likely to play one of three positions in two of the three conceivable patterns. These positions are not equally advantageous, but competition for the best position will be keen and the U.S. may be outmaneuvered. They are, listed in inverse order of relative advantage: outside player in someone else's stable marriage, senior partner in a stable marriage, and pivot player in a romantic triangle.

The outside position in a stable marriage, analogous to the position of "it" in a game of keep-away, is least advantageous because the player is frozen out of amities with either of the others and must cope with two enmities. The position requires greater economic self-reliance and a heavy investment in armaments in order to deter, if not to equal, the combined military prowess of both other players; its sole advantage is to preclude the possibility of cheating or asymmetry by a (nonexistent) partner. Although this attraction is small indeed, it has sufficed to appeal to those political groups characterized by an inordinate national self-confidence and/or a profound suspicion for alliances of convenience: the "Gang of Four" in China, the Soviet "new right,"[35] and the American old right have at different points advocated such a "go it alone" strategy. The U.S. played this position in the 1950s, the P.R.C. in the 1960s, and the U.S.S.R. seems most likely to play it in the 1980s

---

resistance to such revisionism in the course of the debate indicates that these assertions were not merely a propaganda exercise to lull the West.

[35] Alexander Yanov, *The Russian New Right: Right-Wing Ideologies in the Contemporary USSR*, Policy Paper in International Affairs, No. 35 (Berkeley, Calif.: Institute of International Studies, 1978).

—though the United States might be obliged to reassume it in the event of Sino-Soviet collusion.

A rational strategy for a player in this position is to build a cluster of patron-client ties with smaller states in the hope of constituting a bloc strong and cohesive enough to counter the combined strength of the other two players: the United States attempted this in the 1950s with NATO, CENTO, SEATO, and so forth; China in the 1960s tried to adopt the nonaligned movement; more recently, the Soviet Union has attempted to integrate the military forces of the Warsaw Pact and to increase defense spending. It has also adopted an alliance-seeking and base-building approach to Africa, Southeast Asia, and the Middle East. A player who is "it" must shoulder a heavier defense burden than the other members of the triangle in order to maintain a strategic balance. It should also try not to provoke them needlessly—not only because the two-to-one power ratio must be considered forbidding no matter how successful the bloc building or how resourceful the armaments program, but also because the player's ultimate objective should be to court and "seduce" the most susceptible member of the stable marriage, thereby breaking up the opposing combination and opening the way to a new and more advantageous pattern. The incentive for "courting" is greatest for the weakest member of the triangle (viz., China); moreover, its prospects of overcoming two-to-one odds through self-reliance are least realistic.

All this would seem merely prudent, and yet there does seem to be an inherent propensity for players in the pariah position to take a defiant, even an aggressive stance. At no time was the American anti-Communist impulse more militant than in the 1950s, for example; in the 1960s, China took a highly provocative stance toward both "superpowers"; and recent Soviet behavior, with regard both to suppression of domestic dissidents and aid to fraternal regimes in Africa, Southeast Asia, or the "Northern tier," often seems deliberately calculated to antagonize either the United States or China. Such a defiant and provocative posture is perhaps understandable in view of the outside player's beleaguered position, but it is nonetheless irrational and should be avoided, for it only consolidates the opposing coalition.

Senior partnership in a stable marriage—the position vis-à-vis China that the U.S. seems to have inherited from the U.S.S.R.—offers a more advantageous power ratio and more benefits than the "it" position, without the serious danger of disadvantageous asymmetry. The uncertainty is somewhat greater, for partnership entails the risk of cheating or a double-cross. A player in this position must perform two different but interdependent tasks: retain its partner's loyalty, and maintain a modicum of enmity with its opponent.

A partner's loyalty may be retained, first, by ensuring that there is no asymmetry of bilateral relations (the U.S.S.R. forfeited the P.R.C.'s loyalty by taking advantage of such an asymmetry).[36] Unfortunately, there is no quantifiable "balance of trade" in such relations; the assessment of symmetry remains subjective and political, but it is important that neither side (particularly the more vulnerable) *feel* cheated. Second, by increasing tension with the common opponent, it is possible to enhance loyalty by giving the union a *raison d'être*.

Maintaining a modicum of enmity with one's opponent thus implies, on the one hand, that sufficient tension be maintained to retain a "stable marriage." On the other hand, it is advisable not to raise the tension too high, in order to avoid both the costs of an arms race and the risk that a cornered adversary will resort to ill-advised and ill-considered measures. Moreover, it is in the long-term interest of a senior partner in a stable marriage to reach some sort of accommodation with the opponent—if this can be done without alienating one's partner— thereby transforming the pattern to a romantic triangle with the former senior partner as pivot. The junior partner may, however, seek to foreclose such a move by escalating tension with the joint opponent (as China has seemed determined to do since 1978).

The pivot position in a romantic triangle is the most advantageous one available, permitting amities with two other players and enmities with none, thereby maximizing benefits while minimizing expenditures for sanctions. Uncertainty is, however, also maximized (the risk of double-cross is twice that of a stable marriage), but the uncertainty tends to work in the pivot's favor, as the other players are placed in positions of dependency. All the same, the position demands great delicacy and balance and is extremely difficult to play well. The pivot must maintain positive relations with both "wing" players while at the same time attempting to manage the level of tension between them.

In order to maintain positive relations with both wing players, the pivot must be sensitive not only to pivot-wing bilateral issues (such as avoiding asymmetry), but also to the relationship of the wings to each other. Each wing player will be acutely conscious of the possibility that the other may "marry" the pivot and thereby shut it out, and will thus

---

[36] See Dennis M. Ray, "Chinese Perceptions of Social Imperialism and Economic Dependency: The Impact of Soviet Aid," *Stanford Journal of International Studies*, x (Spring 1975), 36-83.

strive to avoid that situation by acting first. The wing players are apt to feel disadvantaged even if bilateral relations are scrupulously "fair," because of the persisting tension with the other wing and the one-sided dependency of both on the pivot. It is probably impossible to remain completely even-handed in dealing with the two wing players, for each will have different interests, different bargaining strategies, different capabilities, and different offers that will be more or less appealing. The important point in maintaining a romantic triangle is to convince each wing player that the pivot's relationship with the other is not based on shared antagonism; to this end, the pivot should be as candid as possible with each wing about its relationship with the other in order to dispel anxieties about collusion (some of which may be expected to persist anyhow). As Kissinger writes:

> We had to walk a narrow path. We would make these agreements with the Soviet Union which we considered in our national interest. But we would give no encouragement to visions of condominium, and we would resist any attempt by Moscow to achieve hegemony over China or elsewhere. We would keep China informed of our negotiations with the Soviet Union in considerable detail; we would take account of Peking's views. But we would not give Peking a veto over our actions.[37]

The reason the initial opening to the P.R.C. brought about a dramatic improvement in Soviet-American relations whereas the normalization of Sino-American relations in December 1978 precipitated a perceptible deterioration in Soviet-American relations may be attributed to a decline in Washington's ability to convince the Soviet Union that the Sino-American relationship was entirely innocent. In fact, the United States tended to react to every new indication of Soviet truculence with overtures to the Chinese for further "complementary actions" to contain the U.S.S.R., confirming the Soviet Union's paranoid suspicions and (from its point of view) justifying a harder line. It was not simply a difference between "playing" and "having played" the China card, but a difference between a noncollusive and a collusive liaison.[38]

Some tension between the two wing players is in the interest of the pivot player, both to forestall collusion and to deflect the targeting of weapons to the wing rivalry that might otherwise be aimed at the pivot. At the same time, too much tension would induce both wings to demand exclusive loyalty from the pivot and thus trigger polarization.

[37] Kissinger (fn. 23), 836-37.
[38] See Garrett (fn. 1); also Garrett, "The China Card: To Play or Not To Play," *Contemporary China*, III (Spring 1979), 3-18.

There is some controversy over the degree of the pivot's discretion in managing tension between the two wings. The last view of the Carter administration on this issue was rather dim, asserting essentially that U.S. relations with the two wing players are basically bilateral, to be determined independently of each other. The present analysis is, however, based on the *inescapable* triangularity of bilateral relationships: the pivot has the capability to exacerbate tension by shifting its weight to one side or the other in the dispute, or to assuage the conflict by declining to take sides.

SYSTEMIC IMPLICATIONS

There are two questions concerning the dynamics of the game as a whole. First, what are the factors that cause the game to shift its pattern dynamics—i.e., to change from a one- to a two-sided game, from a two- to a one-sided game, and so forth, and what are the factors that militate against such shifts? The second, more general question is whether any overall direction of shifts or stabilization points are inherent in the logic of the game.

The factor that seems most conducive to shifts in pattern dynamics is an abrupt increase in the game's general level of tension, followed by a decline in tension. The decline in tension is necessary to permit a realignment of partners that would seem intolerably risky during a crisis; and an increase in tension most clearly reveals stakes and priorities for the actors involved, contributing to a decision to realign once the crisis is over. Thus, the Taiwan Straits crisis of 1958 proved to be the turning point in the Sino-Soviet relationship; the first Soviet-American détente followed the Cuban missile crisis; and Sino-American détente followed the 1969 Sino-Soviet border clash. Crisis engenders a greater need for security and promotes realism, since ideological positioning becomes an unaffordable luxury in view of the high security stakes; resolution of the crisis then offers the opportunity to realign.

Mutual commitment to a common ideology or formal treaty seems to be the most effective way of freezing given pattern dynamics, though it has its limits. Indeed, the Soviet Union and China have become so bitterly estranged in spite of the same ideology that their enmity may constitute the most stable element of the current triangular pattern. How can this paradox be explained? To revert once more to the mating metaphor, friendship treaties and ideologies seem to function in somewhat the same way as marriage vows: on the one hand, they so sanctify the union that it can better endure the vicissitudes of fortune; on the other, they create such a taboo that if the marriage dissolves, it does so at considerable emotional cost and with a lingering sense of outrage. In the case of the Sino-Soviet dispute, the "divorce" was more damaging to the Soviet Union as ex-leader of an ideological crusade than to China as ex-satellite; therefore, the former seems to have clung more tenaciously to the ideology of union and to the hope that the prodigal will return eventually. Amid a world-wide decline in ideological fervor, Chinese foreign policy (like Yugoslav foreign policy, and for similar reasons) seems to have undergone an induced secularization more rapid and complete than that of the U.S.S.R., abandoning a radical challenge to the international status quo in favor of the skillful pursuit of *Realpolitik*. The Chinese punitive incursion into Vietnam in 1979 was a clash of national interests without any ideological rationale, for instance. The Chinese do not even call the CPSU "revisionist" any longer.

The overall direction of shift from one pattern dynamic to another is dependent upon the optimum cumulative benefits, risks, and costs that accrue to all players in the game. If there is an imbalance in this distribution, those placed at a disadvantage may be expected to try to rectify it. The game's developmental propensity will therefore *not* necessarily coincide with the objectives of the individual player, though the latter has an interest in understanding the former in order to plan rational moves. For example, although a pivot position in a romantic triangle is the most advantageous position in the game, this configuration is unstable because of its unequal distribution of benefits and security; this implies that inordinate sensitivity and skill are required to maintain the position against pressures for change from either wing.

If we assume that the game will naturally tend to gravitate to the pattern dynamic that returns the greatest benefit to all players at least cost, it would follow from its premises that it should spiral "upward," from a stable marriage to a romantic triangle to a *ménage à trois*. However, if we examine the evolution of the triangle since World War II, it would seem that in terms of frequency, the opposite tendency prevails: the stable marriage seems to be the norm and the *ménage à trois* has not yet evolved.

Perhaps the most important single reason for the failure of empirical reality to conform to theoretical rationality is the dominant importance of the factor of risk. The threat of massive nuclear destruction that each player poses to the others diminishes such positive inducements as trade flows or cultural exchanges, and creates an atmosphere of intense suspicion. Suspicion is intensified by the technological volatility of the arms race. Although it depletes both participants, usually without enhancing the security of either, the arms race is sustained by the prospect that some dramatic breakthrough will make it possible for one player either pre-emptively to destroy the other's offensive capability or to survive a second strike—thus making a first strike plausible and returning warfare to its classic Clausewitzian role as a continuation of politics by other means.[39] This prospect of qualitative innovation is one of the obstacles that lie in the way of regulation through SALT. Another is, of course, the vested interest that the arms industry and its bureaucratic supporters have acquired in sustaining a given level of productivity.

But the volatility is not merely technological. In the domestic political arena, a politician may cope with a threat either by conciliating the threatening party if the threat is not too grave, or by overcoming and perhaps even eliminating it (depending on domestic political culture). A tendency to transpose the domestic rules of the game to the international arena leads both politicians and their domestic audiences to display a consistent ambivalence about foreign powers who pose a security threat. They are uncertain whether to cooperate in jointly beneficial relationships or to do everything possible to undermine and destroy the other side. Western observers have recognized this ambiguity in the foreign policy of the Soviet Union (and sometimes the P.R.C.), often attributing it to ideological Messianism, but have less frequently detected such tendencies in American foreign policy. Of course, the domestic political payoffs for such broadmindedness are limited; in view of the standing threat posed by the other player, any attempt at cooperation is apt to be viewed as appeasement. Détente tends to coincide with the disintegration of alliances and with the rise of dissident movements, developments particularly threatening to bloc leaders. International polarization tends to concentrate tension, whereas détente tends to disperse it; the former situation is more dangerous, but in some ways more manageable and certainly less ambiguous than the

---

[39] One of the reasons for the deterioration of Soviet-American relations is to be found in recent changes in the nuclear balance, which have led some Western observers to infer that the Soviet Union is on its way to a disabling first-strike capability; these may plausibly have led Soviet observers to the reverse conclusion. Among the technological innovations that make the pre-emptive destruction of land-based hardened missile silos feasible are MIRV capability and the more recent improvements in missile accuracy (which have resulted from unanticipated advances in such areas as computer and engine microminiaturization, order-of-magnitude acceleration of data processing, inertial navigation, American Navstar satellite position fixing of submarines to within 10 meters in three dimensions regardless of weather, gravity and geodesy positioning, real-time satellite reconnaissance of ground information, preprogrammed terminal homing computers in warheads, terrain-matching, and rapid retargeting of both ICBMs and SLBMs). If either side were to achieve a unilateral breakthrough in laser defense against missiles, this could also radically alter the strategic balance.

latter. For détente to be politically feasible, not only should international crises which may be expected to mobilize domestic opposition be avoided; some understanding should also be reached to forbear using social penetration in order to incite dissident movements. Otherwise, the insecurity of the regime will increase (thereby jeopardizing further rapprochement).

Suspicion is probably endemic to the anarchic character of the international arena; any attempt to eliminate it altogether must be dismissed as utopian. The most that might be hoped for is that the principals involved come to understand that they have long-term as well as short-term interests, and that the former require that the interests of the other major actors also be taken into account. The minimal objectives of any prudent foreign policy under current circumstances must be the "national interest"; but more ecumenical arrangements might be adopted as a *maximal* objective, to be striven for whenever it does not jeopardize the minimal objective. Such a viewpoint could certainly be formulated at an ideological level, and might under some circumstances even have an impact upon policy.

STRATEGIC STUDIES AND

ITS CRITICS

By HEDLEY BULL

THE civilian strategic analysts who now constitute a distinct profession in the Western world have from the first been subject to criticism that has called in question the validity of their methods, their utility to society, and even their integrity of purpose.[1] Some of it is directed at particular strategists or at particular techniques they employ, but much of it purports to expose deficiencies that are characteristic of the genre. Some of this is of so scurrilous a nature as not to deserve a reply, but some raises issues of real importance. What are in fact the distinguishing features of the new style of strategic analysis? What has given rise to the criticisms that have been made of it? And what substance do the criticisms have?

Strategy in its most general sense is the art or science of shaping means so as to promote ends in any field of conflict. In the special sense in which I am using it here, the sense in which "strategy" is interchangeable with "military strategy," it is the art or science of exploiting military force so as to attain given objects of policy. If we contrast the strategic thinking of contemporary military analysts with the classical tradition of strategic thought from Clausewitz to Douhet, certain of its peculiarities are at once apparent.

First, strategic thinking at the present time is no longer exclusively concerned with the efficient conduct of war. From the time of Napoleon to that of Hitler, strategy was conceived of as an aspect of war. Contrasting it with tactics, which was the art of winning battles, Clausewitz defined strategy as "the art of employment of battles as a means to gain the object in war."[2] How to gain the object in war remains a central preoccupation of contemporary strategic thinking, but it is no longer the only one or necessarily the most important. Attention has shifted away from war as an instrument of policy toward the threat of war, and studies of actual violence have given place to analyses

---

[1] See, e.g., James R. Newman, review of Herman Kahn's *On Thermonuclear War*, *Scientific American*, CCIV (March 1961), 197-98; P. M. S. Blackett, *Studies of War, Nuclear and Conventional* (New York 1962), chap. 10; Sir Solly Zuckerman, *Scientists and War: The Impact of Science on Military and Civil Affairs* (New York 1967), chap. 5; Irving L. Horowitz, *The War Game: Studies of the New Civilian Militarists* (New York 1963); Anatol Rapoport, *Strategy and Conscience* (New York 1964); Philip Green, *Deadly Logic: The Theory of Nuclear Deterrence* (Columbus 1966).

[2] *On War*, Book III, chap. 1.

of "deterrence," "crisis management," "the manipulation of risk"—or, as we call it when it is practiced by our opponents rather than ourselves, "blackmail." Moreover, gaining the object in war, even when it remains the concern of strategists, is no longer always seen in Clausewitz' sense of attaining victory by imposing our will on the adversary. In discussions of the conduct of strategic nuclear war the object of victory over the opponent has in fact taken second place to that of our own survival. It has sometimes been argued that the chief mission of United States strategic nuclear forces in the event of general war is that of the limitation of damage suffered by the United States and its allies—an object that is not relative to the amount of damage suffered by the enemy, but absolute.

Second, strategic thinking is no longer the preserve of the military. The great strategic writers of the past, like Liddell Hart, Fuller, and Mao Tse-tung in our own time, were soldiers (or sailors or airmen) or ex-soldiers. They were often quite bad soldiers; and they had qualities of mind that soldiers, good and bad, do not often have. But underlying all their theorizing was the assumption that strategy was in some sense a practical business, that experience of the management of forces and weapons in war, even if it was not a sufficient condition of strategic understanding, was at least a necessary one.

The military profession today is very far from having vacated the field of strategy; in wide areas of strategic policy the chiefs of staff responsible to governments remain the preponderant influence. But in the United States and to a lesser extent elsewhere in the Western world, the civilian experts have made great inroads. They have overwhelmed the military in the quality and quantity of their contributions to the literature of the subject; no one would now think of turning to the writings of retired officers rather than to the standard academic treatments of deterrence, limited war, or arms control for illumination of the problems of the nuclear age. They increasingly dominate the field of education and instruction in the subject—the academic and quasi-academic centers of strategic studies have displaced the staff colleges and war colleges, except in narrow fields of professional knowledge. And, most prominently in the United States, the civilian strategists have entered the citadels of power and have prevailed over military advisers on major issues of policy.

A third peculiarity of strategic thinking at the present time is its abstract and speculative character. There has not yet been a nuclear war, and the possibility that there will be one has not yet existed long enough for it to have become clear how the structure of international life will be affected. Anyone who has embarked upon a discussion of what the conditions are under which one country can deter another from doing something, of whether or not limitations are possible in nuclear war, of whether the nuclear stalemate makes conflict at lower levels more likely or less, or of whether one country can credibly threaten to use nuclear weapons on behalf of another must have experienced the sense of being at sea in an argument in which, it seems, almost any position can be plausibly defended and almost none is safe from attack.

Strategic thinking, of course, has always been speculative. It has always had to deal with the future, and it has always involved the making of plans, the fulfilment of which depends on decisions taken by the opponent as well as on those we take ourselves. And the conditions of war and crisis under which these decisions have to be made make them peculiarly difficult to anticipate and peculiarly unlikely to follow the lines of assumed standards of rationality. The advent of nuclear and missile technology, however, has rendered strategic thinking speculative to a degree that it had not previously attained. It is not the physical effects of nuclear explosives and missiles that are speculative; indeed, in this respect war has become more predictable and measurable than before. What cannot be confidently foreseen is how statesmen, governments, and societies will behave under the stress of the use of these weapons or the threat to use them. In a period of vast changes in warfare and its place in human affairs, the relevance of history and experience, and the competence of those whose expertise is founded in them, have rightly been called in question.

A fourth characteristic of strategic thinking at the present time is its sophistication and high technical quality. Many students of strategy today take the view that until our own time military affairs escaped sustained scientific study and received only the haphazard attention of second-rate minds. Accordingly they see themselves as presiding over the birth of a new science, eliminating antiquated methods and replacing them with up-to-date ones. Some take the view that there is a close analogy between strategic studies and economics, and they hold out the hope that the former subject, when it emerges from its birth pangs, will enable us to rationalize our choices and increase our control of our environment to the same extent that the latter has done.

This view does less than justice to the classical tradition of strategic thinking, while it also fails to recognize the very slight extent to which the new scientific rigor in strategic studies has so far circumscribed the domain of speculation. Nevertheless, it is clear that the intellectual resources now being devoted to strategic studies are without precedent and that this has resulted in a literature of higher technical quality and a discussion of a higher standard of sophistication than have existed before. One incidental consequence of this is the emergence of strategic studies as an appropriate subject for inclusion in university curricula. Although I do not myself believe that it is desirable to separate strategic studies from the wider study of international relations, it can be argued that it compares very favorably with some other branches of political science both in its moral and social relevance and as an intellectual discipline.

A number of factors account for the barrage of criticism that the civilian strategists have had to face. For those who feel guilt about modern war or have fear of it—and in some degree this includes all persons who are sensitive and aware—the strategists have undoubtedly provided a scapegoat. The political influence that the civilian strategists have come to command, especially though not exclusively in the United States, has caused resentment—on the one hand among the older generation of soldiers and civil servants whose influence they have displaced, and on the other hand among their fellow intellectuals who have remained outsiders. Their willingness to treat strategy as a specialist's subject, even as an esoteric one, has irritated those who are unable to understand or to emulate them. Their insistence on the complexity of the problems of strategy and arms control has been unwelcome to purveyors of simple solutions of one kind or another. Most basically, perhaps, the position of the professional strategist is and will remain controversial because the legitimacy of the question he sets himself—What shall the state do with its military force?—is itself controversial. While there continues to be disagreement in modern society as to whether or not the state should ever use military force or possess it at all, there will not be general agreement about the worth and utility of students of strategy, in the way in which there is now (although there has not always been) about that of students of medicine, architecture, or economics.

To show that the motives that underlie criticism of the strategist are sometimes discreditable is not, of course, to say that it is only from these sources that criticism arises, still less to provide a rebuttal of the criticisms themselves. Many of the criticisms are worth sympathetic consideration. In my view they do not constitute, either singly or collectively, a valid indictment of the work of the civilian strategists. But we should be grateful that they have been made, for they do draw attention to some false paths along which strategists might stray and sometimes have strayed. Here I shall consider five of the charges.

The first and most common complaint is that the strategists leave morality out of account. Strategists are often said to be technicians and calculators who are indifferent as to the moral standing of the causes for which war is undertaken or of the means by which it is carried on.

There is a sense in which strategic thinking does and should leave morality out of account. Strategy is about the relationship between means and ends, and an exercise in "pure" strategy will exclude consideration of the moral nature of the means and the ends, just as it will exclude anything else that is extraneous. If what is being said is that strategic judgments should be colored by moral considerations or that strategic inquiry should be restricted by moral taboos, this is something that the strategist is bound to reject. If what the critics of Herman Kahn have in mind is that he should not have thought about the unthinkable or that he should have thought about it with his heart instead of his head, then they are obstructing him in his essential task.

What can be said, however, is that while strategy is one thing and morals are another, the decisions that governments take in the field of military policy should not be based on considerations of strategy alone. If the charge against the strategists is that their advice to governments is drawn up in purely strategic terms, as if strategic imperatives were categorical imperatives, or that they themselves have no other dimension in their thinking than the calculation of means and ends, then this is a serious and legitimate complaint.

But so far as one can judge, such a charge is not true of any of the strategists. It is easy to see that their works, dealing as they do with strategy and not with other subjects, might give the impression that decisions should be determined by the logic of this subject alone, but there is no reason to believe that this impression is correct. Strategists as a class, it seems to me, are neither any less nor any more sensitive to moral considerations than are other intelligent and educated persons in the West.

Why, then, is the charge so frequently made? Can all the critics be wrong? Surely as between Herman Kahn and his critic James Newman, as between Irving Horowitz and those he calls "the new civilian militarists," or as between Anatol Rapoport and the various unnamed strategists who are his targets there is some sort of moral disagreement. I believe that there is, but that what is at issue is not whether or not moral questions should be asked before decisions are taken but what the answers to the moral questions are.

In almost any disagreement as to whether or not to resort to war or to threaten it, or as to how a war should be conducted or what risks in it should be run, there are moral arguments to be advanced on both sides. What the critics take to be the strategists' insensitivity to moral considerations is in most cases the strategists' greater sense of the moral stature of American and Western political objectives for which war and the risk of war must be undertaken. The notion that virtue in international conduct lies simply in avoiding risk of war and never in assuming it, always in self-abnegation and never in self-assertion, only in obeying the rules a world community might legislate if it existed and never in pursuing the different moral guides that are appropriate in a situation in which it does not—such a notion is of course untenable. But it forms part of the perspective of many of the critics. What chiefly characterizes the so-called idealist school to which they belong is not (as is often said) that it exaggerates the force of moral considerations, still less that it alone is endowed with moral vision, but that it fails to appreciate the full range of the moral argument, that it embraces what Treitschke called "the monkish type of virtue" without being able to see that there is any other.

There is, I think, a related moral disagreement between the strategists and their critics, which concerns the role of the strategist as an adviser to governments. It is said that there is something unbecoming to an intellectual—or at all events to a university man, with his allegiance to the universal republic of science—in bestowing the fruits of his strategic advice upon any particular government. Since governments use this advice to further their conflicts with one another, the strategic adviser is in a different position from the scholar or scientist who gives advice about the economy or health or education, since in these fields the interests of one nation may be advanced without injuring those of others. The scholar may legitimately proffer advice, if he has any, about the conditions of peace, so the argument goes, but he is disloyal to his calling if he provides advice about war.[3]

Some of this criticism may be met readily enough. One may point out that the strategic interests of nations are not wholly exclusive of one another and that contemporary strategists have been inclined to draw attention to the common interests that nations have in avoiding nuclear war and in limiting it if it occurs. One may say that one of their contributions has been the systematic study of arms control, which may be defined as cooperation among antagonistic states in

[3] See, e.g., Max Teichmann, "Strategic Studies or Peace Research?" *Arena* (Melbourne), No. 12 (Autumn 1967), 9-16.

advancing their perceived common interests in military policy. Arms-control policy is, I should say, subsumed under strategy as a special case. It may also be pointed out that it is facile to regard war and peace as alternative objects of policy, as if peace did not need to be enforced or war were not an outgrowth of diplomacy.

Yet it remains true that the strategic adviser does assist the government he serves to advance its objectives at the expense of those of other governments. But whether or not there is anything in the position of such an adviser unbecoming to a scholar or a scientist will depend on what we take the moral nature of that government and its objectives to be. Few of the critics would, I think, argue that the scientists who assisted the British and American governments during the Second World War, and whose position the contemporary strategists have inherited, were acting in an improper way. Not everyone will agree that the position is the same now; but at least it is not possible to maintain that there is any general incompatibility between assisting a state to augment its relative military position and remaining faithful to scholarly or scientific values.

The second criticism that I wish to discuss is that strategists take for granted the existence of military force and confine themselves to considering how to exploit it, thereby excluding a whole range of policies such as disarmament or nonviolent resistance that are intended to abolish military force or to provide substitutes for it.

It is true that strategists take the fact of military force as their starting point. The question is whether any other starting point is possible at all, whether the doctrine of disarmament that is implicit in this complaint is not inherently untenable. The capacity for organized violence between states is inherent in the nature of man and his environment. The most that can be expected from a total disarmament agreement is that it might make armaments and armed forces fewer and more primitive.

If what is meant by "total disarmament" is a state of affairs in which war is physically impossible, in which states cannot wage war even when they want to (this is what Litvinov meant when he first put forward the proposal in 1927), then we must say that such a state of affairs cannot be. If, on the other hand, what is meant is a situation in which military force has been reduced to very low qualitative and quantitative levels, then this is something that can in principle occur and may well seem worth trying to bring about. But the view that security against war is best provided by a low level of armaments rather than a high one is a particular strategic theory; the arguments for it and against it belong to the same mode of discourse as that we apply in evaluating any other proposition about the relationship between military force and possible ends of policy.

Either, then, the second criticism is a nonsense or it represents an attempt to contribute to strategic reasoning, not a statement about it from outside. In fact, it would seem to me, proposals for radical disarmament and for nonviolent resistance have received a fair hearing within the Western community of strategists. No doubt strategists are inclined to think too readily in terms of military solutions to the problems of foreign policy and to lose sight of the other instruments that are available. But this is the occupational disease of any specialist, and the remedy for it lies in entering into debate with the strategist and correcting his perspective.

The third criticism is that strategists are inclined to make unreal assumptions about international politics and that in comparing alternative strategies and computing their costs and benefits they make assumptions that simplify and distort political reality, that do not allow for change, and that in the course of the subsequent analysis become lost to sight.

This is a complaint that has a great deal of force. The technical rigor and precision of much strategic analysis has been achieved at the cost of losing touch with political variety and change. If the political terms in the strategists' equations were more complex and were changed more frequently, the beauty of much of the ratiocination would be destroyed.

Some of the now-classic analyses of America's problem in choosing her weapons and military posture were founded upon the assumption that there was only one significant relationship in nuclear international politics, that between the United States and the Soviet Union, and that this consisted only of hostility. Not only, as it were, was the game two-person and zero-sum, but the two persons were assumed to be identical twins, Country A and Country B. Even when these analyses were first made they were a simplification of reality, but with their survival into the age of the Soviet-American détente and of the disintegration of the Atlantic Alliance and the Communist bloc, they became dangerously unreal. The greatest absurdities of this sort in recent times formed part of the debate that took place in the United States during the Kennedy administration about the control of nuclear weapons in NATO. The various solutions were set out in programmatic form—a United States nuclear monopoly, national nuclear forces, a NATO nuclear force, a European nuclear force—and their advantages and disadvantages were spelled out on the basis that NATO was a single person and that the sole requirement of that person was to deter attack by the Soviet Union. Not all those who contributed to the debate, of course, formulated the problem in this way, but many a weighty treatise appeared that did so. General de Gaulle has now demonstrated what was perhaps all along clear, that Paris and London are not Washington and that nuclear forces have diplomatic functions as well as military ones; but it is extraordinary for how long, under its own momentum, this strange logic persisted.

All that one can say in defense of the strategists against this charge is that follies of this sort are not inherent in what they do, that technical precision must often be sacrificed so as to allow for political variety and change, and that enough of the strategists are aware of this to ensure that the corrections can come from inside the strategic community.

The fourth criticism is that the civilian strategists are pseudoscientific in their methods, that specialist techniques they employ—such as game theory, systems analysis, simulation, and the writing of scenarios— are bogus when used to arrive at strategic decisions and serve to give an air of expertise to positions arbitrarily and subjectively arrived at. This is the theme of the book *Deadly Logic*, by Philip Green, and it is also part of the meaning of the wrong-headed but subtle and powerful book *Strategy and Conscience*, by Anatol Rapoport.

The crux of the matter is the attack on game theory, which more clearly than any of the other techniques mentioned does represent an impressive expertise. Rapoport presents some strong arguments against the application of game theory to strategic decision-making. Exercises in game theory, he says, deal in numerical probabilities, but these cannot be assigned to unique events. Such exercises assume the unlimited ability of each party to think and compute with no limit of time—which actual decision-makers cannot do. The exercises assume that the goals of each party are single, simple, and unchanging, whereas historical individuals and groups have objectives that are plural, complex, and subject to constant revision. And so on.

This attack on the use of game theory is bewildering. As Donald Brennan has pointed out in a review of Rapoport, the great majority of civilian strategists do not use game theory and indeed would be at a loss to give any account of it.[4] There are, certainly, a number of strategists, like Thomas Schelling, who have mastered this technique, but in their work exercises in game theory serve only to illus-

---

[4] *Bulletin of the Atomic Scientists*, xxi (December 1965), 25-30.

trate points that are independently arrived at; they have not employed game theory in order to determine solutions to strategic problems. As far as I know, the only person who has claimed that game theory presents a method of solving strategic problems is Oskar Morgenstern of Princeton University. Morgenstern collaborated with John von Neumann in producing *Theory of Games and Economic Behavior* and has also written a book on strategy, *The Question of National Defense.*[5] But even in Morgenstern's book, which contains much rhetoric about the value of game theory, it is not possible to find an instance in which he makes use of it. I do not despair of finding an example of what Green and Rapoport are talking about, but I must say I have not so far come across one. It may be that although game theory is not an essential or even a significantly used technique of the civilian strategists, some of the logic of game theory is implicit in the way some strategists do their thinking, and a critique of the former is a way of providing a critique of the latter.[6] The basic point of Philip Green's book, that the technique and rigor that the civilian strategists have brought to the subject do not provide a means of circumventing political choices and that they can be and sometimes are employed as a political weapon in support of one arbitrarily chosen policy or another, is undoubtedly correct. This, however, is an argument for recognizing the limits of rigor and precision and for being on guard against their misuse, not for abandoning rigor and precision in favor of something else.

Both in the domestic defense debates in Western countries today and in international rivalries over arms control or the sharing of military burdens within alliances, the strategist is constantly finding that his works are pressed into the service of political objectives that are pursued on different grounds. The army, the navy, the air force, each has its strategic ideology; the United States, France, and Great Britain, in contending with one another as to how nuclear weapons shall be controlled in NATO, as to where and in what way a war in Europe would be fought, as to what contributions shall be made to the shield forces in central Europe—each develops a strategic doctrine that points

---

[5] *Theory of Games and Economic Behavior* (Princeton 1944); *The Question of National Defense* (Princeton 1959), esp. 61, 164, 269.

[6] In his reply to Brennan's review, Rapoport says, "My complaint against the strategists was not that they use or misuse game theory (although one of my earlier articles was so entitled). On the contrary, my complaint was that they have not learned some important lessons of game theory" (*Bulletin of the Atomic Scientists*, xxi [December 1965], 31-36). This is a slippery reformulation that does not answer Brennan's charge, viz., that Rapoport implies that strategists use game theory, whereas they do not.

to the end it has in view, and each is anxious to exploit the authority of studies independently undertaken and scientifically followed through.

The strategist himself, however, cannot be held responsible for the use that others make of his ideas. Moreover, the fact that strategic expertise has come to have a political function as an ideology is inevitable and, I believe, by no means wholly regrettable. Scientific expertise has become the idiom of debate, within governments and between them, not only in the strategic field but in many others. If it is pressed into service by one party, the other parties must acquire it themselves or go under. The British Foreign Office now finds it necessary to employ its own economic experts to do battle with the Treasury and the Department of Economic Affairs, its own scientific experts to deal with the Ministry of Technology and the Atomic Energy Authority, and its own strategic experts to contend with the Ministry of Defence. The governments of Western Europe in the last decade have found themselves constantly at a most serious political disadvantage in relation to the United States in defense matters because they have not had a body of strategic expertise of their own with which to frustrate American attempts to overawe them. That they will acquire such expertise there can be no doubt.

These developments are not wholly to be regretted because they do raise the standard and tone of strategic debate at the highest levels of decision; the necessity under which governments, and departments of governments, labor of developing strategic ideologies does show that somewhere in the process of decision, independent and expert studies are being carried out and that these cannot be ignored.

Is it the case that the civilian strategists in America have been consistent endorsers of the main lines of United States foreign policy and that they have hidden this policy outlook beneath a pretense of objectivity? The work of the most prominent of these persons originated in criticism and questioning of the established policies of the Eisenhower Administration. No doubt it still has proceeded on the basis of assumptions held in common with official thinking, which looked at from the outside appear as orthodox. In the writings of some of the strategists, more particularly those Rapoport calls the "neo-traditionalists," the assumptions (e.g., about the existence of a "threat," the need for military strength, the morality of providing it, and so on) are spelled out and defended. In the writings of others they are not, and in these cases it is important that critics should identify the assumptions and question them. But the shaping of United

States military policy is not an exercise in philosophy or theology; at some point firm assumptions have to be made, and on the basis of them the costs and benefits of alternatives worked out. It is inevitable that in this process the assumptions will be taken as read and also that books and papers will be written in which the authors address themselves to others who make the same assumptions, rather than to the public at large.

The fifth criticism, although it also comes from Anatol Rapoport, is in some ways at loggerheads with the fourth. It is that the sin of the strategist, far from being his covert commitment to political purposes, is his objectivity. This is really the distinctive contribution of Rapoport's book. The strategist is detached and aloof, but he has no right to be. The effect of his cold appraisal of the world as he sees it is to perpetuate the nightmare around him or to create it where it does not exist. Given the dangers of the world as it is now, the appropriate attitude is not to describe it but to go to work on it. The strategists, who have the ear of the powerful, might accomplish great things if they abandoned the strategic mode of reasoning for the conscientious; but instead they are collaborators in the system and are speeding up its movement toward catastrophe.

If there is a kernel of truth in what Rapoport says it is that the strategist, like all students of social affairs, is related to what he studies not only as subject to object but also as cause to effect. It is always important to recognize in foreign policy, as in the conduct of Western policy toward Russia and China now, that the intentions and goals of a country, whether they are peaceful or aggressive, are not fixed and given, but are always in part the product of our own action toward them.

But this basis of truth does not sustain the strange construction that Rapoport erects upon it. There are certain things that Russia will do whatever policies the United States follows toward her, certain conflicts in the world that simply have to be taken as given. Arthur Burns has pointed out in a review that one of Rapoport's errors is to make the common American assumption of a fundamentally two-person situation.[7] From the perspective of a small country on the sidelines of the international arena, the Soviet-American conflict simply appears as a datum, something that has arisen quite independently of anything that small country did or might have done. It is, to say the least, greatly to exaggerate the influence of the strategists to hold

---

[7] Arthur Lee Burns, "Must Strategy and Conscience Be Disjoined?" *World Politics*, xvii (July 1965), 687-702.

them responsible for the rise of Russian power and for the overflowing beyond Russian borders of the revolution of 1917.

But even if Rapoport is right and America, if not her strategists, has it in her power to mold the behavior of Russia or China, this does not necessarily support the conclusions that Rapoport would like to draw from this. If United States policy in recent years has contributed to the changes that have made the Soviet Union a more satisfied power and a more conservative influence in world affairs, this may have as much to do with America's strength and firmness as will her overtures of conciliation or readiness to make concessions.

The doctrines that the civilian strategic analysts in the West have evolved in the last decade are scarcely the last word on strategy in the nuclear age, but should be seen as first, faltering steps in defining a problem that will be with us for as far into the future as we can see. The three notions that have been most central in these doctrines— "deterrence," "limited war," and "arms control"—have all been elaborated chiefly in the context of the Soviet-American confrontation, and their implications for the more polycentric diplomatic field that now exists have not been thought out. They have all been put forward in relation to classical international conflict between states that are internally stable and armed with the most advanced weapons, and they have not been adapted to the different but now more prominent circumstances of civil conflicts within unstable states with primitive military equipment. Moreover, even in the narrow field in which, quite rightly, the civilian strategists have concentrated their efforts, their most fundamental assumptions are open to challenge, as the debate about ballistic missile defense is now showing.

Yet the work of the civilian strategists has at least charted some reasoned course where otherwise there might well have been only drift. It has provided some solid intellectual fare that subsequent generations, even though they reject it, are at least likely to recognize as a serious attempt to come to grips with the problem. When one asks oneself what the history of strategic policy in the West might have been in the last ten years had this influence not been brought to bear, or when one contemplates the moral and intellectual poverty of the debate about nuclear affairs (or of that part of it we are able to see) in the Soviet Union where in fact no such influence exists, it is difficult to escape the conclusion that even though the civilian strategists have sometimes committed the errors I have been exploring, they have served us well.

TILTING TOWARD THANATOS:
America's "Countervailing" Nuclear Strategy

By LOUIS RENÉ BERES

THE Devil in George Bernard Shaw's *Man and Superman* observes that "Man's heart is in his weapons . . . in the arts of death he outdoes Nature herself . . . when he goes out to slay, he carries a marvel of mechanisms that lets loose at the touch of his finger all the hidden molecular energies. . . ." Since the dawn of the nuclear age in July 1945, these "hidden molecular energies" have brought humankind perilously close to its rendezvous with extinction. Although the United States may still have it within its grasp to prevent such a rendezvous, our leaders continue to refine policies and scenarios of nuclear war-fighting that can only hasten the eventuality of a desolated planet. At present, these leaders behave as if the requirements of stable nuclear deterrence included preparations for "rational" nuclear warfare.[1] In the words of Leon Sloss, who directed this country's nuclear targeting policy review for the Department of Defense in 1978, "The emphasis has shifted from the *survivability* necessary to assure that we can launch a single preplanned strike to the *endurance* necessary to actually fight a war that may extend over some period of time and involve a series of nuclear exchanges."[2]

To understand this shift in emphasis, we must consider the essential elements, assumptions, and historical roots of what has come to be known as the "countervailing" nuclear strategy.[3] Codified in Presidential Directive 59, which was signed on July 25, 1980, and reaffirmed by President Reagan,[4] this strategy represents the latest retreat from the

---

[1] The extreme advocacy for such preparations can be found in Colin S. Gray and Keith Payne, "Victory Is Possible," *Foreign Policy*, No. 39 (Summer 1980), 14-27.

[2] Sloss, "Carter's Nuclear Policy: Going From 'MAD' to Worse"? "No: It's Evolutionary, Not Revolutionary, and Aims to Strengthen Deterrence," *Los Angeles Times*, August 31, 1980, p. 3 (emphasis in original).

[3] The countervailing strategy has, it appears, never been strictly defined. The closest we can come to a definition may be found in Secretary of Defense Harold Brown's *Department of Defense Annual Report for FY 1981*:
For deterrence to operate successfully, our potential adversaries must be convinced that we possess sufficient military force so that if they were to start a course of action which could lead to war, they would be frustrated in their effort to achieve their objective or suffer so much damage that they would gain nothing by their action. . . . The preparation of forces and plans to create such a prospect has come to be referred to as a 'countervailing' strategy (Washington, D.C.: 1980), 65.

[4] Presidential Directive 59 was clarified by Defense Secretary Harold Brown in his "Remarks Delivered at the Convocation Ceremonies for the 97th Naval War College Class," U.S. Naval War College, Newport, Rhode Island, August 20, 1980, p. 6.

doctrine of "massive retaliation" first defined by John Foster Dulles in January 1954.[5] It endorses a "counterforce" targeting plan that is designed to fulfill military tasks at a level far exceeding the requirements of "mutual assured destruction."[6] No longer satisfied with a policy of "minimum deterrence," the countervailing strategy envisions a broad array of nuclear retaliatory options within a carefully defined "spectrum of deterrence." Former Secretary of Defense Harold Brown has stated that

> deterrence remains, as it has been historically, our fundamental strategic objective. But deterrence must restrain a far wider range of threats than just massive attacks on U.S. cities. We seek to deter any adversary from any course of action that could lead to general nuclear war. Our strategic forces must also deter nuclear attacks on smaller sets of targets in the U.S. or on U.S. military forces, and be a wall against nuclear coercion of, or attack on, our friends and allies. And strategic forces, in conjunction with theater nuclear forces, must contribute to deterrence of conventional aggression as well. . . . In our analysis and planning, we are necessarily giving greater attention to how a nuclear war would actually be fought by both sides if deference fails. There is no contradiction between this focus on how a war would be fought and what its results would be, *and* our purpose of insuring continued peace through mutual deterrence. Indeed, this focus helps us achieve deterrence and peace, by ensuring that our ability to retaliate is fully credible.[7]

In essence, this countervailing strategy, which is the outcome of a fundamental review of American targeting policy ordered by President Carter, stresses the capacity to employ strategic nuclear forces "selectively." Anticipating intermediate levels of Soviet aggression, it was designed to impress on Soviet leaders the fact that the United States has both the will and the means to make such aggression irrational. It does this by operationalizing an incremental policy of strategic response that will allegedly make Soviet leaders less adventurous.

Former Secretary Brown stated on several occasions that this is not an altogether new strategic posture. P.D. 59 codifies a series of doctrinal modifications that have been underway for at least 25 years. In the Secretary's words,

> The U.S. has never had a doctrine based simply and solely on reflexive, massive attacks on Soviet cities. Instead, we have always planned both

---

[5] See *New York Times*, January 13, 1954, p. 1.

[6] A *counterforce* strategy emphasizes the targeting of an adversary's military capability, especially its strategic military capability. A *countervalue* strategy emphasizes the targeting of an adversary's cities and industries. *Mutual Assured Destruction* (MAD) is a condition wherein each adversary possesses the ability to inflict an unacceptable degree of damage upon the other after absorbing a first strike.

[7] See Brown (fn. 4), 6.

more selectively (options limiting urban-industrial damage) and more comprehensively (a range of military targets). Previous Administrations, going back well into the 1960s, recognized the inadequacy of a strategic doctrine that would give us too narrow a range of options. The fundamental premises of our countervailing strategy are a natural evolution of the conceptual foundations built over the course of a generation by, for example, Secretaries McNamara and Schlesinger, to name only two of my predecessors who have been most identified with the development of our nuclear doctrine.[8]

The basic shape of the countervailing strategy was outlined by Secretary Brown in his Annual Report to the Congress for FY 1981. There he developed the argument that large-scale countervalue attacks may not be appropriate to deter the full range of potential Soviet threats. Faced with what he saw as a need for deterring Soviet attacks of "less than all-out scale," he proposed options to attack Soviet military and political targets while holding back a significant reserve. Such a strategy, he argued, could preclude an intolerable choice between no effective military response and all-out nuclear war. Instead, we could attack "in a selective and measured way, a range of military, industrial, and political control targets, while retaining an assured destruction capacity in reserve."[9]

At first glance, such a strategy may appear sound and prudent. Upon closer examination, however, it becomes apparent that a policy of calibrating U.S. nuclear retaliation to the particular provocation does not support the overall objective of strategic deterrence. Indeed, careful scrutiny of the policy's underlying principles reveals that it actually contributes to the fulfillment of our long-prophesied nuclear annihilation because it is founded upon an implausible set of assumptions and upon a misunderstanding of interactive effects.

IMPLAUSIBLE ASSUMPTIONS AND IGNORED INTERACTIONS

First, current strategic nuclear policy rests on the assumption that the Soviets might have something to gain by launching a limited first-strike attack on the United States or its allies. This assumption overlooks the fact that the Soviets do not share our view of controlled nuclear conflict, and that they are apt to doubt our declared commitment to proportionate retaliation. Faced with great uncertainty about the nature of an American strategic response, Soviet leaders considering the costs and benefits of striking first could not rationally calculate on the basis of strategic self-restraint.

[8] *Ibid.,* 7.   [9] See Brown (fn. 3), 66.

Sidney Drell has testified before the Senate Subcommittee on Arms Control, that in order to carry out a militarily effective attack against American ICBMs, the Soviets would have to unleash an attack that would bring about approximately 18.3 million American fatalities. Even so extensive a counterforce assault would be far from disabling, since the remaining American ICBMs would still constitute an assuredly destructive retaliatory force.[10] Moreover, Paul C. Warnke, former Director of the U.S. Arms Control and Disarmament Agency, has stated that

> scenarios for limited strategic exchange between the two countries are inherently implausible. Any Soviet attack that would leave untouched the majority of our strategic nuclear delivery vehicles would be an act of insane provocation. To have even a theoretical chance of taking out our more than 1,000 land-based ICBMs, the Soviets would have to launch 2,000 to 3,000 accurate warheads of high yield. This could hardly be described as a limited nuclear war. It would deserve and would receive at least an equally massive response.[11]

Second, current strategic nuclear policy is founded on the idea that the Soviets are more likely to be deterred by the threat of limited American counterforce reprisals than by the threat of overwhelming, total retaliation. What this idea ignores, however, is the Soviets' stated unwillingness to play by American rules. Since the Soviet Union continues to threaten this country with all-out nuclear war once the nuclear threshold has been crossed, the credibility of the U.S. commitment to selective counterforce strikes must be very doubtful. Once again, the asymmetry in strategic doctrine between the superpowers impairs the reasonableness of America's countervailing strategy.

Moscow's viewpoint has repeatedly been voiced in Soviet sources of military doctrine and strategy.[12] Bernard Brodie observed in 1959, "Soviet commentary on the limited-war thinking emanating from the West has thus far been uniformly hostile and derisive. Especially derided has been the thought that wars might remain limited while being fought with atomic weapons."[13] More recently, Sovietologist Richard

---

[10] See Drell's testimony, "Possible Effects on U.S. Society of Nuclear Attacks Against U.S. Military Installations," U.S. Congress, Senate, Subcommittee on Arms Control, International Organizations, and Security Agreements of the Committee on Foreign Relations, 94th Cong., 1st sess. (Washington, D.C.: September 18, 1975), 21.

[11] Warnke, "Carter's Nuclear Policy: Going From 'MAD' to Worse"? "Yes: The Revision of U.S. Strategy Implies a Belief in Limited War," *Los Angeles Times*, August 31, 1980, p. 3.

[12] See, for example, an early article by Colonel V. Mochalov and Major V. Dashichev, "The Smoke Screen of the American Imperialists," *Red Star* (December 17, 1957).

[13] Brodie, *Strategy in the Missile Age* (Princeton: Princeton University Press, 1959), 322n.

Pipes has characterized the position of Soviet leaders: "In the Soviet view, a nuclear war would be total. . . . Limited nuclear war, flexible response, escalation, damage limiting, and all the other numerous refinements of U.S. strategic doctrine find no place in its Soviet counterpart. . . ."[14]

Any remaining doubts about Soviet rejection of the doctrine of limited nuclear war is dispelled by recent writings of Soviet generals. For example, according to General-Major R. Simonyan, an important strategic planner, "the experience of numerous wars attests most clearly to the fact that military conflagrations have hardly ever been successfully kept within their original bounds."[15] Moreover,

> the assertion made by supporters of "limited" nuclear war that it could be kept within pre-planned limits and made "controllable" is altogether false. Every clear-headed person knows that any war unleashed by an aggressor and involving the use of strategic nuclear weapons—even if those weapons were used in limited numbers and against "selected targets"—is fraught with the genuine threat of escalation and development into a strategic (universal) nuclear war with all its fatal consequences.[16]

Third, the countervailing strategy of deterrence is based upon a confusion of the requirement of survivable nuclear forces with the doctrine of employment of counterforce targeting. Although it is clear that a survivable and enduring strategic retaliatory capability is essential to stable deterrence, a provocative targeting doctrine is not only unessential, it is counterproductive. Of course, the Department of Defense and other supporters of the countervailing strategy argue that there can be no reason for making Soviet military targets safe from U.S. ICBMs when comparable targets in this country are at risk from Soviet ICBMs. But this argument is based entirely on the logic of imitation; it does not examine whether the prospective benefits of such a policy actually outweigh the prospective costs. Indeed, considered together with the fact that the United States has not ratified SALT II, the continuing reliance on a policy of nuclear first use, the program to improve long-range theater nuclear forces, and the renewed commitments to Ballistic Missile Defense (BMD) and Civil Defense, the American intention to place a large percentage of Soviet strategic forces in jeopardy provides the U.S.S.R. with a heightened incentive to strike first.

---

[14] Pipes, "Why the Soviet Union Thinks It Could Fight and Win a Nuclear War," *Commentary*, Vol. 64 (July 1977), 30.

[15] Simonyan, "Comments," *Strategic Review*, v (Spring 1977), 100.

[16] *Ibid.*, 107. This view is corroborated by recent remarks of Lieut. General Mikhail A. Milshtein, Director of the Political-Military Department of the Institute on the United States and Canada. See "Limited Nuclear War: The Moscow Approach," *New York Times*, December 7, 1980, p. 8.

We should not be surprised, therefore, when Soviet spokesmen continue to characterize the countervailing strategy as a move toward an eventual American first strike.[17] In assessing this opinion one cannot ignore the fact that a second-strike counterforce strategy is largely a contradiction in terms. A counterforce capability is likely to serve only the country that strikes first. Used in retaliation, counterforce-targeted warheads would only hit empty silos.

Moreover, what is our purpose in placing Soviet military and civilian leaders in particular jeopardy? Is it, as one strategic analyst has suggested, "to destroy the ability of the Soviet leadership to continue to exercise political control over its domestic and 'colonial' territory—either by killing the leadership itself, making it impossible for the leadership to communicate with its subordinates, or destroying the means (people and facilities) by which the leadership's orders are carried out"?[18] If this *is* the purpose, then it is clearly contrary to the essential rationale of a countervailing nuclear strategy: that is, preserving the prospects for limited, controlled nuclear conflict. Indeed, in view of the United States' current inability to support its countervailing strategy with advanced weapons systems,[19] the personal targeting of Soviet leaders actually increases the likelihood of a Soviet first strike in the near term.

But, we must ask, what about the Soviets? Aren't *their* current deployments and capabilities provocative and destabilizing? Aren't *they* continuing to strive for nuclear superiority that is oriented toward a "win the war" potential and augmented by a far-reaching civil defense effort? Consider the following:

—Soviet missile submarine development continues to be geared to the potential for an effective SLBM attack on American bombers.
—Soviet land-based ICBMs, through continued improvements in missile accuracy, MIRVing, and increased throw-weights, are being geared to a hard target counterforce capability which may effectively threaten America's ICBM force.
—Soviet ASW forces, through the continuing proliferation of platforms and the steady improvement of sensor technology, are being geared to the capability to destroy America's SLBM force.

[17] See, for example, "Soviet Charges Reiterated," *New York Times*, August 21, 1980, p. A8.
[18] Jeffrey T. Richelson, "The Dilemmas of Counterpower Targeting," *Comparative Strategy*, II (No. 2, 1980), 226-27.
[19] See, for example, the concerns of CINCSAC General Richard Ellis, in Drew Middleton, "SAC Chief is Critical of Carter's New Nuclear Plan," *New York Times*, September 7, 1980, p. 19.

The evidence is hardly encouraging. The steady growth of Soviet military power has fostered legitimate questions concerning Soviet strategic objectives. It may even be true, as the so-called "Team B" appraisal of 1976 concluded, that Moscow's buildup stems from patently aggressive designs. But it is *not* true, even if our "worst-case" assumptions are correct, that American security is best served by acting in an equally provocative or more provocative manner.

In developing a long-term defense program vis-à-vis the Soviet Union, the Reagan Administration should be guided exclusively by a meticulous comparison of the costs and benefits of alternative courses of action. Such a comparison must take careful note of expected Soviet reactions to American military developments and of the long-range *cumulative effects* of these developments. It would make precious little sense, for example, to substantially increase funding for BMD research and development if the Soviets could be expected to offset the ICBM survivability benefits with a refined offensive strategic capability.

Improving the survivability of the U.S. strategic triad must continue to be an overriding goal of this country's defense posture. But it is by no means clear that this goal will be best served by the mobile, deceptive basing mode of the planned MX system. Again, Soviet countermoves must be anticipated, especially if the future of SALT is in doubt. And it is altogether likely that the search for an associated hard-target kill capacity will do more to undermine deterrence than to provide safety. The fact that the Soviets are already engaged in such a search in in no way supports the rationality of American imitation.

A similar argument may be made concerning renewed American interest in civil defense. If the Reagan Administration's call for funding to implement a "crisis relocation capability" (CRC) were to be subjected to careful scrutiny in terms of expected costs and benefits, it would be revealed as immensely impractical and needlessly provocative. Rather than strengthen deterrence by demonstrating U.S. preparedness (a demonstration that the Soviets no longer seem to need), plans for crisis relocation may underscore Soviet fears of an American first strike. Indeed, even if large-scale civilian evacuation plans were workable, and if a government-directed civilian exodus several days before a nuclear war would not degenerate into chaos, a Soviet nuclear attack could still doom virtually every American.[20]

---

[20] In this connection, one need only consider the *Proceedings* of a recent conference on "The Medical Consequences of Nuclear Weapons and Nuclear War," under the auspices of Physicians for Social Responsibility, Inc., sponsored by the Harvard Medical School and the Tufts University School of Medicine, Cambridge, Mass., February 9 and 10, 1980.

Fourth, current U.S. strategic nuclear policy completely disregards this country's legal commitments to halt proliferation. According to the terms of the Treaty on the Nonproliferation of Nuclear Weapons, the superpowers are obligated to move expeditiously toward meaningful arms control and disarmament. Article VI of the Treaty stipulates:

> Each of the Parties to the Treaty undertakes to pursue negotiations in good faith on effective measures relating to cessation of the nuclear arms race at an early date and to nuclear disarmament, and on a treaty on general and complete disarmament under strict and effective international control.

In the absence of Soviet and American compliance with the Nonproliferation Treaty, it is hard to imagine that non-nuclear-weapons states will continue to bear their restricted condition much longer. Should the United States proceed with its countervailing nuclear strategy, the consequent search for supporting strategic weapons systems would preclude any Soviet-American SALT accord. The resultant spread of nuclear-weapons states would not only create new opportunities for nuclear conflict, but would also heighten the probability of a Soviet-American nuclear war. That is the case because of the increased likelihood of catalytic war (provoked by one or more of the new nuclear powers), of war between new nuclear powers with alliance or interest ties to the superpowers, and of nuclear terrorism.

Fifth, the countervailing strategy of deterrence contributes to the dangerous notion that nuclear war might somehow be endured or even "won." We now have a great deal of scientific and medical evidence to support the conclusion that any nuclear war would have intolerable consequences. One of the first scientists to consider the probable effects of a nuclear attack on the United States was Tom Stonier, a biologist.

> Even before the threat of fallout radiation completely subsided, the country could be thrown into a state of economic and social chaos—including serious outbreaks of famine and disease—and the ensuing shock, loss of morale, and weakened leadership would further hamper relief operations and impede rehabilitation. The effects of this disruption could persist for decades, just as would the somatic damage inflicted on people exposed to radiation. Even individuals who escape the hazards of the explosion and who are themselves uninjured by radiation might carry a legacy of genetic damage, which they would then pass from generation to generation. Perhaps most uncertain, and potentially most disastrous, are the ecological consequences, the imbalances in nature itself, which might well create the preconditions for the disappearance of American civilization as we know it.[21]

[21] Stonier, *Nuclear Disaster* (New York: Meridian, 1964), 24.

Perhaps the most comprehensive and best-known of the recent studies is the 1975 National Academy of Sciences report, *Long-Term
Worldwide Effects of Multiple Nuclear Weapons Detonations*. According to Philip Handler, President of the Academy, it takes as its point
of departure

> a horrendous calamity: a hypothetical exchange involving the detona-
> tion of many nuclear weapons. In the worst case considered, about one
> half of all nuclear weapons in current strategic arsenals, viz., 500 to 1000
> weapons of yield 10 to 20 megatons each and 4000 to 5000 lesser [sic]
> weapons with yields of 1 or 2 megatons each, i.e., a total of 10^4 megatons
> (10,000,000,000 tons) of TNT-equivalent are exchanged among the par-
> ticipants. No report can portray the enormity, the utter horror which
> must befall the targeted areas and adjoining territories. Nor does this
> report so attempt.[22]

What the report does attempt to portray are the long-term, worldwide effects following the exchange of 10,000 megatons of explosive
power in the northern hemisphere, in a plausible mix of low- and high-
yield weapons, and at a variety of altitudes of detonation. Merely
acknowledging the "unimaginable holocaust" that would occur in the
primarily afflicted countries, the report confines its attention to possible
long-term effects on more distant populations and ecosystems, with
special reference to the atmosphere and climate, natural terrestrial ecosystems, agriculture and animal husbandry, the aquatic environment,
and both somatic and genetic effects upon humans.[23]

Although the report concludes that the biosphere and the species
Homo sapiens would survive the hypothetical strategic exchange,[24] it
recognizes that humankind's civilization might not survive such catastrophic insult. This conclusion has nothing to do with the probable
social, political, or economic consequences of the hypothesized nuclear

[22] From Handler's letter of transmittal (August 12, 1975), of the report, *Long-Term
Worldwide Effects of Multiple Nuclear Weapons Detonations*, National Academy of
Sciences (Washington, D.C.: 1975).

[23] *Ibid*.

[24] This point, made by Handler in his letter of transmittal of the report to the U.S.
Arms Control and Disarmament Agency (ACDA), is by no means uncontroversial. In
fact, in the belief that it is an "overstated conclusion," the Federation of American
Scientists issued a public declaration that effectively accused the NAS of inadvertently
encouraging nuclear war. The Federation, whose membership includes half of America's living Nobel laureates, charged that the Academy had reached a "false conclusion"
in suggesting humankind's probable survival. The Federation's statement was prepared
by Jeremy Stone, the organization's director, and was approved by a majority of the
organization's executive committee. The FAS position is supported by Bernard Feld,
Editor-in-Chief of the *Bulletin of the Atomic Scientists*, who believes that the NAS conclusion concerning the survival of the human race is "too sanguine." See Feld, "The
Consequences of Nuclear War," *Bulletin of the Atomic Scientists*, XXXII (June
1976), 13.

exchange (the report deliberately does not address these consequences, which it describes as "entirely unpredictable" effects of "worldwide terror"), but only with the interrelated physical and biological aspects of such a calamity. These aspects include possible temperature changes in either direction, and of different magnitudes; possible major global climatic changes; contamination of foods by radio-nuclides; possible worldwide disease epidemics in crops and domesticated animals because of ionizing radiation; possible shortening of the growing seasons in certain areas; possible irreversible injury to sensitive aquatic species; possible long-term carcinogenesis due to inhalation of plutonium particles; some radiation-induced developmental anomalies in persons *in utero* at the time of detonations; possible increase in the incidence of skin cancer of about 10 percent, which could increase by as much as a factor of 3 if ozone depletion were to rise from 50 to 70 percent; severe sunburn in temperate zones and snow blindness in northern regions in the short term; and an increased incidence of genetic disease that would not be limited to the offspring of the exposed generation, but would extend over many generations.

Predictions of the worldwide consequences of all-out nuclear war between the superpowers are fraught with uncertainty. With this in mind, the participants in the six separate committees that produced the NAS report caution their readers about the limitations of the data upon which their conclusions rest. It would be prudent, therefore, to recognize that the effects expected by the NAS scholars might be only the "tip of the iceberg"—that other, perhaps more significant effects would accompany the exchange. The plausibility of such recognition is underscored by the fact that the magnitude of the war postulated in the report may be much too low. If the superpowers were to exchange between 50,000 and 100,000 megatons of nuclear explosives rather than the 10,000 megatons assumed by the report, global climatological changes would imperil the very survival of humankind. Bernard Feld maintains that

> it is becoming frighteningly plausible to consider the level of nuclear war that would represent the end of humankind: the detonation of one million megatons of nuclear explosives (which may be defined as one "Beach")[25] would result in a global irradiation of around 500 rad.[26] It is very difficult in the present anarchic world, to be sanguine about the fact that we are now about one-tenth of the way toward the possibility

[25] The term "Beach" is taken from Nevil Shute's work of fiction on the aftermath of systemwide nuclear war, *On The Beach* (New York: William Morrow, 1957).

[26] A "rad" is a unit of radiation dose that measures the amount of ionization produced per unit volume by the particles from radioactive decay.

of this ultimate insult (used also in its medical sense) that would certainly spell the end of humankind on planet Earth.[27]

A second reason why the predicted effects of nuclear war between the superpowers are uncertain lies in the unknown interactions between individual effects:

In attempting to project the after-effects of a major nuclear war, we have considered separately the various kinds of damage that could occur. It is also quite possible, however, that interactions might take place among these effects, so that one type of damage would couple with another to produce new and unexpected hazards. For example, we can assess individually the consequences of heavy worldwide radiation fallout and increased solar ultraviolet, but we do not know whether the two acting together might significantly increase human, animal, or plant susceptibility to disease. We can conclude that massive dust injection into the stratosphere, even greater in scale than Krakatoa, is unlikely by itself to produce significant climatic and environmental change, but we cannot rule out interactions with other phenomena, such as ozone depletion, which might produce utterly unexpected results. We have come to realize that nuclear weapons can be as unpredictable as they are deadly in their effects. Despite some 30 years of development and study, there is still much that we do not know. This is particularly true when we consider the global effects of a large-scale nuclear war.[28]

Perhaps the most recent authoritative study of the consequences of nuclear war has been offered in response to a request from the Senate Committee on Foreign Relations for an examination of the effects of nuclear war on the populations and economies of the United States and the Soviet Union. This assessment examines the full range of consequences that nuclear war would have on civilians. In the Foreword, Daniel De Simone, Acting Director of the Office of Technology Assessment, states:

Two of the study's principal findings are that conditions would continue to get worse for some time after a nuclear war ended, and that the effects of nuclear war that cannot be calculated in advance are at least as important as those which analysts attempt to quantify.[29]

The introduction to the Executive Summary goes on to say:

Nuclear war is not a comfortable subject. Throughout all the variations, possibilities, and uncertainties that this study describes, one theme is

[27] Feld (fn. 24), 13.

[28] From a skillful summary of this point, in U.S. Arms Control and Disarmament Agency, *Worldwide Effects of Nuclear War. . . . Some Perspectives* (n.d., but produced after the 1975 NAS report), 23-24.

[29] U.S. Congress, Office of Technology Assessment, *The Effects of Nuclear War* (Washington, D.C.: May 1979), iii.

constant—a nuclear war would be a catastrophe. A militarily plausible nuclear attack, even "limited," could be expected to kill people and to inflict economic damage on a scale unprecedented in American experience: a large-scale nuclear exchange would be a calamity unprecedented in human history. The mind recoils from the effort to foresee the details of such a calamity, and from the careful explanation of the unavoidable uncertainties as to whether people would die from blast damage, from fallout radiation, or from starvation during the following winter.[30]

The Executive Summary also describes the effects of "limited" nuclear exchanges as "enormous." The O.T.A. examined the impact of a "small" attack on economic targets, and found that, "while economic recovery would be possible, the economic damage and social dislocation could be immense." The report continues:

> A review of calculations of the effects on civilian populations and economies of major counterforce attacks found that while the consequences might be endurable (since they would be on a scale with wars and epidemics that nations have endured in the past), the number of deaths might be as high as 20 million. Moreover, the uncertainties are such that no government could predict with any confidence what the results of a limited attack or counterattack would be even if there was no further escalation.[31]

Even these conclusions may be misleading since they stem from the assumed plausibility of *limited* nuclear exchanges. As we have already seen, there is no reason to believe that Soviet objectives would be served by a limited first strike on the United States. Although the Soviet Union would be able to detonate a small number of nuclear weapons over isolated areas in the United States without producing catastrophic effects, there would clearly be no reason for carrying out this type of attack. On the contrary, it would be manifestly irrational.

It is clear, therefore, that the United States has developed a counterforce doctrine which not only understates the potential effects of a limited nuclear war but which also ignores the fact that such a war makes no military sense. There is no clear picture as to what the Soviet Union might gain from the kinds of limited counterforce attacks posited by

[30]*Ibid.*, 3. For additional authoritative information on the expected effects of nuclear war, see "The First Nuclear War Conference," Washington, D.C., December 7, 1978, published as a special report of the *Bulletin of the Atomic Scientists*; "An Open Letter to President Carter and Chairman Brezhnev," Physicians for Social Responsibility, *Newsletter*, 1 (April 1980), 1; *Economic and Social Consequences of Nuclear Attacks on the United States*, a study prepared for The Joint Committee on Defense Production, U.S. Congress, 1979; Kevin N. Lewis, "The Prompt and Delayed Effects of Nuclear War," *Scientific American*, Vol. 241 (July 1979), 35-47; and Louis René Beres, *Apocalypse: Nuclear Catastrophe in World Politics* (Chicago: University of Chicago Press, 1980).
[31]*Effects of Nuclear War* (fn. 29), 4.

current American strategic nuclear policy. Indeed, the same American strategic nuclear policy that assumes the Soviets will cooperate in limiting nuclear war advances the contradictory premise that the U.S.S.R. is preparing to *fight and win* a nuclear war. As a result, current U.S. policy has become increasingly committed to the idea that credible deterrence requires the projection of a parallel capacity to fight and win a nuclear war—an idea that is contrary to the assumption of a limited Soviet first strike.

Apart from these contradictory assumptions of current American strategic nuclear policy, the developing emphasis on a "win-the-war" concept of deterrence is inherently destabilizing. There is no reason to suppose that the Soviet Union can be effectively deterred only by the prospect of complete annihilation—i.e., by the predictable outcome of a no-holds-barred nuclear war. In their assessment of the expected consequences of striking first, Soviet leaders are not likely to calculate that the absorption of a less-than-total American nuclear retaliation would fall within "acceptable" levels. Given the prevailing definition of rationality in world politics, they would make such a calculation only in the expectation of an American first strike. Ironically, that expectation is encouraged rather than diminished by the American search for enhanced deterrence through a capacity for nuclear war-fighting.

Sixth and last, America's countervailing nuclear strategy sustains the myth that peace through nuclear deterrence is capable of working for an indefinite period. At one time or another, in one way or another, the manifestly catastrophic possibilities that now lie latent in nuclear weapons are almost certain to be exploited, either by design or by accident, by misinformation or miscalculation, by lapse from rational decision making or by unauthorized decision.

Despite the successful workings of nuclear deterrence thus far ("successful" being defined in the most limited sense: preventing nuclear war),[32] a nuclear war between the superpowers could come to pass in several ways. It might come about inadvertently through the outcome of competition in risk taking. It might begin through the seizure of nuclear weapons by allied countries. It might be provoked by a smaller power (catalytic war) or by war between smaller powers. It might take place as a result of false warnings. Or it might take place because of

---

[32] Where the workings of nuclear deterrence are considered more broadly in terms of effects on day-to-day life under the threat of nuclear annihilation, they can hardly be termed "successful." For more on these broader considerations, see, for example, Michael Mandelbaum, "The Bomb, Dread, and Eternity," *International Security*, v (Fall 1980), 3-23.

errors in calculating the outcomes of various anticipated courses of action. It might even take place as a consequence of irrationality, through use by unauthorized personnel, or by mechanical/electrical/computer malfunction.

The probability of nuclear war between smaller nuclear powers, or between smaller nuclear powers and one or both of the superpowers, is underscored by the deployment of nuclear weapons to allied countries and by the proliferation of states possessing assembled nuclear weapons or the technology from which these weapons might be manufactured. In the years ahead, the likelihood of a nuclear war that involves "secondary" nuclear powers is apt to be high—not only because of the increasing number of nuclear-weapon states and the corresponding multiplication of existing risks, but also because these risks are certain to be intensified in a milieu of nuclear proliferation.

CREATING AN IMPROVED NUCLEAR REGIME

AROUSING WORLD CONSCIOUSNESS

Nietzsche, in the long critique of faith in his *AntiChrist*, wrote: "'Faith' means not *wanting* to know what is true." Understood in terms of humankind's continuing obliviousness to its tendencies toward self-destruction, Nietzsche's point suggests not only cowardice, but also an irreversible tilt toward *thanatos*, toward collective disintegration. Unless we begin to act upon the recognition of our current nuclear collision course, there is little hope that humankind can escape the fate toward which it is headed at the present.

Spasmodic instances of awareness are not enough. If we are to prevent a nuclear confrontation, we must immediately begin to contemplate the monstrous wreckage of moral, spiritual, and physical being that would descend in the wake of nuclear war.

The general public throughout the world must experience an aroused consciousness of the threat. Rather than continue to be lulled by officially sanctioned pronouncements about the tolerability of nuclear war, it must begin to confront the image of total extinction. The darkly visionary accounts of life after a nuclear catastrophe must be heeded. In order to return to a safer course, we must learn to understand that the growing number of formulations of a livable post-apocalypse world are totally unrealistic.

PROMOTING WORLD ORDER

A far-reaching and feasible agenda for long-term security must be created. Such an agenda must aim at removing incentives for states to acquire, enlarge, or "refine" nuclear forces. These incentives include presumed advantages in terms of strategic deterrence as well as of heightened domestic political support and power over other states.

To develop such an agenda, we require a strengthened regime of international treaties directed at nonproliferation, arms control, and disarmament, as well as a generalized renunciation of the time-dishonored principles of *Realpolitik*. A durable system of global security from nuclear war demands not only the customary restraints under international law, but also a drastic transformation of foreign policy processes. In this connection, the United States has a rare opportunity: it can set an example for other states, by considering cooperation in the world interest to be in its own national interest. Fanciful as such a proposal must appear, it is eminently more realistic than a continuation along the present collision course.

How might this proposal be implemented? The answer lies in several interrelated directions. Most obvious, perhaps, is the need for a bilateral retreat of the superpowers from their growing acceptance of counterforce principles, and for a return to the relatively sane strategy of "minimum deterrence." To make such a retreat possible, the Soviet Union and the United States would have to cooperate in the establishment of a more harmonious style of interaction. This would mean, at a minimum, prompt movement toward a new SALT accord; a joint reversal of current trends toward increased military spending; and a joint commitment to the principles of additional arms control and (ultimately) to the jointly planned obsolescence of existing stockpiles of strategic nuclear weapons.

The move toward minimum deterrence should be augmented by the implementation of the long-sought comprehensive test ban (CTB) and by a joint renunciation of the right to "first use" of nuclear weapons.

COMPREHENSIVE TEST BAN

Although we have the 1963 Partial Test Ban Treaty, the 1974 Treaty on the Limitation of Underground Nuclear Weapon Tests, and the 1976 Treaty on Underground Nuclear Explosions for Peaceful Purposes, only a comprehensive test ban can genuinely inhibit further innovations in nuclear weapons. A CTB was first outlined in the late 1950s; its provisions should be agreed upon by all nuclear-weapon states and by the largest possible number of non-nuclear-weapon states. Even if France and China initially chose to remain outside such an agreement (neither France nor China has yet ratified the Partial Test Ban Treaty of 1963), a CTB's prospective benefits would be significant enough to warrant endorsement. Understood in terms of the super-powers' responsibility to make the avoidance of a nuclear war credible in a world of self-assertive states, a CTB could offer a significant start-ing point for wider imitation and reciprocity.

At the moment, both superpowers continue to be on record in favor of a comprehensive test ban. Former President Carter made such a ban one of the primary objectives of his program for arms control and disarmament. Recognizing the convergence of this country's essential security interests with its legal obligations under Article VI of the Non-proliferation Treaty, the former President first announced his commit-ment to a CTB before the United Nations on March 17, 1977; on Octo-ber 4, 1977, he told the General Assembly: "The time has come to end all explosions of nuclear devices, no matter what their claimed justifica-tion, peaceful or military." In that same month, formal negotiations between the United States, Britain, and the Soviet Union were begun in Geneva on the subject of a comprehensive test ban, and on May 20, 1978, Mr. Carter signed Presidential Decision Memorandum 38, calling for a five-year "zero yield" comprehensive test ban.

In view of the understanding that a CTB would impose an important qualitative restraint on nuclear arms competition, every President since John F. Kennedy has supported a comprehensive test ban treaty that would be verifiable. Nevertheless, although mutual cessation of nuclear testing would contribute significantly to U.S. security by constraining the modernization of Soviet nuclear forces, the Reagan Administration seems ready to abandon the long search for a CTB. This departure from the policies of previous administrations seems to flow from an assumed American inability to detect and positively identify clandestine, low-level Soviet underground nuclear tests by national technical means (seismic and satellite monitoring). Apprehensive that the U.S.S.R. would maintain its nuclear weapons technology base through clandes-tine testing while the U.S. complied with a test ban, President Reagan fears that a long-term asymmetry in superpower nuclear weapons pro-grams would develop.

There is, however, considerable evidence that such concerns are ill-founded. Virtually all of this country's scientific community now agrees that seismological instruments can identify any nuclear explo-sion of 10 kilotons or greater. Many scientists argue that these instru-ments can identify an explosion with as small a yield as one or two kilotons.[33] Such seismological sophistication, together with the current

[33] Dan Caldwell, "CTB: An Effective SALT Substitute," *Bulletin of the Atomic Scientists*, XXXVI (December 1980), 30.

state of satellite reconnaissance and the August 1980 agreement in principle between the United States, the Soviet Union, and Great Britain for verifying a comprehensive test ban, would seem to support arguments for a CTB treaty. The validity of this position is corroborated further by Soviet willingness to accept verification measures that include on-site inspections as well as satellite and seismic technologies.

These arguments do not seem compelling, however, to the Reagan Administration, which appears convinced of the Soviet Union's deceptive intentions and of the enduring wisdom of *Realpolitik*. The ongoing reformulation of national security policy suggests widespread rejection of the principles of a CTB. In addition to doubting that the U.S. ability to detect and positively identify clandestine, low-level Soviet underground nuclear tests is adequate,[34] the Reagan Administration is concerned that the Soviets will continue with peaceful nuclear explosions.

Secretary Brezhnev has announced the Soviet Union's willingness to accept a moratorium on peaceful nuclear explosions in conjunction with a treaty prohibiting nuclear weapons tests, but he has tied this moratorium to a fixed period of time and to a series of continuing negotiations on the issue. The Reagan Administration, disturbed by an alleged Soviet breach of the understanding on a Threshold Test Ban Treaty and by the realization that peaceful nuclear explosions can be used for military testing, seems unprepared to accept these terms.

NO-FIRST-USE PLEDGE

The United States and the Soviet Union should take immediate steps to renounce the first use of nuclear weapons, i.e., the retaliatory use of nuclear weapons in reprisal for non-nuclear attack. At present, both countries reserve the right of first use, although American interest in continuing this right seems to be greater than that of the Soviets. This greater commitment to first use stems from U.S. fears that its conventional forces may be inferior in vital theaters of possible engagement. Faced with growing Soviet military strength, the United States continues to base its deterrence strategy on what it believes to be appropriate responses drawn from a range of available options. Former Secretary of Defense Harold Brown has stated that

> it continues to be U.S. policy that we will resist attacks on the United States and its allies by whatever means necessary, including nuclear weapons. We have made no secret of our view that conventional forces are an essential component of the collective deterrent, and that any con-

---

[34] See, for example, Heritage Foundation, "Developing Arms Control Priorities in 1981," *National Security Record*, No. 29 (January 1981), 2.

ventional aggression should be met initially by conventional means. We also recognize that nuclear decisions—and especially collective nuclear decisions—would be difficult and could be time-consuming, which makes strong non-nuclear capabilities all the more important. But the United States remains determined to do whatever is required to prevent the defeat of its own and allied forces. Our strategic and theater nuclear forces serve as the ultimate backup to our NATO commitments. Not only do they provide the means to strike NATO-related targets; they also dramatize to a potential attacker that any conventional attack could set off a chain of nuclear escalation, the consequences of which would be incalculable.[35]

But why, we might ask, should the American policy of first use appear threatening to the Soviets? After all, it has always been the official policy of the United States not to launch a first strike, i.e., a nuclear strike as an initial, offensive move of war. Is there anything provocative to a nuclear strategy that does not exclude the *retaliatory* use of nuclear weapons to stave off defeat in a conventional conflict?

The answer to this question lies in the fact that, in actual practice, the distinctions between the "first use" of nuclear weapons and a nuclear "first strike" are likely to be meaningless. Once an adversary had committed an act of aggression, the United States would certainly characterize an intended nuclear response as a "first use" rather than as a "first strike." Since the determination that an act of aggression had taken place would necessarily be made by the United States rather than by some specially constituted central arbiter, certain acts that are judged to be aggressive by the United States might be expected to warrant an American nuclear response.

But doesn't the arbitrariness of the distinction between first use and first strike apply equally to the Soviet strategy of first use? Isn't that strategy as threatening to us as ours is to them? The answer to this question, I believe, is clearly "no," since the asymmetry in conventional forces between the two superpowers provides the Soviet Union with little real incentive to initiate an escalation to nuclear conflict.

Together with the consequences of U.S. inferiority in conventional forces, the American policy of first use is especially unsettling to the Soviet Union since it (1) allows for rapid escalation to nuclear conflict; (2) allows for the possibility of disguising a first strike as a first use, either by deliberately creating conditions that lead to "acts of aggression" or by falsely alleging that such acts have taken place; and (3) joins with a targeting doctrine that focuses on Soviet strategic forces.

[35] Brown, *Department of Defense Annual Report for FY 1979*, (Washington, D.C.: February 2, 1978), 68.

Hence, the American policy of first use offers incentives to the Soviet Union to undertake a pre-emptive nuclear strike against the United States. Moreover, this policy creates incentives for *other* nuclear powers to adopt "hair trigger" strategies for protection against possible pre-emptive strikes. These risks are incurred by the United States with little real benefit in terms of deterrence, since any American nuclear retaliation would almost certainly draw a Soviet nuclear response. In view of the enormously high probability of Soviet nuclear counter-retaliation and the terrible destruction that would be visited upon allies "in order to save them," Soviet strategists must entertain grave doubts about U.S. willingness to use theater nuclear forces, in Europe or in any other theater of possible confrontation. Indeed, in the aftermath of an overwhelming conventional assault by the U.S.S.R. against American allies, it might conceivably appear to be rational for the U.S. national command authority to bypass theater nuclear forces altogether, urging instead the immediate resort to a strategic strike.

With these facts in mind, it should be clear that both the United States and the Soviet Union would stand to gain from a joint renunciation of the first-use option. To allow for such a renunciation, the United States must move toward abandonment of the neutron bomb, discontinue NATO plans for the modernization of intermediate-range nuclear weapons in Western Europe, redeploy theater nuclear forces away from frontiers, and—ultimately—remove these forces altogether. These steps, of course, must be accompanied by serious efforts to strengthen American and allied conventional forces in order to preserve a sufficiently high nuclear threshold. However expensive and politically unattractive such efforts may be, their long-term security benefits would surely be worthwhile.

There is growing evidence that the Reagan Administration has already begun to fashion a military strategy that would create huge investments in weapons, ammunition, transport, equipment, and supplies, as well as a vast mobilization of manpower and a revitalization of the defense industry.[36] Although this strategy appears to be founded on the presumed plausibility of protracted conventional war with the Soviet Union (a dangerous presumption since it would underestimate the escalatory potential and reduce inhibitions about confrontations between the superpowers), it may have the stabilizing effect of diminishing reliance on tactical nuclear weapons and of decoupling nuclear and conventional war. Ultimately, however, that effect will con-

[36] Richard Halloran, "U.S. Said to Revise Strategy to Oppose Threats by Soviet," *New York Times*, April 19, 1981, p. 1.

tribute to severing the connection between non-nuclear and nuclear warfare only if it is followed by an explicit rejection of the longstanding reliance on theater nuclear deterrence.

For its part, the Soviet Union should parallel American nuclear concessions by accepting far-reaching curbs on its growing capability to deliver theater nuclear weapons. Warsaw Pact forces are currently equipped with tactical nuclear delivery systems, and Moscow has deployed, in the Soviet Union itself, even longer-range systems, with a theater attack capability. These peripheral attack systems include light and medium bombers, the large MRBM (Medium Range Ballistic Missile) and IRBM (Intermediate Range Ballistic Missile) force being modernized with mobile SS-20 MIRVed missiles, and submarine and surface ships armed with ballistic and cruise missiles. In pursuit of an overall plan to achieve the equalization of conventional forces in the European theater, the Soviet Union should agree to substantial reductions of Warsaw Pact ground manpower and tank forces.

Although initiatives toward no-first-use appear risky, they are considerably less dangerous than continuing on the present course. Current United States strategic policy heightens the chances for nuclear war—without providing credible deterrence against Soviet conventional attack. The supposedly "tough-minded" argument that increased Soviet adventurism and offensive strategic policy need to be countered by a parallel American response is devoid of logical consistency. Understood in terms of careful cost/benefit calculations instead of the inflamed rhetoric of political oratory, American self-interest points unambiguously to taking the initiative of implementing a no-first-use pledge. Only through such an initiative can the United States hope for a reduction in Soviet conventional and theater nuclear forces and for a reciprocal abandonment of the first-use option by the Soviet Union.

Once agreement on no-first-use has been reached between the Soviet Union and the United States, steps should be taken to extend the principles of this agreement to non-nuclear weapons states. Unfortunately, such an extension would have relatively limited credibility, since there would be no concrete set of denuclearization policies to support a commitment by nuclear-weapons states not to use nuclear weapons against non-nuclear-weapons states. Moreover, a no-first-use pledge to non-nuclear weapons states would do nothing to allay the fears of these states concerning the nuclear intentions of non-nuclear adversary states. Therefore, in the absence of assurances that its own compliance with nonproliferation norms would be paralleled by the compliance of non-nuclear adversary states, each non-nuclear weapons state may calculate that the benefits of "going nuclear" would outweigh the costs.

The central problem of extending the protection of no-first-use to non-nuclear-weapons states is not the absence of pertinent declarations or pledges, but the uncertainty of every such state about the intentions of some other states. Although little can be done to relieve this uncertainty as far as it refers to the nuclear-weapons states, some steps can be taken concerning states without nuclear weapons, starting with a cooperative effort by the current nuclear-weapons states and nuclear-supplier states toward the goal of nonproliferation.

To be effective, this effort must be directed at controlling a large number of independent national wills. Such control is an example of the general problem of decision that arises when the benefits of common action are contingent upon the expectation that certain other parties will cooperate. The essential dynamics of this problem were described by Machiavelli:

> The world is a stupendous machine, composed of innumerable parts, each of which being a free agent, has a volition and action of its own; and on this ground arises the difficulty of assuring success in any enterprise depending on the volition of numerous agents. We may set the machine in motion, and dispose every wheel to one certain end; but when it depends on the volition of any one wheel, and the correspondent action of every wheel, the result is uncertain.[37]

In Machiavelli's metaphor, the "enterprise" for which success is sought may be taken to represent nonproliferation; the "parts" of the machine are the non-nuclear-weapons states. Understood in such terms, the metaphor suggests that nonproliferation efforts will remain in doubt as long as they depend upon voluntary compliance by states that expect reciprocal compliance by certain other states. To remove this uncertainty, the current nuclear-weapons and nuclear-supplier states must move deliberately and cooperatively to control the spread of nuclear weapons and sensitive nuclear technologies.[38]

We live at an interface between enduring peace and global destruction. Instead of merely fine-tuning the futile scenarios of strategic bargaining games, the foregoing alternatives to a countervailing nuclear strategy offer hope for a genuinely auspicious nuclear regime. Recognizing the total disutility of a nuclear threat system, this network of

[37] From *The Discourses.*
[38] For a detailed examination of what is needed to achieve such control, see Beres (fn. 30).

obligations and doctrines is shaped by a new calculus of potentiality—a calculus that rejects current strategic thinking in favor of a new world politics. Without such a calculus, we are likely to experience the moment that prompted J. Robert Oppenheimer, upon witnessing the first atomic bomb explosion in July 1945, to recall a passage from the *Bhagavad-Gita*: "I am become Death, the Shatterer of Worlds."

BEYOND RATIONAL DETERRENCE:
The Struggle For New Conceptions

By JOHN STEINBRUNER

. . . the truth that drives men mad must be sought for ere it's found, and it eludes the doltish or myopic hunter. But once 'tis caught and looked on . . . the captor's sole expedient is to force his will upon't ere it work his ruin! . . . One must needs make and seize his soul, and then cleave fast to 't, or go babbling in the corner; one must choose his gods and devils on the run, quill his own name upon the universe and declare, 'Tis I and the world stands such-a-way! One must *assert*, *assert, assert*, or go screaming mad. What other course remains?

—*John Barth**

AS major protagonist in a veritable epic of conflict, intrigue, and struggle for survival, John Barth's literary creation announces in the above words a method for coping and a philosophy for preserving sanity. The setting of the novel is the earliest days of the American colonies, but the theory propounded surely applies to modern times. Indeed, Henry Burlingame's outcry so illuminates one of the more subtle features of the great contemporary problem of survival—the control of nuclear energy—that it deserves serious reflection in that context.

For two decades and more, the threat of nuclear destruction has been carried in the dynamics of confrontation between the governments of the United States and the Soviet Union. For that same period, some of the most active minds of our society have labored to impose some coherent theory on this threat which would render it comprehensible and manageable, which would provide a foothold for sanity. This effort has been substantially successful, as these things go. Nuclear strategy has been given a core logic revolving around the concept of deterrence. That logic has been related to the realities of technology and economics. A series of resulting concepts—assured destruction, counterforce, first strike, second strike, pre-emption, flexible response, stability, sufficiency, escalation, and so forth—have entered the public consciousness, have been intensely discussed in professional circles, and to some extent have affected the decisions of contemporary governments. Above all, though there has been serious and occasionally violent political conflict, nuclear war has not occurred.

* Henry Burlingame in *The Sot-Weed Factor* (New York: Bantam Books 1969) 373.

As a result of this success, nuclear strategy has settled into a ·reasonably stable state and no longer seems to compel the intellectual effort it once did. The logic of deterrence has been established, and its most tractable derivations have been worked out. Though recognized as bald assumption and though plagued with internal paradox and unanswered questions, the theory has had no serious competition. Given this, most who concern themselves with the matter are willing to consider the foothold on sanity which deterrence strategy provides to be an adequate place to stand for the indefinite future. The miliary balance between the superpowers has evolved to a state of rough parity, at least moderately buttressed by recent agreements; besieged Western governments have many other problems to worry about. Though there are articulate dissenters, in the main the human spirit has adjusted to living against a background of potential terror, and general public opinion does not appear to be very alarmed by continuing weapons deployments. The entire topic has become established, familiar, middle-aged and—let us admit—rather boring.

Therein lies a major problem. Boredom, though it has its defenders, is surely premature. The enormity of potential disaster alone guarantees that, and the level of world conflict is such that the destructive power of deployed strategic forces cannot be taken casually. In principle, our society ought to spare no effort to drive understanding of the problem of nuclear defense to the very limits of human comprehension; but we are hardly doing that. Our knowledge is very uneven, and we have come to accept that. At great effort and expense we have developed at least partial understanding of the central technologies and their immediate implications—of nuclear warheads, aircraft, submarines, and ballistic missiles; of the physical effects of nuclear explosions; and of the basic economics of weapons production. We understand far less about the actual decision processes by means of which the weapons of the superpowers are designed, deployed, and controlled during moments of crisis—even though these decision processes are at the very core of the strategic problem.

This imbalance in understanding is not the result of simple oversight. In part it reflects the more advanced development of the natural sciences in our culture as a whole, and that itself presumably has something to do with the inherent structure and regularity of the physical world as opposed to social, political, and psychological events. But that is by no means the entire story. The imbalance also reflects the fact that technical matters and abstract economics are safely remote from the exercise of power. Knowledge can be developed in these areas without the threat of an immediate and direct impact on those who control the necessary resources. By comparison, the study of decision processes is far less neutral, and in all societies, including our own, it is far more constrained. In sum, rather than seriously promoting an ever developing, ever more penetrating analysis of the process of decision, we rely on a set of coherent but unavoidably simplistic assumptions which we now routinely assert much in the spirit of Barth's Henry Burlingame.

For all the importance of the topic, therefore, it is not easy to resist boredom, not easy to battle for new departures in strategic thinking. The odds are unfavorably stacked. Nonetheless, over the past decade conceptions of the decision process have developed which promise an alternative basis for analysis to that provided by rational formulations underlying the accepted theory of deterrence. These conceptions may already be used to introduce some new lines of argument into the continuing debate over strategy, force posture, and arms control. The new arguments are not likely to replace the more established analysis entirely—nor would that be desirable—but they do seem to offer healthy competition. Intellectual competition is a force against complacency and conceptual stagnation; it is a hedge against self-delusion and its consequences.

FAMILIAR ASSUMPTIONS

It is well known that the established strategy of deterrence in the United States is explicitly based upon the rational theory of decision. In its purest and most abstract conceptualization the strategic problem is presented as a game between two players each rationally calculating the expected pay-off of his actions across the range of possible consequences. The players are assumed to be fundamentally hostile toward each other, and therefore it is expected that each of them will act to minimize the damage that his opponent might do to him in the course of play. Deterrence consists in one player's threatening his opponent with such severe retaliation to attack (i.e., a large negative pay-off delivered with significant probability) that the rationally calculating opponent will always choose not to attack. Mutual deterrence exists when both players exercise such a threat against each other.

The use of rational decision theory to provide a basic conception of the strategic problem is natural, indeed virtually inevitable. That theory represents the clearest, most coherent, most developed conception of the decision process which is available at the moment. It is the theory with the most widely credited normative claim, and the one with the greatest intellectual acceptance within our culture.[1] Where else would we choose to place one of the most serious intellectual burdens of our time?

Unfortunately, however, rational decision theory remains highly abstract and remote from the actual events of human life. In order to apply the strategic logic derived from it to the actual problems of defense, it is necessary to adopt the truly heroic assumption that the behavior of very large modern governments—notably those of the United States and the Soviet Union—will approximate the behavior of rationally calculating individual players in the simple prototype game (or at least that it can be made to do so). No one is very comfortable with such an obviously questionable assumption, but in the absence of a compelling alternative it must be made. The core problem of nuclear strategy is thus defined as that of preventing war started by a deliberate, rationally calculated attack.

In tacit recognition of the extreme act of faith that is involved in such logic, force planners and political decision-makers in the United States have developed very conservative assumptions about what is required to achieve the conditions of deterrence. These decision-makers have insisted on stockpiling strategic forces in such numbers and with such technical capability that their ability to retaliate, after even the worst attack the enemy could conceivably undertake, cannot be seriously questioned. They insist, moreover, that the destruction that would

---

[1] Rational decision theory is fundamental to modern economic analysis and to the techniques of systems analysis which have been developed over the past 30 years. The influential work by Charles Hitch and Roland McKean, *The Economics of Defense in the Nuclear Age* (New York: Atheneum 1965), provides a textbook on the logic involved, as do Herman Kahn's *On Thermonuclear War* (Princeton: Princeton University Press 1961) and Thomas Schelling's *The Strategy of Conflict* (Cambridge: Harvard University Press 1960). Graham Allison, in *Essence of Decision* (Boston: Little, Brown & Company 1972), has documented the pervasive influence of rational assumptions while attacking their most simplistic embodiment in highly aggregated models of government behavior. This has stimulated a discussion regarding the degree to which political analysis should disaggregate governments—whether, for example, the Soviet Union is to be interpreted as a single, coherent entity or as a disaggregated collection of organizational units, different pressure groups, and differing individuals. It is now widely conceded that the degree of disaggregation does powerfully affect the character of political analysis, and that reasonable disaggregation is required to achieve adequate understanding of modern governments. Disaggregation does not change the fundamental character of rational logic, however. Even highly sophisticated models of bureaucratic and political behavior are generally built upon the assumption that constituent actors are driven by rational calculations of their institutional and personal interests.

The conceptions of the decision process under discussion in this paper have to do with basic theories that can be worked out at any level of aggregation. Very simple examples of rational analysis are used for illustrative purposes, but the same argument applies to the more sophisticated, more disaggregated forms.

be visited on the opponent in retaliation approximate the maximum amount that could be achieved under any circumstances; and that that amount be estimated very cautiously—crediting only that damage which established knowledge renders both certain and calculable.[2] The planning calculations are made under such rigid criteria in order to make the desired conclusions compelling even for an opponent with only a very tenuous hold on rationality. The idea is to make the threat so stark and so obvious that it swamps all misperceptions arising, for example, from cultural differences, individual idiosyncracies, and the complexities of internal politics. This line of reasoning, in conjunction with the initial assumption that the strategic opponent is at least potentially hostile, has established conservative planning as a dominant principle of strategic decision making.

It is possible to rationalize the very large strategic forces deployed by the United States in terms of this logic of deterrence. The strategic forces which we have now programmed will have over 10,000 warheads in the latter part of this decade; these will represent the explosive power of 4000-5000 one-megaton bombs.[3] Conservative damage estimates indicate that one-tenth of this force actually exploded on urban-industrial targets in the Soviet Union would destroy *at least* 30 per cent of the population and 70 per cent of industrial capacity. Most observers feel that if the threat of destruction works at all, it will work at these levels.[4] Thus, if the United States force posture is interpreted in terms of strategic reason, it might be said that up to 90 per cent of these forces are deployed in service of the conservative planning principle as a hedge against errors in the rational decision process.[5] That translates into an average annual effort over the past decade of as much as 20 billion constant 1974 dollars, depending on the accounting assumptions applied.[6]

[2] Fred Iklé, in "Can Deterrence Last Out the Century?" *Foreign Affairs*, Vol. 51 (January 1973), 267-85, discusses the conservative assumptions used in damage calculations.

[3] The aggregate measure in terms of equivalent megatonnage depends upon how the bomber force is counted. A frequently quoted public estimate can be found in the Brookings budget review: Barry M. Blechman, Edward M. Gramlich, and Robert W. Hartman, *Setting National Priorities: The 1975 Budget* (Washington, D.C., Brookings Institution 1974), 111.

[4] U.S. Congress, House, Committee on Armed Services, *Hearings on Military Posture*, 90th Cong., 2nd sess., 1968, pp. 8507 ff.

[5] 90% is obviously the high end of the range of possible estimates. It includes additional forces procured to insure that the residual force surviving a massive first strike —the most catastrophic failure of deterrence—would be of sufficient size to impose unacceptable damage.

[6] $20 billion is again the high end of the range of possible estimates. It is derived from calculations done by the Brookings Institution, which include a full accounting of

The conservative planning principle, the extensive technical effort that stands behind it, and the continuing absence of general war have combined to bring a fundamental sense of confidence to nuclear strategy, and have enabled a broad consensus to form behind rational deterrence as the appropriate conceptual basis of defense policy. Over two decades and more, the central assumptions of this policy have been built into detailed force-planning calculations that structure decisions at virtually every level of the defense bureaucracy. In the process, these assumptions have gained the enormous policy momentum which only the set routine of very large organizations can impart. The intellectual and organizational position of the rational deterrence strategy could hardly be more firmly established.

That does not mean, however, that conceptual issues are all settled and that rational deterrence is merely a matter of implementing established logic. Quite the contrary. There are at least two internal paradoxes within the theory which have not found stable resolution. Each of these has called forth what might be called second-order applications of rational logic, and it is here that we encounter the sharpest issues of contemporary defense policy.

CONTINUING ANOMALIES

The unresolved problems of rational deterrence involve the issues of force size and design on one hand and force operations on the other. Though there tend to be significant interactions between these issues, the difficulties for rational theory are minimized if they are treated separately. The most recent development of strategic doctrine tends to emphasize this separation.

First, let us consider the problems of force size and design. If the conservative planning principle operates on both sides of the strategic confrontation, which is certainly the natural presumption, then—even under technologically stable conditions of mutual deterrence—there is no natural limit to strategic arms deployments. In fact, if both sides undertake a continuous search for qualitative improvements in their forces and otherwise hedge against the threat of the other (as again it is natural to expect), then a sequence of interactive deployments should occur which would drive both sides to higher levels of potential destruc-

---

direct costs and attribute a portion of administrative defense costs to the strategic forces. See Edward R. Fried, Alice M. Rivlin, Charles C. Schultze, and Nancy H. Teeter, *Setting National Priorities: The 1974 Budget* (Washington, D.C., Brookings Institution 1973), 296. Official DoD budget figures, which do not include indirect costs and even exclude some categories of direct cost, have averaged under $10 billion per year for the strategic forces.

tiveness. In brief, straightforward rational logic predicts some form of arms competition.

A number of specific models have been advanced to illustrate this effect mathematically. There has also been a reasonably extensive empirical discussion focused on the question as to whether or not the strategic deployments of the United States and the Soviet Union over the past thirty years actually reflect such a pattern.[7] Though the empirical discussion has been inconclusive, most strategic analysts have come to assume that there is an inherent tendency for the opposing strategic forces to interact upward. The prevention of that tendency has become a second-order strategic problem.

If force structure decisions are to be made under the principle of conservative planning, then the solution to increasing force deployments must involve a reasonably formal procedure by means of which both sides adopt symmetric constraints. The constraints, moreover, must be so specified and so protected that cheating is believably rendered difficult and unlikely. The United States has attempted, of course, to achieve such mutual constraints by engaging in formal strategic arms negotiations with the Soviet Union. The agreement of May 1972 represents a significant success, and the guidelines resulting from the Vladivostok summit conference represent a potentially significant further development. The fundamental problem nonetheless remains, for the mere fact of formal negotiations, of practical results, and of serious proposals for additional constraints does not contain the underlying dynamic. Both superpowers have continued very active force deployments following the 1972 treaty; the force ceilings announced in the Vladivostok guidelines leave ample scope for this process to continue. By what means, then, by what second-order strategy does one motivate the adversary to accept binding constraints?

An answer to this question, it appears, has been adduced by applying the central idea of the retaliatory threat to the ongoing negotiation process. Just as the rationally calculating adversary is to be deterred from attack by the threat of massive destruction in return, so the same

[7] Two recent articles by Albert Wohlstetter attack some of the more simplistic models of an arms race, and present data to indicate that the U.S.-U.S.S.R. arms competition, whatever its actual character, has not produced monotonic increases in some standard force measurements—e.g., budget levels, gross megatonnage, and equivalent megatonnage. See Albert Wohlstetter, "Is There a Strategic Arms Race?" *Foreign Policy* Nos. 15 and 16 (Summer and Fall 1974). When destructive capability is measured more directly, however, with qualitative improvements in accuracy and delivery-vehicle flexibility taken into account, it is clear that the capacity of both sides has increased monotonically; few would deny that there is some form of interaction between the opposing strategic forces of the United States and the Soviet Union.

opponent is to be deterred from increasing his force deployments—and thereby motivated to accept agreement—by the threat of matching or even overmatching deployments. This secondary application of the logic is reflected in recent policy statements of the U.S. Government, which relate continuing strategic deployments by the United States directly to the Soviet Union's force deployments, and explicitly assert that "undesirable and unnecessary" deployments will be undertaken unless constraining, symmetrical agreements are reached. Lending substance to the threat is the fact that the current five-year defense program is quite aggressive, containing development programs for advanced designs of virtually every component of the strategic force plus such new strategic weapons as cruise missiles and terminally guided warheads. Though much of the basic policy is either being left to imagination or hidden in the classified record, it is fairly clear that more is involved here than is suggested by the ubiquitously used image of bargaining chips. The explicitly articulated connection between Soviet offensive missile deployment and programs to improve the performance of U.S. warheads against hard targets carries the implication that, in the absence of appropriate arms limitations, the United States will seek the capacity to destroy those parts of the Soviet force considered to be most objectionable.[8] The threat of retaliation, even preemption—in terms of weapons development and deployment—has become a major if not dominant element of the United States bargaining strategy.

The fact that the 1972 and 1974 agreements have followed the pursuit of this coercive bargaining strategy will undoubtedly strengthen its political status. As a conceptual matter, however, this secondary application of rational deterrence to the process of strategic bargaining is destined to be far more difficult and less widely accepted than primary deterrence. The threat is exercised not against the extreme and all but unprecedented action of a massive nuclear attack, but rather against the established, routine behavior of the opposing government. In order to accede to our demands the Soviets are not required to desist from doing something they have never done, but rather to contain the natural momentum of a very large research, development, and production process. They must stop an effort in which they have been engaged on a priority basis for over a decade. There is grave difficulty,

---

[8] The message is reasonably clearly conveyed in the 1974 Posture Statement, U.S. Department of Defense, *Report of the Secretary of Defense James R. Schlesinger to the Congress on the FY 1975 Defense Budget and the FY 1975–79 Defense Program* [hereafter referred to as *Posture Statement*], March 4, 1974, p. 40 f.

moreover, in controlling the threat. Even if the Soviets are motivated to accept truly binding constraints, the United States predictably will have trouble controlling the momentum of its own process of weapons acquisition. At the moment that process is not postured to operate on the contingent basis which the rational bargaining strategy requires.[9] In all, we must seriously contemplate the possible failure of the bargaining strategy and hence the possibility that the threat being used to control arms deployments will ultimately have precisely the opposite effect.

The second major internal problem is that rational deterrence strategy involves force operations—that is, the actual use of the strategic forces once they have been designed and procured. The established strategy of rational deterrence has long been plagued by the paradox that if deterrence should fail and war should begin (a possibility which cannot be entirely eliminated), then it would not be rational actually to carry out the threat of massive retaliation upon which deterrence is based. Once attacked, a rationally calculating player has nothing substantial to gain by massive retaliation. Even the inevitable desire for revenge must yield to more serious needs—notably the continuing necessity to exercise deterrence against any residual capacity of the opponent. Though it is assumed that strategic forces, in order to deter, must have a real *capacity* to retaliate massively, such retaliation is not at all what the rational calculator would undertake in the actual event of war. This twist to the logic is very bothersome under the principle of conservative planning. To the extent that carrying out the retaliatory threat is irrational, the entire strategy of deterrence is undermined, and conservative planning tends to magnify any such difficulty.

If simple, direct, and perfect rationality existed on both sides of the strategic confrontation, this paradox of the retaliatory threat would presumably lead to a pre-emptive counterforce attack by the first side truly understanding the conundrum. Adding irony to paradox, however, the presence of imperfection in the rational process prevents such a self-defeating conclusion. A realistic attacker could not be certain that his severely provoked victim could control the urge to retaliate; and as long as the capacity to retaliate exists, there is significant chance that it will be used. The threat that leaves something to chance

[9] This argument is developed in more detail in John Steinbruner and Barry Carter, "The Organizational Dimensions of the Strategic Posture: The Case for Reform," *Daedalus* (Summer 1975), 131-54; issued as Vol. 104, No. 3 of the *Proceedings of the American Academy of Arts and Sciences.*

is sufficient to deter, Schelling persuasively argues, and that gives an adequate solution to the theoretical problem.[10]

This theoretical solution does entail some compromise of the conservative planning principle, however, and therefore does present some difficulty in actual strategic application. To be sure, few analysts believe this compromise threatens primary deterrence as long as there is symmetry in the assumptions being applied to both sides. A massive attack on urban-industrial targets still seems sufficiently likely to call forth a similar retaliatory response that mutual deterrence of such attacks is not seriously questioned. Conservative planning, nonetheless, does generate fears of assymetrical situations. Under conservative assumptions, limited attacks might not be deterred by the threat of disproportionate retaliatory response on urban-industrial targets.

This problem again requires a second-order application of rational theory supplemental to the basic strategy of rational deterrence. Such an application is under development, it appears, in the recently articulated doctrine of limited counterforce.[11]

For over a decade now the concept of counterforce response has been advanced as the basic answer to the paradox of the retaliatory threat. The doctrine requires that any actual retaliatory attack be conducted not against populated and industrial centers, as threatened in advance, but rather against the remaining military forces of the attacker—a response which delivers direct benefits and is therefore more credible. The well-rehearsed problem with this conception is that, under the conditions imposed by known technology, it tends to give strong impetus to additional arms deployments since it readily generates requirements for very large and/or extremely accurate strategic offensive forces which are specifically pegged to the opponent's deployments. The doctrine of limited counterforce offers a potential means of avoiding this defect by focusing exclusively on force operations, by tying the concept solely to the objective of deterrence, and by stressing the limited nature of the response envisaged.

In pure form, limited counterforce is a targeting policy that imposes no additional requirements on the size, design, or composition of the strategic forces. The forces required to implement the doctrine are automatically provided by the normal operation of conservative assumptions which produce forces far in excess of realistic requirements.

---

[10] Thomas C. Schelling (fn. 1).

[11] The term "limited counterforce" is applied to the currently articulated defense policy by Ted Greenwood and Michael Nacht, "The New Nuclear Debate: Sense or Nonsense?" *Foreign Affairs*, Vol. 52 (July 1974), 761-80. The doctrine is officially articulated in the *Posture Statement* (fn. 8).

Moreover, the doctrine entails no strategic objective beyond deterrence. Though the idea of counterforce has been associated in the past with additional objectives, such as limiting damage and achieving a military advantage, any meaningful contribution to such objectives does seem to require significant additional procurement, and thus does stimulate arms competition. By defining a retaliatory threat of sharply restricted character, limited counterforce allows proportionate response to low-level threats or attacks,[12] and thus presumably strengthens deterrence against such attacks. Since actual force-targeting plans have apparently not allowed for very limited retaliation against strictly military targets, the doctrine of limited counterforce promises a substantial improvement in the force posture and at least a partial answer to the inherent paradox of the retaliatory threat, without driving deployment levels upward.

As with the strategic bargaining strategy, however, limited counterforce is not destined to enjoy the broad support that the primary deterrence strategy has achieved. There are theoretical objections from those who feel that a doctrine which creates the capacity, organizational posture, and mental outlook required for a very limited, precisely controlled use of nuclear weapons will damage rather than bolster deterrence, will erode the stark barrier that guards the entrance to nuclear violence, and will increase rather than decrease the aggregate probability of war. There are practical objections as well from those who doubt whether the pure concept of limited counterforce can be implemented, whether even its conceptual evolution can be held to the rational interpretation just advanced. The United States has development programs for highly accurate warheads and a bargaining strategy that contemplates either qualitative or quantitative advances in the strategic forces in the absence of highly detailed, precisely symmetrical, and truly constraining agreements. It will be very difficult to avoid a connection between these programs and the counterforce doctrine—a connection made both in the mind of the adversary and in the domestic policies associated with weapons acquisition. If that natural connection is established, it will be extremely difficult to keep the counterforce doctrine strictly limited. At least in the current public record, the limits of the concept are not well enough defined to offer much resistance to the trend toward increasing strategic force capabilities.

---

[12] "Low" here is a relative term whose reference is the annihilating damage that modern nuclear arsenals could produce if fully utilized. It remains true that even a very limited nuclear attack would produce levels of damage properly judged enormous if compared to the standards of previous warfare. Nonetheless, the problem of deterrence persists as long as the strategic forces have not yet been used at full strength.

Unfortunately, these secondary applications of rational logic—strategic bargaining and limited counterforce—are not merely matters of intellectual doubt and disagreement. The issues of strategic doctrine are strongly energized by the broader dynamics of weapons development and procurement. The United States and the Soviet Union over recent years have undertaken very extensive but asymmetrical developments of their strategic forces. The Soviet Union has increased the number of launchers and the overall throw-weight of its missile forces. The United States has increased the number of warheads that can be independently assigned to strategic targets. In addition, the United States has been making significant technical improvements in the overall accuracy of its missile forces and in the efficiency of weapons design.[13] Advances in both areas are expected of the Soviet forces as well, though probably on a schedule lagging significantly behind the American force. Even under the arms limitations now being projected to 1985 these trends can be expected to continue and to produce increasingly pessimistic calculations of the possible strategic exchange. In the United States at least, force planners are now seized with the possibility of the American land-based missile force becoming vulnerable to attack, and thus constituting both an unreliable component of the deterrent forces and a destabilizing one in crisis situations.

In sum, strong technical and organizational forces are pushing upward on the arms procurement cycle, and these forces threaten to carry strategic logic right along. The extent to which strategic policy can bring reasoned discipline to force deployments is a matter of considerable uncertainty, but strategic policy nonetheless represents a major point of human leverage which cannot be casually abandoned. The difficulties encountered by rational theory in application to second-order strategic problems are a matter of practical as well as theoretical concern.

ALTERNATIVE CONCEPTIONS

Rational decision theory, for all its sophistication, coherence, and utility, has always suffered from inherent implausibility. The calculations required of decision-makers in any extensive application of the

[13] The United States program and the relative force balances are discussed and estimated by Secretary Schlesinger in the 1974 *Posture Statement* (fn. 8). Increases in accuracy and in the explosive power which can be achieved by a weapon of given weight and size serve to increase the capability of conducting counterforce attacks against hardened land-based missile sites. Since both sides significantly rely on hardened land-based missiles for their retaliatory threat, such developments seem to jeopardize their primary deterrent posture—particularly under the principle of conservative planning.

theory are readily demonstrated to be impossibly burdensome. One of the favorite examples is the game of chess, where the most direct rational solution would require an evaluation of the consequences of all possible moves and a selection of the best move at each point of choice. The number of possible move sequences is so enormous, however (larger by far than the number of atoms in the universe), that such a procedure is obviously impossible. In general, despite the traditional normative exhortation of rational theorists, it is clear that at best, real political decision-makers can achieve only the faintest approximation of the theory's requirements, and it is not likely that they do even that without unusual (and hence infrequent) effort.

Inspired by such arguments, some theorists have labored to explain how it is that decision-makers—having limited capacities and facing the staggering variety inherent in any serious decision problem—can nonetheless rapidly and reliably make basically successful decisions. All human beings in their daily lives constantly solve decision problems of great complexity; their very survival depends on it. If it is not plausible that they are constantly carrying out the calculations required by rational decision theory, then there must be another way of accomplishing equivalent results. By approaching the issue in this way, theorists in a number of related disciplines have gradually developed a coherent account of decision processes which are extremely simple but nonetheless very effective under the proper circumstances. This account differs sharply from central assumptions of rational decision theory and thus promises a competitive theoretical base for application to policy problems. It may be labeled "cybernetic theory of decision," to reflect the central role played by highly structured feedback cycles that confine the decision process within strict limits.[14] The limits have to do both with the information that the decision-maker attends to and with the range of response contemplated within any given time period.

Cybernetic decision theory is only very abstractly developed at the moment; its distinctiveness from rational theory is not widely acknowledged; and there is virtually no experience in applying it to serious problems of public policy. It thus competes under a severe handicap and we would be foolish to impose extravagant expectations upon it. Nonetheless the cybernetic theory does serve to illuminate some of the more troublesome underlying assumptions of rational theory, and it does inspire a set of practical propositions that challenge central tenets

---

[14] The logic of cybernetic decision theory and the distinction between that and the rational theory of decision is discussed in Steinbruner, *The Cybernetic Theory of Decision* (Princeton: Princeton University Press 1974).

of the rational deterrence strategy based on these underlying assumptions. This is a limited but important role.

What, then, are the distinctive characteristics of a cybernetic process? Perhaps the major point is that cybernetic theory defines the fundamental decision problem not as a matter of maximizing expected utility (or any loose approximation), but rather as a question of simplifying an incomprehensibly complex world. Because his central problem is that of achieving a workable simplification of his environment, the cybernetic decision-maker does not make probabilistic judgments and analytic evaluations of the consequences of his actions. He does not make elaborate outcome calculations at all. Rather, the cybernetic decision-maker performs a set of procedures under simulation of *very narrowly constrained* information input. The procedures do produce decisions that do in turn affect outcomes in the environment; in cases of successfully operating cybernetic processes the consequences return information on a feedback channel. The pure cybernetic decision-maker, however, can be and often is perfectly blind to all that. He perceives only the highly specific information input and the limited procedures he performs. Moreover, given a broad view of cybernetic logic set in contrast to specific assumptions of rational theory, it can be demonstrated that the cybernetic decision-maker does not resolve value conflicts; that is, that he does not seek to produce an optimally balanced return to competing objectives. Rather, the cybernetic decision-maker breaks such problems into separate decision processes and operates at any one time solely in terms of a single objective with a single expected outcome.[15]

In order to get some concrete sense of what these abstractions mean, let us consider that prototype strategic game known as "chicken." A famous form of that game consists in two players driving automobiles at 70 mph directly at each other down the center of an isolated road. An audience of peers looks on. The player who swerves off of the center line to avoid a head-on collision is labeled a chicken and suffers the contempt of his peers. Thomas Schelling has provided a solution to the game under rational assumptions.[16] He has pointed out that that player will win who first establishes an irreversible commitment to the center of the road—say, by throwing his steering wheel out of the window and climbing in the back seat. The other player then faces but two choices—a finite loss of honor or a certainty of death—and everyone knows how a rational calculator will solve that conflict of values.

[15] *Ibid.*, chaps. 3 and 4.   [16] Schelling (fn. 1).

Under cybernetic assumptions the game readily generates a disaster. A pure prototype of the cybernetic decision-maker would assume from the start that the other player must yield to his resolve, and he would not observe his opponent's behavior at all as the cars approached each other. Rather, he would execute a pre-established program for driving down the center of the road and would notice only whether the line still ran between his wheels. There would be no resolution of the conflicting values—conscious or unconscious—until fate imposed one as an unintended result of his primitive calculations. The important point is that the cybernetic theory predicts tragedy not from any failure in rational calculation or execution, not from random error, but rather from the result of normally operating decision processes that are functional under most circumstances. It may be hard to imagine such a blind process actually operating in the starkly defined game of chicken, but real strategic confrontations usually occur under far more complex, more ambiguous situations. The cybernetic process is far more plausible under the decision-making burdens of complex environments.

The moral of the story is not that cybernetic processes necessarily produce strategic disaster, but rather that they work very differently from rational processes, and that under the same circumstances cybernetic and rational decision processes can produce very different outcomes.

STRATEGIC IMPLICATIONS

Strategic policy in the United States is sufficiently suffused with rational logic that there are many points at which the distinction between rational and cybernetic decision processes has interesting and potentially important implications. As illustrations we can consider the topics raised above—the principle of conservative planning, arms interactions, and force operations. Since these questions all revolve around difficulties in the rational deterrence strategy, they are of obvious significance.

Influential American strategists have long held to the opinion that stable deterrence is difficult to achieve, and that it depends very much on the fine details of the technical balance.[17] Under the principle of conservative planning, this line of argument has focused attention on the technical vulnerability of United States forces to a massive, calculated, optimally coordinated first strike. It has generally been assumed

---

[17] See Albert Wohlstetter, "The Delicate Balance of Terror," *Foreign Affairs*, XXXVII (January 1959), 211-35, for an influential articulation of this argument.

that the opponent's ability to conduct such an attack would be constrained (in the worst case) only by the number and technical characteristics of his forces.

If one uses cybernetic logic to understand the opponent, this argument comes under very serious doubt for a number of reasons. First, in even contemplating a first strike, a cybernetic decision process would not be very sensitive to fine details of the technical force balance. The destructiveness of nuclear weapons delivered in retaliation, even in modest numbers, is compelling enough to dominate the attention and behavior of cybernetic decision-makers under most circumstances, and even clearly demonstrable technical advantages would have very little effect on this basic result. To the extent that, in a cybernetic decision process, deterrence can be achieved at all by a retaliatory threat, it does not appear difficult to achieve under anything like the currently projected balance of technology and deployed weapons.

Second, the fully coordinated first strike that would minimize the victim's ability to retaliate would be *extremely* difficult to implement with even a strong advantage in strategic forces. Again, given anything like current force levels, it is very likely that a cybernetic decision process would itself impose the binding constraints—limiting the accuracy and the reliability of individual weapons and the overall coordination of a large force well below the best technically feasible levels, particularly under the conditions of extreme secrecy necessary to achieve strategic surprise. The simple reason is that such an attack succeeds or fails on the first attempt—allowing for little feedback and virtually no evolutionary learning process. Third, the circumstances under which a cybernetic process might not readily achieve deterrence by the retaliatory threat would not be much affected by the increased levels of threat or increased probabilities of response produced by conservative force planning. The power and significance of a cybernetic decision process lies in the fact that it frees the decision-maker from the potentially overwhelming burdens of elaborate outcome calculations. The cybernetic decision-maker in a crisis would not be sensitive to even quite broad differences in the level of retaliatory threat; he would utilize instead rather unrefined categorical judgments—either expecting retaliation or not expecting it, without giving much attention to distinguishing levels of retaliation. In general, under cybernetic assumptions the problem of a calculated, massive first strike looses its premier position as a strategic problem, and it appears unlikely that the principle of conservative planning and the large forces it generates actually do provide the protection they are meant to provide.

But the doubts are more serious than that. The force posture logically generated by conservative planning—a posture with a great deal of excess retaliatory capacity in which forces are kept on high alert, particularly in times of crisis—is directly dangerous under cybernetic assumptions. These assumptions drive home the point that any large-scale decision process is inevitably disaggregated and that any coherent action depends upon the simultaneous operation of a number of routinized procedures. Each actor has a part to play, triggered by cues from other actors, almost none of whom have much discretionary power over their actions. The cybernetic theorist finds that the rigidities of such a process and the difficulties of controlling it are vastly underestimated in the established strategy. Though it is probably possible to achieve, by technical means, a high degree of centralized *negative* control—so that the strategic forces cannot operate without high-level authorization—the problems of positive control are much more formidable, particularly if the planners envisage flexibility in the use of forces. Under cybernetic assumptions the great problem of deterrence is that an attempt to use the strategic forces in any active way runs a grave risk of initiating an uncontrollable process leading to an imperfect implementation of an established war plan. Deterrence in a cybernetic process, in other words, is most likely to fail *not* as a result of a technical accident, an unauthorized action, or a cold-blooded calculation, but rather as an unintended and unexpected consequence of a limited strategic maneuver.[18] The chicken game described above is a simple prototype. Those who feel that that example is too bizarre to be helpful should find Barbara Tuchman's study of the outbreak of World War I ample stimulus to the imagination.[19] Under cybernetic assumptions the rigidities of the mobilization plans cannot simply be ascribed to stupidity on the part of their designers; they are inherent in the nature of large organizations, the complexity of the world, and the limits of the human mind.

The foregoing logic, then, brings doubt to bear on both of the secondary applications of the rational deterrence strategy—the limited counterforce doctrine and the theory of strategic bargaining.

The clearest and most immediate problem with the counterforce

[18] The word "escalation," which is often used to label this phenomenon, belongs to the rational tradition and in popular connotation does not convey the dynamic involved. Escalation frequently suggests a more or less consciously intended sequence of increasingly violent attacks meant to put pressure on the opponent for bargaining purposes. "Evolution" or even some appropriately grotesque construct such as "cybelation" would better suggest the unwitting process involved.

[19] *The Guns of August* (New York: Macmillan 1962).

doctrine, under cybernetic assumptions, is the difficulty of setting limits.
The rationally articulated idea of limited counterforce must be implemented by a sizable bureaucracy, contained largely within the United
States Air Force, whose mission it is to identify strategic targets in the
Soviet Union (and presumably elsewhere as well), and to make plans
for attacking these targets. It is a demanding task full of technical
complexity and its successful performance is a necessary condition for
exercising any real strategic capability. Over the course of the nuclear
era the United States has devoted large resources to the problem, and
has created elaborate planning procedures that have been devoted
primarily to the task of preparing for maximally damaging retaliatory
attacks on the potential enemy. Though the entire area is shrouded
(appropriately) in unusual secrecy, public knowledge suggests that the
established target list has always been very large, that there is a great
deal of redundancy in the targeting plans, and that regardless of governing doctrines, war plans have always included both civilian and
military targets. That is, the United States has been planning truly
massive responses.[20] The existence of a highly developed organization
for exercising a massive retaliatory threat, supplied with large forces,
will make it very difficult to redirect the effort to emphasize very small,
precisely limited attacks. Perhaps the organization can be induced to
create limited options, but it is quite another thing to make it behave in
a limited way under fire or to accept the limitation on strategic forces
ultimately implied.

Within the rational tradition, this problem of dealing with organizational inertia is treated as a detail of implementation, and is not
usually raised at the level of fundamental policy formulation. So the
United States Army and Tactical Air Forces, trained for the type of
combat operations encountered in World War II and in Korea, were
sent to Vietnam with the expectation that the adjustment to very different conditions would somehow be made. Under cybernetic assumptions the problem of adjustment appears to be much more fundamental;
the effort required to accomplish it is judged to be much more extensive. The doctrine of limited counterforce appears to require such an
adjustment.

Doubts may also be raised regarding perceptions of the opponent.
As noted above, under established strategic assumptions the damage
that the United States forces would do to the Soviet Union is conserva-
tively estimated to protect against misperceptions that might weaken

[20] See, for example, Milton Leitenberg, "The Race to Oblivion," *Bulletin of the Atomic Scientists*, xxx (September 1974), 12 ff.

deterrence. Under cybernetic assumptions, however, there is far greater worry about misperceptions in the other direction—the tendency to regard any nuclear attack as a mortal blow, however limited it might be. Cybernetic analysis seems to require a very expansive estimation of the damage to the enemy which limited counterforce attacks might produce, as well as a clear definition of a rather low secondary threshold of damage beyond which retaliation cannot be realistically considered to be limited because the opponent—with vast retaliatory power—would not see it so. (The primary threshold, of course, is the first use of nuclear weapons.) It is notoriously difficult to find a break in the continuum of violence once nuclear weapons are employed at all. Unless a clearly defined and widely acknowledged secondary threshold can be established at a very low level, however, limited counterforce does not appear to be a very workable doctrine under cybernetic assumptions. It seems more likely to provoke the enemy than to control him—like sticking needles in an enraged bull.

Finally there is the critical question as to whether the doctrine of limited counterforce, even if appropriately defined and implemented, would make the outbreak of war more likely. The application of cybernetic assumptions does not, of course, overcome the central problem that the most directly pertinent data cannot be gathered and that uncertainty on this question is therefore acute. If all else remains the same, however—the size of the strategic forces, the established assumptions of strategic logic, and particularly the theory of coercive bargaining—then cybernetic analysis yields a very strong suspicion that creating limited options will indeed make their use more likely. That argument does not translate by any means into endorsement of a targeting policy exclusively focused on urban-industrial retaliation, but it does identify a very serious problem that cannot be wished away.

Cybernetic analysis also presents doubts as to the validity of the bargaining strategy that appears to underlie the current United States approach to strategic arms limitation. If the U.S. is indeed relying on the threat of counter-deployments and ultimately even of missile silo-targeting to induce Soviet agreement to serious constraints on strategic forces, then the cybernetic theory of decision contains a sharp warning. The central point is that a cybernetic decision process does not directly balance conflicting objectives. When presented with actual conflicts between objectives, cybernetic decision-makers tend to perceive two problems and to oscillate between single-minded pursuit of each of the two conflicting objectives.[21] The bargaining strategy seems to depend on

---

[21] Steinbruner (fn. 14), chap. 4.

a rational balancing of such conflicts, however, in that the essence of the threat is to attach a predictably negative consequence to an otherwise positively valued course of action in hopes of inducing the desired decision to stop procuring particular weapons. A threat exercised against a cybernetic decision-maker is likely to become a separate issue in itself and is likely to induce a counter-threat; it is not likely to produce the immediate response desired.

At the very least, cybernetic analysis suggests that there is a critical question of timing. It may be possible to induce a strategic opponent to accept the rational construction that the bargaining strategy requires, but cybernetic analysis suggests that that is not the natural pattern and is likely to require time and patience. To attempt to work the bargaining strategy either too quickly or too harshly is likely to overload the politics of the opponent.

The same analysis applies to the doctrine of limited counterforce. It remains implicit in the concept that limited retaliation would serve the purpose of coercing the opponent to accept some trade-off problem in the desired fashion before the cycle of violence reaches the levels of enormous destruction that nuclear weapons can produce. Cybernetic analysis raises the question whether the decision process on either side would work in the required fashion.

PRINCIPLES

What then is to be done? Cybernetic analysis suggests that decision processes on both sides of the strategic confrontation are coherent and basically functional, but far more primitive than normally assumed. To the extent that it is credited, that analysis bodes serious trouble for current strategic policies. We cannot leap directly to counsel a drastic change in the established strategy, however. Cybernetic analysis is neither sufficiently developed nor sufficiently accepted to carry that degree of responsibility or impact. In a more modest spirit, therefore, let us set forth some principles that can be applied to specific decisions of force posture, and that would give some effect to cybernetic arguments without presuming any radical shift in basic defense policy.

The major principle is that the United States should hedge against instabilities in the strategic balance primarily with a broad-ranging research and development effort, and *not* by means of offensive force deployments. Though the U.S. is undertaking a substantial R&D effort at the moment, the focus, the balance, and the organizational posture of that effort are not what the principle requires. The current research and development effort is too narrow, too much tied to anticipated procurement of specific weapons projects, and too dominantly focused on offensive capability. An R&D effort used as a strategic hedge would undertake more long-term developments independent of anticipated procurement, would develop competing technologies to the prototype stage, and would give greater emphasis than now is the case to defense—particularly the protection of strategic forces. The central purpose of such an effort would be a broad, protective accumulation both of basic knowledge and of developed technology, and this would provide a base for wide choice and rapid response should a truly serious challenge to the strategic balance actually develop. The R&D would be so organized that even very successful technical developments could be held short of deployment in the absence of gross strategic imbalances.

As a corollary to the strategy of hedging with developed technical capability and not with actual force deployments, the United States should be prepared to tolerate, if necessary, substantial disparities in static force characteristics as long as it maintains undeniable deterrent capability. The Vladivostok guidelines give the Soviet Union an inherent advantage in missile throw-weight which can ultimately be translated into an advantage in independently targetable warheads. Concern has arisen that this will render the American land-based missile force relatively more vulnerable to attack, and that this realization will lead to a political disadvantage in dealing with the Soviet Union and other nations on the many issues of the times. It would be desirable of course if force disparities of this sort could be avoided—either by unilateral forebearance or by additional agreements—but even if disparities should occur, the U.S. should not rush to match the Soviet forces as it has threatened to do. Such simplistic force matching is an inherent tendency of interacting cybernetic decision processes, and it is very much in the interest of the United States to control this phenomenon. The American ability to threaten massive retaliation and actually to conduct limited counterforce response is not very sensitive to substantial force disparities; the hypothetical political effects of these disparities range from very speculative to highly implausible. At very least, the United States should delay response to Soviet deployments rather than anticipating them, thus using the flexibility allowed by the impressive technical advantage in accuracy and multiple-targeting capability which has been achieved and will be maintained well into the next decade.

A third principle is that the United States should be extremely cautious about the interaction between technical capabilities and human decision processes. Since both formal knowledge and practical experience is far more developed on the technical side, there is continuous danger that technical analysis will dominate force planning and lead to very serious miscalculations. This problem is perhaps most acute in dealing with the issues of force targeting and the use of highly accurate missile delivery systems.

It is obvious that the rapidly developing technical ability of the U.S. to attack selected military targets with accurate, low-yield weapons offers significant strategic advantages in terms of the established strategy. This trend can be expected to make the doctrine of *limited* counterforce retaliation technically feasible, and thus to diminish a major anomaly of the rational deterrence posture. It cannot be emphasized too strongly, however, that the validity of the doctrine and the utility of the weapons designed to implement it critically depend upon the response of a human decision process. Limited counterforce attacks would cause pain and injury to an opponent, but they would not cripple him. They would leave him with substantial capacity to retaliate. If a strategy of threatening or actually conducting such attacks is to succeed in controlling the terror of nuclear war, then it must induce the opponent to accept some political accommodation. The United States must recognize that the question as to whether reasonable accommodation can be brought about by limited nuclear attack or the threat of it is a matter of the greatest uncertainty. The weight of historical experience seems to suggest the contrary: that violence once begun is not readily terminated. The third principle implies, then, that those arguing the merits of limited counterforce, the broad political effects of the strategic balance, and the necessity of additional force deployments for either purpose should bear the burden of proof. That requirement cannot be met by a simple appeal to the rational theory of deterrence or by unanalyzed judgments regarding the effects of coercive bargaining.

In aggregate, these principles lead to a working proposition; namely, that at the moment and for the foreseeable future the United States has already programmed for deployment all the strategic offensive capability which it is desirable to have. It must be conceded that the progress of formal strategic arms limitation is disappointing in many respects and that leeway exists for very provocative Soviet arms deployments. Precisely for these reasons, however, the U.S. must concern itself with the problems of achieving restraint and reason in its own force posture. The problems that should command priority attention involve the internal management of weapons systems—their design, development, procurement, and operation—and the integration of military capability with international political purposes. The nation's defense in the coming years will depend far more on these things than on additional deployment of strategic weapons.

WHY BIG NATIONS LOSE SMALL WARS: THE POLITICS OF ASYMMETRIC CONFLICT

By ANDREW MACK*

A cursory examination of the history of imperialist expansion in the late nineteenth and early twentieth century reveals one thing very clearly: Third-World resistance, where it existed, was crushed with speedy efficiency. In terms of conventional military thinking such successes were not unexpected. Indeed, together with the Allied experience in the first and second World Wars, they served to reinforce and to rigidify the pervasive notion that superiority in military capability (conventionally defined) will mean victory in war. However, the history of a number of conflicts in the period following World War II showed that military and technological superiority may be a highly unreliable guide to the outcome of wars. In Indochina (1946–54), Indonesia (1947–49), Algeria, Cyprus, Aden, Morocco, and Tunisia, local nationalist forces gained their objectives in armed confrontations with industrial powers which possessed an overwhelming superiority in conventional military capability. These wars were not exclusively a colonial phenomenon, as was demonstrated by the failure of the United States to defeat its opponents in Vietnam.

For some idea of the degree to which the outcome of these wars presents a radical break with the past, it is instructive to examine the case of Indochina. The French successfully subjugated the peoples of Indochina for more than sixty years with a locally based army only fifteen thousand strong. The situation changed dramatically after 1946, when the Vietnamese took up arms in guerrilla struggle. By 1954 the nationalist forces of the Vietminh had forced the French— who by this time had deployed an expeditionary force of nearly two hundred thousand men—to concede defeat and withdraw their forces in ignominy. Within twenty years, a vast U.S. military machine with an expeditionary force five hundred thousand strong had also been forced to withdraw.

The purpose of this paper is to attempt to provide a "pre-theoretical

* Research for this article was supported by the British Social Science Research Council. An ongoing project examining a number of case histories of "asymmetric conflicts" is currently being supported by the Rockefeller Foundation.

perspective" within which the *outcome* of such "asymmetric conflicts" may be explained. In the field of conflict research, the study of the outcome and the conduct of wars, as against that of their *etiology*, has received remarkably little attention.[1] The outcome of "asymmetric conflicts" as described in this paper has been almost totally neglected.[2]

Arguably, it is easier to explain why the insurgents were *not* defeated than it is to explain the related but more interesting question—namely, how and why the external power was forced to withdraw. Since the former problem has been the subject of intense investigation both by specialists in counter-insurgency and strategists of guerrilla warfare, the greater part of this paper will deal with the latter problem. However, a few fairly obvious points need to be made before going on.

In analyzing the successes of the British at Omdurman against the Sudanese and the Italians in their war against local insurgents in Abyssinia, Mao Tse-tung has noted that defeat is the invariable outcome where native forces fight with inferior weapons against modernized forces *on the latter's terms*. Katzenbach writes in this context: "By and large, it would seem that what made the machinery of European troops so successful was that native troops saw fit to die, with glory, with honor, en masse, and in vain."[3] Second, it should be noted that in general this type of war met with little domestic opposition; success only served to increase public support.[4] Two interesting exceptions were the Boer War and the Irish Rebellion (1916–22); it is significant that in these conflicts the resistance to the British was both protracted and bitter and, in the metropolis, generated domestic opposition to the war.[5] Thus, the first condition for avoiding defeat is to refuse to confront the enemy on his own terms. To avoid being crushed,

[1] See Berenice A. Carroll, "War Termination and Conflict Theory," and William T. R. Fox, "The Causes of Peace and the Conditions of War," both in *How Wars End, Annals of the American Academy of Political and Social Science*, Vol. 392 (November 1970); and Elizabeth Converse, "The War of All Against All: A Review of the Journal of Conflict Resolution, 1957–68," *Journal of Conflict Resolution*, XII (December 1968).

[2] Exceptions are found in E. L. Katzenbach, "Time, Space and Will: The Politico-Military Strategy of Mao Tse-tung," in Lt. Col. T. N. Greene, ed., *The Guerrilla and How To Fight Him* (New York 1962); Robert Taber, *The War of the Flea* (New York 1965); and Joseph S. Kraemer, "Revolutionary Guerrilla Warfare and the Decolonization Movement," *Polity*, IV (Winter 1971).

[3] Katzenbach (fn. 2), 15.

[4] See, for example, H. Wehler, "Industrial Growth and Early German Imperialism" in Robert Owen and Robert Sutcliffe, eds., *Theories of Imperialism* (London 1972).

[5] Two excellent recent studies dealing directly with domestic opposition to these wars are: Stephen Koss, *The Pro-Boers: The Anatomy of an Anti-War Movement* (Chicago 1973), and D. G. Boyce, *Englishmen and Irish Troubles: British Public Opinion and the Making of Irish Policy 1918–22* (London 1972).

the insurgent forces must retain a degree of invulnerability, but the defensive *means* to this end will depend on the conditions of the war. In guerrilla warfare in the classical sense, the "people sea" forms a sanctuary of popular support for the "guerrilla fish"; in urban guerrilla warfare the anonymity of the city provides protection. Operating in uninhabited areas and supplied from without (e.g., the post-1968 North Vietnamese operations along the Ho Chi Minh Trail in the Vietnam War), the insurgents may simply rely on the mountains and forests to conceal and protect them.

For students of strategy the importance of these wars lies in the fact that the simplistic but once prevalent assumption—that conventional military superiority necessarily prevails in war—has been destroyed. What is also interesting is that although the metropolitan powers did not *win* militarily, neither were they *defeated* militarily. Indeed the military defeat of the metropolis itself was impossible since the insurgents lacked an invasion capability. In every case, success for the insurgents arose not from a military victory on the ground—though military successes may have been a contributory cause—but rather from the progressive attrition of their opponents' *political* capability to wage war. In such asymmetric conflicts, insurgents may gain political victory from a situation of military stalemate *or even defeat*.

The most recent and obvious example of this type of conflict is the American war in Vietnam, which has brought home several important lessons. First, it has provided the most obvious demonstration of the falsity of the assumptions that underlie the "capability" conception of power.[6] Not only does superiority in military force (conventionally defined) not guarantee victory; it may, under certain circumstances, be positively counter-productive.[7] Second, the Vietnam conflict has demonstrated how, under certain conditions, the theatre of war extends well beyond the battlefield to encompass the polity and social institutions of the external power. The Vietnam war may be seen as having been fought on two fronts—one bloody and indecisive in the forests and mountains of Indochina, the other essentially nonviolent— but ultimately more decisive—within the polity and social institutions of the United States. The nature of the relationship between these two

[6] Problems with different conceptions of power in this context are examined in Andrew Mack, "The Concept of Power and its Uses in Explaining Asymmetric Conflict," Richardson Institute for Conflict and Peace Research (London 1974).

[7] The least ambiguous demonstrations of this apparently paradoxical assertion are to be found in the relatively rare cases of successful nonviolent resistance to armed aggression. See Anders Boserup and Andrew Mack, *War Without Weapons: Non-Violence in National Defence* (London 1974).

conflicts—which are in fact different facets of the same conflict—is critical to an understanding of the outcome of the war. However, the American experience was in no sense unique, except to Americans. In 1954 the Vietminh destroyed the French forces which were mustered at Dien Bien Phu in a classic set piece battle. The direct military costs to the French have been much exaggerated; only 3 per cent of the total French forces in Indochina were involved. The psychological effects—like those of the Tet offensive some fourteen years later— were shattering, however. The Vietminh did not of course defeat France militarily. They lacked not only the capability but also any interest in attempting such a move. Dien Bien Phu, however, had the effect of destroying the *political* capability ("will" in the language of classical strategy) of the French Government to mobilize further troops and to continue the struggle—this despite the fact that the greater part of the financial costs of the war were being borne by the United States. Third, the Vietnam war, which for the Vietnamese revolutionaries has now lasted over a quarter of a century, has emphasized the enormous importance which guerrilla strategists place on "protracted warfare." This is articulated most clearly in Mao Tse-tung's works, but it is also found in the military writings of General Giap and Truong Chinh and in the works of the leading African guerrilla strategists, Cabral and Mondlane. The certainty of eventual victory which is the result of intensive political mobilization by the guerrilla leadership is the key to what Rosen sees as a critical factor in such conflicts—namely, the willingness to absorb costs.[8] Katzenbach has noted of Mao's strategic theory that it is based on the premise that "if the totality of the population can be made to resist surrender, this resistance can be turned into a war of attrition which will eventually and inevitably be victorious."[9] Or, as Henry Kissinger more succinctly observed in 1969: "The guerrilla wins if he does not lose."[10]

Above all, Vietnam has been a reminder that in war the ultimate aim must be to affect the will of the enemy. Most strategic theorists would of course concur with this view. But in practice, and at the risk of oversimplification, it may be noted that it is a prevalent military belief that if an opponent's military capability to wage war can be destroyed, his "will" to continue the struggle is irrelevant since the means to that end are no longer available. It is not surprising that this

[8] Steven Rosen, "War Power and the Willingness to Suffer," in Bruce M. Russett, ed., *Peace, War, and Numbers* (London 1972).

[9] Katzenbach (fn. 2), 18.

[10] Henry A. Kissinger, "The Vietnam Negotiations," *Foreign Affairs*, XLVII (January 1969), 214.

should be a prevalent belief in modern industrial societies: strategic doctrine tends to mold itself to available technology, as critics of strategic weapons deployment have forcefully pointed out. Neither is it surprising that guerrilla strategists should see strategy in very different terms. Lacking the technological capability or the basic resources to destroy the external enemy's military capability, they must of necessity aim to destroy his political capability. If the external power's "will" to continue the struggle is destroyed, then its military capability—no matter how powerful—is totally irrelevant. One aim of this paper is to show how and why, in certain types of conflict, conventional military superiority is not merely useless, but may actually be counter-productive. The implications for those military systems which rely almost wholly on industrial power and advanced technology need hardly be spelled out.

As I have noted above, in none of the asymmetric conflicts did the local insurgents have the capability to invade their metropolitan opponents' homeland. It *necessarily* follows that insurgents can only achieve their ends if their opponents' *political* capability to wage war is destroyed. This is true whether the insurgents are revolutionaries or right-wing nationalists, whether they rely on guerrilla warfare, urban terrorism, or even nonviolence. The destruction of the external power's forces in the field places no *material* obstacle in its path which will prevent it from simply mobilizing more forces at home and dispatching them to the battlefront. The constraints on mobilization are political, not material. In none of the conflicts noted was more than a fraction of the total *potential* military resources of the metropolitan power in fact mobilized. The U.S. war in Vietnam has by any measure had the greatest impact on international and American domestic politics of any conflict since World War II, but the maximum number of U.S. troops in Vietnam at the peak of the ground war in 1968 amounted to less than one quarter of one per cent of the American population. The political constraints operating against full mobilization of the metropolitan forces arise as a consequence of the conflicts in the metropolis—both within the political elite and in the wider society—which the war, *by its very nature*, will inevitably tend to generate. To paraphrase Clausewitz, politics may become the continuation of war by other means. Therefore the military struggle on the ground must be evaluated not in terms of the narrow calculus of military tactics, but in terms of its political impact in the metropolis: "Battles and campaigns are amenable to analysis as rather self-contained contests of military power. . . . By contrast, the final outcome of wars depends on a much wider range of factors, many of them highly elusive—such as the war's impact on domestic politics. . . ."[11] The significance of particular battles does not lie in their outcome as "self-contained contests of military power." Thus, although the United States could contend that the 1968 Tet offensive marked a dramatic defeat for the revolutionary forces in terms of the macabre military calculus of "body counts," the offensive was in fact a major strategic defeat for the U.S., marking the turning point in the war. The impact of Tet on American domestic politics led directly to the incumbent President's decision not to stand for another term of office. And, for the first time, military requests for more resources (a further 200,000 men) were refused *despite the fact* that the military situation had worsened.

Even where military victory over the insurgents is unambiguous—as in General Massu's destruction of the FLN infrastructure in the notorious Battle of Algiers—this is still no sure guide to the outcome of the conflict. Despite the fact that the FLN never regained the military initiative, the French abandoned their struggle within four years. Indeed, the barbarous methods used by Massu to achieve that victory, including the widespread use of torture, were instrumental in catalyzing opposition to the war in metropolitan France.

The Algerian war is an instructive example of our thesis. Between 1954 and 1962 there was a radical shift in the balance of political forces in metropolitan France. The *colon* (white settler) class of Algeria was the chief political victim. A few days after fighting broke out, the leftist Minister of the Interior, François Mitterand, responded to a suggestion that Paris should negotiate with the rebels by stating flatly that in the Algerian *départements* "the only negotiation is war." Yet seven and a-half years later, De Gaulle had not only granted the rebels all their initial demands (including some they had not even considered when fighting broke out), but received overwhelming support from the majority of the French population in doing so. Significantly, the last task of the French Army (which had itself attempted a coup against the Gaullist government) was to hunt down the terrorists of the OAS—the diehard remnants of the *colon* class in whose interests the military had intervened in the first place.

French policy throughout this conflict—as metropolitan policy in other asymmetric conflicts—was beset by what Mao Tse-tung calls "contradictions." The initial military repression directed against the rebels achieved for the militants what they had been unable to achieve

---

[11] Fred Charles Iklé, *Every War Must End* (London 1971), 1-2.

for themselves—namely, the political mobilization of the masses against the French.

As the rebellion became more broadly based, more numerous forces and ever more extreme methods were used to attempt to quell it. The French also tried to buy off nationalist aspirations by offering to grant some of the political demands which had initially been made by the insurgents—only to find that these had been radically escalated. Offers of concessions were—as is frequently the case in such conflicts—both too small and too late. The more forces the French deployed (ultimately four hundred thousand men), the greater was the impact which the war had in the metropolis. It was not so much the inhumanity of the war *per se* that generated opposition in France; the majority of French men and women were no more sympathetic to the FLN than were the majority of Americans to the NLF in Vietnam. The major cause of opposition lay not in the enormous costs of the war to the *Algerians* (though this was a factor), but in the costs of the war to the French themselves. The progressively greater human, economic, and political costs gave rise to the phenomenon of "war weariness" which many writers have described without analyzing, and to the "loss of political will" of the government to which the military invariably ascribed the defeat. Thus it can be seen that the shift in the balance of political forces in metropolitan France was of critical importance in determining the outcome of the war. Political leaders in such conflicts do not grant insurgent demands because they undergo a sudden change of heart. They concede because they have no choice.

Why are asymmetries in structure important, and what do we in fact mean by "asymmetry" in this context? We must first note that the *relationship* between the belligerents is *asymmetric*. The insurgents can pose no direct threat to the survival of the external power because, as already noted, they lack an invasion capability. On the other hand, the metropolitan power poses not simply the threat of invasion, but the reality of occupation. This fact is so obvious that its implications have been ignored. It means, crudely speaking, that for the insurgents the war is "total," while for the external power it is necessarily "limited." Full mobilization of the total military resources of the external power is simply not politically possible. (One might conceive of cases where this is not the case—as in a popularly backed "holy war" for example— but such possibilities are of no relevance to the present discussion.) Not only is full mobilization impossible politically, it is not thought to be in the least *necessary*. The asymmetry in conventional military capability is so great and the confidence that military might will prevail is so pervasive that expectation of victory is one of the hallmarks of the initial endeavor.

The fact that one belligerent possesses an invasion capability and the other does not is a function of the differences in level of industrial and technological capability of the two sides. The asymmetric *relationship* is thus a function of the asymmetry in "resource power."

Some strategic implications of symmetric and asymmetric conflict relations may now be spelled out. The insurgents, faced with occupation by a hostile external power, are able to capitalize on those powerful forces to which political scientists have given the label "nationalism." What this means essentially is that disparate and sometimes conflicting national groups may find a common unity—a national interest—in opposing a common enemy. In that case the cohesion generated is only *indirectly* a consequence of the asymmetry in resource power: its social and psychological bonds are to be found in the common hostility felt toward the external enemy.

Clausewitz noted that war only approximates to its "pure form" when a "grand and powerful purpose" is at stake.[12] Only then will the full mobilization of national resources become a possibility, and only then will the diverse and sometimes conflicting goals that various national groups pursue in time of peace be displaced by a single overriding strategic aim—"the overthrow of the enemy." In a *symmetric*, "total war" situation where the survival of *both sides* is at stake, both have a "grand and powerful purpose" to defend. Thus, other things being equal, the potential for internal divisions arising in either camp is small relative to the potential for domestic conflict in the homeland of the metropolitan power involved in an *asymmetric* conflict. In symmetric conflicts, *ceteris paribus,* the absence of constraints on the mobilization and the use of conventional military force maximize the strategic utility of conventional warfare. Examples of *symmetric* "total wars" are the first and second World Wars and civil wars in which the struggle can be seen in zero-sum terms—as one of survival. However, although the external-enemy/internal-cohesion thesis of sociologists like Simmel and Coser has been widely accepted, the relationship is not as simple as some writers appear to think. Coser follows Williams in agreeing that there has to be a minimal consensus that the group (or nation) is a "going concern," and that there must be recognition of an outside threat which is thought to menace the group *as a whole*, not just some part of it. Coser notes of the second World War that "attempts at centralization by the

---

[12] The final chapter of Boserup and Mack (fn. 7) discusses Clausewitzian strategic theory and its application to "asymmetric conflicts."

French Government were unavailing and could not mend the basic cleavages nor remedy the lack of social solidarity."[13] We may add to this two more conditions which will affect national unity in the face of external threat. First, resistance must be perceived as a viable alternative to surrender. It is noteworthy that after the collapse of the Nazi-Soviet Pact in the second World War, resistance to the Nazis in occupied Europe was very often led by Communists for whom surrender meant extermination. A majority of the population of the occupied countries perceived surrender as a more viable alternative than resistance—at least until it appeared that the tide of the war had turned against the Nazis. Resistance movements whose members share a revolutionary ideology which has as one of its basic tenets the belief that "protracted war" will ultimately be victorious, will, by definition, see resistance as an obvious alternative to surrender. Second, since occupation is likely to have adverse consequences for all groups, but much worse for some than for others, such national unity as does occur will not be unshakable. But it will be enormously reinforced by what may be called the "bandwagon effect."[14] Dissent will be heavily proscribed and sanctioned socially as well as by the leadership.

Even though it is not possible to be precise about the conditions which *necessarily* generate national solidarity in the face of an external threat, we may note the following two points with respect to asymmetric conflicts:

(a) An external threat is a necessary if not sufficient condition for the emergence of a popular front.

(b) Occupation and military repression by the metropolitan power has *in fact* produced the nationalist unity predicted by the Coser-Simmel thesis. (One interesting exception is the confrontation in Malaysia, where there was a deep cleavage dividing the Chinese insurgents from the Malays.) Indeed, it is possible to argue that in some cases the repression did not so much intensify a pre-existing basic consensus as create one.

(c) More importantly, there was no comparable unifying external force in the case of the metropolitan power. On the contrary, in every case where the insurgents won, the war was a profoundly divisive issue.

Those scholars who are expounding the "paradox" that external conflict will both increase and decrease domestic conflict (see below) are guilty of creating a false dichotomy. Contrast the situation in the United

---

[13] Lewis A. Coser, *The Functions of Social Conflict* (New York 1956), 87-110.
[14] Boserup and Mack (fn. 7), chap. 1.

States, as the war escalated in Vietnam, with that of Britain facing the Nazis in the second World War. In the former case we see the progressive escalation of domestic opposition to the war creating deep divisions within U.S. society. In the latter, "The Nazi attack appreciably increased the internal cohesion of the British social system, temporarily narrowing the various political, social and economic fissures that existed in British society."[15] In Britain the electoral process was suspended for the duration of the conflict in order to form a coalition "national government." In the various "wars of national liberation" we see precisely the same process in the formation of "popular fronts." Indeed, the label "National Liberation Front" is found in some guise in nearly all these conflicts, though rarely in civil wars.[16]

It is my contention that the process of political attrition of the metropolitan power's capability to continue to wage war is *not* the consequence of errors of generalship, though these may well occur. Rather, it is a function of the *structure* of the conflict, of the nature of the conflictual relationship between the belligerents. Where the war is perceived as "limited"—because the opponent is "weak" and can pose no direct threat—the prosecution of the war does not take automatic primacy over other goals pursued by factions within the government, or bureaucracies or other groups pursuing interests which compete for state resources. In a situation of total war, the prosecution of the war *does* take automatic primacy above all other goals. Controversies over "guns or butter" are not only conceivable in a Vietnam-type conflict, but inevitable. In a total-war situation they would be inconceivable: guns would get *automatic* priority. In contrast to the total-war situation, the protagonists of a limited war have to compete for resources—human, economic, and political—with protagonists of other interests—governmental, bureaucratic, "interest groups," and so forth. Clearly, if the war is terminated quickly and certain benefits are believed to be accruing from victory (as in the case of the mini-wars of colonial expansion) the *potential* for divisive domestic conflict on the war issue will not be realized. But this is simply another way of stating that if the insurgents are to win, they must not lose.

In his highly prophetic paper published in 1969, Henry Kissinger observed of America's war in Vietnam: "We fought a military war; our opponents fought a political one. We sought physical attrition; our opponents aimed for our psychological exhaustion. In the process, we

---

[15] Coser (fn. 13), 87-110; quotation from p. 95.

[16] The obvious point here is that "nationalism" is normally a meaningless concept except in relation to an external environment. "Nationalism" may be significant in civil wars that are based on an ethnic conflict but not on class conflict.

lost sight of one of the cardinal maxims of guerrilla warfare: the guerrilla wins if he does not lose. The conventional army loses if it does not win."[17]

In a similar vein, E. L. Katzenbach in 1962 described Mao Tse-tung's general strategic approach as follows: "Fundamental to all else, Mao says, is the belief that countries with legislative bodies simply cannot take a war of attrition, either financially or, in the long run, psychologically. Indeed, the very fact of a multi-party structure makes commitment to a long war so politically suicidal as to be quite impossible. . . . When the financial burden increases from month to month, the outcry against the war will itself weaken the ability of the troops to fight. The war that Mao's theory contemplates is the cheapest for him to fight and the most expensive for the enemy."[18]

In order to avoid defeat, the insurgents must retain a minimum degree of invulnerability. In order to *win*, they must be able to impose a steady accumulation of "costs" on their opponent. They must not only be undefeated; they must be *seen* to be undefeated. Strategically, the insurgents' aim must be to provoke the external power into escalating its forces on the ground. This *in itself* will incur economic and political costs in the metropolis. Such a process of escalation did in fact mark the history of the conflicts in Indochina, Algeria, Portuguese Africa, Vietnam, and the current conflict in Ulster. The *direct* costs the insurgents impose on the external power will be the normal costs of war—troops killed and matériel destroyed. But the aim of the insurgents is not the destruction of the military capability of their opponents as an *end in itself*. To attempt such a strategy would be lunatic for a small Third-World power facing a major industrial power. Direct costs become of strategic importance when, and only when, they are translated into indirect costs. These are psychological and political: their objective is to amplify the "contradictions in the enemy's camp."

In the metropolis, a war with no visible payoff against an opponent who poses no direct threat will come under increasing criticism as battle casualties rise and economic costs escalate. Obviously there will still be groups in the metropolis whose ideological commitments will lead them to continue to support the government's war policy; others (munitions manufacturers, for example) may support the war because they have more material interests at stake. But if the war escalates dramatically, as it did in Algeria and Vietnam, it makes a definite impact on the economic and political resources which might otherwise have been allocated to, say, public welfare projects. Tax increases may be

[17] Kissinger (fn. 10), 214.   [18] Katzenbach (fn. 2), 18.

necessary to cover the costs of the war, a draft system may have to be introduced, and inflation will be an almost certain by-product. Such costs are seen as part of the "necessary price" when the security of the nation is directly threatened. When this is not the case, the basis for consensus disappears. In a limited war, it is not at all clear to those groups whose interests are adversely affected why such sacrifices are necessary.[19]

But that is only part of the story. Just as important is the fact that the necessity for the sacrifices involved in fighting and risking death will appear less obvious to the conscripts and even the professional soldiers when the survival of the nation is not directly at stake. American soldiers fought well in the second World War, but the last years in Vietnam were marked by troop mutinies, widespread drug addiction, high levels of desertion, and even the murders of over-zealous officers intent on sending their men out on dangerous patrols. This in fact led to a strong feeling among some senior U.S. Army officers that it was necessary to get out of Vietnam before morale collapsed completely. It is impossible to explain such a dramatic deterioration of morale within the army and the massive opposition to the draft without reference to the *type* of war being fought.

There is also the question of the morality of the war. When the survival of the nation is not directly threatened, and when the obvious asymmetry in conventional military power bestows an underdog status on the insurgent side, the morality of the war is more easily questioned. It is instructive to note that during World War II the deliberate Allied attempt to terrorize the working-class populations of Dresden and other German cities generated no moral outrage in Britain. This despite the fact that the thousand-bomber raids were designed to create fire storms so devastating in effect that more people died in one night of bombing over Dresden than perished in the Hiroshima holocaust. On the other hand, the aerial bombardment of civilian localities in Vietnam, the use of herbicides and defoliants, napalm, and anti-personnel weapons have been all met with widespread controversy and protest. One should not deduce from this that the British public was more callous to the effects of human suffering than was the American.

---

[19] Some interesting and recent theoretical work in the "issue area" literature is relevant to this discussion; see in particular Theodore J. Lowi, "Making Democracy Safe for the World: National Politics," in James Rosenau, ed., *Domestic Sources of Foreign Policy* (New York 1967); and William Zimmerman, "Issue Area and Foreign Policy Process," *American Political Science Review*, LXVII (December 1973). The literature on "bureaucratic politics" and "linkage politics" is also relevant.

Moral outrage is in large part a function of the interests perceived to be at stake in the conflict. Where survival is the issue, the propensity to question and protest the morality of the means used to defeat the enemy is markedly attenuated.

As the war drags on and the costs steadily escalate without the "light at the end of the tunnel" becoming more visible, the divisions generated within the metropolis become *in themselves* one of the political costs of the war. The government—or, more precisely, that faction of the government which is committed to the war—will continue to argue that prosecuting the war *is* in the national interest, that vital security interests *are* at stake, that the international credibility and prestige of the nation is at issue, and so forth. Whether or not these claims bear any relationship to reality—whether they are wholly true or wholly false—is quite immaterial. What counts in the long run is what the opponents of the war believe to be at stake and how much political capital they can muster.

Finally, another word about "contradiction." Mao and Giap have repeatedly emphasized that the principal contradiction which the imperialist army must confront on the ground derives from the fact that forces dispersed to control territory become spread so thinly that they are vulnerable to attack. If forces are concentrated to overcome this weakness, other areas are left unguarded. For the external power to overcome this contradiction requires a massive increase in metropolitan forces; but this immediately increases the domestic costs of the war. On the other hand, if the imperialists wish to pacify the opposition at home by withdrawing some of their forces, the contradiction on the battlefronts is sharpened. Any attempt to resolve one contradiction will magnify the other. The guerrilla strategists understand perfectly that the war they fight takes place on two fronts and the conflict must be perceived as an integrated whole. From this perspective, those who oppose the war in the metropolis act *objectively*—regardless of their subjective political philosophies—as a strategic resource for the insurgents. Governments are well aware of this, since it is they who have to confront the political constraints. Yet government accusations that those opposed to the war are "aiding the enemy" are contemptuously rejected. They are nevertheless objectively correct. From this perspective we can also see why the slogan "imperialism is a paper tiger" is by no means inaccurate. It is not that the material resources of the metropolitan power are in themselves underestimated by the revolutionaries; rather, there is an acute awareness that the political constraints on their maximum deployment are as real as if those resources did not exist, and that these constraints become more rather than less powerful as the war escalates.

Few attempts have been made to analyze the outcome of asymmetric conflicts systematically. Among those few, even fewer have seen the asymmetries which characterize the conflict as being critical to an understanding of the outcome. However, some aspects have been touched on. Rosen considers the asymmetry in power and "willingness to suffer costs"; Katzenbach examines the asymmetry in "tangible" and "intangible resources"; Galtung distinguishes between "social" and "territorial defense" (asymmetry in goals); Kissinger, as already noted, mentions asymmetry in overall strategy (physical versus psychological attrition); and Kraemer distinguishes "colonial" versus "non-colonial" guerrilla wars.[20] An examination of the conflict in the light of any of *these* asymmetries provides certain insights into particular aspects of the war, but misses the overall picture. The asymmetries described in this paper—in the interests perceived to be at stake, in mobilization, in intervention capability, in "resource power," and so forth—are abstracted from their context for the sake of analytical clarity. But the whole remains greater than the sum of its parts, and it is the conflict *as a whole* which must be studied in order to understand its evolution and outcome.

Some writers interested in the *etiology* of conflict have argued that the nature of the state polity mediates the link between internal and external conflict.[21] The same question is of relevance with respect to the relatively neglected problem of understanding the *outcome* of international conflicts. *Is* the process of attrition of the political capability to wage war, which we observe so clearly in the Vietnam and Algerian conflicts, a function of the nature of the polity of the metropolitan powers involved? Some writers clearly believe that it is. With respect to Vietnam, Edmund Ions notes: "Whilst the freedom to demonstrate —even for defeatism in foreign policy—is clearly one of the strengths of a free society, *it is also one of its weaknesses so far as power politics is concerned.*"[22] The argument of Ions and other writers is roughly as follows. In contrast to "open" societies, where dissent is permitted, dissent is repressed in "closed" or "totalitarian" societies. Therefore

---

[20] Rosen (fn. 8); Katzenbach (fn. 2); Kissinger (fn. 10); Kraemer (fn. 2); see also Johan Galtung, "Mot et Nytt Forsvarsbegrep," *Pax*, No. 1 (Oslo 1965).

[21] E.g., Jonathan Wilkenfeld, "Models for the Analysis of Foreign Conflict Behavior of States," in Russett (fn. 8).

[22] Edmund Ions, "Dissent in America: The Constraints on Foreign Policy," *Conflict Studies*, No. 18 (London 1971); emphasis in original.

totalitarian societies will not be troubled by the domestic constraints which have bedeviled U.S. policy-makers on Vietnam, for instance. In some of the best-known examples of asymmetric conflict in which the insurgents gained their objectives—Indochina, Algeria, Cyprus, Aden, Palestine, and Indonesia—the metropolitan power which conceded defeat was a "democracy." Asymmetric conflicts in which the external power successfully crushed the opposition (or has yet to be beaten) include Hungary (1956), Czechoslovakia (1968), and Portugal's ongoing war in Africa. In these cases, the metropolitan regime may be described as "closed," "centrist," "totalitarian," or whatever; in any case, popular domestic opposition is not tolerated. In addition to the government proscribing opposition, it may be withholding information. The brutalities inflicted on civilians may go unreported, the costs of the war to the economy concealed, and the number of troops killed minimized. Ions in the paper quoted, and other supporters of the U.S. war in Indochina, have come close to recommending censorship for precisely these reasons. The French military strategist Trinquier, with greater concern for logic than for political reality, argues that in order to prevent the rot of "defeatism" or "lack of political will" from betraying the troops in the field, the entire structure of the metropolitan society must be altered.[23] The general point has some validity. In Laos, a greater number of civilian refugees was created by U.S. bombing missions than in Vietnam, yet the "secret war" in Laos attracted far less attention and controversy because the press was specifically excluded from the battle zones. Despite these obvious points, my main contention—that limited wars by their very nature will generate domestic constraints if the war continues—is not disproved. In terms of the argument put forward here, "politics" under *any* political system involves conflict over the allocation of resources. In closed or centrist polities, these conflicts will by and large be confined to the ruling elite—but not necessarily so. The argument may be exemplified by examining the case of Portugal.* Clearly, popular opposition to the war in Angola, Mozambique, and Guinea Bissau could not manifest itself in Portugal as did opposition to the Vietnam war in the United States. But there were nevertheless major controversies within the ruling Portuguese elite concerning the desirability —the costs and benefits—of continuing war in Africa: "[T]here seem

[23] P. Trinquier, *Modern Warfare* (New York 1964).
*This article was completed before the Spinola coup in Portugal in the spring of 1974. A brief discussion of the implications of the coup, and those of the recent developments in the Ulster crisis, has been added to the conclusion.

to be three main currents when it comes to the major direction of orientation for Portugal: the colonialist tradition in various versions which still believe in 'Portuguese Africa,' the old 'Lucitanian tradition' that would base Portuguese future on the Portugal/Brazil axis, and the 'Europeans' for whom the European Community must appear as a very attractive haven of escape."[24] The younger generation of "modernizing technocrats" clearly see Portugal's future as allied with the European Community and realize equally clearly that the price of a closer association with the EEC is the cessation of the war in Africa. Portugal is also an interesting case in the sense that, in addition to domestic constraints, there are also powerful *international* constraints, Portugal being critically dependent on the NATO countries for the arms needed to fight the war in Africa. This support is, needless to say, highly undependable, not only because it has already come under sustained attack from some of the north-European NATO powers, but more obviously because Portugal has a far greater dependence on NATO than NATO has on Portugal. Finally, popular domestic opposition has in the past manifested itself *indirectly*, as thousands of Portuguese "voted with the feet" by emigrating to the European Community.

It remains to be explained why Portugal, the oldest and weakest of imperial powers, should have clung to her colonies long after her more powerful rivals surrendered by granting independence to their colonial dependencies. The usual explanation is that it is a matter of an ideological—and essentially irrational—obsession with "manifest destiny." However, without denying that there may be a powerful contingent of genuine ideologues within the Portuguese polity who support the war for these reasons, this does not provide the whole answer. Those most loyal to the "Portuguese connection" are the Portuguese settlers in the territories themselves—loyal in the sense of total opposition to black rule. But this loyalty—like the loyalty of Ulster Protestants, white Rhodesians or white *colons* in Algeria—is highly unreliable.[25] The settler class will bitterly resist any attempt to hand over control to the

[24] Johan Galtung, *The European Community: A Superpower in the Making* (London 1973), 166.
[25] As Emmanuel notes of the "settler class" in "colonial" situations: "They benefitted from colonialism and therefore promoted it, without reserve or contradiction—and for that very reason they were basically anti-imperialist, however paradoxical that may seem. From the very beginning they were in conflict with their parent countries . . . objectively so at all times, subjectively so at times of crisis, going so far as to take up arms against it." Argirihi Emmanuel, "White Settler Colonialism and the Myth of Investment Imperialism," *New Left Review*, No. 73 (May/June 1972), 38-39.

indigenous population; it thereby provides a powerful brake on any move towards independence.

For the settler class, *qua* settler class, the granting of independence to the indigenous population poses a direct threat to local European hegemony in both the political and economic spheres. If pressures in the metropolis are such that withdrawal from the colonies appears likely —as seems highly possible following the Spinola coup of the spring of 1974—there may well be moves by the settlers to attempt a type of go-it-alone, Unilateral Declaration of Independence strategy along Rhodesian lines. The *colons* in Algeria tried this strategy when it became obvious that De Gaulle was going to give in to Moslem demands for independence. They failed, but the white Rhodesians succeeded. In the current Ulster crisis there is little doubt that such a strategy would be attempted—and would most likely succeed if it became clear to the Protestant majority that the British were going to withdraw—as seems increasingly possible. The "settlers" exhibit "ultra-loyalism" towards the "mother country" up to the moment at which they appear to have been deserted. If the break *does* succeed, the structure of the conflict changes completely. If the metropolitan power does not intervene against the settlers' rebellion (Algeria) but instead simply makes nonmilitary protests (Britain against Rhodesia) then the conflict becomes symmetric: a zero-sum struggle for ascendancy, essentially a civil war in which the settler class has a survival stake in the outcome. The settlers will in many ways prove to be a more formidable enemy than was the vastly more powerful metropolitan power, because the constraints against the use of force will be almost completely absent in their case. Thus the task of nationalist movements trying to bring down the settler regimes in Israel, Rhodesia, and South Africa is extremely onerous. The question for these regimes is not *whether* to fight the insurgents but *how*. In other words, despite superficial similarities in tactics and in descriptive language—"Palestinian guerrillas," "national liberation struggle,"—the "settler-regime" conflicts are fundamentally different from asymmetric conflicts.

There is another, perhaps equally powerful reason why the Portuguese resisted independence so bitterly. It is extremely difficult to calculate the economic costs and benefits which Portugal derives from her overseas territories, in part because exchange controls are artificially manipulated. However, even if it could be unequivocally demonstrated that the costs of the war exceed by a wide margin the *present* economic benefits which Portugal derives from her colonies—most particularly

Angola—it would not invalidate the hypothesis that a major Portuguese interest in maintaining the colonial possessions is economic. Oil in large quantities has already been discovered in the overseas territories, and there are also extensive and as yet barely exploited mineral reserves. Portugal therefore has a considerable economic interest in trying to maintain control in these areas.[26] When France and Britain relinquished their African colonies, they relinquished also the economic costs of administration while retaining whatever benefits they derived from their investments and from special trade relationships. Portugal is in a very different position. Since Portugal is relatively underdeveloped economically, the benefits she derives from her overseas territories are based on political rather than economic control. The key economic enterprises in the overseas territories are increasingly dominated by non-Portuguese capital (in contrast to the situation in French and British African colonies before independence). If Portugal were to relinquish political control in Africa, she would lose not only the present economic benefits but also the more important future benefits. The so-called neo-colonial solution is not a possibility for the Portuguese.

In discussing Portugal by way of exemplification of my argument, I have raised three possible hypotheses, which might be formulated as follows:

(1) The political attrition of the metropolitan power's war-making capability appears to be positively correlated with the degree of "openness" of the political system and negatively correlated with the degree of "closeness" of the political system. Democratic polyarchies are apparently most susceptible to internal opposition to external wars, while totalitarian "centrist" states are less susceptible to such opposition. This argument is subject to severe qualification (see below).

(2) Where a metropolitan settler class exists in the insurgents' homeland, it will have a survival interest in the conflict and will thus act as a powerful countervailing "brake" to forces in the metropolis which favor a pull-out. If the latter forces prevail, there will be a strong push from the settler class for a U.D.I.-type break with the metropolis along Rhodesian lines. If this succeeds, the conflict ceases to be asymmetric as defined here.

(3) In a limited war, despite the fact that there is no direct threat to physical survival of the metropolis, there may well be other power-

[26] For a detailed argument of this point see Eduardo de Sousa Ferreira, *Portuguese Colonialism from South Africa to Europe* (Freiburg 1972).

ful interests to be protected. The greater the salience of these interests, the greater the resistance to withdrawal will be in the
metropolis.

The last point brings us to the two other examples noted above—
the Russian interventions in Hungary (1956) and Czechoslovakia
(1968). It is obvious that one of the necessary conditions noted earlier
for the process of political attrition to manifest itself was absent. In both
cases the local resistance was effectively and rapidly crushed.[27]

From the Soviet point of view, the security interest, while not one
of a direct threat of invasion, was nevertheless highly salient. For example, Russian interests in maintaining Czechoslovakia under Soviet
control were two-fold. As Zeman notes, Czechoslovakia had a key
position in the Soviet system: "It is a workshop where a lot of Russian
and East-European raw material is processed; the country's territory
forms a tunnel leading from western Europe directly to the Soviet
Union."[28] Second, for the U.S.S.R., twice invaded this century from
the West at a cost of millions of lives, a certain fixation on security interests was understandable. But the strategic costs of relinquishing control over Czechoslovakia were not simply the direct costs of creating a
physical gap in the chain of satellite buffer states. The real risk from
the Soviet point of view was that the subversive ideology of national
determination, of "socialism with a human—i.e., non-Russian—face"
might spread first to the other satellite states of Eastern Europe and
ultimately to the Soviet Union itself. The Soviet intervention in Hungary in 1956 is a similar case in point.

These examples show that it is virtually impossible to produce a model
of asymmetric conflict which would be sufficiently flexible to account
for the outcome of the cases of conflict that might be included under
that rubric. Neither is it evident that this would be desirable. The problem with using models to explain conflicts is that there is a natural
tendency to attempt to force the data to fit the requirements of the
theory. The risks lie in ignoring other factors which might fall within
the category sometimes labeled "accidents of history," but which may
nevertheless be of critical importance in determining the outcome of
a particular conflict.

Most of the discussion thus far has dealt with the *domestic* constraints
which will be generated in the metropolis as a consequence of asymmetries in the structure of the conflict. We can quite easily point to the

---

[27] For an analysis of the breakdown of the resistance in the Czech case see Boserup
and Mack (fn. 7), chap. VI.
[28] Z. A. B. Zeman, *Prague Spring* (London 1969).

mechanisms that generate such constraints—though the *form* they will take in practice will vary according to the interests perceived to be at stake and according to the nature of the polity of the external power. But little or nothing can be said with respect to *external* constraints. For example, there were few external constraints bearing down on British policy in the Mau Mau rebellion in Kenya, yet in the case of the nationalist struggle in Indonesia against the Dutch the situation was very different. The critical factor here was the U.S. threat to cut off Marshall Plan aid to the Dutch if they failed to make a settlement with the Indonesian nationalists. A completely different set of potential external pressures could be brought to bear against Portugal vis-à-vis the Portuguese wars in Africa, and so on.

In an asymmetric conflict, the *potential* for the generation of internal divisions in the metropolitan power exists *regardless* of the historical epoch, the nature of the polity of the external power, the interests perceived to be at stake, and the international context in which the conflict takes place. Though these factors may influence the form and intensity taken by these internal divisions in any particular conflict, the *cause* of these divisions is independent from all of them. It arises from the nature of the asymmetric relationships which exist between the belligerents. On the other hand, nothing can be said in the abstract about any *external* constraints which may be brought to bear on the external power. These are dependent on the conditions of a particular historical epoch.

SUMMARY

The initial problem was one of explaining how the militarily powerful could be defeated in armed confrontation with the militarily weak. This was not just idle speculation; in a number of critically important conflicts in the post-World War II epoch, industrial powers *have* failed to gain their objectives in wars fought on foreign soil against local nationalist forces. In all of these cases the superiority in conventional military capability of the external power was overwhelming. In a sense, these wars may be seen as a replay of the mini-wars of colonial conquest which took place in the late nineteenth and early twentieth centuries, but with a critical difference. In the earlier era, the industrial powers used minimal force to achieve rapid success, whereas in the post-World War II conflicts, the same industrial powers confronted the same Third-World countries with massive forces and lost.

In explaining the successes of the "weaker" party, I pointed out that an obvious minimal requirement for victory was that the insurgents should not lose. They achieved this by refusing to confront the industrial powers on their own terms and by resorting instead to "unconventional" forms of warfare—guerrilla war, urban terrorism, or even nonviolent action. However, I did not examine this aspect of the problem in any detail. I took the fact that the insurgents did not lose as a "given" when I inquired into the more interesting problem—namely, how did they *win*? I noted that one of the key asymmetries which characterized the relationships of the belligerents was that, as a consequence of the asymmetry in wealth and economic and technological development, the insurgents lacked the physical capability to attack the metropolitan power. It thus followed *logically* that the metropolitan power could not be defeated militarily. In turn, victory for the insurgents could only come about as a consequence of the destruction of the external power's *political* capability to wage war. The historical evidence of the outcome of the post-World War II conflicts confirms the logic of the argument.

As a next step, I examined the dynamics of the process of political attrition, arguing that the asymmetries which characterized the conflict provided the basis, not only for the initial restraints on mobilization of military forces, but also for the emergence of internal divisions as the war dragged on and costs accumulated. The fact that the war was by definition "limited" also provided the basis for a sustained moral critique of the military means employed—from torture to napalm—while reducing the willingness of troops to risk their lives in combat and of the domestic population to make economic sacrifices. However, the process of attrition was not seen as arising primarily from a steady across-the-board increment of "war weariness," as some writers have suggested; still less was it seen as a process of conversion at the top whereby the political leadership was gradually persuaded of the immorality or undesirability of its policies. The controversies *themselves* became one of the costs of the war. Time is a resource in politics, and the bitter hostilities such wars generate may come to dominate political debate to the detriment of the pursuit of other objectives. Provided the insurgents can maintain a steady imposition of "costs" on their metropolitan opponent, the balance of political forces in the external power will *inevitably* shift in favor of the anti-war factions.

Although the main discussion dealt essentially with domestic constraints, I also recognized that *international* constraints were often of great importance in asymmetric conflicts. However, whereas the mechanisms giving rise to internal constraints could be identified, it was impossible to say anything in the abstract about external constraints.

Having outlined in fairly general terms the conditions under which the process of political attrition might be expected to manifest itself in practice, I then briefly examined the countervailing forces. I noted that the nature of the polity of the external power might either inhibit or facilitate the generation of domestic conflict. But I also argued that internal divisions were primarily a function of the conflict *relationship* and not of differences in the political structure of the metropolis. Finally, I noted that the salience of the interest which the external power —or rather factions within it—had in pursuing the war would also affect the process of political attrition.

NOTE ON METHODOLOGY

Examples of the types of hypotheses which this analysis might suggest were given earlier in the paper. It would be easy to think of others, for instance:

> The greater the interest a particular metropolitan faction has in the prosecution of the war and the wider the basis of its domestic support, the greater will be the support for continuing the war.

Another example would be:

> The weaker and more dependent the external power is on external support in order to prosecute the war, the more important external constraints will be in determining the outcome.

The objections to these alternative approaches—other than for the purpose of illustrating points in the argument—are several. First, they would slice the conflict up into parts (either temporally or spatially) which are then examined in relative isolation. I have argued that a full understanding can only come from an analysis of the conflict as a whole. Second, there is the technical problem of operationalizing such vague concepts as "interest" or "faction." Third, even if operationalization were possible, the hypotheses would remain untestable by the traditional statistical significance tests. That is a problem which has been largely ignored in most of the quantitative studies in conflict research where conflicts tend to get lumped together—symmetric and asymmetric and across periods of up to a hundred years or more—in order to obtain a sufficiently large sample for statistical manipulation. Thus the quantitative studies undertaken by Rummel and Tanter with the object of testing the relationship between external and internal conflicts arrive at the conclusion that no such relationship exists.[29] However, the relationships may well exist but be hidden by precisely the methodological methods intended to reveal them. Contrary to writers like Stohl and Wilkenfeld, there is no "paradox" in the *apparently* contradictory assertions that, on the one hand, external conflicts cause internal conflict and, on the other, that they create internal solidarity.[30] Whether or not this *is* the case is a function of the nature of the conflict. But since the *type* of conflict is not identified, the relationships are lost in the aggregation of data. It is not possible to consider asymmetric conflicts (as defined here) on their own, since the size of the sample is far too small. The only way out of this dilemma is to attempt a "time series" analysis.[31] Here, instead of many conflicts being examined once, the data matrix is filled by examining one conflict (or a few) over many time intervals. The methodological and epistemological problems with this type of analysis are enormous, however, and the results produced thus far are extremely modest.

If we move away from the quantitative literature to examine other attempts at explaining the outcome of asymmetric conflicts, different problems arise. The literature on counter-insurgency, for example, concentrates almost exclusively on the development of the war on the ground and ignores its impact on the metropolis. Iklé notes: "When it comes to actual fighting, the scores that count are, for instance, the number of enemy units destroyed, square miles of territory gained, and other successes or failures in battle. Where such an attitude prevails, professional military men would consider it unusual, if not somewhat improper, to ask whether these 'mid-game' successes will improve the ending."[32] Counter-insurgency theorists can thus provide a partial explanation of why insurgents may *lose*, but they cannot, almost by definition, grasp how it is that they may *win*. Awareness that insurgent successes are a consequence of "lack of political will" or "defeatism" on the part of the metropolitan governments is of course there, but this is seen as a contingent phenomenon almost wholly unrelated to the con-

[29] R. J. Rummel, "Dimensions of Conflict Behavior Within and Between Nations," *General Systems Yearbook*, VIII (1963), 1-50; and Raymond Tanter, "Dimensions of Conflict Behavior Within and Between Nations, 1958-60," *Journal of Conflict Resolution*, x (March 1966), 41-64.

[30] Michael Stohl, "Linkages between War and Domestic Political Violence in the United States, 1890-1923" in J. Caporaso and L. Roos, eds., *Quasi-Experimental Approaches* (Evanston 1973); and Jonathan Wilkenfeld, "Introduction" to Wilkenfeld, ed., *Conflict Behavior and Linkage Politics* (New York 1973).

[31] See Robert Burrowes and Bertram Spector, "The Strength and Direction of Relationships Between Domestic and External Conflict and Cooperation: Syria, 1961-67" in Wilkenfeld, *ibid.*; also Stohl (fn. 30).

[32] Iklé (fn. 11).

duct of the war. More sophisticated works in the counter-insurgency field *do* consider political factors in the *insurgents'* homeland—namely, the payoffs of social and economic reform as a means of reducing popular support for the insurgents. But only Trinquier provides a sustained analysis of the political and social changes necessary in the *metropolis* if such wars are to succeed—and in this case the demands of logic are followed with no regard for political reality.

Although much of the research literature on conflict deals with events leading up to the outbreak of war, there has been a recent renewal of interest in "war-termination studies."[33] However, these concentrate on the final phases of the war, in particular those leading to negotiations or offering possibilities for third-party mediation. The *evolution* of the war and its wider sociopolitical dimensions are largely ignored.

A number of excellent historical case studies of the various asymmetric conflicts have been mentioned in this paper. Many of them have a virtue manifestly lacking in other works, namely that of treating the conflict as a whole rather than examining particular "technical" dimensions or temporal slices. However, individual case studies can provide no conceptual basis for distinguishing between what might in this context be called "structural necessity" from historically unique factors. Since narrative history is unable to discriminate between the universal and the particular when analyzing conflicts, it is a most unreliable guide to the future. Military history is replete with "Maginot lines," illustrating the dangers of relying on historical precedents.

Specific problems raised by these different methodological approaches to asymmetric conflicts and the different foci of interest which have been employed will be dealt with in depth in a forthcoming study.[34] In particular, that study will examine the writings of the leading revolutionary strategists. In the present paper, I have dealt essentially with the *process* of attrition as a function of the asymmetries which characterize the conflict. An asymmetric *strategy* would be one which sought to amplify this process of attrition *indirectly*. An outline of the basic requirements of such an "asymmetric strategy" (derived from the strategic writings of Clausewitz, Glucksman, and Mao Tse-tung) is provided in the final chapter of *War Without Weapons*.[35]

Finally, it should be obvious that my aim in this paper has not been to provide a "model" which may then be "tested" by applying it

[33] Carroll (fn. 1); Fox (fn. 1); Iklé (fn. 11); and R. F. Randle, *The Origins of Peace* (New York 1973).
[34] Andrew Mack, "Working Papers on Asymmetric Conflict," Nos. I-VI, Richardson Institute (London 1974).
[35] Boserup and Mack (fn. 7).

mechanically and ahistorically to a wide range of conflicts. Rather, it has been to construct a conceptual framework which will provide a focus for empirical studies. Like the "paradigm" of the physical sciences which Thomas Kuhn has described, this conceptual framework functions essentially to direct the researcher's attention toward particular aspects of the real world—to distinctions and relationships which "common sense" often does not take into account. The framework defines the necessary questions which must be asked; it does not seek to provide automatic answers.

CONCLUSION

Recent developments in two ongoing asymmetric conflicts have tended to bear out the main thrust of my argument. The most dramatic development has been the Spinola coup in Portugal which clearly has far-reaching implications for the wars of national liberation in Angola, Mozambique, and Guinea Bissau.* The second is the conflict in Ulster. The spring of 1974 saw the emergence, in England, of significant domestic opposition to the war, with several campaigns for troop withdrawal attracting growing support from very different political constituencies. Since the British Government has exhausted all the obvious "initiatives" (juggling the local Ulster leadership, direct rule, the Northern Ireland Assembly, and the Council of Ireland) to no avail, and since the I.R.A. remains not only undefeated but capable of escalating its offensive where necessary, it seems certain that the campaign for withdrawal will gather strength. One of the most significant aspects of current I.R.A. activity is its role in maintaining and solidifying Protestant "extremism." The bombing functions essentially to prevent the "moderate" political solution, favored by the Westminster government and the Catholic and Protestant center groups which dominate the Assembly, from coming to fruition. The Spinola government in Portugal faces a similar problem. Having explicitly abandoned the belief that the war is winnable, the regime's current strategy is to seek a "political" solution. General Spinola advocates greatly increased autonomy, but "the overseas territories must be an integral part of the Portuguese nation." It is already obvious that such a solution is ac-

---

* Since this conclusion was written, the new Portuguese Government has abandoned the earlier insistence that the "overseas territories must be an integral part of the Portuguese nation." The threat of a possible settler bid for a unilateral declaration of independence was briefly raised in Mozambique, but evaporated with the considerable exodus of whites to Portugal and South Africa. In Angola, with a larger settler population, far greater mineral resources, and deep divisions between competing liberation movements, the situation remains unclear.

ceptable neither to the European settlers nor to the liberation movements. Withdrawal is now clearly a serious political option for both metropolitan powers. In admitting that the colonial wars are unwinnable, General Spinola has in fact admitted defeat: "the conventional army loses if it does not win." In both countries the key question is no longer whether to withdraw but rather when and how.

To conclude, it hardly needs pointing out that—if correct—the implications of the foregoing analysis for industrial powers which become embroiled in long drawn-out wars in the Third World are far-reaching. Governments which become committed to such wars for whatever reason should realize that, over time, the costs of the war will inevitably generate widespread opposition at home. The causes of dissent lie beyond the control of the political elite; they lie in the structure of the conflict itself—in the type of war being pursued and in the asymmetries which form its distinctive character. Anti-war movements, on the other hand, have tended to underestimate their political effectiveness. They have failed to realize that in every asymmetric conflict where the external power has been forced to withdraw, it has been as a consequence of internal dissent. Thus, any analysis of the outcome of asymmetric conflicts must of necessity take into account and explain not only the tenacity and endurance of the nationalist forces, but also the generation of internal divisions in the homeland of their metropolitan enemy. In this type of conflict, anti-war movements—and this includes all the social forces that oppose the war—have, despite their short-term failures and frustrations, proven to be remarkably successful in the long run.

HYPOTHESES ON MISPERCEPTION

By ROBERT JERVIS*

I N determining how he will behave, an actor must try to predict how others will act and how their actions will affect his values. The actor must therefore develop an image of others and of their intentions. This image may, however, turn out to be an inaccurate one; the actor may, for a number of reasons, misperceive both others' actions and their intentions. In this research note I wish to discuss the types of misper-ceptions of other states' intentions which states tend to make. The concept of intention is complex, but here we can consider it to com-prise the ways in which the state feels it will act in a wide range of future contingencies. These ways of acting usually are not specific and well-developed plans. For many reasons a national or individual actor may not know how he will act under given conditions, but this problem cannot be dealt with here.

I. Previous Treatments of Perception in International Relations

Although diplomatic historians have discussed misperception in their treatments of specific events, students of international relations have generally ignored this topic. However, two sets of scholars have applied content analysis to the documents that flowed within and between governments in the six weeks preceding World War I. But the data have been put into quantitative form in a way that does not produce accurate measures of perceptions and intentions and that makes it impossible to gather useful evidence on misperception.[1]

The second group of theorists who have explicitly dealt with general questions of misperception in international relations consists of those, like Charles Osgood, Amitai Etzioni, and, to a lesser extent, Kenneth Boulding and J. David Singer, who have analyzed the cold war in

* I am grateful to the Harvard Center for International Affairs for research support. An earlier version of this research note was presented at the International Studies Association panel of the New England Political Science Association in April 1967. I have benefited from comments by Robert Art, Alexander George, Paul Kecskemeti, Paul Leary, Thomas Schelling, James Schlesinger, Morton Schwartz, and Aaron Wildavsky.

[1] See, for example, Ole Holsti, Robert North, and Richard Brody, "Perception and Action in the 1914 Crisis," in J. David Singer, ed., *Quantitative International Politics* (New York 1968). For a fuller discussion of the Stanford content analysis studies and the general problems of quantification, see my "The Costs of the Quantitative Study of International Relations," in Klaus Knorr and James N. Rosenau, eds., *Contending Approaches to International Politics* (forthcoming).

terms of a spiral of misperception.[2] This approach grows partly out of the mathematical theories of L. F. Richardson[3] and partly out of findings of social and cognitive psychology, many of which will be discussed in this research note.

These authors state their case in general, if not universal, terms, but do not provide many historical cases that are satisfactorily explained by their theories. Furthermore, they do not deal with any of the numerous instances that contradict their notion of the self-defeating aspects of the use of power. They ignore the fact that states are not individuals and that the findings of psychology can be applied to organizations only with great care. Most important, their theoretical analysis is for the most part of reduced value because it seems largely to be a product of their assumption that the Soviet Union is a basically status-quo power whose apparently aggressive behavior is a product of fear of the West. Yet they supply little or no evidence to support this view. Indeed, the explanation for the differences of opinion between the spiral theorists and the proponents of deterrence lies not in differing general views of international relations, differing values and morality,[4] or differing methods of analysis,[5] but in differing perceptions of Soviet intentions.

II. THEORIES—NECESSARY AND DANGEROUS

Despite the limitations of their approach, these writers have touched on a vital problem that has not been given systematic treatment by theorists of international relations. The evidence from both psychology and history overwhelmingly supports the view (which may be labeled Hypothesis 1) that decision-makers tend to fit incoming information into their existing theories and images. Indeed, their theories and images play a large part in determining what they notice. In other words, actors tend to perceive what they expect. Furthermore (Hypothesis 1a), a theory will have greater impact on an actor's interpretation of data (a) the greater the ambiguity of the data and (b) the

---

[2] See, for example, Osgood, *An Alternative to War or Surrender* (Urbana 1962); Etzioni, *The Hard Way to Peace* (New York 1962); Boulding, "National Images and International Systems," *Journal of Conflict Resolution*, III (June 1959), 120-31; and Singer, *Deterrence, Arms Control, and Disarmament* (Columbus 1962).

[3] *Statistics of Deadly Quarrels* (Pittsburgh 1960) and *Arms and Insecurity* (Chicago 1960). For nonmathematicians a fine summary of Richardson's work is Anatol Rapoport's "L. F. Richardson's Mathematical Theory of War," *Journal of Conflict Resolution*, I (September 1957), 249-99.

[4] See Philip Green, *Deadly Logic* (Columbus 1966); Green, "Method and Substance in the Arms Debate," *World Politics*, XVI (July 1964), 642-67; and Robert A. Levine. "Facts and Morals in the Arms Debate," *World Politics*, XIV (January 1962), 239-58.

[5] See Anatol Rapoport, *Strategy and Conscience* (New York 1964).

higher the degree of confidence with which the actor holds the theory.[6]

For many purposes we can use the concept of differing levels of perceptual thresholds to deal with the fact that it takes more, and more unambiguous, information for an actor to recognize an unexpected phenomenon than an expected one. An experiment by Bruner and Postman determined "that the recognition threshold for . . . incongruous playing cards (those with suits and color reversed) is significantly higher than the threshold for normal cards."[7] Not only are people able to identify normal (and therefore expected) cards more quickly and easily than incongruous (and therefore unexpected) ones, but also they may at first take incongruous cards for normal ones.

However, we should not assume, as the spiral theorists often do, that it is necessarily irrational for actors to adjust incoming information to fit more closely their existing beliefs and images. ("Irrational" here describes acting under pressures that the actor would not admit as legitimate if he were conscious of them.) Abelson and Rosenberg label as "psycho-logic" the pressure to create a "balanced" cognitive structure—i.e., one in which "all relations among 'good elements' [in one's attitude structure] are positive (or null), all relations among 'bad elements' are positive (or null), and all relations between good and bad elements are negative (or null)." They correctly show that the "reasoning [this involves] would mortify a logician."[8] But those who have tried to apply this and similar cognitive theories to international relations have usually overlooked the fact that in many cases there are important logical links between the elements and the processes they describe which cannot be called "psycho-logic." (I am here using the term "logical" not in the narrow sense of drawing only those conclusions that follow necessarily from the premises, but rather in the sense of conforming to generally agreed-upon rules for the treating of evidence.) For example, Osgood claims that psycho-logic is displayed when the Soviets praise a man or a proposal and people in the West react by distrusting the object of this praise.[9] But if a person believes that the Russians are aggressive, it is logical for him to be suspicious of their moves. When we say that a decision-maker "dislikes" another

[6] Floyd Allport, *Theories of Perception and the Concept of Structure* (New York 1955), 382; Ole Holsti, "Cognitive Dynamics and Images of the Enemy," in David Finlay, Ole Holsti, and Richard Fagen, *Enemies in Politics* (Chicago 1967), 70.

[7] Jerome Bruner and Leo Postman, "On the Perceptions of Incongruity: A Paradigm," in Jerome Bruner and David Krech, eds., *Perception and Personality* (Durham, N.C., 1949), 210.

[8] Robert Abelson and Milton Rosenberg, "Symbolic Psycho-logic," *Behavioral Science*, III (January 1958), 4-5.

[9] P. 27.

state this usually means that he believes that that other state has policies conflicting with those of his nation. Reasoning and experience indicate to the decision-maker that the "disliked" state is apt to harm his state's interests. Thus in these cases there is no need to invoke "psycho-logic," and it cannot be claimed that the cases demonstrate the substitution of "emotional consistency for rational consistency."[10]

The question of the relations among particular beliefs and cognitions can often be seen as part of the general topic of the relation of incoming bits of information to the receivers' already established images. The need to fit data into a wider framework of beliefs, even if doing so does not seem to do justice to individual facts, is not, or at least is not only, a psychological drive that decreases the accuracy of our perceptions of the world, but is "essential to the logic of inquiry."[11] Facts can be interpreted, and indeed identified, only with the aid of hypotheses and theories. Pure empiricism is impossible, and it would be unwise to revise theories in the light of every bit of information that does not easily conform to them.[12] No hypothesis can be expected to account for all the evidence, and if a prevailing view is supported by many theories and by a large pool of findings it should not be quickly altered. Too little rigidity can be as bad as too much.[13]

This is as true in the building of social and physical science as it is

---

[10] *Ibid.*, 26.

[11] I have borrowed this phrase from Abraham Kaplan, who uses it in a different but related context in *The Conduct of Inquiry* (San Francisco 1964), 86.

[12] The spiral theorists are not the only ones to ignore the limits of empiricism. Roger Hilsman found that most consumers and producers of intelligence felt that intelligence should not deal with hypotheses, but should only provide the policy-makers with "all the facts" (*Strategic Intelligence and National Decisions* [Glencoe 1956], 46). The close interdependence between hypotheses and facts is overlooked partly because of the tendency to identify "hypotheses" with "policy preferences."

[13] Karl Deutsch interestingly discusses a related question when he argues, "Autonomy . . . requires both intake from the present and recall from memory, and selfhood can be seen in just this continuous balancing of a limited present and a limited past. . . . No further self-determination is possible if either openness or memory is lost. . . . To the extent that [systems cease to be able to take in new information], they approach the behavior of a bullet or torpedo: their future action becomes almost completely determined by their past. On the other hand, a person without memory, an organization without values or policy . . . —all these no longer steer, but drift: their behavior depends little on their past and almost wholly on their present. Driftwood and the bullet are thus each the epitome of another kind of loss of self-control . . ." (*Nationalism and Social Communication* [Cambridge, Mass., 1954], 167-68). Also see Deutsch's *The Nerves of Government* (New York 1963), 98-109, 200-256. A physicist makes a similar argument: "It is clear that if one is too attached to one's preconceived model, one will miss all radical discoveries. It is amazing to what degree one may fail to register mentally an observation which does not fit the initial image. . . . On the other hand, if one is too open-minded and pursues every hitherto unknown phenomenon, one is almost certain to lose oneself in trivia" (Martin Deutsch, "Evidence and Inference in Nuclear Research," in Daniel Lerner, ed., *Evidence and Inference* [Glencoe 1958], 102).

in policy-making.[14] While it is terribly difficult to know when a finding throws serious doubt on accepted theories and should be followed up and when instead it was caused by experimental mistakes or minor errors in the theory, it is clear that scientists would make no progress if they followed Thomas Huxley's injunction to "sit down before fact as a mere child, be prepared to give up every preconceived notion, follow humbly wherever nature leads, or you will learn nothing."[15]

As Michael Polanyi explains, "It is true enough that the scientist must be prepared to submit at any moment to the adverse verdict of observational evidence. But not blindly. . . . There is always the possibility that, as in [the cases of the periodic system of elements and the quantum theory of light], a deviation may not affect the essential correctness of a proposition. . . . The process of explaining away deviations is in fact quite indispensable to the daily routine of research," even though this may lead to the missing of a great discovery.[16] For example, in 1795, the astronomer Lalande did not follow up observations that contradicted the prevailing hypotheses and could have led him to discover the planet Neptune.[17]

Yet we should not be too quick to condemn such behavior. As Thomas Kuhn has noted, "There is no such thing as research without counter-instances."[18] If a set of basic theories—what Kuhn calls a paradigm—has been able to account for a mass of data, it should not be lightly trifled with. As Kuhn puts it: "Lifelong resistance, particularly from those whose productive careers have committed them to an older tradition of normal science [i.e., science within the accepted paradigm], is not a violation of scientific standards but an index to the nature of scientific research itself. The source of resistance is the assurance that the older paradigm will ultimately solve all its problems, that nature

---

[14] Raymond Bauer, "Problems of Perception and the Relations Between the U.S. and the Soviet Union," *Journal of Conflict Resolution*, v (September 1961), 223-29.

[15] Quoted in W. I. B. Beveridge, *The Art of Scientific Investigation*, 3rd ed. (London 1957), 50.

[16] *Science, Faith, and Society* (Chicago 1964), 31. For a further discussion of this problem, see *ibid.*, 16, 26-41, 90-94; Polanyi, *Personal Knowledge* (London 1958), 8-15, 30, 143-68, 269-98, 310-11; Thomas Kuhn, *The Structure of Scientific Revolutions* (Chicago 1964); Kuhn, "The Function of Dogma in Scientific Research," in A. C. Crombie, ed., *Scientific Change* (New York 1963), 344-69; the comments on Kuhn's paper by Hall, Polanyi, and Toulmin, and Kuhn's reply, *ibid.*, 370-95. For a related discussion of these points from a different perspective, see Norman Storer, *The Social System of Science* (New York 1960), 116-22.

[17] "He found that the position of one star relative to others . . . had shifted. Lalande was a good astronomer and knew that such a shift was unreasonable. He crossed out his first observation, put a question mark next to the second observation, and let the matter go" (Jerome Bruner, Jacqueline Goodnow, and George Austin, *A Study of Thinking* [New York 1962], 105).

[18] *The Structure of Scientific Revolutions*, 79.

can be shoved into the box the paradigm provides. Inevitably, at times of revolution, that assurance seems stubborn and pig-headed as indeed it sometimes becomes. But it is also something more. That same assurance is what makes normal science or puzzle-solving science possible."[19]

Thus it is important to see that the dilemma of how "open" to be to new information is one that inevitably plagues any attempt at understanding in any field. Instances in which evidence seems to be ignored or twisted to fit the existing theory can often be explained by this dilemma instead of by illogical or nonlogical psychological pressures toward consistency. This is especially true of decision-makers' attempts to estimate the intentions of other states, since they must constantly take account of the danger that the other state is trying to deceive them.

The theoretical framework discussed thus far, together with an examination of many cases, suggests Hypothesis 2: scholars and decision-makers are apt to err by being too wedded to the established view and too closed to new information, as opposed to being too willing to alter their theories.[20] Another way of making this point is to argue that actors tend to establish their theories and expectations prematurely. In politics, of course, this is often necessary because of the need for action. But experimental evidence indicates that the same tendency also occurs on the unconscious level. Bruner and Postman found that "perhaps the greatest single barrier to the recognition of incongruous stimuli is the tendency for perceptual hypotheses to fixate after receiving a minimum of confirmation. . . . Once there had occurred in these cases a partial confirmation of the hypothesis . . . it seemed that nothing could change the subject's report."[21]

---

[19] *Ibid.*, 150-51.

[20] Requirements of effective political leadership may lead decision-makers to voice fewer doubts than they have about existing policies and images, but this constraint can only partially explain this phenomenon. Similar calculations of political strategy may contribute to several of the hypotheses discussed below.

[21] P. 221. Similarly, in experiments dealing with his subjects' perception of other people, Charles Dailey found that "premature judgment appears to make new data harder to assimilate than when the observer withholds judgment until all data are seen. It seems probable . . . that the observer mistakes his own inferences for facts" ("The Effects of Premature Conclusion Upon the Acquisition of Understanding of a Person," *Journal of Psychology*, xxx [January 1952], 149-50). For other theory and evidence on this point, see Bruner, "On Perceptual Readiness," *Psychological Review*, LXIV (March 1957), 123-52; Gerald Davison, "The Negative Effects of Early Exposure to Suboptimal Visual Stimuli," *Journal of Personality*, xxxII (June 1964), 278-95; Albert Myers, "An Experimental Analysis of a Tactical Blunder," *Journal of Abnormal and Social Psychology*, LXIX (November 1964), 493-98; and Dale Wyatt and Donald Campbell, "On the Liability of Stereotype or Hypothesis," *Journal of Abnormal and Social Psychology*, XLIV (October 1950), 496-500. It should be noted that this tendency makes "incremental" decision-making more likely (David Braybrooke and Charles Lindblom, *A Strategy of Decision* [New York 1963]), but the results of this process may lead the actor further from his goals.

However, when we apply these and other findings to politics and discuss kinds of misperception, we should not quickly apply the label of cognitive distortion. We should proceed cautiously for two related reasons. The first is that the evidence available to decision-makers almost always permits several interpretations. It should be noted that there are cases of visual perception in which different stimuli can produce exactly the same pattern on an observer's retina. Thus, for an observer using one eye the same pattern would be produced by a sphere the size of a golf ball which was quite close to the observer, by a baseball-sized sphere that was further away, or by a basketball-sized sphere still further away. Without other clues, the observer cannot possibly determine which of these stimuli he is presented with, and we would not want to call his incorrect perceptions examples of distortion. Such cases, relatively rare in visual perception, are frequent in international relations. The evidence available to decision-makers is almost always very ambiguous since accurate clues to others' intentions are surrounded by noise[22] and deception. In most cases, no matter how long, deeply, and "objectively" the evidence is analyzed, people can differ in their interpretations, and there are no general rules to indicate who is correct.

The second reason to avoid the label of cognitive distortion is that the distinction between perception and judgment, obscure enough in individual psychology, is almost absent in the making of inferences in international politics. Decision-makers who reject information that contradicts their views—or who develop complex interpretations of it— often do so consciously and explicitly. Since the evidence available contains contradictory information, to make any inferences requires that much information be ignored or given interpretations that will seem tortuous to those who hold a different position.

Indeed, if we consider only the evidence available to a decision-maker at the time of decision, the view later proved incorrect may be supported by as much evidence as the correct one—or even by more. Scholars have often been too unsympathetic with the people who were proved wrong. On closer examination, it is frequently difficult to point to differences between those who were right and those who were wrong with respect to their openness to new information and willingness to modify their views. Winston Churchill, for example, did not open-mindedly view each Nazi action to see if the explanations provided by the appeasers accounted for the data better than his own beliefs. Instead,

[22] For a use of this concept in political communication, see Roberta Wohlstetter, *Pearl Harbor* (Stanford 1962).

like Chamberlain, he fitted each bit of ambiguous information into his own hypotheses. That he was correct should not lead us to overlook the fact that his methods of analysis and use of theory to produce cognitive consistency did not basically differ from those of the appeasers.[23]

A consideration of the importance of expectations in influencing perception also indicates that the widespread belief in the prevalence of "wishful thinking" may be incorrect, or at least may be based on inadequate data. The psychological literature on the interaction between affect and perception is immense and cannot be treated here, but it should be noted that phenomena that at first were considered strong evidence for the impact of affect on perception often can be better treated as demonstrating the influence of expectations.[24] Thus, in international relations, cases like the United States' misestimation of the political climate in Cuba in April 1961, which may seem at first glance to have been instances of wishful thinking, may instead be more adequately explained by the theories held by the decision-makers (e.g., Communist governments are unpopular). Of course, desires may have an impact on perception by influencing expectations, but since so many other factors affect expectations, the net influence of desires may not be great.

There is evidence from both psychology[25] and international relations that when expectations and desires clash, expectations seem to be more important. The United States would like to believe that North Vietnam is about to negotiate or that the USSR is ready to give up what the United States believes is its goal of world domination, but ambiguous

---

[23] Similarly, Robert Coulondre, the French ambassador to Berlin in 1939, was one of the few diplomats to appreciate the Nazi threat. Partly because of his earlier service in the USSR, "he was painfully sensitive to the threat of a Berlin-Moscow agreement. He noted with foreboding that Hitler had not attacked Russia in his *Reichstag* address of April 28. . . . So it went all spring and summer, the ambassador relaying each new evidence of the impending diplomatic revolution and adding to his admonitions his pleas for decisive counteraction" (Franklin Ford and Carl Schorske, "The Voice in the Wilderness: Robert Coulondre," in Gordon Craig and Felix Gilbert, eds., *The Diplomats*, Vol. II [New York 1963] 573-74). His hypotheses were correct, but it is difficult to detect differences between the way he and those ambassadors who were incorrect, like Neville Henderson, selectively noted and interpreted information. However, to the extent that the fear of war influenced the appeasers' perceptions of Hitler's intentions, the appeasers' views did have an element of psycho-logic that was not present in their opponents' position.

[24] See, for example, Donald Campbell, "Systematic Error on the Part of Human Links in Communications Systems," *Information and Control*, 1 (1958), 346-50; and Leo Postman, "The Experimental Analysis of Motivational Factors in Perception," in Judson S. Brown, ed., *Current Theory and Research in Motivation* (Lincoln, Neb., 1953), 59-108.

[25] Dale Wyatt and Donald Campbell, "A Study of Interviewer Bias as Related to Interviewer's Expectations and Own Opinions," *International Journal of Opinion and Attitude Research*, IV (Spring 1950), 77-83.

evidence is seen to confirm the opposite conclusion, which conforms to the United States' expectations. Actors are apt to be especially sensitive to evidence of grave danger if they think they can take action to protect themselves against the menace once it has been detected.

III. Safeguards

Can anything then be said to scholars and decision-makers other than "Avoid being either too open or too closed, but be especially aware of the latter danger"? Although decision-makers will always be faced with ambiguous and confusing evidence and will be forced to make inferences about others which will often be inaccurate, a number of safeguards may be suggested which could enable them to minimize their errors. First, and most obvious, decision-makers should be aware that they do not make "unbiased" interpretations of each new bit of incoming information, but rather are inevitably heavily influenced by the theories they expect to be verified. They should know that what may appear to them as a self-evident and unambiguous inference often seems so only because of their preexisting beliefs. To someone with a different theory the same data may appear to be unimportant or to support another explanation. Thus many events provide less independent support for the decision-makers' images than they may at first realize. Knowledge of this should lead decision-makers to examine more closely evidence that others believe contradicts their views.

Second, decision-makers should see if their attitudes contain consistent or supporting beliefs that are not logically linked. These may be examples of true psycho-logic. While it is not logically surprising nor is it evidence of psychological pressures to find that people who believe that Russia is aggressive are very suspicious of any Soviet move, other kinds of consistency are more suspect. For example, most people who feel that it is important for the United States to win the war in Vietnam also feel that a meaningful victory is possible. And most people who feel defeat would neither endanger U.S. national security nor be costly in terms of other values also feel that we cannot win. Although there are important logical linkages between the two parts of each of these views (especially through theories of guerrilla warfare), they do not seem strong enough to explain the degree to which the opinions are correlated. Similarly, in Finland in the winter of 1939, those who felt that grave consequences would follow Finnish agreement to give Russia a military base also believed that the Soviets would withdraw their demand if Finland stood firm. And those who felt that concessions would not lead to loss of major values also believed that Russia would fight if need be.[26] In this country, those who favored a nuclear test ban tended to argue that fallout was very harmful, that only limited improvements in technology would flow from further testing, and that a test ban would increase the chances for peace and security. Those who opposed the test ban were apt to disagree on all three points. This does not mean, of course, that the people holding such sets of supporting views were necessarily wrong in any one element. The Finns who wanted to make concessions to the USSR were probably correct in both parts of their argument. But decision-makers should be suspicious if they hold a position in which elements that are not logically connected support the same conclusion. This condition is psychologically comfortable and makes decisions easier to reach (since competing values do not have to be balanced off against each other). The chances are thus considerable that at least part of the reason why a person holds some of these views is related to psychology and not to the substance of the evidence.

Decision-makers should also be aware that actors who suddenly find themselves having an important shared interest with other actors have a tendency to overestimate the degree of common interest involved. This tendency is especially strong for those actors (e.g., the United States, at least before 1950) whose beliefs about international relations and morality imply that they can cooperate only with "good" states and that with those states there will be no major conflicts. On the other hand, states that have either a tradition of limited cooperation with others (e.g., Britain) or a strongly held theory that differentiates occasional from permanent allies[27] (e.g., the Soviet Union) find it easier to resist this tendency and need not devote special efforts to combating its danger.

A third safeguard for decision-makers would be to make their assumptions, beliefs, and the predictions that follow from them as explicit as possible. An actor should try to determine, before events occur, what evidence would count for and against his theories. By knowing what to expect he would know what to be surprised by, and surprise could indicate to that actor that his beliefs needed reevaluation.[28]

A fourth safeguard is more complex. The decision-maker should try

[26] Max Jakobson, *The Diplomacy of the Winter War* (Cambridge, Mass., 1961), 136-39.
[27] Raymond Aron, *Peace and War* (Garden City 1966), 29.
[28] Cf. Kuhn, *The Structure of Scientific Revolutions*, 65. A fairly high degree of knowledge is needed before one can state precise expectations. One indication of the lack of international relations theory is that most of us are not sure what "naturally" flows from our theories and what constitutes either "puzzles" to be further explored with the paradigm or "anomalies" that cast doubt on the basic theories.

to prevent individuals and organizations from letting their main task, political future, and identity become tied to specific theories and images of other actors.[29] If this occurs, subgoals originally sought for their contribution to higher ends will take on value of their own, and information indicating possible alternative routes to the original goals will not be carefully considered. For example, the U.S. Forest Service was unable to carry out its original purpose as effectively when it began to see its distinctive competence not in promoting the best use of lands and forests but rather in preventing all types of forest fires.[30]

Organizations that claim to be unbiased may not realize the extent to which their definition of their role has become involved with certain beliefs about the world. Allen Dulles is a victim of this lack of understanding when he says, "I grant that we are all creatures of prejudice, including CIA officials, but by entrusting intelligence coordination to our central intelligence service, which is excluded from policy-making and is married to no particular military hardware, we can avoid, to the greatest possible extent, the bending of facts obtained through intelligence to suit a particular occupational viewpoint."[31] This statement overlooks the fact that the CIA has developed a certain view of international relations and of the cold war which maximizes the importance of its information-gathering, espionage, and subversive activities. Since the CIA would lose its unique place in the government if it were decided that the "back alleys" of world politics were no longer vital to U.S. security, it is not surprising that the organization interprets information in a way that stresses the continued need for its techniques.

Fifth, decision-makers should realize the validity and implications of Roberta Wohlstetter's argument that "a willingness to play with material from different angles and in the context of unpopular as well as popular hypotheses is an essential ingredient of a good detective, whether the end is the solution of a crime or an intelligence estimate."[32] However, it is often difficult, psychologically and politically, for any one person to do this. Since a decision-maker usually cannot get "unbiased" treatments of data, he should instead seek to structure conflicting biases into the decision-making process. The decision-maker, in other words, should have devil's advocates around. Just as, as Neustadt points out,[33] the decision-maker will want to create conflicts among his

---

[29] See Philip Selznick, *Leadership in Administration* (Evanston 1957).
[30] Ashley Schiff, *Fire and Water: Scientific Heresy in the Forest Service* (Cambridge, Mass., 1962). Despite its title, this book is a fascinating and valuable study.
[31] *The Craft of Intelligence* (New York 1963), 53.
[32] P. 302. See Beveridge, 93, for a discussion of the idea that the scientist should keep in mind as many hypotheses as possible when conducting and analyzing experiments.
[33] *Presidential Power* (New York 1960).

subordinates in order to make appropriate choices, so he will also want to ensure that incoming information is examined from many different perspectives with many different hypotheses in mind. To some extent this kind of examination will be done automatically through the divergence of goals, training, experience, and information that exists in any large organization. But in many cases this divergence will not be sufficient. The views of those analyzing the data will still be too homogeneous, and the decision-maker will have to go out of his way not only to cultivate but to create differing viewpoints.

While all that would be needed would be to have some people examining the data trying to validate unpopular hypotheses, it would probably be more effective if they actually believed and had a stake in the views they were trying to support. If in 1941 someone had had the task of proving the view that Japan would attack Pearl Harbor, the government might have been less surprised by the attack. And only a person who was out to show that Russia would take objectively great risks would have been apt to note that several ships with especially large hatches going to Cuba were riding high in the water, indicating the presence of a bulky but light cargo that was not likely to be anything other than strategic missiles. And many people who doubt the wisdom of the administration's Vietnam policy would be somewhat reassured if there were people in the government who searched the statements and actions of both sides in an effort to prove that North Vietnam was willing to negotiate and that the official interpretation of such moves as the Communist activities during the Têt truce of 1967 was incorrect.

Of course all these safeguards involve costs. They would divert resources from other tasks and would increase internal dissension. Determining whether these costs would be worth the gains would depend on a detailed analysis of how the suggested safeguards might be implemented. Even if they were adopted by a government, of course, they would not eliminate the chance of misperception. However, the safeguards would make it more likely that national decision-makers would make conscious choices about the way data were interpreted rather than merely assuming that they can be seen in only one way and can mean only one thing. Statesmen would thus be reminded of alternative images of others just as they are constantly reminded of alternative policies.

These safeguards are partly based on Hypothesis 3: actors can more easily assimilate into their established image of another actor information contradicting that image if the information is transmitted and considered bit by bit than if it comes all at once. In the former case, each piece of discrepant data can be coped with as it arrives and each of the conflicts with the prevailing view will be small enough to go unnoticed, to be dismissed as unimportant, or to necessitate at most a slight modification of the image (e.g., addition of exceptions to the rule). When the information arrives in a block, the contradiction between it and the prevailing view is apt to be much clearer and the probability of major cognitive reorganization will be higher.

IV. Sources of Concepts

An actor's perceptual thresholds—and thus the images that ambiguous information is apt to produce—are influenced by what he has experienced and learned about.[34] If one actor is to perceive that another fits in a given category he must first have, or develop, a concept for that category. We can usefully distinguish three levels at which a concept can be present or absent. First, the concept can be completely missing. The actor's cognitive structure may not include anything corresponding to the phenomenon he is encountering. This situation can occur not only in science fiction, but also in a world of rapid change or in the meeting of two dissimilar systems. Thus China's image of the Western world was extremely inaccurate in the mid-nineteenth century, her learning was very slow, and her responses were woefully inadequate. The West was spared a similar struggle only because it had the power to reshape the system it encountered. Once the actor clearly sees one instance of the new phenomenon, he is apt to recognize it much more quickly in the future.[35] Second, the actor can know about a concept but not believe that it reflects an actual phenomenon. Thus Communist and Western decision-makers are each aware of the other's explanation of how his system functions, but do not think that the concept cor-

[34] Most psychologists argue that this influence also holds for perception of shapes. For data showing that people in different societies differ in respect to their predisposition to experience certain optical illusions and for a convincing argument that this difference can be explained by the societies' different physical environments, which have led their people to develop different patterns of drawing inferences from ambiguous visual cues, see Marshall Segall, Donald Campbell, and Melville Herskovits, *The Influence of Culture on Visual Perception* (Indianapolis 1966).

[35] Thus when Bruner and Postman's subjects first were presented with incongruous playing cards (i.e., cards in which symbols and colors of the suits were not matching, producing red spades or black diamonds), long exposure times were necessary for correct identification. But once a subject correctly perceived the card and added this type of card to his repertoire of categories, he was able to identify other incongruous cards much more quickly. For an analogous example—in this case, changes in the analysis of aerial reconnaissance photographs of an enemy's secret weapons-testing facilities produced by the belief that a previously unknown object may be present—see David Irving, *The Mare's Nest* (Boston 1964), 66-67, 274-75.

responds to reality. Communist elites, furthermore, deny that anything *could* correspond to the democracies' description of themselves. Third, the actor may hold a concept, but not believe that another actor fills it at the present moment. Thus the British and French statesmen of the 1930's held a concept of states with unlimited ambitions. They realized that Napoleons were possible, but they did not think Hitler belonged in that category. Hypothesis 4 distinguishes these three cases: misperception is most difficult to correct in the case of a missing concept and least difficult to correct in the case of a recognized but presumably unfilled concept. All other things being equal (e.g., the degree to which the concept is central to the actor's cognitive structure), the first case requires more cognitive reorganization than does the second, and the second requires more reorganization than the third.

However, this hypothesis does not mean that learning will necessarily be slowest in the first case, for if the phenomena are totally new the actor may make such grossly inappropriate responses that he will quickly acquire information clearly indicating that he is faced with something he does not understand. And the sooner the actor realizes that things are not—or may not be—what they seem, the sooner he is apt to correct his image.[36]

Three main sources contribute to decision-makers' concepts of international relations and of other states and influence the level of their perceptual thresholds for various phenomena. First, an actor's beliefs about his own domestic political system are apt to be important. In some cases, like that of the USSR, the decision-makers' concepts are tied to an ideology that explicitly provides a frame of reference for viewing foreign affairs. Even where this is not the case, experience with his own system will partly determine what the actor is familiar with and what he is apt to perceive in others. Louis Hartz claims, "It is the absence of the experience of social revolution which is at the heart of the whole American dilemma. . . . In a whole series of specific ways it enters into our difficulty of communication with the rest of the world. We find it difficult to understand Europe's 'social question'. . . . We are not familiar with the deeper social struggles of Asia and hence tend to interpret even reactionary regimes as 'democratic.'"[37] Similarly, George Kennan argues that in World War I the Allied powers, and especially America, could not understand the bitterness and violence of others' internal conflicts: ". . . The inability of the Allied statesmen to picture to themselves the passions of the Russian civil war [was partly caused

---

[36] Bruner and Postman, 220.
[37] *The Liberal Tradition in America* (New York 1955), 306.

by the fact that] we represent . . . a society in which the manifestations of evil have been carefully buried and sublimated in the social behavior of people, as in their very consciousness. For this reason, probably, despite our widely traveled and outwardly cosmopolitan lives, the mainsprings of political behavior in such a country as Russia tend to remain concealed from our vision."[38]

Second, concepts will be supplied by the actor's previous experiences. An experiment from another field illustrates this. Dearborn and Simon presented business executives from various divisions (e.g., sales, accounting, production) with the same hypothetical data and asked them for an analysis and recommendations from the standpoint of what would be best for the company as a whole. The executives' views heavily reflected their departmental perspectives.[39] William W. Kaufmann shows how the perceptions of Ambassador Joseph Kennedy were affected by his past: "As befitted a former chairman of the Securities Exchange and Maritime Commissions, his primary interest lay in economic matters. . . . The revolutionary character of the Nazi regime was not a phenomenon that he could easily grasp. . . . It was far simpler, and more in accord with his own premises, to explain German aggressiveness in economic terms. The Third Reich was dissatisfied, authoritarian, and expansive largely because her economy was unsound."[40] Similarly it has been argued that Chamberlain was slow to recognize Hitler's intentions partly because of the limiting nature of his personal background and business experiences.[41] The impact of training and ex-

[38] *Russia and the West Under Lenin and Stalin* (New York 1962), 142-43.
[39] DeWitt Dearborn and Herbert Simon, "Selective Perception: A Note on the Departmental Identification of Executives," *Sociometry*, XXI (June 1958), 140-44.
[40] "Two American Ambassadors: Bullitt and Kennedy," in Craig and Gilbert, 358-59.
[41] Hugh Trevor-Roper puts this point well: "Brought up as a business man, successful in municipal politics, [Chamberlain's] outlook was entirely parochial. Educated Conservative aristocrats like Churchill, Eden, and Cranborne, whose families had long been used to political responsibility, had seen revolution and revolutionary leaders before, in their own history, and understood them correctly; but the Chamberlains, who had run from radical imperialism to timid conservatism in a generation of life in Birmingham, had no such understanding of history or the world: to them the scope of human politics was limited by their own parochial horizons, and Neville Chamberlain could not believe that Hitler was fundamentally different from himself. If Chamberlain wanted peace, so must Hitler" ("Munich—Its Lessons Ten Years Later," in Francis Loewenheim, ed., *Peace or Appeasement?* [Boston 1965], 152-53). For a similar view see A. L. Rowse, *Appeasement* (New York 1963), 117.
But Donald Lammers points out that the views of many prominent British public figures in the 1930's do not fit this generalization (*Explaining Munich* [Stanford 1966], 13-140). Furthermore, arguments that stress the importance of the experiences and views of the actors' ancestors do not explain the links by which these influence the actors themselves. Presumably Churchill and Chamberlain read the same history books in school and had the same basic information about Britain's past role in the world. Thus what has to be demonstrated is that in their homes aristocrats like Churchill learned different things about politics and human nature than did middle-class people

perience seems to be demonstrated when the background of the appeasers is compared to that of their opponents. One difference stands out: "A substantially higher percentage of the anti-appeasers (irrespective of class origins) had the kind of knowledge which comes from close acquaintance, mainly professional, with foreign affairs."[42] Since members of the diplomatic corps are responsible for meeting threats to the nation's security before these grow to major proportions and since they have learned about cases in which aggressive states were not recognized as such until very late, they may be prone to interpret ambiguous data as showing that others are aggressive. It should be stressed that we cannot say that the professionals of the 1930's were more apt to make accurate judgments of other states. Rather, they may have been more sensitive to the chance that others were aggressive. They would then rarely take an aggressor for a status-quo power, but would more often make the opposite error.[43] Thus in the years before World War I the permanent officials in the British Foreign Office overestimated German aggressiveness.[44]

A parallel demonstration in psychology of the impact of training on perception is presented by an experiment in which ambiguous pictures were shown to both advanced and beginning police-administration students. The advanced group perceived more violence in the pictures than did the beginners. The probable explanation is that "the law enforcer may come to accept crime as a familiar personal experience, one which he himself is not surprised to encounter. The acceptance of crime as a familiar experience in turn increases the ability or readiness to perceive violence where clues to it are potentially available."[45] This

---

like Chamberlain and that these experiences had a significant impact. Alternatively, it could be argued that the patterns of child-rearing prevalent among the aristocracy influenced the children's personalities in a way that made them more likely to see others as aggressive.

[42] *Ibid.*, 15.

[43] During a debate on appeasement in the House of Commons, Harold Nicolson declared, "I know that those of us who believe in the traditions of our policy, . . . who believe that one great function of this country is to maintain moral standards in Europe, to maintain a settled pattern of international relations, not to make friends with people who are demonstrably evil . . . —I know that those who hold such beliefs are accused of possessing the Foreign Office mind. I thank God that I possess the Foreign Office mind" (quoted in Martin Gilbert, *The Roots of Appeasement* [New York 1966], 187). But the qualities Nicolson mentions and applauds may be related to a more basic attribute of "the Foreign Office mind"—suspiciousness.

[44] George Monger, *The End of Isolation* (London 1963). I am also indebted to Frederick Collignon for his unpublished manuscript and several conversations on this point.

[45] Hans Toch and Richard Schulte, "Readiness to Perceive Violence as a Result of Police Training," *British Journal of Psychology*, LII (November 1961), 392 (original italics omitted). It should be stressed that one cannot say whether or not the advanced police students perceived the pictures "accurately." The point is that their training pre-

experiment lends weight to the view that the British diplomats' sensitivity to aggressive states was not totally a product of personnel selection procedures.

A third source of concepts, which frequently will be the most directly relevant to a decision-maker's perception of international relations, is international history. As Henry Kissinger points out, one reason why statesmen were so slow to recognize the threat posed by Napoleon was that previous events had accustomed them only to actors who wanted to modify the existing system, not overthrow it.[46] The other side of the coin is even more striking: historical traumas can heavily influence future perceptions. They can either establish a state's image of the other state involved or can be used as analogies. An example of the former case is provided by the fact that for at least ten years after the Franco-Prussian War most of Europe's statesmen felt that Bismarck had aggressive plans when in fact his main goal was to protect the status quo. Of course the evidence was ambiguous. The post-1871 Bismarckian maneuvers, which were designed to keep peace, looked not unlike the pre-1871 maneuvers designed to set the stage for war. But that the post-1871 maneuvers were seen as indicating aggressive plans is largely attributable to the impact of Bismarck's earlier actions on the statesmen's image of him.

A state's previous unfortunate experience with a type of danger can sensitize it to other examples of that danger. While this sensitivity may lead the state to avoid the mistake it committed in the past, it may also lead it mistakenly to believe that the present situation is like the past one. Santayana's maxim could be turned around: "Those who remember the past are condemned to make the opposite mistakes." As Paul Kecskemeti shows, both defenders and critics of the unconditional surrender plan of the Second World War thought in terms of the conditions of World War I.[47] Annette Baker Fox found that the Scandinavian countries' neutrality policies in World War II were strongly influenced by their experiences in the previous war, even though vital aspects of the two situations were different. Thus "Norway's success [during the First World War] in remaining non-belligerent though

---

disposed them to see violence in ambiguous situations. Whether on balance they would make fewer perceptual errors and better decisions is very hard to determine. For an experiment showing that training can lead people to "recognize" an expected stimulus even when that stimulus is in fact not shown, see Israel Goldiamond and William F. Hawkins, "Vexierversuch: The Log Relationship Between Word-Frequency and Recognition Obtained in the Absence of Stimulus Words," *Journal of Experimental Psychology*, LVI (December 1958), 457-63.

[46] *A World Restored* (New York 1964), 2-3.
[47] *Strategic Surrender* (New York 1964), 215-41.

pro-Allied gave the Norwegians confidence that their country could again stay out of war."[48] And the lesson drawn from the unfortunate results of this policy was an important factor in Norway's decision to join NATO.

The application of the Munich analogy to various contemporary events has been much commented on, and I do not wish to argue the substantive points at stake. But it seems clear that the probabilities that any state is facing an aggressor who has to be met by force are not altered by the career of Hitler and the history of the 1930's. Similarly the probability of an aggressor's announcing his plans is not increased (if anything, it is decreased) by the fact that Hitler wrote *Mein Kampf*. Yet decision-makers are more sensitive to these possibilities, and thus more apt to perceive ambiguous evidence as indicating they apply to a given case, than they would have been had there been no Nazi Germany.

Historical analogies often precede, rather than follow, a careful analysis of a situation (e.g., Truman's initial reaction to the news of the invasion of South Korea was to think of the Japanese invasion of Manchuria). Noting this precedence, however, does not show us which of many analogies will come to a decision-maker's mind. Truman could have thought of nineteenth-century European wars that were of no interest to the United States. Several factors having nothing to do with the event under consideration influence what analogies a decision-maker is apt to make. One factor is the number of cases similar to the analogy with which the decision-maker is familiar. Another is the importance of the past event to the political system of which the decision-maker is a part. The more times such an event occurred and the greater its consequences were, the more a decision-maker will be sensitive to the particular danger involved and the more he will be apt to see ambiguous stimuli as indicating another instance of this kind of event. A third factor is the degree of the decision-maker's personal involvement in the past case—in time, energy, ego, and position. The last-mentioned variable will affect not only the event's impact on the decision-maker's cognitive structure, but also the way he perceives the event and the lesson he draws. Someone who was involved in getting troops into South Korea after the attack will remember the Korean War differently from someone who was involved in considering the possible use of nuclear weapons or in deciding what messages should be sent to the Chinese. Greater personal involvement will usually give the event greater impact, especially if the decision-maker's own views

[48] *The Power of Small States* (Chicago 1959), 81.

were validated by the event. One need not accept a total application of learning theory to nations to believe that "nothing fails like success."[49] It also seems likely that if many critics argued at the time that the decision-maker was wrong, he will be even more apt to see other situations in terms of the original event. For example, because Anthony Eden left the government on account of his views and was later shown to have been correct, he probably was more apt to see as Hitlers other leaders with whom he had conflicts (e.g., Nasser). A fourth factor is the degree to which the analogy is compatible with the rest of his belief system. A fifth is the absence of alternative concepts and analogies. Individuals and states vary in the amount of direct or indirect political experience they have had which can provide different ways of interpreting data. Decision-makers who are aware of multiple possibilities of states' intentions may be less likely to seize on an analogy prematurely. The perception of citizens of nations like the United States which have relatively little history of international politics may be more apt to be heavily influenced by the few major international events that have been important to their country.

The first three factors indicate that an event is more apt to shape present perceptions if it occurred in the recent rather than the remote past. If it occurred recently, the statesman will then know about it at first hand even if he was not involved in the making of policy at the time. Thus if generals are prepared to fight the last war, diplomats may be prepared to avoid the last war. Part of the Anglo-French reaction to Hitler can be explained by the prevailing beliefs that the First World War was to a large extent caused by misunderstandings and could have been avoided by farsighted and nonbelligerent diplomacy. And part of the Western perception of Russia and China can be explained by the view that appeasement was an inappropriate response to Hitler.[50]

V. The Evoked Set

The way people perceive data is influenced not only by their cognitive structure and theories about other actors but also by what they are concerned with at the time they receive the information. Information

---

[49] William Inge, *Outspoken Essays*, First Series (London 1923), 88.

[50] Of course, analogies themselves are not "unmoved movers." The interpretation of past events is not automatic and is informed by general views of international relations and complex judgments. And just as beliefs about the past influence the present, views about the present influence interpretations of history. It is difficult to determine the degree to which the United States' interpretation of the reasons it went to war in 1917 influenced American foreign policy in the 1920's and 1930's and how much the isolationism of that period influenced the histories of the war.

is evaluated in light of the small part of the person's memory that is presently active—the "evoked set." My perceptions of the dark streets I pass walking home from the movies will be different if the film I saw had dealt with spies than if it had been a comedy. If I am working on aiding a country's education system and I hear someone talk about the need for economic development in that state, I am apt to think he is concerned with education, whereas if I had been working on, say, trying to achieve political stability in that country, I would have placed his remarks in that framework.[51]

Thus Hypothesis 5 states that when messages are sent from a different background of concerns and information than is possessed by the receiver, misunderstanding is likely. Person A and person B will read the same message quite differently if A has seen several related messages that B does not know about. This difference will be compounded if, as is frequently the case, A and B each assume that the other has the same background he does. This means that misperception can occur even when deception is neither intended nor expected. Thus Roberta Wohlstetter found not only that different parts of the United States government had different perceptions of data about Japan's intentions and messages partly because they saw the incoming information in very different contexts, but also that officers in the field misunderstood warnings from Washington: "Washington advised General Short [in Pearl Harbor] on November 27 to expect 'hostile action' at any moment, by which it meant 'attack on American possessions from without,' but General Short understood this phrase to mean 'sabotage.' "[52] Washington did not realize the extent to which Pearl Harbor considered the danger of sabotage to be primary, and furthermore it incorrectly believed that General Short had received the intercepts of the secret Japanese diplomatic messages available in Washington which indicated that surprise attack was a distinct possibility. Another implication of this hypothesis is that if important information is known to only part of the government of state A and part of the government of state B, international messages may be misunderstood by those parts of

---

[51] For some psychological experiments on this subject, see Jerome Bruner and A. Leigh Minturn, "Perceptual Identification and Perceptual Organization" *Journal of General Psychology*, LIII (July 1955), 22-28; Seymour Feshbach and Robert Singer, "The Effects of Fear Arousal and Suppression of Fear Upon Social Perception," *Journal of Abnormal and Social Psychology*, LV (November 1957), 283-88; and Elsa Sippoal, "A Group Study of Some Effects of Preparatory Sets," *Psychology Monographs*, XLVI, No. 210 (1935), 27-28. For a general discussion of the importance of the perceiver's evoked set, see Postman, 87.

[52] Pp. 73-74.

the receiver's government that do not match, in the information they have, the part of the sender's government that dispatched the message.[53]

Two additional hypotheses can be drawn from the problems of those sending messages. Hypothesis 6 states that when people spend a great deal of time drawing up a plan or making a decision, they tend to think that the message about it they wish to convey will be clear to the receiver.[54] Since they are aware of what is to them the important pattern in their actions, they often feel that the pattern will be equally obvious to others, and they overlook the degree to which the message is apparent to them only because they know what to look for. Those who have not participated in the endless meetings may not understand what information the sender is trying to convey. George Quester has shown how the German and, to a lesser extent, the British desire to maintain target limits on bombing in the first eighteen months of World War II was undermined partly by the fact that each side knew the limits it was seeking and its own reasons for any apparent "exceptions" (e.g., the German attack on Rotterdam) and incorrectly felt that these limits and reasons were equally clear to the other side.[55]

Hypothesis 7 holds that actors often do not realize that actions intended to project a given image may not have the desired effect because the actions themselves do not turn out as planned. Thus even without appreciable impact of different cognitive structures and backgrounds, an action may convey an unwanted message. For example, a country's representatives may not follow instructions and so may give others impressions contrary to those the home government wished to convey. The efforts of Washington and Berlin to settle their dispute over Samoa in the late 1880's were complicated by the provocative behavior of their agents on the spot. These agents not only increased the intensity of the local conflict, but led the decision-makers to become more suspicious of the other state because they tended to assume that their agents were obeying instructions and that the actions of the other side represented official policy. In such cases both sides will believe that the other is reading hostility into a policy of theirs which is friendly. Similarly,

---

[53] For example, Roger Hilsman points out, "Those who knew of the peripheral reconnaissance flights that probed Soviet air defenses during the Eisenhower administration and the U-2 flights over the Soviet Union itself . . . were better able to understand some of the things the Soviets were saying and doing than people who did not know of these activities" (*To Move a Nation* [Garden City 1967], 66). But it is also possible that those who knew about the U-2 flights at times misinterpreted Soviet messages by incorrectly believing that the sender was influenced by, or at least knew of, these flights.

[54] I am grateful to Thomas Schelling for discussion on this point.

[55] *Deterrence Before Hiroshima* (New York 1966), 105-22.

Quester's study shows that the attempt to limit bombing referred to above failed partly because neither side was able to bomb as accurately as it thought it could and thus did not realize the physical effects of its actions.[56]

VI. FURTHER HYPOTHESES FROM THE PERSPECTIVE OF THE PERCEIVER

From the perspective of the perceiver several other hypotheses seem to hold. Hypothesis 8 is that there is an overall tendency for decision-makers to see other states as more hostile than they are.[57] There seem to be more cases of statesmen incorrectly believing others are planning major acts against their interest than of statesmen being lulled by a potential aggressor. There are many reasons for this which are too complex to be treated here (e.g., some parts of the bureaucracy feel it is their responsibility to be suspicious of all other states; decision-makers often feel they are "playing it safe" to believe and act as though the other state were hostile in questionable cases; and often, when people do not feel they are a threat to others, they find it difficult to believe that others may see them as a threat). It should be noted, however, that decision-makers whose perceptions are described by this hypothesis would not necessarily further their own values by trying to correct for this tendency. The values of possible outcomes as well as their probabilities must be considered, and it may be that the probability of an unnecessary arms-tension cycle arising out of misperceptions, multiplied by the costs of such a cycle, may seem less to decision-makers than the probability of incorrectly believing another state is friendly, multiplied by the costs of this eventuality.

Hypothesis 9 states that actors tend to see the behavior of others as more centralized, disciplined, and coordinated than it is. This hypothesis holds true in related ways. Frequently, too many complex events are squeezed into a perceived pattern. Actors are hesitant to admit or even see that particular incidents cannot be explained by their theories.[58] Those events not caused by factors that are important parts of the perceiver's image are often seen as though they were. Further, actors see others as more internally united than they in fact are and generally overestimate the degree to which others are following a coherent policy. The degree to which the other side's policies are the product of internal

[56] *Ibid.*
[57] For a slightly different formulation of this view, see Holsti, 27.
[58] The Soviets consciously hold an extreme version of this view and seem to believe that nothing is accidental. See the discussion in Nathan Leites, *A Study of Bolshevism* (Glencoe 1953), 67-73.

bargaining,[59] internal misunderstandings, or subordinates' not follow-ing instructions is underestimated. This is the case partly because actors tend to be unfamiliar with the details of another state's policy-making processes. Seeing only the finished product, they find it simpler to try to construct a rational explanation for the policies, even though they know that such an analysis could not explain their own policies.[60]

Familiarity also accounts for Hypothesis 10: because a state gets most of its information about the other state's policies from the other's for-eign office, it tends to take the foreign office's position for the stand of the other government as a whole. In many cases this perception will be an accurate one, but when the other government is divided or when the other foreign office is acting without specific authorization, misper-ception may result. For example, part of the reason why in 1918 Allied governments incorrectly thought "that the Japanese were preparing to take action [in Siberia], if need be, with agreement with the British and French alone, disregarding the absence of American consent,"[61] was that Allied ambassadors had talked mostly with Foreign Minister Motono, who was among the minority of the Japanese favoring this policy. Similarly, America's NATO allies may have gained an inac-curate picture of the degree to which the American government was committed to the MLF because they had greatest contact with parts of the government that strongly favored the MLF. And states that tried to get information about Nazi foreign policy from German diplomats were often misled because these officials were generally ignorant of or out of sympathy with Hitler's plans. The Germans and the Japanese sometimes purposely misinformed their own ambassadors in order to deceive their enemies more effectively.

Hypothesis 11 states that actors tend to overestimate the degree to which others are acting in response to what they themselves do when the others behave in accordance with the actor's desires; but when the behavior of the other is undesired, it is usually seen as derived from internal forces. If the *effect* of another's action is to injure or threaten

---

[59] A. W. Marshall criticizes Western explanations of Soviet military posture for failing to take this into account. See his "Problems of Estimating Military Power," a paper presented at the 1966 Annual Meeting of the American Political Science Asso-ciation, 16.

[60] It has also been noted that in labor-management disputes both sides may be apt to believe incorrectly that the other is controlled from above, either from the inter-national union office or from the company's central headquarters (Robert Blake, Herbert Shepard, and Jane Mouton, *Managing Intergroup Conflict in Industry* [Houston 1964], 182). It has been further noted that both Democratic and Republican members of the House tend to see the other party as the one that is more disciplined and united (Charles Clapp, *The Congressman* [Washington 1963], 17-19).

[61] George Kennan, *Russia Leaves the War* (New York 1967), 484.

the first side, the first side is apt to believe that such was the other's *purpose*. An example of the first part of the hypothesis is provided by Kennan's account of the activities of official and unofficial American representatives who protested to the new Bolshevik government against several of its actions. When the Soviets changed their position, these representatives felt it was largely because of their influence.[62] This sort of interpretation can be explained not only by the fact that it is gratifying to the individual making it, but also, taking the other side of the coin mentioned in Hypothesis 9, by the fact that the actor is most familiar with his own input into the other's decision and has less knowledge of other influences. The second part of Hypothesis 11 is illustrated by the tendency of actors to believe that the hostile behavior of others is to be explained by the other side's motives and not by its reaction to the first side. Thus Chamberlain did not see that Hitler's behavior was related in part to his belief that the British were weak. More common is the failure to see that the other side is reacting out of fear of the first side, which can lead to self-fulfilling prophecies and spirals of misperception and hostility.

This difficulty is often compounded by an implication of Hypothesis 12: when actors have intentions that they do not try to conceal from others, they tend to assume that others accurately perceive these intentions. Only rarely do they believe that others may be reacting to a much less favorable image of themselves than they think they are projecting.[63]

For state A to understand how state B perceives A's policy is often difficult because such understanding may involve a conflict with A's image of itself. Raymond Sontag argues that Anglo-German relations before World War I deteriorated partly because "the British did not like to think of themselves as selfish, or unwilling to tolerate 'legitimate' German expansion. The Germans did not like to think of themselves as aggressive, or unwilling to recognize 'legitimate' British vested interest."[64]

---

[62] *Ibid.*, 404, 408, 500.

[63] Herbert Butterfield notes that these assumptions can contribute to the spiral of "Hobbesian fear. . . . You yourself may vividly feel the terrible fear that you have of the other party, but you cannot enter into the other man's counter-fear, or even understand why he should be particularly nervous. For you know that you yourself mean him no harm, and that you want nothing from him save guarantees for your own safety; and it is never possible for you to realize or remember properly that since he cannot see the inside of your mind, he can never have the same assurance of your intentions that you have" (*History and Human Conflict* [London 1951], 20).

[64] *European Diplomatic History 1871-1932* (New York 1933), 125. It takes great mental effort to realize that actions which seem only the natural consequence of defending your vital interests can look to others as though you are refusing them any

Hypothesis 13 suggests that if it is hard for an actor to believe that the other can see him as a menace, it is often even harder for him to see that issues important to him are not important to others. While he may know that another actor is on an opposing team, it may be more difficult for him to realize that the other is playing an entirely different game. This is especially true when the game he is playing seems vital to him.[65]

The final hypothesis, Hypothesis 14, is as follows: actors tend to overlook the fact that evidence consistent with their theories may also be consistent with other views. When choosing between two theories we have to pay attention only to data that cannot be accounted for by one of the theories. But it is common to find people claiming as proof of their theories data that could also support alternative views. This phenomenon is related to the point made earlier that any single bit of information can be interpreted only within a framework of hypotheses and theories. And while it is true that "we may without a vicious circularity accept some datum as a fact because it conforms to the very law for which it counts as another confirming instance, and reject an allegation of fact because it is already excluded by law,"[66] we should be careful lest we forget that a piece of information seems in many cases to confirm a certain hypothesis only because we already believe that hypothesis to be correct and that the information can with as much validity support a different hypothesis. For example, one of the reasons why the German attack on Norway took both that country and England by surprise, even though they had detected German ships moving toward Norway, was that they expected not an attack but an attempt by the Germans to break through the British blockade and reach the

---

chance of increasing their influence. In rebutting the famous Crowe "balance of power" memorandum of 1907, which justified a policy of "containing" Germany on the grounds that she was a threat to British national security, Sanderson, a former permanent undersecretary in the Foreign Office, wrote, "It has sometimes seemed to me that to a foreigner reading our press the British Empire must appear in the light of some huge giant sprawling all over the globe, with gouty fingers and toes stretching in every direction, which cannot be approached without eliciting a scream" (quoted in Monger, 315). But few other Englishmen could be convinced that others might see them this way.

[65] George Kennan makes clear that in 1918 this kind of difficulty was partly responsible for the inability of either the Allies or the new Bolshevik government to understand the motivations of the other side: "There is . . . nothing in nature more egocentrical than the embattled democracy. . . . It . . . tends to attach to its own cause an absolute value which distorts its own vision of everything else. . . . It will readily be seen that people who have got themselves into this frame of mind have little understanding for the issues of any contest other than the one in which they are involved. The idea of people wasting time and substance on any *other* issue seems to them preposterous" (*Russia and the West*, 11-12).

[66] Kaplan, 89.

Atlantic. The initial course of the ships was consistent with either plan, but the British and Norwegians took this course to mean that their predictions were being borne out.[67] This is not to imply that the interpretation made was foolish, but only that the decision-makers should have been aware that the evidence was also consistent with an invasion and should have had a bit less confidence in their views.

The longer the ships would have to travel the same route whether they were going to one or another of two destinations, the more information would be needed to determine their plans. Taken as a metaphor, this incident applies generally to the treatment of evidence. Thus as long as Hitler made demands for control only of ethnically German areas, his actions could be explained either by the hypothesis that he had unlimited ambitions or by the hypothesis that he wanted to unite all the Germans. But actions against non-Germans (e.g., the takeover of Czechoslovakia in March 1939) could not be accounted for by the latter hypothesis. And it was this action that convinced the appeasers that Hitler had to be stopped. It is interesting to speculate on what the British reaction would have been had Hitler left Czechoslovakia alone for a while and instead made demands on Poland similar to those he eventually made in the summer of 1939. The two paths would then still not have diverged, and further misperception could have occurred.

[67] Johan Jorgen Holst, "Surprise, Signals, and Reaction: The Attack on Norway," *Cooperation and Conflict*, No. 1 (1966), 34. The Germans made a similar mistake in November 1942 when they interpreted the presence of an Allied convoy in the Mediterranean as confirming their belief that Malta would be resupplied. They thus were taken by surprise when landings took place in North Africa (William Langer, *Our Vichy Gamble* [New York 1966], 365).

FAILURES IN NATIONAL INTELLIGENCE ESTIMATES:
The Case of the Yom Kippur War

By AVI SHLAIM

I. STRATEGIC SURPRISE

A FORMER Israeli Chief of Staff, Lieutenant-General Chaim Bar-Lev, divides strategic surprise or surprise at war into three types: surprise in method, surprise in place, and surprise in time.[1] According to Bar-Lev, in October 1973 the only type of surprise achieved by the Arabs concerned the timing of the attack. But it is arguable that Israel was taken by surprise in all three spheres.[2] As far as the method of warfare is concerned, the Israeli armed forces were not adequately prepared for the dense deployment of antiaircraft and antitank missiles by the Egyptians and the Syrians, nor were they fully equipped for an amphibious crossing. As far as the place of the attack is concerned, Bar-Lev assumed that there could be no doubt that if the enemy launched an attack, it would be on the defensive lines built by Israel. But it should be recalled that Israel's official theory of "secure borders" precluded the possibility of an attack. The theory assumed that the June 1967 borders were so secure that an enemy attack was bound to fail, and that this would deter the enemy from launching a full-scale war in the first place. Seen in this perspective, Israel was surprised not only by the timing, but also by the method and place of the Yom Kippur attack. Military history offers few parallels for strategic surprise as complete as that achieved by Egypt and Syria on October 6, 1973.

"In security matters," wrote Israel's Defense Minister Shimon Peres, "the problem of advance warning is a problem of life and death," quoting the example of America's investment of millions of dollars to gain a few additional minutes of warning.[3] Israel's own defense doctrine was based on maintaining a small standing force which could be reinforced in a crisis by highly trained reserves through the operation of a swift and efficient system of mobilization. Advance warning was a

---

[1] *Ma'ariv*, 1 August 1975.
[2] This was argued by Major-General (Res.) Matityahu Peled in *Ma'ariv*, 8 August 1975.
[3] Peres, *Hashlav Haba* [The Next Phase] (Tel-Aviv: HaSefer Publishers 1965), 114; this and all following translations from Hebrew by the author.

crucial element in this conception; to ensure it, Israel developed an intelligence service of near-legendary competence. The strategic surprise attained by the combined Arab attack of October 6, 1973, provides a dramatic illustration of the momentous consequences which a failure in national intelligence estimates can have. It enabled the Arabs to dictate the opening moves in the war and to secure their initial successes. More significantly, it radically changed the whole political and psychological balance of power in the Middle East to Israel's disadvantage.

When a nation suffers such setbacks as a result of being caught unprepared, a search for scapegoats frequently takes place; the blame is often laid at the door of the intelligence community. After the defeat of June 1967, for example, President Nasser dismissed the Egyptian intelligence chief although all the evidence indicates that a first strike by Israel was an integral part of Nasser's strategy. Following the Yom Kippur War, the Israeli Director of Military Intelligence was removed from his post. (He was not dismissed from the army.) But the fact that failures in national intelligence estimates have taken place so frequently and ubiquitously, and that they have not been confined to services of low professional standing, would suggest that it is misleading to attribute responsibility for mistakes of this kind to the incompetence of the officers most directly concerned, and that there are deeper and more pervasive factors which need to be taken into account. In the present article I seek to use the Yom Kippur episode as a basis for an exploration of these basic factors which are conducive to incorrect evaluation. The argument is based on the conviction that intelligence failures display similarities that make it legitimate to generalize by using a case study drawn out of a specific context to illuminate questions of broader and continuing significance. The task must be approached with the greatest caution, however, mindful of de Tocqueville's warning that misapplied lessons from history may be more dangerous than ignorance of the past.

What the Israeli national intelligence failure has in common with a large number of other historical examples is that it was not due to any dearth of information but to an incorrect evaluation of the available information.[4] This point cannot be over-emphasized: had the failure

---

[4] The Chinese intervention in the Korean War, for example, came as a surprise to the Truman Administration although the Chinese had explicitly stated that they would intervene if the American forces crossed the 38th parallel. From the study of the documents, H. A. de Weerd has concluded that the evidence available to the policy makers was good enough for reasonably vigilant statesmen to take seriously the threat of full-

been the result of inadequate information about the war preparations of the other side, the simple conclusion to be drawn from the episode would have been the need to expand and improve Israel's fact-gathering services. But the interest of the episode and the lessons to be learned from it lie precisely in the fact that enemy intentions were misperceived until the last moment, although there was not shortage of information about enemy moves and preparations.

That this was so is by now abundantly clear. Chaim Bar-Lev, now the Minister of Commerce and Industry, who was dispatched to assist the high command upon the outbreak of war because of his previous military experience, emphasized the point in a newspaper article: "It is worth pointing out that no lack of reliable information caused this situation. *Zahal* [the Israel Defense Forces] had all the information about the enemy's power, his deployment and the advanced weapons in his possession. The mistake lay in the evaluation of the intelligence data and not in the absence of accurate and reliable information."[5]

In the article mentioned earlier, Bar-Lev noted that, on the eve of the German invasion in 1941, Russia had details on a scale never enjoyed by another country before; in his opinion, that record of accurate details in the possession of a country which was subjected to a surprise attack has passed from the Soviet Union to Israel.[6]

In discussing the information available on an approaching crisis, it is useful to distinguish between what Roberta Wohlstetter has called "signals" and "noise." "By the 'signal' of an action is meant a sign, a clue, a piece of evidence that points to the action or to an adversary's intention to undertake it, and by 'noise' is meant the background of irrelevant and inconsistent signals, signs pointing in the wrong direction, that tend always to obscure the signs pointing the right way."[7] Signals rarely come in a pure or isolated form. They are embedded in a complex network of competing and contradictory signals, some inadvertently created by the receiver, some by chance, and some deliberately projected by the adversary in an effort to conceal his true intentions. Pearl Harbor, as Wohlstetter points out, "shows how hard it is to hear a signal against the prevailing noise, in particular when you are listening for the wrong signal, and even when you have a wealth of in-

---

scale Chinese intervention: "It was not the absence of intelligence which led us into trouble but our unwillingness to draw unpleasant conclusions from it." "Strategic Surprise in the Korean War," *Orbis*, vi (Fall 1962).

[5] *Ma'ariv*, 9 November 1973.

[6] *Ma'ariv*, 1 August 1975.

[7] Wohlstetter, "Cuba and Pearl Harbor: Hindsight and Foresight," *Foreign Affairs*, xliii (July 1965).

formation. (Or perhaps especially then. There are clearly cases when riches can be embarrassing)."[8] To understand the phenomenon of surprise, it is essential to examine not only the signals but also the noise that obscures them and can prevent them from being understood correctly.

Here a word of warning must be interjected. Signals that announce an impending disaster appear much more stark and clear after the disaster has taken place than at the time they are originally received. After the event it is much easier to sort out the relevant from the irrelevant signals. A retrospective examination can be compared to the construction of a familiar jigsaw puzzle: one can pick out the appropriate pieces and fit them into a coherent pattern which is seen to have heralded the imminent attack clearly and unmistakenly. Even the accounts of the participants themselves display a common tendency to allow the memories of the doubts, the confusions, and the ambiguities to fade away, leaving the signals perceived to stand as an inexorable chain of evidence pointing firmly in the right direction. But the commentator must take care not to allow the benefit of hindsight to distort his vision and not to be too unsympathetic with the people who were proved wrong: on closer examination, it is frequently difficult to point to differences between those who were right and those who were wrong in their interpretation of the data at hand.

II. The Agranat Report

Although the full story of the Israeli intelligence failure of October 1973 is not yet known and may never be known, the essential components of this failure are fully documented in the Interim Report of the Agranat Commission of Inquiry which was published in April 1974.[9] This five-man Commission, which was chaired by the President of the Supreme Court, Dr. S. Agranat, and included two former Chiefs of Staff, was appointed by the Government to examine the responsibility of the military and civilian authorities for the failure to anticipate the Yom Kippur War and for the lapses in the initial conduct of the war. Its Report is of the highest interest not only for practitioners of the intelligence craft, but also for historians and social scientists whose

---

[8] *Ibid.*

[9] *Interim Report of the Agranat Commission of Inquiry*, Jerusalem, 1 April 1974. An additional interim report was published on 10 July 1974, and the final report was submitted on 30 January 1975. These, however, have not been made public and all the references in the present article are to the first Interim Report. The subsequent reports deal, *inter alia*, with the performance of the intelligence services after the outbreak of hostilities, a subject that falls outside the scope of this article.

access to material on which to base their research is severely limited by the necessity for secrecy in the work of the intelligence services. Since the Report provides the bulk of the material for this portrait of the Israeli intelligence failure, and since it is not available in English, a detailed account of its relevant parts follows.

The opening of the war by Egypt and Syria on Saturday, October 6, 1973, at 14:00 hours surprised the Israel Defense Forces (IDF): until the early morning, the high command and the political leaders did not realize that a general war was about to break out; when they finally did, the high command assumed, mistakenly, that this would happen at 18:00.

The responsibility for these mistakes is attributed by the Commission primarily to the Director of Military Intelligence and his principal assistant who heads the research department, the only body in the country which deals with intelligence evaluation. These officers failed in that the warning they gave to the IDF was totally inadequate. At 4:30 on the morning of October 6, the Director of Military Intelligence announced, on the basis of new evidence, that the enemy would attack on both fronts at 18:00. This short warning did not permit an orderly mobilization of the reserves in accordance with the established timetables and procedures. The additional mistake of four hours concerning the actual timing of the attack further impaired the preparedness of the standing forces at the front and the deployment of the reserves.

The Commission indicates three reasons for the error of those charged with evaluation. First, their stubborn adherence to "the conception," resting on two assumptions: (a) Egypt would not go to war until she was able to stage deep air strikes into Israel, particularly against her major military airfields, in order to neutralize Israel's Air Force; (b) Syria would not launch a full-scale war against Israel unless Egypt was in the struggle too. This conception may have been correct at the time it was formulated, but its first and crucial part was not reassessed in the light of political and military changes in the area.

Second, the Director of Military Intelligence had guaranteed that his department would give sufficient advance warning of such an all-out attack to permit the orderly call-up of the reserves. This promise became the firm foundation of the IDF's defense plans. The Commission tersely observes that it found no grounds for such a definitive guarantee.

Third, during the days that preceded the war, the research department possessed considerable information about threatening enemy moves which were supplied by the intelligence and other agencies. But the Director of Military Intelligence and his assistants did not correctly evaluate the warning this information contained because of their doctrinaire adherence to "the conception" and their willingness to explain away the enemy's deployment at the front lines—although it was unprecedented in its scale and direction—as evidence of a defensive move in Syria and a multidivision exercise in Egypt.

The Military Intelligence's belief in the correctness of its evaluation did not begin to falter until the morning of October 5, when a particularly clear piece of evidence was difficult to reconcile with the assumption of a harmless exercise and defensive maneuver. Even then, the right conclusion was not drawn and the chances of war were given in the military jargon as "low probability" and even as "lower than low." It was on the basis of this confidence that Prime Minister Golda Meir and Defense Minister Moshe Dayan concluded that full mobilization was not yet necessary, and the Chief of Staff merely placed the standing army on full alert. Only at the dawn of Yom Kippur, after receiving an additional piece of clear-cut information, did the Director conclude that war would break out that very day.

The Agranat Commission's separate recommendations for dealing with the intelligence personnel shed further light on the causes of what has come to be known in Israel as "the breakdown." Major-General Eliyahu Zeira, the Director of Military Intelligence, had only been at his post for one year before the war and had found established patterns of work. But he adopted "the conception" whose rigidity destroyed the openness required in confronting inflowing information.

With Lt. Col. Yonah Bendman, the head of the Egypt branch in the research department, the belief in "the conception" reached its peak. This is evident from a report he issued on October 5, containing a long list of offensive Egyptian preparations. His conclusion was that, although the deployment showed apparent signs of offensive intent, no change had taken place in the Egyptian view of the balance of power between them and the IDF, and that consequently the likelihood that they intended to renew the war was low.

Military Intelligence actually suppressed views contradicting its senior officers' unconcern. On October 1, a young intelligence officer, Lieutenant Benjamin Siman-Tov, presented a startling document entitled "Movement in the Egyptian Army—the possibility of resumption of hostilities." This document summarized and analyzed the information concerning the build-up across the Suez Canal. On October 3, Siman-Tov presented a second and more detailed report. In these two reports he pointed to a number of important facts that could not be squared with the view of the Egyptian moves as an exercise. On the basis of these facts the Lieutenant gave his evaluation that the exercise camouflaged the final phases of preparation for all-out war.

Siman-Tov's reports got no further than the senior intelligence officer in the Southern Command, Lt. Col. David Geddaliah. Geddaliah's reports to GHQ in Tel-Aviv contained no trace of Siman-Tov's dissenting conclusions. He had "erased" the penetrating questions which were apt to arouse doubts about the nonoffensive intentions of the Egyptians because "they stood in contradiction to Headquarters' evaluation that an exercise was taking place in Egypt." His thinking, the Commission concludes, was trapped in a vicious circle. He did not fulfil his duty as an intelligence officer to treat every item of information and every evaluation without prejudice. His conduct was particularly reprehensible because the evidence of a picture taken by a reconnaissance flight on October 4, which showed an alarming reinforcement of the Egyptian forces, should have assumed a special significance in the light of Siman-Tov's evaluation.

The members of the Commission of Inquiry explicitly state that, in criticizing the intelligence community, they were mindful not to fall into the trap of "wisdom after the event" and endeavored to see matters in the perspective of the situation as it was at the time the evaluations were made and the decisions were taken. But the Report shows that to some extent they succumbed to the all too human tendency of distinguishing much more clearly between signals and noise with hindsight than would have been possible at the time; they dwell on the signals which after the event are clearly seen to have heralded the attack, paying insufficient regard to the plethora of conflicting signs which pointed in the wrong direction. In addition to the obstacles to clear perception which the intelligence officers created themselves and which are so skilfully analyzed in the Report, there were all kinds of noises which either occurred by chance or were deliberately created by the enemy and which, in the perspective of the time, were no less relevant. An example of the "objective" barrier was provided by Lieutenant-General David Elazar, the Israeli Chief of Staff at the time of the war, when he explained that "the objective data which we had as a warning this time were different from those in the past. In addition to threats by Arab rulers, the armies of Egypt and Syria were all deployed along the ceasefire line, not as in the 1967 war when the entry of the Egyptian Army into Sinai signalled the need for us to mobilize our reserves."[10] Nor were the signs of escalation a definitive signal: three previous mobilizations had taken place since 1971 without the subsequent launching of a strike. In the absence of clear "objective" indicators, Israeli intelligence experts had to rely on their reading of the enemy leaders' intentions as a source of advance warning to the IDF.

Arab deception strategy was a further and significant reason behind the Israeli intelligence failure. Unlike the Wohlstetter model, which sees strategic surprise primarily as the result of ambiguous information, the model developed by Barton Whaley singles out deception as the key to surprise. His study of the German invasion of Russia in 1941 contends that Stalin had been surprised by Hitler's action not because the warnings were ambiguous, but precisely because the Germans had managed to reduce their ambiguity. In other words, surprise had been inflicted by the deliberately false "signals" and not by the ambiguous "signals," much less by the merely distracting "noise."[11] Whaley's study of this and other cases leads him to conclude that "deception and surprise are so closely linked that their intensities are directly related. That is, the greater the deception effort, the greater the degree of surprise gained."[12] This model, which should be seen as complementing rather than competing with Wohlstetter's, helps to explain the surprise achieved in the Yom Kippur War.

The Arabs went far beyond mere secrecy and resorted to active deception designed to create a misleading impression concerning their capabilities, plans, and intentions. Their efforts ranged from welcoming Dr. Kissinger's peace initiatives in September 1973 to planting news items in a Lebanese newspaper about the neglect and deterioration of the Soviet equipment in the Suez Canal zone, and from staging the kidnapping of Soviet Jews by Palestinian terrorists in Austria as a decoy plan to positioning Syrian tanks "hull down," dug in to resist retaliative assault rather than to attack.[13] These efforts were part of an imaginative, intensive, and well-orchestrated strategy of deception

[10] SWB (Summary of World Broadcasts) Second Series ME/4437, 30 October 1973, published by the Monitoring Service of the BBC.

[11] Barton Whaley, *Codeword Barbarossa* (Cambridge: MIT Press 1973).

[12] Barton Whaley, "The Causes of Surprise in War," Paper delivered at the Conference on Strategic Issues, The Leonard Davis Institute of International Relations, The Hebrew University of Jerusalem, 7-9 April 1975.

[13] For details of the Arab deception strategy, see Mohamed Heikal, *The Road to Ramadan* (London: Collins 1975), chap. I; The Insight Team of the Sunday Times, *The Yom Kippur War* (London: André Deutsch 1975), 80-81, 101-11; John Bullock, *The Making of a War* (London: Longman 1974), 206-9; and Zeev Schiff, *October Earthquake* (Tel Aviv: University Publishing Projects 1974), 23-26.

which brought rich rewards. Particularly effective was the exploitation of Israeli weaknesses by deliberately acting in such a way as to confirm the Israeli leaders' known belief that the Arabs were not ready and not willing to go to war.

It must also be remembered that there is such a thing as the cry-wolf syndrome. Repeated warnings which are not followed up by action have the effect of eroding the alertness of the threatened party. President Sadat had named 1971 as "the year of decision," and he made himself a laughing stock by repeating his threats noisily at a time when he was incapable of carrying them out. As Coral Bell put it, "the unfulfilled threats of the two previous years had left a pervasive impression of military irresolution which operated as a conscious or unconscious *ruse de guerre* for the Egyptians, concealing their intentions."[14] False alarms and repeated alerts that turn out to have been unnecessary are also connected with this syndrome, for their effect in the long run is to obscure the signals that herald the advent of a real crisis. This effect is what Prime Minister Meir had in mind when she said plaintively: "No one in this country realises how many times during the past year we received information from the same source that war would break out on this or that day, without war breaking out. I will not say this was good enough. I do say it was fatal."[15]

The neglect of details such as these and many others led the Commission of Inquiry to present a somewhat unbalanced picture. As one critic has pointed out, its conclusions crystallized in the light of history and the chain of events as they occurred, and not in accordance with the internal logic of the various facts and the evaluations seen in the light of the original circumstances in which they were collected and formed.[16] Notwithstanding this deficiency, there is much in the Interim Report that is useful in underpinning an investigation of the causes of failure in national intelligence estimates. The causes can be divided into two categories, the psychological and the institutional, although to some extent they overlap.

III. The Psychological Roots of Surprise

The possibilities of surprise are inherent in the limitations of human perception. Surprise is essentially a psychological phenomenon that has

---

[14] Bell, "The October Middle East War: a Case Study in Crisis Management During Detente," *International Affairs*, Vol. 50 (October 1974), 534.

[15] *Jerusalem Post Weekly*, 11 December 1973.

[16] Abraham Ben-Zvi, "Military Intelligence and its Evaluations," *Ma'ariv*, 18 April 1974.

its roots in human nature.[17] Since the facts do not speak for themselves but need to be interpreted, it is inevitable that the individual human propensities of an intelligence officer will enter into the process of evaluation. Images, beliefs, ideological bias, wishful thinking, natural optimism or pessimism, confidence or the lack of it, all play a part in determining which facts the observer will notice and which he will ignore, the weight he will attach to the selected facts, the pattern into which he will fit them, and the conclusions which he will draw from them. It is arguable, therefore, that the discipline of psychology is as relevant to the study of surprise as that of military history. Both its commonplaces and some of its more tentative ideas should help us to understand the roots of surprise.

Images, which may be defined as the organized representation of an object in an individual's cognitive system, play an all-important part in the process of making intelligence evaluations. Actors do not respond to the "objective" facts—whatever that may mean—but to their individual perceptions of reality. Any assessment they make of a situation is bound to be affected in varying degrees by a series of personal images they hold, notably the image of the antagonistic out-group they are combatting. In their deliberations they will tend to convey to each other oversimplified images embodied in long-standing ideological stereotypes instead of seeking to apply to the issue at hand varied concepts derived from an open-minded inquiry. Images serve as screens for the selective reception of new messages, and they often control the perception and interpretation of those messages which are not completely ignored, rejected or suppressed.[18] The tendency of observers to interpret incoming information in a way that confirms their images sometimes extends to the actual suppression of messages that are difficult to reconcile with these images.

The same is true of preconceived ideas and theories. Evidence from both history and psychology overwhelmingly supports the view that people tend to fit incoming information into their existing views and theories. That intelligence analysts should hold theories is in a way inevitable, because without them the mass of information with which they have to cope would become unmanageable. But they can easily become the prisoners of their theories, with those theories acting as blinkers to exclude any evidence that does not conform to their ex-

[17] Y. Harkabi, *Nuclear War and Nuclear Peace* (Jerusalem: Israel Program for Scientific Translations 1966), 51.
[18] Karl W. Deutsch and Richard L. Merritt, "Effects of Events on National and International Images," in Herbert C. Kelman, ed. *International Behavior* (New York: Holt, Rinehart & Winston 1966), 134.

pectations. Moreover, in conditions of uncertainty they would tend to cling to their theories all the more tenaciously; the greater the ambiguity of the information, the greater the impact of the established theory.[19] As Robert Jervis has pointed out, this phenomenon has several implications. First, since actors tend to perceive what they expect to perceive, a signal in accord with the receiver's expectations can be quite subtle and still have the desired impact. Indeed, such signals may be perceived even if they are not sent. The other side of this coin is that signals that go against the established view will have to be much clearer to be noticed, let alone understood.[20] Another way of putting it would be to say that the recognition threshold for signals which confirm the theory of the receiver is lower than that for signals which contradict it; and the higher the degree of confidence with which the receiver holds the theory, the higher this recognition threshold will be for signals which contradict it.[21]

The Agranat Report provides a convincing analysis of the barriers to clear perception which stem from too rigid an adherence to a theory. Although the evidence about the enemy's intentions was ambiguous, General Zeira did not seek additional evidence from any of the other sources at his disposal, but accepted as valid the interpretation that did not conflict with "the conception." Lt. Col. Bendman's confidence in "the conception" was such that he perceived but did not grasp the import of the signals that were in conflict with it. Lt. Col. Geddaliah went to the length of silencing an evaluation that called the validity of the Intelligence Branch's theories into question, instead of re-examining these theories in the light of the dissenting evaluation and the facts on which it was based.

It needs to be pointed out, however, that theories held by intelligence services, particularly theories that command such an impressive consensus as "the conception," do not spring out of thin air. They are the product of the collective wisdom, knowledge, and experience of the organization. Usually such a theory has stood the test of time and proved its usefulness. "The conception" is a case in point: it appeared to have been vindicated only a few months before it was so spectacularly demolished. In May 1973, the Israeli Intelligence assessed correctly the

[19] Floyd Allport, *Theories of Perception and the Concept of Structure* (New York: Wiley 1955), 382.

[20] Jervis, *The Logic of Images in International Relations* (Princeton: Princeton University Press 1970), 132.

[21] Ole Holsti, "Cognitive Dynamics and Images of the Enemy," in David Finlay, Ole Holsti, and Richard Fagen, *Enemies in Politics* (Chicago: Rand McNally 1967), 29-33, 70.

limited repercussions of the Lebanese crisis which threatened to spread, Balkan-fashion—despite Syria's conspicuously threatening maneuvers, Egypt's war-like preparations, and President Sadat's speeches announcing the "phase of total confrontation." This success enhanced confidence in the established theories and predisposed the intelligence community to make the same evaluation in September-October. At the same time the Chief of Staff, who had not accepted the Intelligence Branch's estimate of the low probability of war in May and ordered a partial mobilization which was severely criticized at the time as costly and unnecessary, had become less willing to enter into another contest with the intelligence professionals.

Since the adoption of theories as a basic working tool has both its uses and its pitfalls, a question arises as to the proper role of theory and the dilemma of how "open" to be to new information. It would probably be true to say (although it cannot be quantified), that intelligence officers are apt to err by being too wedded to a theory and too closed to new information, as opposed to being too willing to alter their theories. This assumption, if correct, would suggest the need to employ theories more tentatively and experimentally than the senior Israeli officers did, and to make a conscious effort to re-assess them constantly and critically in the light of fresh, incongruent data.

Much of the improper use of evidence made in connection with the employment of theories can be traced to the hypothesis advanced by Jervis, that "actors tend to overlook the fact that evidence consistent with their theories may also be consistent with other views."[22] It is indeed common to find people claiming as proof of their theories data that could also support alternative views. To avoid falling into this trap, it is advisable to work with more than one hypothesis so that the evidence that comes to hand will not confirm the preferred hypothesis simply because it is already believed to be correct.

Just as actors tend to perceive what they expect, so—in conditions of great uncertainty—they will tend to predict that events they want to happen actually will happen, i.e., overrate the probability of a desirable event.[23] That is the well-known phenomenon usually referred to as wishful thinking. The greater the actor's preference for a particular outcome, the greater the perceptual distortion. Ambiguous signals will be misinterpreted even when an actor realizes that they are signals rather than noise. The vast literature on the impact of affect on perception

---

[22] Robert Jervis, "Hypotheses on Misperception," *World Politics*, xx (April 1968), 478.
[23] J. David Singer, "Inter-State Influence: A Formal Model," *American Political Science Review*, LVII (June 1963), 426.

cannot be treated here, but a distinction should be made between wishful thinking and probabilistic thinking, with which it is often confused. Wishful thinking permits the observer's individual wishes and aspirations to suppress uncomfortable evidence. Probabilistic thinking proceeds to predict an adversary's behavior in conditions of uncertainty on the basis of patterns of expectations formed by past experience. The Agranat Report contains evidence that would suggest that the line of demarcation between the two is so fine that a slide from probabilistic to wishful thinking can take place without the actor actually being aware of it.

The fact that intelligence evaluation is not the product of individual effort but of a group has important consequences; group dynamics necessarily come into play. The maintenance of group solidarity is usually a central value, with the effect of predisposing members of the group to focus on one interpretation or option, to stress consensus, and to underplay their personal doubts and differences. Group dynamics act not only as a potent instrument for conformity but also lead to overlooking dangers and taking a more optimistic view of a situation than individual members would take in isolation from one another.[24] The individual who wishes to gain the confidence of his colleagues finds it expedient to place himself within the secure framework of shared norms and assumptions even if in fact his position differs fundamentally and not marginally from the collective wisdom. And there is substantial evidence that stress reduces tolerance by members of a group for those who deviate from its norms.[25] Lt. Col. Geddaliah's erasure of the discordant notes struck by Lt. Siman-Tov is an extreme example of such intolerance.

Pressures for conformity operate not only within a professional group but also between professional groups. This at any rate is suggested by the interactions between Israeli and American intelligence agencies in the period preceding the October War. As early as May 1973, the CIA and the State Department's own Intelligence and Research Bureau gave the American Government a generalized warning that war in the Middle East was coming "soon."[26] This estimate was supported by

[24] For a detailed and interesting discussion of the nature and impact of group dynamics on foreign policy decisions and fiascoes, see Irving L. Janis, *Victims of Groupthink* (Boston: Houghton Mifflin 1972).
[25] Leonard Weller, "The Effects of Anxiety on Cohesiveness and Rejection," *Human Relations*, xvi (1963); Lewis Coser, *The Functions of Social Conflict* (New York: Free Press 1956), 103-4.
[26] Insight Team of the Sunday Times (fn. 13), 71. See chap. 6 for further details on contacts between American and Israeli intelligence prior to the outbreak of the war.

information which came in during September from America's excellent monitoring system with its highly secret base in southern Iran and its SAMOS satellites. The Israeli Intelligence was alerted, but dismissed the forecasts of war; in turn, the American intelligence community's evaluation of the extensive indicators that had been picked up was heavily influenced by the opinion of its Israeli opposite number. Dr. Kissinger has revealed that "We asked our intelligence, as well as the Israeli intelligence, on three separate occasions during the week prior to the outbreak of hostilities to give us their assessment of what might happen. There was the unanimous view that hostilities were unlikely to the point of there being no chance of it happening." Questioned about why U.S. intelligence miscalculated the intentions of the Arabs, he added: "Surprise would never be possible if there were no misjudgments of intentions. And obviously the people most concerned, with the reputation of the best intelligence service in the area, were also surprised, and they have the principal problem of answering the question which you put to me."[27] Given the early misgivings of the American intelligence community and the quantity and accuracy of information it possessed which pointed toward war, the acceptance of its Israeli counterpart's estimate of Arab intentions may be regarded as a remote form of group dynamics making for conformity.

In addition to enumerating specific barriers to clear perception which have their roots in human nature, an analysis of the causes of a national failure to anticipate an attack must examine the impact on the intelligence community of the society it serves. The political attitudes of intelligence professionals, like those of all other groups, are affected by the prevailing social and political climate. In post-1967 Israel, complacency was the hallmark of this climate. The ruling elite in its actions and utterances propagated the view that the status quo had overwhelming advantages for Israel and that it could be perpetuated indefinitely. After the crushing defeat which the Arabs had suffered in the Six-Day War, it was thought that they would not risk an attempt to change the status quo by force; the superpowers were divided and the international community could not impose a settlement. The Israeli Government could, therefore, sit tight on the secure borders won in the war and wait until the Arabs were prepared to make peace on its terms. Following the ending of the war of attrition in August 1970, the beginning of the cease-fire, the death of Nasser, the civil war in Jordan, and ultimately the expulsion of the Soviet advisers from Egypt, a feeling developed in the Israeli defense establishment that a considerable

[27] *Jerusalem Post Weekly,* 16 October 1973.

period of time would elapse before the Arabs would be ready for war—
a feeling that was strengthened by a lack of belief in Arab ability to
wage a coordinated modern war. As a former Director of Israeli Military Intelligence observed, "a mixture of conceit and complacency
tended to color the evaluation of future developments in the area."[28]
Moshe Dayan was particularly instrumental in propagating the view
that war was not to be expected for another ten years. On July 23,
1973, he said in an interview with *Time Magazine* that over the next
decade Israel's borders would freeze along the then prevailing lines.
On August 10, 1973, he told the IDF's Staff College that "the balance
of forces is so much in our favor that it neutralizes the Arab considerations and motives for the immediate renewal of hostilities."[29] This political outlook had its counterpart in "the conception" of the army high
command.[30] The intelligence professionals were not unaffected by this
national consensus which in their case was translated into a very significant reduction in the perception of external threat. Threat perception may be said to equal estimated capability multiplied by the estimated intent.[31] Had the intelligence chiefs not been influenced by the
current views about the Arabs' intent, they might have given more
weight in their evaluations to the demonstrable increase in Arab
capabilities which preceded the outbreak of war.

The most difficult and most crucial element in the intelligence craft
lies in estimating the enemy's *intentions*. It is one thing to estimate
the enemy's capability on the basis of hard evidence that is relatively
easy to obtain (although even here there is room for error). It is quite
another to adduce the enemy's intention, which is notoriously elusive,
on the basis of evidence that is necessarily incomplete and frequently
unreliable. And knowledge about capability does not supply an infallible clue to intentions. As George F. Kennan has observed:

> In everything that can be statistically expressed—expressed, that is, in
> such a way as not to imply any judgment on our motivation—I believe
> the Soviet Government to be excellently informed about us. I am sure
> that their information on the development of our economies, on the

[28] Major-General Chaim Herzog, *The War of Atonement* (London: Weidenfeld and
Nicolson 1975), 41.

[29] Quoted in *Al-Hamishmar*, 14 September 1975.

[30] The army's mood of overconfidence is illustrated by the following comment of an
eminent Israeli general: "Israel's principal enemy in the 1970s is the Soviet Union. . . .
The Arabs are merely secondly enemies who harass Israel in the area of relatively
minor defence problems." Uzi Narkiss, "The Israel Defence Forces in the 1970s,"
Brassey's Annual, 1972, 91.

[31] J. David Singer, "Threat Perception and the Armament-Tension Dilemma," *Journal
of Conflict Resolution*, II (March 1958), 94; D. G. Pruitt, "Definition of the Situation
as a Determinant of International Action," in Kelman (fn. 18), 400.

state of our military preparations, on our scientific progress, etc., is absolutely first-rate. But when it comes to the analysis of our motives, to the things that make our life tick as it does, I think this whole great system of intelligence-gathering breaks down seriously . . . because . . . the Communist Party has made it impossible for the people who collect the factual information to accompany that information with any really objective analysis of the nature of Western society. The Soviet diplomatic representative or journalist abroad has no choice but to cast his analytic report in terms of Marxist-Leninist ideology. . . . In this way the Soviet leaders find themselves committed to a badly distorted image of the outside world. . . . Thus . . . they apprehend everything about us but the main things. They view us as one might view the inhabitants of another planet, through a very powerful telescope. Everything is visible; one sees in the greatest detail the strange beings of that other world going about their daily business . . . but what one does not see is the motivation that drives them on their various pursuits. This remains concealed; and thus the entire image, clear and intelligible in detail, becomes incomprehensible in its totality.[32]

The difficulty in understanding the enemy's intentions despite the wealth of information about his capabilities is not, of course, confined to the Soviet Union or to countries with closed political systems; nor is Marxist-Leninist ideology the only distorting prism that stands in the way of an objective analysis. The problem is a universal one. Any national intelligence estimate must be very largely concerned with the enemy's intentions. In assessing these intentions, intelligence analysts employ models, theories, or conceptions that are the functional equivalents of an ideology. These too make certain assumptions about the target country. The commonest mistake is to make an uncritical interpretation of the enemy's intentions by applying a theory or model based on assumptions that may be correct about oneself, but are not necessarily correct about the enemy. Failure of an intelligence prediction can be reduced, in the last analysis, to a misunderstanding of the foreigners' conceptual framework—i.e., a failure to understand properly the assumptions or interpretations of the situation upon which foreigners base their decisions.[33]

After isolating the use of inapplicable assumptions within the framework of a theory or model or set of expectations as the critical source of faulty intelligence evaluations, one can advance the analysis further with the help of concepts that have been developed by Klaus Knorr.

[32] Kennan, *Russia, The Atom and the West* (New York: Harper and Row 1957), 21-22.
[33] Benno Wasserman, "The Failure of Intelligence Prediction," *Political Studies,* VIII (June 1962), 166-67.

Knorr distinguishes between "technical surprise" and what, for lack of a less inelegant term, he calls "behavioral surprise." A "technical surprise" is one not incompatible with the prevalent set of expectations. It occurs because the opponent was successful in concealing a particular capability or in keeping a particular course of action shrouded in secrecy. "Behavioral surprise" occurs when the opponent's behavior is incompatible with our set of expectations. There are three causes of "behavioral surprise."[34]

First, the opponent may act irrationally.[35] Highly irrational behavior is, of course, extremely difficult to predict since it may follow directions that make no sense to the rational mind.

Second, the regnant set of expectations may be unrealistic because intelligence bodies are incompetent or strongly under the influence of "national images" of the outside world that are based more on myth or wishfulness than on objective perception.

Third, an opponent's pattern of behavior may change as a result of changes in leadership or various other important conditions; a set of expectations, though realistic in the past, may not register this change quickly and correctly. The set, in other words, may be out of date.

The surprise caused by the Arab attack of October 6, 1973, was a "behavioral surprise"; its origins can be traced to the third cause enumerated by Knorr. "The conception" (which is taken here as the equivalent of what Knorr calls "a set of expectations") was probably valid for the immediate aftermath of the 1967 war. The basic assumption on which it was based, namely, that Egypt would not begin a war unless she could neutralize Israel's air superiority, was probably a correct assumption. But the situation changed radically when Egypt advanced a network of SAM missiles to the Suez Canal as the cease-fire came into force in August 1970.[36] This meant that Egypt's forces could operate on the East side of the Canal under an air umbrella, obviating the necessity to strike directly at Israeli airfields. On the political front, President Sadat's increasingly untenable position prompted him to decide to unfreeze the status quo by initiating hostilities against Israel with the hope that this would spark off intervention by the superpowers who would impose a settlement on Israel. Far from

---

[34] Klaus Knorr, "Failures in National Intelligence Estimates: The Case of the Cuban Missiles," *World Politics*, xvi (April 1964), 462-63.

[35] For a discussion of the question of rationality see Sidney Verba, "Assumptions of Rationality and Non-Rationality in Models of the International System," *World Politics*, xiv (October 1961).

[36] The former Israeli Air Force Chief, Major-General Ezer Weizmann, had argued at the time that if the missile-sites were not destroyed, Egypt would be able to launch a war at any time that suited her.

being an irrational and suicidal act, as Israeli doctrine assumed, Sadat's decision under the conditions of 1973 represented a subtle combination of force and diplomacy at the service of rational and limited aims. In other words, "the conception" was simply out of date, having failed to register the important strategic and political changes that took place between 1970 and 1973. It is true that the crisis of May 1973 appeared to vindicate "the conception," but that crisis was not part of Sadat's plan of action; the fact that war on this occasion was not precipitated by the Arabs did not in itself make the basic assumption of "the conception" any less inapplicable.

IV. The Institutional Roots of Surprise

Bureaucratic organizations are not immune to the limitations and weaknesses that lead individuals to make faulty evaluations, or to the tendency to interpret incoming information in such a way as to confirm established theories and to eschew any radical criticism and the jettisoning of cherished ideas. Indeed, institutional factors may increase the human and psychological propensity for error. A circular process may evolve: a newspaper or a diplomatic service adopts a policy, sends out men to report on facts pertinent to it, selects the reports and men that seem favorable to the policy, and then receives from these men further reports more favorable, and so on.[37] Individuals who work for an organization that displays a strong commitment to a policy or outlook will be tempted to send back news which shows that they are on the right side, and to ignore or underplay uncomfortable facts so as not to risk unpopularity with their colleagues and superiors.[38] In these circumstances it is not always possible to distinguish between what is seen and what is regarded as expedient to see.

Once a circular process becomes entrenched in an organization, reality testing is no longer possible. As Kenneth Boulding has noted,

[37] Otto Klineberg, *The Human Dimension of International Relations* (New York: Holt, Rinehart & Winston 1965), 93-94.
[38] David Halberstam, in his study of the American decision-making process on Vietnam, provides numerous examples of this circular process. General Paul Harkins, the American Commander in Saigon, was told by his superior, General Maxwell Taylor, to be optimistic in his reporting on the war. Harkins had his ear tuned not to the field but to Washington and the Pentagon. He reported just what his military superiors wanted to hear: everything was right on schedule, the war was being won, and victory was in the offing. When President Kennedy, increasingly doubtful about the progress of the war, sent a list of specific questions, Harkins sent a reply that was based on the debate in Washington rather than on the situation in Saigon. The reason was that he had received a cable from General Taylor outlining which of Kennedy's questions Harkins should answer, and precisely how to answer them. *The Best and the Brightest* (London: Pan Books 1974), 247, 331-32.

"All organizations operate as information filters which filter out and condense information as it passes up through the hierarchy, so that by the time that information reaches the powerful decision-makers it has been filtered many, many times. If the powerful decision-makers are able to control their information receivers they are likely to find themselves in an essentially schizophrenic position in which reality testing, in the sense of change of images through disappointment, becomes almost impossible."[39]

Any attempt to deal with this danger must focus on the relationship between the policy makers and the intelligence professionals—a relationship that is of the utmost importance in determining the efficiency with which the national intelligence machinery functions. If the intelligence service is dominated by a group of powerful decision makers, it will become the prisoner of these decision makers' images, dogmas, and preconceptions. Instead of challenging these dogmas and correcting these images when they clash with its objective findings, the intelligence service will be no more than a rubber stamp of these preconceptions. Instead of examining carefully every piece of evidence according to the basic rule that nothing is permanent, it will be reduced to the subservient role of seeking supportive material for already established policy. The failure of the Israeli national intelligence estimates in October 1973 vividly illustrates the disastrous consequences that excessive domination by the political leadership can have. The Intelligence chiefs were not insulated from political pressures, but were in regular contact with the Cabinet and particularly close contact with the *ad hoc* forum in which a small caucus of powerful ministers took all the important decisions on national security—a forum known as "Golda's Kitchen Cabinet."[40] The Intelligence chiefs were consequently ill-disposed toward challenging the dogmas and firmly held beliefs of these politicians who dominated the war-peace establishment. Consciously or unconsciously, they slanted information, analyses, and estimates so they would fit the established policy.

This case points to the need to free the intelligence service of a country from control by the political authority, and lends weight to the

[39] Kenneth E. Boulding, "Social Systems Analysis and the Study of International Conflict," in Alastair Buchan, ed., *Problems of Modern Strategy* (London: Chatto and Windus 1970), 85.

[40] For a more detailed discussion of the deficiencies in the Israeli decision-making system, see Shlaim, "Crisis Decision-Making in Israel: The Lessons of October 1973," *The International Yearbook of Foreign Policy Analysis*, I (London: Croom-Helm 1975). For a comprehensive treatment, see Michael Brecher, *The Foreign Policy System of Israel: Setting, Images, Process* (London: Oxford University Press 1972).

frequently made but rarely heeded pleas of intelligence chiefs for autonomy and independence. Their argument was clearly summed up by Allen Dulles, the former Director of the CIA, when he wrote that "for the proper judging of the situation in any foreign country it is important that information should be processed by an agency whose duty it is to weigh facts, and to draw conclusions from those facts, without having either the facts or the conclusions warped by the inevitable and even proper prejudices of the men whose duty it is to determine policy and who, having once determined a policy, are too likely to be blind to any facts which might tend to prove the policy to be faulty."[41]

To argue for a clear demarcation of functions between intelligence producers and intelligence consumers is not to argue for the absence of any contact between them, or for mutual ignorance. Good intelligence management must begin with a decision of what needs to be known; such a decision cannot be taken independently of the preoccupations of those in charge of policy. Intelligence is not knowledge for its own sake but for the practical purpose of taking action. To perform its task, the intelligence organization needs to know the issues and problems with which the policy makers are concerned. Without this knowledge, the organization's fact gathering will be diffuse and unsystematic, and the policy makers will not be provided with the relevant information on which to base their policy. An intelligence community is more alert and efficient, and the information it supplies is more accurate and timely, when it is given the right political guidelines and is asked the right questions. This guidance must be provided while at the same time the organization's political independence and administrative autonomy must be fully respected.

If the first danger is that intelligence will be dominated by policy, the second is that it will be too remote and sealed off from the world in which policy is planned to serve a useful purpose. No hard and fast formula for governing the relationship between intelligence producers and consumers can be provided. It is a question of striking the right balance in each particular national context. Only a general rule can be suggested; it has been stated by Sherman Kent: "Intelligence must be close enough to policy, plans and operations to have the

---

[41] U.S., Congress, Senate, "Memorandum Respecting Section 202 (Central Intelligence Agency) to the Bill to provide for a National Defense Establishment, submitted by Allen W. Dulles, April 25, 1947"; *Hearings Before the Committee on Armed Services*, 80th Cong., 1st sess., 525.

greatest amount of guidance, and must not be so close that it loses its objectivity and integrity of judgment."[42]

The Yom Kippur failure illustrates not only the danger of subordinating intelligence to a dominant and centralizing political authority, but also the danger of dependence by the political authorities on a single source of intelligence evaluation. There were at least four agencies that carried out intelligence work in Israel before the last war: Military Intelligence; the Central Institute for Intelligence and Security (*Hammosad*), which operates primarily in foreign countries; the *Shin Beth*, which is responsible for internal security, counterespionage, and combatting Arab terrorist activity; and the research department in the Foreign Office, a small unit which deals with political intelligence. But Military Intelligence had a monopoly over national intelligence evaluation. It alone provided the civilian authorities with evaluations on such vital questions as: Would war break out? Where would the attack come from and when? What would be the scale of the war and what is the capability of the attacker? In its analysis of the failure to anticipate the Arab attack, the Agranat Commission stressed the decisive influence exercised by the Director of Military Intelligence and his research department on the assessment of information about enemy plans and intentions. That influence stemmed from their position as the sole center in the country where military intelligence was evaluated, as well as from their position as the guardians of all the intelligence information received from the other intelligence-gathering agencies. It was they who processed all the data, gave an evaluation of them as intelligence, and decided what should be distributed, in what form, and to which body.[43]

The observation that Israel's leadership held excessive sway over Military Intelligence and that it was unduly dependent on that agency

[42] Kent, *Strategic Intelligence for American World Policy* (Connecticut: Archon Books 1965), 180. The relationship between intelligence producers and consumers is also discussed in Roger Hilsman, *Strategic Intelligence and National Decisions* (Glencoe, Ill.: Free Press 1956); Washington Platt, *Strategic Intelligence Production* (New York: Praeger 1957); Harry H. Ransom, *Central Intelligence and National Security* (Cambridge: Harvard University Press 1958); Wasserman (fn. 33); William J. Barnds, "Intelligence and Foreign Policy: Dilemmas for a Democracy," *Foreign Affairs*, XLVII (January 1969); and the following review articles: Willmoore Kendall, "The Function of Intelligence," *World Politics*, I (July 1949); Allan Evans, "Intelligence and Policy Formation," *World Politics*, XII (October 1959); and Harry H. Ransom, "Strategic Intelligence and Foreign Policy," *World Politics*, XXVII (October 1974).

[43] This monopoly of evaluation by one agency has no parallel in the intelligence systems of the major Western powers or even in the leading Communist powers. For a concise description of the intelligence systems of the United States, Britain, France, the Soviet Union, and China, see *Encyclopaedia Britannica*, 15th ed., s.v. "Intelligence and Counter-intelligence," by Harry H. Ransom.

may sound paradoxical, but it is nonetheless an accurate description of the situation which prevailed from 1967 on. In contrast to David Ben-Gurion who, in his capacity as Defense Minister, always insisted on reporting personally to the Cabinet on military and intelligence matters, Moshe Dayan regularly invited high-ranking officers to brief the Cabinet, a practice that tended to blur the line of division between ministerial and military responsibility. Moreover, in the absence of any machinery or staff work at Cabinet level capable of providing an evaluation of its own or checking the evaluations presented by the Director of Military Intelligence, the acceptance of the latter's estimates was a foregone conclusion.[44] The influence of Military Intelligence was also enhanced by the absence of an orderly procedure for the formulation of national intelligence estimates, a situation that left it to the professionals to tell the politicians what they thought the politicians should know, instead of the usual practice whereby the politicians tell the professionals what information they need to have. In her account, Golda Meir, the Israeli Prime Minister at the time of the October War, suggests that it would have been unreasonable for mere civilians like herself to challenge the confidently presented estimates of the military experts,[45] but this is surely an anomalous position for the head of a democratic state to find herself in. The responsibility for permitting such a situation ever to emerge rests entirely with the politicians and not with the military.

The monopolistic structure of the intelligence community was largely responsible for the narrow, dogmatic, and monolithic thinking that characterized the estimates presented to the policy makers. It precluded the wider vision, depth, and subtlety which the confrontation of independent evaluations and opposing points of view can produce. It is true that the task of the policy makers of deciding on a course of action will not be made easier if they are presented with a full and variegated intelligence picture that contains multiple appraisals of the situation, but the chances of a fatal error will also be reduced. It is a matter for speculation whether the Israeli Government would have decided on general mobilization before it actually did, or would have sanctioned a preemptive strike, if it had been given two evaluations one of which predicted an Arab attack. In any case, its awareness of the dangers confronting the state would undoubtedly have been more acute. If this sounds like wisdom after the event, it is pertinent to recall that the case for greater pluralism in the organization of intelli-

[44] Herzog (fn. 28), 40-41.
[45] Golda Meir, My Life (London: Weidenfeld and Nicolson 1975), 357-59.

gence was argued as early as 1963 in a report commissioned by Prime Minister David Ben-Gurion.[46] The authors of this report felt that "it is vital that the Prime Minister should have estimates on political security and other matters which are balanced and based on varying points of view and do not necessarily come from a single channel." To this end they recommended the reinforcement of the research department of the Foreign Ministry so as to enable it to present independent evaluations, and the appointment of a special intelligence adviser to the Prime Minister with extensive powers of surveillance and investigation.

The Agranat Commission of Inquiry deprecated the failure to implement these recommendations and noted that, far from being strengthened, the research department of the Foreign Ministry had actually been whittled down. In its conclusion it stated that "the state of affairs which existed until the Yom Kippur War—in which independent evaluation of political strategic, operational and tactical intelligence was prevented through centralization in one organization and under one authority on the one hand and the absence of a special intelligence adviser to the Prime Minister on the other—was an important factor in the inability to get a full intelligence picture in all its dimensions."

A sound and comprehensive intelligence evaluation is the product not merely of accurate technical data but also of background political knowledge that helps the analyst to lift the signals out of the confusion of noise. He can then interpret them in the broad perspective of regional and international mutations that have a bearing on the adversary's perceptions and calculations. Evaluations by politically informed amateurs can consequently display more sensitivity than those of military intelligence professionals. Roberta Wohlstetter, for example, in comparing the top-secret intelligence evaluations of Japanese intentions before the attack at Pearl Harbor with estimates in the contemporary press, was struck by the relative soundness of the less privileged judgments, and concluded that general knowledgeability in the world of international affairs and close observation of overt developments are the most useful ingredients in making such estimates.[47] This conclusion is supported by the fact that Israeli observers who stood outside the centers of decision and had no access to classified information estimated enemy intentions correctly. As early as May 1973, Gabriel Cohen,

[46] The report, drawn up by Y. Yadin and Z. Sharef, was presented to Ben-Gurion's successor, Levi Eshkol, on July 31, 1963.

[47] Wohlstetter, *Pearl Harbor: Warning and Decision* (Stanford: Stanford University Press 1962), 169.

a historian and political scientist, and Yair Evron, an analyst of the country's international relations, were predicting a war in the autumn.[48] The fact that the national intelligence estimates were wholly the work of Military Intelligence—as the Foreign Ministry had long since given up trying to put its own view of things across—is, therefore, particularly significant. Nadav Safran was surely right in suggesting that "the faulty evaluation may have had a structural rather than an accidental basis—the absence of appropriate or sufficient representation of political analysts in the intelligence-evaluation apparatus concerned."[49]

V. Safeguards

In the course of the discussion of the causes of failure in national intelligence estimates, I have made some observations on methods of minimizing errors. In the present section I will explore more fully some safeguards whose implementation would tend to reduce the frequency of error.

The view that adherence to rigid conceptions or theories is an important cause of misperception is underlined not only by the case study here examined but also by a number of other historical examples. The Stennis Report attributed the intelligence failure that preceded the Cuban missile crisis of 1962 primarily to the "predisposition of the intelligence community to the philosophical conviction that it would be incompatible with Soviet policy to introduce strategic missiles into Cuba."[50] It was a preconception about Soviet behavior that, according to the Report, did not permit "the indications to the contrary" to be "given proper weight."[51] Similarly, the North Korean aggression in 1950 took the Truman Administration by surprise because its estimates had been based on the theory that the Soviet Union would not engage in overt forms of aggression, involving the risk of a general war, for several years to come.[52] Once a preconception or a theory about the enemy's behavior becomes settled, it is very hard to shake until it is too late because of the stubborn human attachment to old beliefs and the equally stubborn resistance to new material that will upset them.

Yet, the making of assumptions and the employment of hypotheses

---

[48] *Times Literary Supplement*, 12 July 1974.

[49] Safran, "The War and the Future of the Arab-Israeli Conflict," *Foreign Affairs*, Vol. 52 (January 1974), 216.

[50] U.S., Congress, Senate, *Investigation of the Preparedness Program*, Interim Report on the Cuban Military Buildup by the Preparedness Investigating Sub-Committee, Committee on Armed Services, 88th Cong., 1st sess. (Washington 1963), 2.

[51] *Ibid.*, 11.

[52] Alexander L. George, "American Policy-making and the North Korean Aggression," *World Politics*, vii (January 1955).

and theories is not a luxury for the intelligence analyst, but a necessity. They are required for selecting and interpreting facts, estimating the likelihood of various contingencies, and clarifying the range of responses available. Pure empiricism is bound to be defeated by the sheer volume and disparity of the evidence. Even if we assume that such a thing as the "unbiased and objective presentation of the facts as they are" were possible, the result would be an encyclopedic accumulation of details, which is not the same as analytic and predictive intelligence geared to the exigencies of sound decision making.

The first safeguard, therefore, is to make the assumptions about the adversary's behavior, and the theories and predictions which are based on them, as explicit as possible. The more explicit they are, the greater will be the likelihood that once they cannot be squared with fresh pieces of evidence, that fact will not go unnoticed, and that a revision of the assumptions will take place rather than an unconscious suppression or distortion of the evidence. The greater the analyst's awareness of the subjective factors which are liable to distort his vision and color his interpretation of the facts he perceives, the better placed he will be to reduce the impact of these subjective factors. Herein lies the advantage of not leaving images, beliefs, preconceptions, and assumptions about the adversary at the level of the subconscious, but bringing them to the surface and reflecting continually and critically upon them.

A second safeguard for intelligence analysts is to examine their attitudes for consistent or supporting beliefs that are not logically linked. These may be examples of psycho-logic.[53] An evaluation in which elements that are not logically connected support the same conclusion should arouse their suspicion. The chances are considerable in such a case that the reasons for a particular evaluation are related to psychology and not to the substance of the evidence.

Third, those who have the primary responsibility for predicting the adversary's plans can only avoid surprise if they constantly revise and update their assumptions and expectations. They must take account of any appreciable change in the military balance of power or a barely perceived change by the enemy of his own capability, as well as political changes in the region and outside which might lead to a shift in the policy of the target country. To this end the gathering of accurate information about political and military developments will not be sufficient. The significance of these developments must be appraised from the vantage point of the other side. Different political cultures

[53] Jervis (fn. 22), 462-63.

produce different hierarchies of values and preferences; to ignore these would court failure because the enemy's considerations may be set in a totally different psychological and political context, leading to decisions quite different from those one would normally expect. Pearl Harbor is an outstanding example of strategic surprise caused by inability to imagine the enemy's psychology and to examine the policy alternatives from the enemy leaders' point of view, as well as the attribution to the enemy of inapplicable standards of logic. As Roberta Wohlstetter has put it, "our own standards, as we have observed them in military and State Department documents, reckoned the risks to the Japanese as too large, and therefore not likely to be taken. They were too large but they were going to be taken. And we missed this apparently illogical connection because we did not include in our reckoning any consideration of the alternative of 'gradual exhaustion' and the danger of encirclement and defeat without having struck a single blow."[54]

A fourth safeguard consists of applying several hypotheses or theories to the data available so as to avoid becoming the slave of the dominant theory. To quote Wohlstetter again: "A willingness to play with material from different angles and in the context of unpopular as well as popular hypotheses is an essential ingredient of a good detective, whether the end is the solution of a crime or an intelligence estimate. This sort of flexibility is probably not good for one's reputation as a sound estimator, since one index to sound judgment is agreement with the hypothesis on which current departmental policy is based. But intelligence is always confronted with this choice: whether to be popular or alert."[55] This fourth safeguard is most difficult to implement in the context of a small and homogeneous group of analysts. A large and diverse group would facilitate multiple advocacy and the probing of information from different perspectives so as to guard against the fallibility of all the individuals involved.

Joseph de Rivera has taken this idea a step further in his suggestion that the organization itself must institutionalize a procedure that forces officials to try to disprove their own beliefs by setting up a routine procedure for systematically searching out information that goes against their view of reality. A group should always be assigned to make the opposition case. This group should:

1. Be composed of competent men who are identified with the office, department or administration, and who have the trust and confidence of the leadership and access to it.

[54] Wohlstetter (fn. 47), 354.
[55] *Ibid.*, 302.

2. Be given a fair opportunity to periodically present their case.
3. Be given feedback so that they are assured that the leadership understands the case they present.
4. Be given the authority to ask the leadership to state the assumptions on which the policy is based.[56]

It is important, says de Rivera, for such a group to continue its work *after* the organization is committed to a particular view or policy. Usually, after a decision has been made, all persons are expected to pull together. Those who cannot commit themselves generally leave the organization. Consequently, once it is committed to a policy, the organization becomes even blinder than a single individual would be.

The suggested group would:

1. Continue to actively look for information contrary to the office, department or administration's ideas and plans.
2. Serve as a repository for such negative information.
3. Insure that filters in the information system were properly placed, that adequate feedback was being given, and that unpopular views were being heard at high levels.
4. Make out the most reasonable case possible for alternative beliefs and plans.
5. Be ready to suggest new policy if and when changing conditions substantiate the opposition's viewpoint.[57]

An alternative method of institutionalizing the process of confrontation of ideas and the consideration of unpopular hypotheses and evaluations is the appointment of a devil's advocate within the intelligence apparatus.

The idea of a devil's advocate is of course not a new one, but success in implementing it appears to be inversely related to the frequency with which it is advanced. That this should be so is not surprising because decision makers as a rule have little time or inclination to engage in protracted debates; the whole emphasis is on reaching swift and unequivocal decisions. Moreover, they tend to surround themselves with advisers who share their views; the capacity to tolerate, let alone benefit from, protracted dissent is the exception rather than the rule. Joachim von Ribbentrop, for example, Hitler's Foreign Minister, had an unshakeable conviction that Great Britain would never go to war against Germany. All members of his staff received a warning: "If it came to my notice that anyone had expressed a contrary opinion I would kill him myself in his office, and take responsibility before the

[56] De Rivera, *The Psychological Dimension of Foreign Policy* (Columbus, Ohio: Charles E. Merrill Publishing Co. 1968), 61-62.
[57] *Ibid.*, 62.

Führer for it."[58] As Ole Holsti, who quotes this example, wryly remarks, even a less extreme warning would no doubt have sufficed to protect von Ribbentrop from the discomforts of dissent. Individuals who "rock the boat," particularly if they do this persistently and vociferously, are neither welcomed nor rewarded in government, and rarely stay there for very long. For devil's advocates to work effectively, therefore, it is not enough to appoint them and then to tolerate with ill-disguised impatience their questioning of agreed assumptions and their challenges to the conventional wisdom. Unless they are actively supported and encouraged by the people at the top, and are seen to be supported and valued, their views will carry little weight, and their colleagues will conclude that the only safe position is that which confirms what the leaders are presumed to prefer.[59]

VI. Institutional Reform

Unlike the preceding discussion of safeguards, any discussion of the institutional reforms for the improvement of intelligence estimates must focus directly on the specific national organization, because reforms that might be useful in one country may well be unnecessary or even counterproductive in another. The Agranat Commission made five proposals for reform which are worth quoting at length; although they refer directly to the Israeli intelligence services, the ideas that underlie them are of general interest and, with appropriate modifications, are applicable elsewhere.

The first proposal calls for the appointment of a special intelligence adviser to the Prime Minister, backed by a small but highly able team that would permit the Prime Minister and the Cabinet to undertake an independent political-strategic intelligence evaluation by drawing on all the material gathered by the various agencies. At the same time, such an adviser must not isolate the heads of the intelligence community from direct contact with the Prime Minister.[60]

[58] Gilles Perrault, *The Secrets of D-Day* (Boston: Little, Brown 1965), 171.
[59] Holsti, *Crisis Escalation War* (Montreal: McGill-Queen's University Press 1972), 208-12.
[60] If this last point is not observed, the danger is that the Prime Minister will not be acquainted with the conflicting views that exist within the intelligence apparatus, and become excessively dependent for information and evaluations on his adviser—with all the dangers that this involves. Walt Rostow's use of his power as Special Assistant to President Johnson to screen the flow of information and keep dissident experts away from the White House—which had the desired effect of preventing the President from becoming fully aware of the extent of disaffection with the Vietnam War and the grounds for it—suggests that the existence of a powerful adviser with strong views of his own can defeat the objective of making the Prime Minister better informed. See Janis (fn. 24), 124.

Second, the Commission urges the reinforcement of the research department of the Foreign Ministry by organizing it as an independent body within the Ministry, and by allocating to it the appropriate staff from the point of view of quantity and quality. One of the principal tasks of the department would be the carrying out of independent political-strategic evaluations especially on the basis of the special material at its disposal.

Third, the Commission recommends the fixing of clear rules to govern the distribution and feedback of the raw intelligence material by the gathering agencies to the various research setups and to the Defense Minister and Prime Minister. The significance of this apparently humdrum suggestion can be gauged from the statement of the Chief of Staff at the time of the October War that Military Intelligence received some four hundred messages during the run-up to the war; some of them, referring explicitly to the impending outbreak of war, were not shown to him. If he had seen them, they might have led him to adopt a different estimate regarding the likelihood of war.[61]

A fourth recommendation calls for the substantive restructuring of Military Intelligence to ensure that the center of gravity of research and evaluation will be in the sphere of military, strategic, operational, and tactical intelligence; to give encouragement and adequate opportunity for expression to the different and conflicting views held by members of the research department in the evaluations that are transmitted by Military Intelligence to other bodies; to secure the appointment of suitable personnel, including civilians, to the research department, with optimal channels of promotion and rotation within and outside the department; and to maintain continuous surveillance of intelligence estimates.

Finally, the Commission suggests that an evaluation unit should be set up inside the Central Institute of Intelligence and Security (*Hammosad*) to evaluate the information collected by the Institute.

All these proposals are evidently inspired by the desire to introduce and maintain a degree of pluralism in the structures and processes for reaching national intelligence estimates. But it should be pointed out that pluralism is not an infallible remedy for the problems that beset the Israeli or any other intelligence system. Pluralism has its own drawbacks and attendant dangers, such as the diversion of resources, the duplication of effort, and the growth of friction and jealousies be-

[61] Lieutenant-General (Res.) David Elazar, "Memorandum on the Report of the Commission of Inquiry on the Yom Kippur War," unpub. memo, Tel-Aviv, May 1975.

tween the various branches of the intelligence community. The structural complexity of American wartime intelligence, for example, accentuated the blocks to communication which exist in any large organization, and the intraservice and interservice rivalries that were occasionally carried to the point of withholding secret information. That complexity was among the important causes of the failure to decode properly the mass of signals announcing the impending Japanese attack. Once again, there are no simple solutions. A *modus vivendi* must be sought which minimizes the dangers inherent in rigid homogeneity and centralization on the one hand and excessive fragmentation and pluralism on the other.

An idea that has attracted considerable attention in the course of the intense public debate on the war-peace establishment in Israel which was unleashed by "the breakdown" is that of setting up a National Security Council. Many alternative versions have been advanced, but the central idea is that the task of making national intelligence estimates would be entrusted to an independent body consisting of official and outside experts on defense, intelligence, economics, foreign policy, and international relations. This body would not replace any of the existing intelligence agencies, but would draw on all their raw data and processed information. It would have no decision-making power of its own, but would be required to present to the Cabinet a comprehensive and variegated intelligence picture, giving alternative evaluations of the situation and outlining the main options available. The Council should intimate to the Cabinet which evaluation commands the strongest support and which option it favors for dealing with a situation. Under no circumstances should it confine itself to a single evaluation and recommendation. Such a system would appear to combine many of the ingredients of a healthy intelligence organization—such as flexibility, the adequate representation of political analysts, the careful consideration of information from a variety of angles, and the ability to promote openness and caution on the part of policy makers by not presenting them with a shallow and one-dimensional evaluation based on the lowest common denominator of agreement. At the same time, it would avoid the consequences of subordination to the preconceptions of the political leaders and the monopoly of the army over national security matters, which played such a decisive role in the failure of October 1973. It is noteworthy that a number of defense experts and former Directors of Military Intelligence have put the weight of their authority behind the proposal for a National Security Council.[62]

VII. Conclusions

The search for an infallible system of advance warning of an attack is the search for a will-o'-the-wisp. Neither history nor reflection, and certainly nothing that has been said in the present article, warrant the foolhardy conclusion that strategic surprise can be completely eliminated. National intelligence estimates are concerned both with enemy capability and enemy intentions; however accurate the estimate of the former may be, estimates of the latter will always contain an irreducible element of uncertainty.

It is one of the great paradoxes of intelligence that its greatest successes may be indistinguishable from failures because of the intrinsic uncertainty of strategic warning. This uncertainty is the consequence of the fact that predictions of an enemy's intention to attack must be based on moves that are almost invariably reversible at short notice. Had, for example, American intelligence issued an unambiguous warning of a Japanese attack, leading to an alert at Pearl Harbor, the Japanese, implementing their plans for just such a contingency, would have called off the attack. Since the success of the intelligence services would have been expressed in the falsification of its predictions, it would have been difficult to rebutt charges of a misconstrual of Japanese intentions.

In view of the intrinsic uncertainty of strategic warning, to base strategic doctrine on the assumption that in the event of an attack adequate warning would be forthcoming is to gamble with the nation's security. By making such an unwarranted assumption an explicit and fundamental element of their strategic doctrine, Israeli planners took an incalculable risk. The heavy price that had to be paid for this faulty premise should serve to discourage similar complacency in other countries.

Superficially, the view that technological advance has the effect of making a surprise attack less likely appears attractive. War preparations on any significant scale can be easily detected with the aid of aerial photography, electronic surveillance, sophisticated cryptographic devices, and the like. But a closer examination points to the conclusion that technological advance has shifted the balance of advantage in

---

[62] Major-General (Res.) Matityahu Peled, "The Management of Defense," *Ma'ariv*, 28 December 1973; Amos Perlmutter, "The Politicization of the Army and the Militarization of Politics," *Ma'ariv*, 19 April 1974; and former intelligence chiefs Meir Amit and Aharon Yariv in interviews in *Ma'ariv*, 5 April 1974 and 26 April 1974 respectively.

favor of the surprise attacker. In the first place, the monumental increase in the information collected has not been matched by advances in processing this information. The problem of how to cope with the enormous quantity of incoming information is a major difficulty facing many intelligence services. Second, the perfection of means of communication and consequent centralization of the decision-making power has greatly reduced the number of people in the know and thereby the number of potential leaks. Third, the significance of advances in decoding is reduced by the widespread use of "one-time" codes based on random numbers. As Dr. Martin van Creveld has pointed out, these developments lead, on balance, to the conclusion that, in spite of the perfection of means of surveillance and detection, surprise attacks are now more feasible than ever.[63]

The only safe assumption on which to base national defense, therefore, is that there will not be an advance warning of the enemy's plan to attack. If such a warning is in fact provided by the intelligence services, it should be exploited fully. But it must not be counted upon. Unless national defense plans are designed to operate without advance warning, unless they take into account the feasibility of a surprise attack, there is no cause for confidence that setbacks similar to those sustained by Israel in October 1973, or even greater ones, will not occur again.

The history of the Israeli intelligence failure, like the Pearl Harbor episode with which it has so many affinities, provides a number of insights into the phenomenon of strategic surprise, and considerably enriches our understanding of the circumstances in which failures of perception and evaluation are liable to occur. The point of the foregoing discussion of the psychological and structural roots of surprise has been to identify the basic factors that are conducive to faulty perception and evaluation, based on the belief that a recognition and an understanding of these factors can help to reduce their incidence and their impact. No claim of infallibility can be made in respect of the safeguards and institutional reforms that have been suggested. No amount of technical and administrative ingenuity can completely eradicate the human propensity to be caught by surprise. The most that I would assert is that if an intelligence service is soundly organized and its members observe the necessary precautions, the frequency of failure will be reduced and overall performance will be improved.

In the process of increasing the accuracy and reliability of national

[63] See the section on "Intelligence" in Walter Laqueur, *Confrontation: The Middle East War and World Politics* (London: Abacus 1974), 111-12.

intelligence estimates by means of a more profound understanding of the human and organizational dynamics involved, historians and social scientists have a role to play which has not been adequately recognized. Both the mistrust of "intellectuals" and the secrecy in which intelligence work is usually shrouded constitute a barrier to a fruitful interplay between conceptual enterprise and empirical research. The objective of this interplay should be the gradual development of a theory of intelligence that will link together a large body of fragmentary insights, testable hypotheses, and partial theories produced by cumulative research and that is of more than purely academic interest. In the absence of theory, as Klaus Knorr has argued, "we have no criteria (indicators!) for judging whether intelligence work . . . is done well or badly or for specifying ways of improving it."[64]

The investigation of historical case studies is of distinct utility in the building up of a theory of intelligence. The interests of the social scientist, however, do lead him to attempt to go beyond the narrative of events and the enumeration of relevant factors into a search for explanatory theory that transcends the bounds of the particular case. The fact that most theorists have a low opinion of case studies may be simply the result of the atheoretical character of the case studies made in the past. What we need is a new kind of case study which tests hypotheses, refines propositions, and in general seeks to advance conceptual enquiry with the aid of empirical research.

Ultimately, a well-substantiated theory of intelligence should have valuable practical applications to the formulation of effective prescriptions. As Kurt Lewin pointed out, "Nothing is so practical as a good theory." But until we have a good theory—one that is supported by systematic research and case studies—we must recognize that any prescriptions we draw up are tentative inferences based on what little we know about when and why intelligence failures occur.

[64] Knorr, *Foreign Intelligence and the Social Sciences*, Center of International Studies, Princeton University, Research Monograph No. 17 (Princeton 1964), 47.

ANALYSIS, WAR, AND DECISION:
Why Intelligence Failures Are Inevitable

By RICHARD K. BETTS*

MILITARY disasters befall some states, no matter how informed their leaders are, because their capabilities are deficient. Weakness, not choice, is their primary problem. Powerful nations are not immune to calamity either, because their leaders may misperceive threats or miscalculate responses. Information, understanding, and judgment are a larger part of the strategic challenge for countries such as the United States. Optimal decisions in defense policy therefore depend on the use of strategic intelligence: the acquisition, analysis, and *appreciation* of relevant data. In the best-known cases of intelligence failure, the most crucial mistakes have seldom been made by collectors of raw information, occasionally by professionals who produce finished analyses, but most often by the decision makers who consume the products of intelligence services. Policy premises constrict perception, and administrative workloads constrain reflection. Intelligence failure is political and psychological more often than organizational.

Observers who see notorious intelligence failures as egregious often infer that disasters can be avoided by perfecting norms and procedures for analysis and argumentation. This belief is illusory. Intelligence can be improved marginally, but not radically, by altering the analytic system. The illusion is also dangerous if it abets overconfidence that systemic reforms will increase the predictability of threats. The use of intelligence depends less on the bureaucracy than on the intellects and inclinations of the authorities above it. To clarify the tangled relationship of analysis and policy, this essay explores conceptual approaches to intelligence failure, differentiation of intelligence problems, insurmountable obstacles to accurate assessment, and limitations of solutions proposed by critics.

I. Approaches to Theory

Case studies of intelligence failures abound, yet scholars lament the lack of a theory of intelligence.[1] It is more accurate to say that we lack

* For corrections or comments whose usefulness exceeded my ability to accommodate them within space limitations, thanks are due to Bruce Blair, Thomas Blau, Michael Handel, Robert Jervis, Klaus Knorr, H. R. Trevor-Roper, and members of the staff of the National Foreign Assessment Center.
[1] For example, Klaus Knorr, "Failures in National Intelligence Estimates: The Case

a positive or normative theory of intelligence. Negative or descriptive theory—the empirical understanding of how intelligence systems make mistakes—is well developed. The distinction is significant because there is little evidence that either scholars or practitioners have succeeded in translating such knowledge into reforms that measurably reduce failure. Development of a normative theory of intelligence has been inhibited because the lessons of hindsight do not guarantee improvement in foresight, and hypothetical solutions to failure only occasionally produce improvement in practice. The problem of intelligence failure can be conceptualized in three overlapping ways. The first is the most reassuring; the second is the most common; and the third is the most important.

1. *Failure in perspective.* There is an axiom that a pessimist sees a glass of water as half empty and an optimist sees it as half full. In this sense, the estimative system is a glass half full. Mistakes can happen in any activity. Particular failures are accorded disproportionate significance if they are considered in isolation rather than in terms of the general ratio of failures to successes; the record of success is less striking because observers tend not to notice disasters that do not happen. Any academician who used a model that predicted outcomes correctly in four out of five cases would be happy; intelligence analysts must use models of their own and should not be blamed for missing occasionally. One problem with this benign view is that there are no clear indicators of what the ratio of failure to success in intelligence is, or whether many successes on minor issues should be reassuring in the face of a smaller number of failures on more critical problems.[2] In the thermonuclear age, just *one* mistake could have apocalyptic consequences.

2. *Pathologies of communication.* The most frequently noted sources of breakdowns in intelligence lie in the process of amassing timely

---

of the Cuban Missiles," *World Politics,* xvi (April 1964), 455, 465-66; Harry Howe Ransom, "Strategic Intelligence and Foreign Policy," *World Politics,* xxvii (October 1974), 145.

2 "As that ancient retiree from the Research Department of the British Foreign Office reputedly said, after serving from 1903–50: 'Year after year the worriers and fretters would come to me with awful predictions of the outbreak of war. I denied it each time. I was only wrong twice.' " Thomas L. Hughes, *The Fate of Facts in a World of Men—Foreign Policy and Intelligence-Making* (New York: Foreign Policy Association, Headline Series No. 233, December 1976), 48. Paradoxically, "successes may be indistinguishable from failures." If analysts predict war and the attacker cancels his plans because surprise has been lost, "success of the intelligence services would have been expressed in the falsification of its predictions," which would discredit the analysis. Avi Shlaim, "Failures in National Intelligence Estimates: The Case of the Yom Kippur War," *World Politics,* xxviii (April 1976), 378.

data, communicating them to decision makers, and impressing the latter with the validity or relevance of the information. This view of the problem leaves room for optimism because it implies that procedural curatives can eliminate the dynamics of error. For this reason, official post mortems of intelligence blunders inevitably produce recommendations for reorganization and changes in operating norms.

3. *Paradoxes of perception*. Most pessimistic is the view that the roots of failure lie in unresolvable trade-offs and dilemmas. Curing some pathologies with organizational reforms often creates new pathologies or resurrects old ones;[3] perfecting intelligence production does not necessarily lead to perfecting intelligence consumption; making warning systems more sensitive reduces the risk of surprise, but increases the number of false alarms, which in turn reduces sensitivity; the principles of optimal analytic procedure are in many respects incompatible with the imperatives of the decision process; avoiding intelligence failure requires the elimination of strategic preconceptions, but leaders cannot operate purposefully without some preconceptions. In devising measures to improve the intelligence process, policy makers are damned if they do and damned if they don't.

It is useful to disaggregate the problem of strategic intelligence failures in order to elicit clues about which paradoxes and pathologies are pervasive and therefore most in need of attention. The crucial problems of linkage between analysis and strategic decision can be subsumed under the following categories:

1. *Attack warning*. The problem in this area is timely prediction of an enemy's immediate intentions, and the "selling" of such predictions to responsible authorities. Major insights into intelligence failure have emerged from catastrophic surprises: Pearl Harbor, the Nazi invasion of the U.S.S.R., the North Korean attack and Chinese intervention of 1950, and the 1973 war in the Middle East. Two salient phenomena characterize these cases. First, evidence of impending attack was available, but did not flow efficiently up the chain of command. Second, the fragmentary indicators of alarm that did reach decision makers were dismissed because they contradicted strategic estimates or assumptions. In several cases hesitancy in communication and disbelief on the part of leaders were reinforced by deceptive enemy maneuvers that cast doubt on the data.[4]

[3] Compare the prescriptions in Peter Szanton and Graham Allison, "Intelligence: Seizing the Opportunity," with George Carver's critique, both in *Foreign Policy*, No. 22 (Spring 1976).
[4] Roberta Wohlstetter, *Pearl Harbor: Warning and Decision* (Stanford: Stanford

2. *Operational evaluation.* In wartime, the essential problem lies in judging the results (and their significance) of interacting capabilities. Once hostilities are under way, informed decision making requires assessments of tactical effectiveness—"how we are doing"—in order to adapt strategy and options. In this dimension, the most interesting insights have come from Vietnam-era memoirs of low-level officials and from journalistic muckraking. Again there are two fundamental points. First, within the context of a glut of ambiguous data, intelligence officials linked to operational agencies (primarily military) tend to indulge a propensity for justifying service performance by issuing optimistic assessments, while analysts in autonomous non-operational units (primarily in the Central Intelligence Agency and the late Office of National Estimates) tend to produce more pessimistic evaluations. Second, in contrast to cases of attack warning, fragmentary tactical indicators of *success* tend to override more general and cautious strategic estimates. Confronted by differing analyses, a leader mortgaged to his policy tends to resent or dismiss the critical ones, even when they represent the majority view of the intelligence community, and to cling to the data that support continued commitment.[5] Lyndon Johnson railed at his Director of Central Intelligence (DCI) at a White House dinner: "Policy making is like milking a fat cow. You see the milk coming out, you press more and the milk bubbles and flows, and just as the bucket is full, the cow with its tail whips the bucket and all is

University Press 1962); Barton Whaley, *Codeword Barbarossa* (Cambridge: The M.I.T. Press 1973); Harvey De Weerd, "Strategic Surprise in the Korean War," *Orbis,* vi (Fall 1962); Alan Whiting, *China Crosses the Yalu* (New York: Macmillan 1960); James F. Schnabel, *Policy and Direction: The First Year* (Washington, D.C.: Department of the Army 1972), 61-65, 83-85, 274-78; Michael I. Handel, *Perception, Deception, and Surprise: The Case of the Yom Kippur War* (Jerusalem: Leonard Davis Institute of International Relations, Jerusalem Paper No. 19, 1976); Shlaim (fn. 2); Abraham Ben-Zvi, "Hindsight and Foresight: A Conceptual Framework for the Analysis of Surprise Attacks," *World Politics,* xxviii (April 1976); Amos Perlmutter, "Israel's Fourth War, October 1973: Political and Military Misperceptions," *Orbis,* xix (Summer 1975); U.S., Congress, House, Select Committee on Intelligence [hereafter cited as HSCI], *Hearings, U.S. Intelligence Agencies and Activities: The Performance of the Intelligence Community,* 94th Cong., 1st sess., 1975; Draft Report of the House Select Committee on Intelligence, published in *The Village Voice,* February 16, 1976, pp. 76-81.

[5] David Halberstam, *The Best and the Brightest* (New York: Random House 1972); Morris Blachman, "The Stupidity of Intelligence," in Charles Peters and Timothy J. Adams, eds., *Inside the System* (New York: Praeger 1970); Patrick J. McGarvey, "DIA: Intelligence to Please," in Morton Halperin and Arnold Kanter, eds., *Readings in American Foreign Policy: A Bureaucratic Perspective* (Boston: Little, Brown 1973); Chester Cooper, "The CIA and Decision-Making," *Foreign Affairs,* Vol. 50 (January 1972); Sam Adams, "Vietnam Cover-Up: Playing War With Numbers," *Harper's,* Vol. 251 (June 1975); Don Oberdorfer, *Tet!* (Garden City, N.Y.: Doubleday 1971). For a more detailed review, see Richard K. Betts, *Soldiers, Statesmen, and Cold War Crises* (Cambridge: Harvard University Press 1977), chap. 10.

spilled. That's what CIA does to policy making."[6] From the consensus-seeking politician, this was criticism; to a pure analyst, it would have been flattery. But it is the perspective of the former, not the latter, that is central in decision making.

3. *Defense planning*. The basic task in using intelligence to develop doctrines and forces for deterrence and defense is to estimate threats posed by adversaries, in terms of both capabilities and intentions, over a period of several years. Here the separability of intelligence and policy, analysis and advocacy, is least clear. In dealing with the issue of "how much is enough" for security, debates over data merge murkily into debates over options and programs. As in operational evaluation, the problem lies more in data mongering than in data collecting. To the extent that stark generalizations are possible, the basic points in this category are the reverse of those in the previous one.

First, the justification of a mission (in this case, preparedness for future contingencies as opposed to demonstration of current success on the battlefield) prompts pessimistic estimates by operational military analysts; autonomous analysts without budgetary axes to grind, but with biases similar to those prevalent in the intellectual community, tend toward less alarmed predictions.[7] Military intelligence inclines toward "worst-case" analysis in planning, and toward "best-case" analysis in operational evaluation. (Military intelligence officials such as Lieutenant General Daniel Graham were castigated by liberals for *under*estimating the Vietcong's strength in the 1960's but for *over*-estimating Soviet strength in the 1970's.) Air Force intelligence over-estimated Soviet air deployments in the "bomber gap" controversy of the 1950's, and CIA-dominated National Intelligence Estimates (NIE's) underestimated Soviet ICBM deployments throughout the 1960's (over-reacting, critics say, to the mistaken prediction of a "missile gap" in 1960).[8]

---

[6] Quoted in Henry Brandon, *The Retreat of American Power* (Garden City, N.Y.: Doubleday 1973), 103.

[7] Betts (fn. 5), 160-61, 192-95. On bias within CIA, see James Schlesinger's comments in U.S., Congress, Senate, Select Committee to Study Governmental Operations with Respect to Intelligence Activities [hereafter cited as SSCI], *Final Report, Foreign and Military Intelligence*, Book I, 94th Cong., 2d sess., 1976, 76-77.

[8] *Ibid.*, Book IV, 56-59; William T. Lee, *Understanding the Soviet Military Threat: How CIA Estimates Went Astray* (New York: National Strategy Information Center, Agenda Paper No. 6, 1977), 24-37; Albert Wohlstetter: "Is There a Strategic Arms Race?" *Foreign Policy*, No. 15 (Summer 1974); Wohlstetter, "Rivals, But No Race," *Foreign Policy*, No. 16 (Fall 1974); Wohlstetter, "Optimal Ways to Confuse Ourselves," *Foreign Policy*, No. 20 (Fall 1975). There are exceptions to this pattern of military and civilian bias: see *ibid.*, 185-88; Lieutenant General Daniel Graham, USA (Ret.), "The Intelligence Mythology of Washington," *Strategic Review*, IV (Summer

Second, in the context of peacetime, with competing domestic claims on resources, political leaders have a natural interest in at least partially rejecting military estimates and embracing those of other analysts who justify limiting allocations to defense programs. If the President had accepted pessimistic CIA operational evaluations in the mid-1960's, he might have withdrawn from Vietnam; if he had accepted pessimistic military analyses of the Soviet threat in the mid-1970's, he might have added massive increases to the defense budget.

Some chronic sources of error are unique to each of these three general categories of intelligence problems, and thus do not clearly suggest reforms that would be advisable across the board. To compensate for the danger in conventional attack warning, reliance on worst-case analysis might seem the safest rule, but in making estimates for defense planning, worst-case analysis would mandate severe and often unnecessary economic sacrifices. Removing checks on the influence of CIA analysts and "community" staffs[9] might seem justified by the record of operational evaluation in Vietnam, but would not be warranted by the record of estimates on Soviet ICBM deployments. It would be risky to alter the balance of power systematically among competing analytic components, giving the "better" analysts more status. Rather, decision makers should be encouraged to be more *and* less skeptical of certain agencies' estimates, *depending on the category of analysis involved.*

Some problems, however, cut across all three categories and offer a more general basis for considering changes in the system. But these general problems are not very susceptible to cure by formal changes in process, because it is usually impossible to disentangle intelligence failures from policy failures. Separation of intelligence and policy making has long been a normative concern of officials and theorists, who have seen both costs and benefits in minimizing the intimacy between intelligence professionals and operational authorities. But, although the personnel can be segregated, the functions cannot, unless intelligence is defined narrowly as the collection of data, and analytic responsibility is reserved to decision makers. Analysis and decision are interactive

---

1976), 61-62, 64; Victor Marchetti and John Marks, *The CIA and the Cult of Intelligence* (New York: Knopf 1974), 309.

[9] The U.S. intelligence *community* includes the CIA, Defense Intelligence Agency (DIA), National Security Agency, the intelligence branches of each military service, the State Department Bureau of Intelligence and Research, the intelligence units of the Treasury and Energy Departments, and the FBI. Before 1973, coordination for national estimates was done through the Office of National Estimates, and since then, through the National Intelligence Officers. The Intelligence Community Staff assists the Director of Central Intelligence in managing allocation of resources and reviewing the agencies' performance.

rather than sequential processes. By the narrower definition of intelligence, there have actually been few major failures. In most cases of mistakes in predicting attacks or in assessing operations, the inadequacy of critical data or their submergence in a viscous bureaucracy were at best the proximate causes of failure. The ultimate causes of error in most cases have been wishful thinking, cavalier disregard of professional analysts, and, above all, the premises and preconceptions of policy makers. Fewer fiascoes have occurred in the stages of acquisition and presentation of facts than in the stages of interpretation and response. Producers of intelligence have been culprits less often than consumers. Policy perspectives tend to constrain objectivity, and authorities often fail to use intelligence properly. As former State Department intelligence director Ray Cline testified, defending his analysts' performance in October 1973 and criticizing Secretary Kissinger for ignoring them:

> Unless something is totally conclusive, you must make an inconclusive report. . . . by the time you are sure it is always very close to the event. So I don't think the analysts did such a lousy job. What I think was the lousy job was in bosses not insisting on a new preparation at the end of that week [before war broke out]. . . . the reason the system wasn't working very well is that people were not asking it to work and not listening when it did work.[10]

II. Basic Barriers to Analytic Accuracy

Many constraints on the optimal processing of information lie in the structure of authority and the allocation of time and resources. Harold Wilensky argues persuasively that the intelligence function is hindered most by the structural characteristics of hierarchy, centralization, and specialization.[11] Yet it is precisely these characteristics that are the essence of any government. A related problem is the dominance of operational authorities over intelligence specialists, and the trade-off between objectivity and influence. Operators have more influence in decision making but are less capable of unbiased interpretation of evidence because they have a vested interest in the success of their operations; autonomous analysts are more disinterested and usually more objective, but lack influence. Senior generalists at the policy level often distrust or discount the judgments of analytic professionals and place more weight on reports from operational sources.[12] In response to this

---

[10] HSCI, *Hearings* (fn. 4), 656-57.
[11] Wilensky, *Organizational Intelligence* (New York: Basic Books 1967), 42-62, 126, 179.
[12] *Ibid., passim.* The counterpoint of Cooper (fn. 5) and McGarvey (fn. 5) presents a perfect illustration.

phenomenon, the suggestion has been made to *legislate* the requirement that decision makers consider analyses by the CIA's Intelligence Directorate (now the National Foreign Assessment Center) before establishing policy.[13] Such a requirement would offer no more than wishful formalism. Statutory fiat cannot force human beings to value one source above another. "No power has yet been found," DCI Richard Helms has testified, "to force Presidents of the United States to pay attention on a continuing basis to people and papers when confidence has been lost in the originator."[14] Moreover, principals tend to believe that they have a wider point of view than middle-level analysts and are better able to draw conclusions from raw data. That point of view underlies their fascination with current intelligence and their impatience with the reflective interpretations in "finished" intelligence.[15]

The dynamics of decision are also not conducive to analytic refinement. In a crisis, both data and policy outpace analysis, the ideal process of staffing and consultation falls behind the press of events, and careful estimates cannot be digested in time. As Winston Churchill recalled of the hectic days of spring 1940, "The Defence Committee of the War Cabinet sat almost every day to discuss the reports of the Military Co-ordination Committee and those of the Chiefs of Staff; and their conclusions or divergences were again referred to frequent Cabinets. All had to be explained or reexplained; and by the time this process was completed, the whole scene had often changed."[16] Where there is ample time for decision, on the other hand, the previously mentioned bureaucratic impediments gain momentum.[17] Just as information processing is frustrated by constraints on the time that harried principals can spend scrutinizing analytic papers, it is constrained by the funds that a government can spend. To which priorities

[13] Graham Allison and Peter Szanton, *Remaking Foreign Policy: The Organizational Connection* (New York: Basic Books 1976), 204.

[14] Quoted in SSCI, *Final Report* (fn. 7), I, 82.

[15] *Ibid.*, 267, 276; SSCI, *Staff Report, Covert Action in Chile 1963–1973*, 94th Cong., 1st sess., 1975, 48-49. The Senate Committee deplored the tendency of decision makers to focus on the latest raw data rather than on refined analyses, a practice that contributed to the intelligence failure in the 1974 Cyprus crisis. SSCI, *Final Report* (fn. 7), I, 443. But the failure in the October War was largely due to the *reverse* phenomenon: disregarding warning indicators because they contradicted finished intelligence that minimized the possibility of war. HSCI Draft Report (fn. 4), 78; Ben-Zvi (fn. 4), 386, 394; Perlmutter (fn. 4), 453.

[16] Churchill, *The Gathering Storm* (Boston: Houghton Mifflin 1948), 587-88.

[17] "Where the end is knowledge, as in the scientific community, time serves intelligence; where the end is something else—as in practically every organization but those devoted entirely to scholarship—time subverts intelligence, since in the long run, the central institutionalized structures and aims (the maintenance of authority, the accommodation of departmental rivalries, the service of established doctrine) will prevail." Wilensky (fn. 11), 77.

should scarce resources be allocated? The Schlesinger Report of 1971, which led to President Nixon's reorganization of U.S. intelligence, noted that criticisms of analytic products were often translated into demands for more extensive collection of data, but "Seldom does anyone ask if a further reduction in uncertainty, however small, is worth its cost."[18] Authorities do not always know, however, which issues require the greatest attention and which uncertainties harbor the fewest potential threats. Beyond the barriers that authority, organization, and scarcity pose to intelligence lie more fundamental and less remediable intellectual sources of error.

1. *Ambiguity of evidence.* Intelligence veterans have noted that "estimating is what you do when you do not know,"[19] but "it is inherent in a great many situations that after reading the estimate, you will still not know."[20] These observations highlight an obvious but most important obstacle to accuracy in analysis. It is the role of intelligence to extract certainty from uncertainty and to facilitate coherent decision in an incoherent environment. (In a certain and coherent environment there is less need for intelligence.) To the degree they reduce uncertainty by extrapolating from evidence riddled with ambiguities, analysts risk oversimplifying reality and desensitizing the consumers of intelligence to the dangers that lurk within the ambiguities; to the degree they do not resolve ambiguities, analysts risk being dismissed by annoyed consumers who see them as not having done their job. Uncertainty reflects inadequacy of data, which is usually assumed to mean *lack* of information. But ambiguity can also be aggravated by an *excess* of data. In attack warning, there is the problem of "noise" and deception; in operational evaluation (particularly in a war such as Vietnam), there is the problem of overload from the high volume of finished analyses, battlefield statistics, reports, bulletins, reconnaissance, and communications intercepts flowing upward through multiple channels at a rate exceeding the capacity of officials to absorb or scrutinize them judiciously. (From the CIA alone, the White House received current intelligence dailies, Weekly Reports, daily Intelligence Information Cables, occasional Special Reports and specific memoranda, and analyses from the CIA Vietnam Working Group.) Similarly, in estimates for defense planning, there is the problem of innumerable and endlessly refined indices of the strategic balance, and the

[18] Quoted in SSCI, *Final Report* (fn. 7), I, 274.
[19] Sherman Kent, "Estimates and Influence," *Foreign Service Journal*, XLVI (April 1969), 17.
[20] Hughes (fn. 2), 43.

dependence of assessments of capabilities on complex and variable as-sumptions about the doctrine, scenarios, and intentions that would govern their use.

Because it is the job of decision makers to decide, they cannot react to ambiguity by deferring judgment.[21] When the problem is an en-vironment that lacks clarity, an overload of conflicting data, and lack of time for rigorous assessment of sources and validity, ambiguity abets instinct and allows intuition to drive analysis. Intelligence can fail be-cause the data are too permissive for policy judgment rather than too constraining. When a welter of fragmentary evidence offers support to various interpretations, ambiguity is exploited by wishfulness. The greater the ambiguity, the greater the impact of preconceptions.[22] (This point should be distinguished from the theory of cognitive dissonance, which became popular with political scientists at the time it was being rejected by psychologists.)[23] There is some inverse relation between the importance of an assessment (when uncertainty is high) and the like-lihood that it will be accurate. Lyndon Johnson could reject pessimistic NIE's on Vietnam by inferring more optimistic conclusions from the reports that came through command channels on pacification, inter-diction, enemy casualties, and defections. Observers who assume Soviet malevolence focus on analyses of strategic forces that emphasize missile throw-weight and gross megatonnage (Soviet advantages); those who assume more benign Soviet intentions focus on analyses that emphasize missile accuracy and numbers of warheads (U.S. advantages). In as-sessing the naval balance, Secretary of Defense Rumsfeld focused on numbers of ships (Soviet lead), and Congressman Les Aspin, a critic of the Pentagon, focused on total tonnage (U.S. lead).

[21] "The textbooks agree, of course, that we should only believe reliable intelligence, and should never cease to be suspicious, but what is the use of such feeble maxims? They belong to that wisdom which for want of anything better scribblers of systems and compendia resort to when they run out of ideas." Carl von Clausewitz, *On War*, ed. and trans. by Michael Howard and Peter Paret (Princeton: Princeton University Press 1976), 117.

[22] Robert Jervis, *The Logic of Images in International Relations* (Princeton: Prince-ton University Press 1970), 132; Jervis, *Perception and Misperception in International Politics* (Princeton: Princeton University Press 1976), chap. 4; Floyd Allport, *Theories of Perception and the Concept of Structure*, cited in Shlaim (fn. 2), 358. Cognitive theory suggests that uncertainty provokes decision makers to separate rather than integrate their values, to deny that inconsistencies between values exist, and even to see contradictory values as mutually supportive. John Steinbruner, *The Cybernetic Theory of Decision* (Princeton: Princeton University Press 1974), 105-8.

[23] See William J. McGuire, "Selective Exposure: A Summing Up," in R. P. Abelson and others, eds., *Theories of Cognitive Consistency* (Chicago: Rand McNally 1968), and Irving L. Janis and Leon Mann, *Decision Making: A Psychological Analysis of Con-flict, Choice, and Commitment* (New York: Free Press 1977), 213-14.

2. *Ambivalence of judgment.* Where there are ambiguous and conflicting indicators (the context of most failures of intelligence), the imperatives of honesty and accuracy leave a careful analyst no alternative but ambivalence. There is usually *some* evidence to support *any* prediction. For instance, the CIA reported in June 1964 that a Chinese instructor (deemed not "particularly qualified to make this remark") had told troops in a course in guerrilla warfare, "We will have the atom bomb in a matter of months."[24] Several months later the Chinese did perform their first nuclear test. If the report had been the only evidence, should analysts have predicted the event? If they are not to make a leap of faith and ignore the data that do not mesh, analysts will issue estimates that waffle. In trying to elicit nuances of probability from the various possibilities not foreclosed by the data, cautious estimates may reduce ambivalence, but they may become Delphic or generalized to the point that they are not useful guides to decision. (A complaint I have heard in conversations with several U.S. officials is that many past estimates of Soviet objectives could substitute the name of any other great power in history—Imperial Rome, 16th-century Spain, Napoleonic France—and sound equally valid.) Hedging is the legitimate intellectual response to ambiguity, but it can be politically counterproductive, if the value of intelligence is to shock consumers out of wishfulness and cognitive insensitivity. A wishful decision maker can fasten onto that half of an ambivalent analysis that supports his predisposition.[25] A more objective official may escape this temptation, but may consider the estimate useless because it does not provide "the answer."

3. *Atrophy of reforms.* Disasters always stimulate organizational changes designed to avert the same failures in the future. In some cases these changes work. In many instances, however, the changes persist formally but erode substantively. Standard procedures are constant. Dramatic failures occur only intermittently. If the reforms in procedure they have provoked do not fulfill day-to-day organizational needs—or

24 CIA Intelligence Information Cable, "Remarks of the Chief of the Nanking Military Academy and Other Chinese Leaders on the Situation in South Vietnam," June 25, 1964, in Lyndon B. Johnson Library National Security Files, Vietnam Country File [hereafter cited as LBJL/NSF-VNCF], Vol. XII, item 55.

25 See for example, U.S., Department of Defense, *The Senator Gravel Edition: The Pentagon Papers* (Boston: Beacon Press 1971) [hereafter cited as *Pentagon Papers*], Vol. II, 99; Frances Fitzgerald, *Fire in the Lake* (Boston: Atlantic–Little, Brown 1972), 364; Special National Intelligence Estimate 53-64, "Chances for a Stable Government in South Vietnam," September 18, 1964, and McGeorge Bundy's covering letter to the President, in LBJL/NSF-VNCF, Vol. XIII, item 48.

if, as often happens, they complicate operations and strain the organization's resources—they fall into disuse or become token practices. After the postmortem of North Korea's downing of a U.S. EC-121 monitoring aircraft in 1969, there was, for several months, a great emphasis on risk assessments for intelligence collection missions. Generals and admirals personally oversaw the implementation of new procedures for making the assessments. Six months later, majors and captains were doing the checking. "Within a year the paperwork was spot-checked by a major and the entire community slid back to its old way of making a 'quick and dirty' rundown of the JCS criteria when sending in reconnaissance mission proposals."[26] The downing of the U-2 over the Soviet Union in 1960 and the capture of the intelligence ship *Pueblo* in 1968 had been due in part to the fact that the process of risk assessment for specific collection missions, primarily the responsibility of overworked middle-level officers, had become ponderous, sloppy, or ritualized.[27] At a higher level, a National Security Council Intelligence Committee was established in 1971 to improve responsiveness of intelligence staff to the needs of policy makers. But since the subcabinet-level consumers who made up the committee were pressed by other responsibilities, it lapsed in importance and was eventually abolished.[28] A comparable NSC committee that *did* serve tangible day-to-day needs of consumers to integrate intelligence and policy—the Verification Panel, which dealt with SALT—was more effective, but it was issue-oriented rather than designed to oversee the intelligence process itself. Organizational innovations will not improve the role of intelligence in policy unless they flow from the decision makers' views of their own needs and unless they provide frequent practical benefits.

None of these three barriers are accidents of structure or process. They are inherent in the nature of intelligence and the dynamics of work. As such, they constitute severe constraints on the efficacy of structural reform.

[26] Patrick J. McGarvey, *CIA: The Myth and the Madness* (Baltimore: Penguin 1974), 16.
[27] David Wise and Thomas B. Ross, *The U-2 Affair* (New York: Random House 1962), 56, 176, 180; Trevor Armbrister, *A Matter of Accountability* (New York: Coward-McCann 1970), 116-18, 141-45, 159, 187-95; U.S., Congress, House, Committee on Armed Services, *Report, Inquiry Into the U.S.S. Pueblo and EC-121 Plane Incidents* [hereafter cited as *Pueblo and EC-121 Report*], 91st Cong., 1st sess., 1969, 1622-24, 1650-51; U.S., Congress, House, Committee on Armed Services, *Hearings, Inquiry Into the U.S.S. Pueblo and EC-121 Plane Incidents* [hereafter cited as *Pueblo and EC-121 Hearings*], 91st Cong., 1st sess., 1969, 693-94, 699-700, 703-7, 714, 722, 734, 760, 773-78, 815-16.
[28] SSCI, *Final Report* (fn. 7), I, 61-62; HSCI Draft Report (fn. 4), 82.

III. THE ELUSIVENESS OF SOLUTIONS

If they do not atrophy, most solutions proposed to obviate intelligence dysfunctions have two edges: in reducing one vulnerability, they increase another. After the seizure of the *Pueblo*, the Defense Intelligence Agency (DIA) was reprimanded for misplacing a message that could have prevented the incident. The colonel responsible developed a careful microfilming operation in the message center to ensure a record of transmittal of cables to authorities in the Pentagon. Implementing this check, however, created a three-to-four hour delay—another potential source of failure—in getting cables to desk analysts whose job was to keep reporting current.[29] Thus, procedural solutions often constitute two steps forward and one step back; organizational fixes cannot transcend the basic barriers. The lessons of Pearl Harbor led to the establishment of a Watch Committee and National Indications Center in Washington. Although this solution eliminated a barrier in the communication system, it did not prevent the failure of timely alert to the Chinese intervention in Korea or the 1973 October War, because it did not eliminate the ambiguity barrier. (Since then, the Watch Committee has been replaced by the DCI's Strategic Warning Staff.) DIA was reorganized four times within its first ten years; yet it continued to leave most observers dissatisfied. The Agranat Commission's review of Israel's 1973 intelligence failure produced proposals for institutional reform that are striking because they amount to copying the American system of the same time—which had failed in exactly the same way as the Israeli system.[30] Reform is not hopeless, but hopes placed in solutions most often proposed—such as the following—should be circumscribed.

1. *Assume the worst.* A common reaction to traumatic surprise is the recommendation to cope with ambiguity and ambivalence by acting on the most threatening possible interpretations. If there is *any* evidence of threat, assume it is valid, even if the *apparent* weight of contrary indicators is greater. In retrospect, when the point of reference is an

---

[29] McGarvey (fn. 26), 16.

[30] Shlaim (fn. 2), 375-77. The proposals follow, with their U.S. analogues noted in parentheses: appoint a special intelligence adviser to the Prime Minister (Director of Central Intelligence) to supplement the military chief of intelligence; reinforce the Foreign Ministry's research department (Bureau of Intelligence and Research); more autonomy for non-military intelligence (CIA); amend rules for transmitting raw intelligence to research agencies, the Defense Minister, and the Prime Minister (routing of signals intelligence from the National Security Agency); restructure military intelligence (creation of DIA in 1961); establish a central evaluation unit (Office of National Estimates). On the U.S. intelligence failure in 1973, see the HSCI Draft Report (fn. 4), 78-79.

actual disaster attributable to a mistaken calculation of probabilities, this response is always justifiable, but it is impractical as a guide to standard procedure. Operationalizing worst-case analysis requires extraordinary expense; it risks being counterproductive if it is effective (by provoking enemy countermeasures or pre-emption), and it is likely to be ineffective because routinization will discredit it. Many Israeli observers deduced from the 1973 surprise that defense planning could only rest on the assumption that no attack warning will be available, and that precautionary mobilization should always be undertaken even when there is only dubious evidence of impending Arab action.[31] Similarly, American hawks argue that if the Soviets' intentions are uncertain, the only prudent course is to assume they are seeking the capability to win a nuclear war.

In either case, the norm of assuming the worst poses high financial costs. Frequent mobilizations strain the already taut Israeli economy. Moreover, countermobilization can defeat itself. Between 1971 and 1973, the Egyptians three times undertook exercises similar to those that led to the October attack; Israel mobilized in response, and nothing happened. It was the paradox of self-negating prophecy.[32] The Israeli Chief of Staff was sharply criticized for the unnecessary cost.[33] The danger of hypersensitivity appeared in 1977, when General Gur believed Sadat's offer to come to Jerusalem to be a camouflage for an Egyptian attack; he began Israeli maneuvers in the Sinai, which led Egypt to begin maneuvers of its own, heightening the risk of accidental war.[34] To estimate the requirements for deterrence and defense, worst-case assumptions present an open-ended criterion. The procurement of all the hedges possible for nuclear war-fighting—large increments in offensive forces, alert status, hardening of command-control-and-communications, active and passive defenses—would add billions to the U.S. defense budget. Moreover, prudent hedging in policy should be distinguished from net judgment of probabilities in estimates.[35]

Alternatively, precautionary escalation or procurement may act as self-fulfilling prophecies, either through a catalytic spiral of mobiliza-

[31] Shlaim (fn. 2), 379; Handel (fn. 4), 62-63.

[32] Ibid., 55.

[33] Shlaim (fn. 2), 358-59. The Israeli command estimated a higher probability of attack in May 1973 than it did in October. Having been proved wrong in May, Chief of Staff Elazar lost credibility in challenging intelligence officers, complained that he could no longer argue effectively against them, and consequently was unable to influence his colleagues when he was right. Personal communication from Michael Handel, November 15, 1977.

[34] Washington Post, November 27, 1977, p. A17.

[35] Raymond Garthoff, "On Estimating and Imputing Intentions," International Security, II (Winter 1978), 22.

tion (à la World War I) or an arms race that heightens tension, or doctrinal hedges that make the prospect of nuclear war more "thinkable." Since evidence for the "action-reaction" hypothesis of U.S. and Soviet nuclear policies is meager, and arms races can sometimes be stabilizing rather than dangerous, the last point is debatable. Still, a large unilateral increase in strategic forces by either the United States or the Soviet Union would, at the least, destroy the possibility of gains desired from SALT. A surprise attack or defeat make the costs of *under*estimates obvious and dramatic; the unnecessary defense costs due to *over*estimates can only be surmised, since the minimum needed for deterrence is uncertain. Worst-case analysis as a standard norm would also exacerbate the "cry wolf" syndrome. *Unambiguous* threat is not an intelligence problem; rather, the challenge lies in the response to fragmentary, contradictory, and dubious indicators. Most such indicators turn out to be false alarms. Analysts who reflexively warn of disaster are soon derided as hysterical. General William Westmoreland recalled that the warnings that had been issued before the 1968 Tet Offensive were ignored. U.S. headquarters in Saigon had each year predicted a winter-spring offensive, "and every year it had come off without any dire results. . . . Was not the new offensive to be more of the same?"[36]

Given the experience of intelligence professionals that most peacetime indicators of suspicious enemy activity lead to nothing, what Colonel who has the watch some night will risk "lighting up the board" in the White House simply on the basis of weak apprehension? How many staffers will risk waking a tired President, especially if they have done so before and found the action to be needless? How many distracting false alarms will an overworked President tolerate before he makes it clear that aides should exercise discretion in bothering him? Even if worst-case analysis is promulgated in principle, it will be compromised in practice. Routinization corrodes sensitivity. Every day that an expected threat does not materialize dulls receptivity to the reality of danger. As Roberta Wohlstetter wrote of pre-Pearl Harbor vigilance, "We are constantly confronted by the paradox of pessimistic realism of phrase coupled with loose optimism in practice."[37] Seeking to cover all contingencies, worst-case analysis loses focus and salience; by providing a theoretical guide for everything, it provides a practical guide for very little.

[36] Westmoreland, *A Soldier Reports* (Garden City, N.Y.: Doubleday 1976), 316. See the postmortem by the President's Foreign Intelligence Advisory Board, quoted in Herbert Y. Schandler, *The Unmaking of a President* (Princeton: Princeton University Press 1977), 70, 76, 79-80.
[37] Wohlstetter (fn. 4), 69.

2. *Multiple advocacy*. Blunders are often attributed to decision makers' inattention to unpopular viewpoints or to a lack of access to higher levels of authority by dissident analysts. To reduce the chances of such mistakes, Alexander George proposes institutionalizing a balanced, open, and managed process of debate, so that no relevant assessments will be submerged by unchallenged premises or the bureaucratic strength of opposing officials.[38] The goal is unobjectionable, and formalized multiple advocacy certainly would help, not hinder. But confidence that it will help systematically and substantially should be tentative. In a loose sense, there has usually been multiple advocacy in the U.S. policy process, but it has not prevented mistakes in deliberation or decision. Lyndon Johnson did not decide for limited bombing and gradual troop commitment in Vietnam in 1965 because he was not presented with extensive and vigorous counterarguments. He considered seriously (indeed solicited) Under Secretary of State George Ball's analysis, which drew on NIE's and lower-level officials' pessimistic assessments that any escalation would be a mistake. Johnson was also well aware of the arguments by DCI John McCone and the Air Force from the other extreme—that massive escalation in the air war was necessary because gradualism would be ineffective.[39] The President simply chose to accept the views of the middle-of-the-road opponents of *both* Ball and McCone.

To the extent that multiple advocacy works, and succeeds in maximizing the number of views promulgated and in supporting the argumentive resources of all contending analysts, it may simply highlight ambiguity rather than resolve it. In George's ideal situation, the process would winnow out unsubstantiated premises and assumptions about ends-means linkages. But in the context of data overload, uncertainty, and time constraints, multiple advocacy may in effect give all of the various viewpoints an aura of empirical respectability and allow a leader to choose whichever accords with his predisposition.[40] The

---

[38] George, "The Case for Multiple Advocacy in Making Foreign Policy," *American Political Science Review*, Vol. 66 (September 1972). My usage of the term multiple advocacy is looser than George's.

[39] Henry F. Graff, *The Tuesday Cabinet* (Englewood Cliffs, N.J.: Prentice-Hall 1970), 68-71; Leslie H. Gelb with Richard K. Betts, *The Irony of Vietnam: The System Worked* (Washington, D.C.: Brookings, forthcoming), chap. 4; Ball memorandum of October 5, 1964, reprinted as "Top Secret: The Prophecy the President Rejected," *Atlantic Monthly*, Vol. 230 (July 1972); McCone, memorandum of April 2, 1965, in LBJL/NSF-VNCF, Troop Decision folder, item 14b.

[40] Betts (fn. 5), 199-202; Schandler (fn. 36), 177. George (fn. 38), 759, stipulates that multiple advocacy requires "no major maldistribution" of power, influence, competence, information, analytic resources, and bargaining skills. But, except for resources and the right to representation, the foregoing are subjective factors that can rarely be equalized by design. If they are equalized, in the context of imperfect data and time

efficacy of multiple advocacy (which is greatest under conditions of manageable data and low ambiguity) may vary inversely with the potential for intelligence failure (which is greatest under conditions of confusing data and high uncertainty). The process could, of course, bring to the surface ambiguities where false certainty had prevailed; in these cases, it would be as valuable as George believes. But if multiple advocacy increases ambivalence and leaders do *not* indulge their instincts, it risks promoting conservatism or paralysis. Dean Acheson saw danger in presidential indecisiveness aggravated by debate: " 'I know your theory,' he grumbled to Neustadt. 'You think Presidents should be warned. You're wrong. Presidents should be given confidence.' "[41] Even Clausewitz argued that deference to intelligence can frustrate bold initiative and squander crucial opportunities. Critics charged Henry Kissinger with crippling U.S. intelligence by refusing to keep analysts informed of his intimate conversations with foreign leaders.[42] To do so, however, would have created the possibility of leaks and might thereby have crippled his diplomatic maneuvers. It is doubtful that Nixon's initiative to China could have survived prior debate, dissent, and analysis by the bureaucracy.

It is unclear that managed multiple advocacy would yield markedly greater benefits than the redundancy and competitiveness that have long existed. (At best it would perfect the "market" of ideas in the manner that John Stuart Mill believed made liberalism conducive to the emergence of truth.) The first major reorganization of the American intelligence community in 1946-1947 emphasized centralization in order to avert future Pearl Harbors caused by fragmentation of authority; the latest reorganization (Carter's 1977 extension of authority of the Director of Central Intelligence over military intelligence programs) emphasized centralization to improve efficiency and coherence. Yet decentralization has always persisted in the overlapping division of labor between several separate agencies. Recent theorists of bureaucracy see such duplication as beneficial because competition exposes disagreement and presents policy makers with a wider range of views. Redundancy inhibits consensus, impedes the herd instinct in the decision process, and

---

pressure, erroneous arguments as well as accurate ones will be reinforced. Non-expert principals have difficulty arbitrating intellectually between experts who disagree.

[41] Quoted in Steinbruner (fn. 22), 332.

[42] Clausewitz (fn. 21), 117-18; HSCI, *Hearings* (fn. 4), 634-36; William J. Barnds, "Intelligence and Policymaking in an Institutional Context," in U.S., Commission on the Organization of the Government for the Conduct of Foreign Policy [hereafter cited as Murphy Commission], *Appendices* (Washington, D.C.: G.P.O., June 1975), Vol. VII, 32.

thus reduces the likelihood of failure due to unchallenged premises or cognitive errors. To ensure that redundancy works in this way, critics oppose a process that yields coordinated estimates—negotiated to the least common denominator, and cleared by all agencies before they are passed to the principals. George's "custodian" of multiple advocacy could ensure that this does not happen. There are, of course, trade-off costs for redundancy. Maximization of competition limits specialization. In explaining the failure of intelligence to predict the 1974 coup in Portugal, William Hyland pointed out, "if each of the major analytical components stretch their resources over the same range, there is the risk that areas of less priority will be superficially covered."[43]

The problem with arguing that the principals themselves should scrutinize numerous contrasting estimates in their integrity is that they are constantly overwhelmed by administrative responsibilities and "action items"; they lack the time to read, ponder, and digest that large an amount of material. Most intelligence products, even NIE's, are never read by policy makers; at best, they are used by second-level staffers as background material for briefing their seniors.[44] Consumers want previously coordinated analyses in order to save time and effort. In this respect, the practical imperatives of day-to-day decision contradict the theoretical logic of ideal intelligence.

3. *Consolidation.* According to the logic of estimative redundancy, more analysis is better than less. Along this line of reasoning, Senate investigators noted critically that, as of fiscal year 1975, the U.S. intelligence community still allocated 72 percent of its budget for collection of information, 19 percent for processing technical data, and less than 9 percent for production of finished analyses. On the other hand, according to the logic of those who focus on the time constraints of leaders and the confusion that results from innumerable publications, quantity counteracts quality. The size of the CIA's intelligence directorate and the complexity of the production process "precluded close association between policymakers and analysts, between the intelligence product and policy informed by intelligence analysis."[45] For the sake of clarity and acuity, the intelligence bureaucracy should be streamlined.

[43] HSCI, *Hearings* (fn. 4), 778.
[44] SSCI, *Final Report* (fn. 7), IV, 57; Roger Hilsman, *Strategic Intelligence and National Decisions* (Glencoe, Ill.: Free Press 1956), 40. During brief service as just a low-level staff member of the National Security Council, even I never had time to read all the intelligence analyses relevant to my work.
[45] SSCI, *Final Report* (fn. 7), I, 344, and IV, 95 (emphasis deleted).

This view is consistent with the development of the Office of National Estimates (ONE), which was established in 1950 and designed to coordinate the contributions of the various organs in the intelligence community for the Director of Central Intelligence. DCI Walter Bedell Smith envisioned an operation of about a thousand people. But William L. Langer, the scholar Smith imported to organize ONE, wanted a tight group of excellent analysts and a personnel ceiling of fifty. Langer prevailed, and though the number of staff members in ONE crept upwards, it probably never exceeded a hundred in its two decades of existence.[46] Yet ONE could not eliminate the complexity of the intelligence process; it could only coordinate and integrate it for the production of National Intelligence Estimates. Other sources found conduits to decision makers (to Cabinet members through their own agencies, or to the President through the National Security Council). And some policy makers, though they might dislike the cacophony of multiple intelligence agencies, were suspicious of the consolidated NIE's, knowing that there was pressure to compromise views in order to gain agreement. Over time, the dynamics of bureaucracy also blunted the original objectives of ONE's founder. From a cosmopolitan elite corps, it evolved into an insular unit of senior careerists from the CIA. The National Intelligence Officer system that replaced ONE reduced the number of personnel responsible for coordinating NIE's, but has been criticized on other grounds such as greater vulnerability to departmental pressures. Bureaucratic realities have frustrated other attempts to consolidate the intelligence structure. The Defense Intelligence Agency was created in 1961 to unify Pentagon intelligence and reduce duplicative activities of the three service intelligence agencies, but these agencies regenerated themselves; in less than a decade they were larger than they had been before DIA's inception.[47]

The numerous attempts to simplify the organization of the analytic process thus have not solved the major problems. Either the streamlining exercises were short-lived, and bureaucratization crept back, or the changes had to be moderated to avoid the new dangers they entailed. Contraction is inconsistent with the desire to minimize failure by "plugging holes" in intelligence, since compensating for an inadequacy usually requires *adding* personnel and mechanisms; pruning the structure that contributes to procedural sluggishness or complexity may create lacunae in substantive coverage.

46 Ray S. Cline, *Secrets, Spies, and Scholars* (Washington, D.C.: Acropolis 1976), 20.
47 Gilbert W. Fitzhugh and others, *Report to the President and the Secretary of Defense on the Department of Defense, By the Blue Ribbon Defense Panel* (Washington, D.C.: G.P.O., July 1970), 45-46.

4. *Devil's advocacy.* Multiple advocacy ensures that all views held by individuals within the analytic system will be granted serious attention. Some views that should receive attention, however, may not be held by anyone within the system. Virtually no analysts in Israel or the United States believed the Arabs would be "foolish" enough to attack in 1973. Many observers have recommended institutionalizing dissent by assigning to someone the job of articulating apparently ridiculous interpretations to ensure that they are forced into consideration. Establishing an official devil's advocate would probably do no harm (although some argue that it may perversely facilitate consensus-building by domesticating true dissenters or providing the illusory comfort that all views have been carefully examined;[48] worse, it might delude decision makers into believing that *uncertainties* have been resolved). But in any case, the role is likely to atrophy into a superfluous or artificial ritual. By the definition of the job, the devil's advocate is likely to be dismissed by decision makers as a sophist who only makes an argument because he is supposed to, not because of its real merits. Institutionalizing devil's advocacy is likely to be perceived in practice as institutionalizing the "cry wolf" problem; "There are limits to the utility of a 'devil's advocate' who is not a true devil."[49] He becomes someone to be indulged and disregarded. Given its rather sterile definition, the role is not likely to be filled by a prestigious official (who will prefer more "genuine" responsibility); it will therefore be easier for policy makers to dismiss the arguments. In order to avert intelligence failures, an analyst is needed who tells decision makers what they don't want to hear, dampening the penchant for wishful thinking. But since it is the job of the devil's advocate to do this habitually, and since he is most often wrong (as would be inevitable, since otherwise the conventional wisdom would eventually change), he digs his own grave. If the role is routinized and thus ritualized, it loses impact; but if it is not routinized, there can be no assurance that it will be operating when it is needed.

Despite the last point, which is more important in attack warning than in operational evaluation or defense planning, there is a compromise that offers more realistic benefits: *ad hoc* utilization of "real devils." This selective or biased form of multiple advocacy may be achieved by periodically giving a platform within the intelligence process to minority views that can be argued more persuasively by prestigious analysts outside the bureaucracy. This is what the President's Foreign Intelli-

[48] Alexander George, "The Devil's Advocate: Uses and Limitations," Murphy Commission, *Appendices* (fn. 42), II, 84-85; Jervis, *Perception and Misperception* (fn. 22), 417.
[49] *Ibid.*, 416.

gence Advisory Board and DCI George Bush did in 1976 by commissioning the "Team B" critique of NIE's on Soviet strategic objectives and capabilities. Dissenters within the intelligence community who were skeptical of Soviet intentions were reinforced by a panel of sympathetic scholars, with a mandate to produce an analysis of their own.[50] This controversial exercise, even if it erred in many of its own ways (as dovish critics contend), had a major impact in promoting the re-examination of premises and methodology in U.S. strategic estimates. The problem with this option is that it depends on the political biases of the authorities who commission it. If it were balanced by a comparable "Team C" of analysts at the opposite extreme (more optimistic about Soviet intentions than the intelligence community consensus), the exercise would approach regular multiple advocacy, with the attendant limitations of that solution. Another variant would be intermittent designation of devil's advocates in periods of crisis, when the possibility of disaster is greater than usual. Since the role would then be fresh each time, rather than ritualized, the advocate might receive a more serious hearing. The problem here is that receptivity of decision makers to information that contradicts preconceptions varies inversely with their personal commitments, and commitments grow as crisis progresses.[51]

5. *Sanctions and incentives.* Some critics attribute intelligence failures to dishonest reporting or the intellectual mediocrity of analysts. Suggested remedies include threats of punishment for the former, and inducements to attract talent to replace the latter. Other critics emphasize that, will or ability aside, analytic integrity is often submerged by the policy makers' demands for intelligence that suits them; "the NIEs ought to be responsive to the evidence, not the policymaker."[52] Holders of this point of view would institutionalize the analysts' autonomy. Unobjectionable in principle (though if analysts are totally unresponsive to the consumer, he will ignore them), these implications cannot easily be operationalized without creating as many problems as they solve.

Self-serving operational evaluations from military sources, such as optimistic reports on progress in the field in Vietnam or pessimistic strategic estimates, might indeed be obviated if analysts in DIA, the service intelligence agencies, and command staffs were credibly threat-

[50] U.S., Congress, Senate, Select Committee on Intelligence, *Report, The National Intelligence Estimates A-B Team Episode Concerning Soviet Capability and Objectives,* 95th Cong., 2d sess., 1978; *New York Times,* December 26, 1976, pp. 1, 14; *Washington Post,* January 2, 1977, pp. A1, A4.

[51] George H. Poteat, "The Intelligence Gap: Hypotheses on the Process of Surprise," *International Studies Notes,* III (Fall 1976), 15.

[52] Cline (fn. 46), 140.

ened with sanctions (firing, nonpromotion, reprimand, or disgrace). Such threats theoretically could be a countervailing pressure to the career incentives analysts have to promote the interests of their services. But, except in the most egregious cases, it is difficult to apply such standards without arbitrariness and bias, given the problem of ambiguity; it simply encourages an alternative bias or greater ambivalence. Moreover, military professionals would be in an untenable position, pulled in opposite directions by two sets of authorities. To apply the sanctions, civil authorities would have to violate the most hallowed military canon by having civilian intelligence officials interfere in the chain of command. In view of these dilemmas, it is easier to rely on the limited effectiveness of redundancy or multiple advocacy to counteract biased estimates.

Critics concerned with attracting better talent into the analytic bureaucracy propose to raise salaries and to provide more high-ranking positions (supergrades) to which analysts can aspire. Yet American government salaries are already very high by academic standards. Those who attribute DIA's mediocrity (compared to CIA), to an insufficient allocation of supergrades and a consequent inability to retain equivalent personnel are also mistaken; as of 1975 the difference in the grade structures of DIA and CIA had been negligible.[53] And the fact that CIA analysts cannot rise to a supergrade position (GS-16 to 18) without becoming administrators is not convincing evidence that good analysts are underpaid; GS-15 salaries are higher than the maximum for most tenured professors.

Non-military analysts, or high-ranking soldiers with no promotions to look forward to, have fewer professional crosspressures to contend with than military intelligence officers. But an analyst's autonomy varies inversely with his influence, and hortatory injunctions to be steadfast and intellectually honest cannot ensure that he will be; they cannot transcend political realities or the idiosyncrasies of leaders. Richard Helms notes that "there is no way to insulate the DCI from unpopularity at the hands of Presidents or policymakers if he is making assessments which run counter to administrative policy. That is a built-in hazard of the job. Sensible Presidents understand this. On the other hand they are human too." Integrity untinged by political sensitivity courts professional suicide. If the analyst insists on perpetually

---

[53] SSCI, *Final Report* (fn. 7), I, 352. A valid criticism is that military personnel systems and promotion standards penalized intelligence officers, thus encouraging competent officers to avoid intelligence assignments. This situation was rectified in the service intelligence agencies by the early 1970's, but not within DIA. *Ibid.*; Betts (fn. 5), 196-97.

bearing bad news, he is likely to be beheaded. Helms himself succumbed to policy makers' pressures in compromising estimates of the MIRV capabilities of the Soviet SS-9 missile in 1969, and the prospects for Cambodia in 1970.[54] The same practical psychological constraints are reflected in an incident in which Chief of Naval Operations Elmo Zumwalt, who had already infuriated Nixon and Kissinger several times with his strategic estimates, was determined to present yet another unwelcome analysis; Secretary of Defense Schlesinger dissuaded him with the warning, "To give a briefing like that in the White House these days would be just like shooting yourself in the foot."[55]

6. *Cognitive rehabilitation and methodological consciousness.* The intertwining of analysis and decision and the record of intelligence failures due to mistaken preconceptions and unexamined assumptions suggest the need to reform the intelligence consumers' attitudes, awareness, and modes of perception. If leaders were made self-conscious and self-critical about their own psychologies, they might be less vulnerable to cognitive pathologies. This approach to preventing intelligence failure is the most basic and metaphysical. If policy makers focused on the methodologies of competing intelligence producers, they would be more sensitive to the biases and leaps of faith in the analyses passed to them. "In official fact-finding . . . the problem is not merely to open up a wide range of policy alternatives but to create incentives for persistent criticism of evidentiary value."[56] Improvement would flow from mechanisms that force decision makers to make explicit rather than unconscious choices, to exercise judgment rather than engage in automatic perception, and to enhance their awareness of their own preconceptions.[57]

Unlike organizational structure, however, cognition cannot be altered by legislation. Intelligence consumers are political men who have risen by being more decisive than reflective, more aggressive than introspective, and confident as much as cautious. Few busy activists who have achieved success by thinking the way that they do will change their way of thinking because some theorist tells them to. Even if they could be forced to confront scholarly evidence of the dynamics of misperception, it is uncertain that they could consistently internalize it. Preconception cannot be abolished; it is in one sense just another word for "model" or

[54] SSCI, *Final Report* (fn. 7), I, 77-82. See also U.S., Congress, Senate, Committee on Foreign Relations, *Hearings, National Security Act Amendment,* 92d Cong., 2d sess., 1972, 14-24.

[55] Zumwalt, *On Watch* (New York: Quadrangle 1976), 459.

[56] Wilensky (fn. 11), 164.

[57] Jervis, *Perception and Misperception* (fn. 22), 181-87.

"paradigm"—a construct used to simplify reality, which any thinker needs in order to cope with complexity. There is a grain of truth in the otherwise pernicious maxim that an open mind is an empty mind. Moreover, the line between *perception* and *judgment* is very thin, and consumers cannot carefully scrutinize, compare, and evaluate the methodologies of competing analyses, for the same prosaic reason (the problem of expertise aside) that impedes many proposed reforms: they do not have the *time* to do so. Solutions that require principals to invest more attention than they already do are conceptually valid but operationally weak. Ideally, perhaps, each principal should have a Special Assistant for Rigor Enforcement.

Although most notable intelligence failures occur more often at the consuming than the producing end, it is impractical to place the burden for correcting those faults on the consumers. The most realistic strategy for improvement would be to have intelligence professionals anticipate the cognitive barriers to decision makers' utilization of their products. Ideally, the Director of Central Intelligence should have a theoretical temperament and personal skills in forcing unusual analyses to the attention of principals; he might act as George's "custodian" of the argumentation process. To fulfill this function, the DCI should be not only a professional analyst and an intellectual (of the twelve DCI's since 1946, only James Schlesinger met those criteria, and he served for only three months), but also a skilled bureaucratic politician. These qualifications seldom coincide. The DCI's coordinating staff and National Intelligence Officers should be adept at detecting, making explicit, and exposing to consumers the idiosyncracies in the assessments of various agencies—the *reasons* that the focus and conclusions of the State Department's Bureau of Intelligence and Research differ from those of DIA, or of naval intelligence, or of the CIA. For such a procedure to work, the consumers would have to favor it (as opposed to negotiated consensual estimates that would save them more time). There is always a latent tension between what facilitates timely decision and what promotes thoroughness and accuracy in assessment. The fact that there is no guaranteed prophylaxis against intelligence failures, however, does not negate the value of incremental improvements. The key is to see the problem of reform as one of modest refinements rather than as a systematic breakthrough.

IV. LIVING WITH FATALISM

Organizational solutions to intelligence failure are hampered by three basic problems: most procedural reforms that address specific pathologies introduce or accent other pathologies; changes in analytic processes can never fully transcend the constraints of ambiguity and ambivalence; and more rationalized information systems cannot fully compensate for the predispositions, perceptual idiosyncrasies, and time constraints of political consumers. Solutions that address the psychology and analytic style of decision makers are limited by the difficulty of changing human thought processes and day-to-day habits of judgment by normative injunction. Most theorists have thus resigned themselves to the hope of marginal progress, "to improve the 'batting average'—say from .275 to .301—rather than to do away altogether with surprise."[58]

There is some convergence in the implications of all three ways of conceptualizing intelligence failures. Mistakes should be expected because the *paradoxes* are not resolvable; minor improvements are possible by reorganizing to correct *pathologies*; and despair is unwarranted because, seen *in perspective*, the record could be worse. Marginal improvements have, in fact, been steadily instituted since World War II. Although many have indeed raised new problems, most have yielded a net increase in the rationalization of the system. The diversification of sources of estimates of adversaries' military power has grown consistently, obviating the necessity to rely exclusively on military staffs. The resources and influence of civilian analysts of military data (principally in the CIA's Office of Strategic Research but also in its Directorate of Science and Technology) are unparalleled in any other nation's intelligence system. At the same time, the DCI's mechanism for coordinating the activities of all agencies—the Intelligence Community Staff—has grown and become more diverse and representative, and less an extension of the CIA, as more staffers have been added from the outside. In 1972, a separate Product Review Division was established within the staff to appraise the "objectivity, balance, and responsiveness" of intelligence studies on a regular basis. It has conducted postmortems of intelligence failures since then (the Yom Kippur War, the Cyprus crisis of 1974, the Indian nuclear test, and the seizure of the *Mayaguez*).[59] (Previously, postmortems had been conducted by the analysts who had failed, a procedure that hardly guaranteed objectivity.)

[58] Knorr (fn. 1), 460.
[59] SSCI, *Final Report* (fn. 7), I, 276, and IV, 85; U.S., Congress, House, Committee on Appropriations, *Hearings, Supplemental Appropriations for Fiscal Year 1977*, 95th Cong., 2d sess., 1977, 515-621; *Washington Post*, February 15, 1977, p. A6; Paul W. Blackstock, "The Intelligence Community Under the Nixon Administration," *Armed Forces and Society*, 1 (February 1975), 238.

Within the Pentagon, capabilities for estimates relevant to planning were enhanced with the establishment of an office for Net Assessment, which analyzes the significance of foreign capabilities in comparison with U.S. forces. (CIA, DIA, and NIE's only estimate foreign capabilities.) Civilian direction of military intelligence was reinforced by an Assistant Secretary of Defense for Intelligence after the 1970 recommendation of the Fitzhugh Commission, and an Under Secretary for Policy in 1978. Experiments in improving communication between producers and consumers have been undertaken (such as, for example, the testing of a Defense Intelligence Board in late 1976). The dominance of operators within the intelligence community has also waned—especially since the phasing out of paramilitary operations in Southeast Asia and the severe reductions in size and status of CIA's covert action branch that began in 1973. Dysfunctions in the military communications system, which contributed to crises involving intelligence collection missions in the 1960's (the Israeli attack on the U.S.S. *Liberty* and North Korea's seizure of the *Pueblo*) were alleviated (though not cured) by new routing procedures and by instituting an "optimal scanning system" in the Pentagon.[60] Statistical analyses of strategic power have become progressively more rigorous and comprehensive; as staffs outside the executive branch—such as the Congressional Budget Office—have become involved in the process, they have also become more competitive.[61]

Few of the changes in structure and process have generated more costs than benefits. (Some critics believe, however, that the abolition of the Office and Board of National Estimates and their replacement with National Intelligence Officers was a net loss.) But it is difficult to prove that they have significantly reduced the incidence of intelligence failure. In the area of warning, for instance, new sophisticated coordination mechanisms have recently been introduced, and since the institution at the time of the 1974 Cyprus crisis of DCI "alert memoranda"—"brief notices in a form which cannot be overlooked"[62]—no

---

[60] Joseph C. Goulden, *Truth is the First Casualty* (Chicago: Rand McNally 1969), 101-4; Phil G. Goulding, *Confirm or Deny* (New York: Harper & Row 1970), 130-33, 269; *Pueblo and EC-121 Hearings* (fn. 27), 646-47, 665-73, 743-44, 780-82, 802-3, 865-67, 875, 880, 897-99; *Pueblo and EC-121 Report* (fn. 27), 1654-56, 1662-67; Armbrister (fn. 27), 196ff, 395; U.S., Congress, House, Committee on Armed Services, *Report, Review of Department of Defense Worldwide Communications: Phase I*, 92d Cong., 1st sess., 1971, and *Phase II*, 2d sess., 1972.

[61] See, for example, James Blaker and Andrew Hamilton, *Assessing the NATO/Warsaw Pact Military Balance* (Washington, D.C.: Congressional Budget Office, December 1977).

[62] SSCI, *Final Report* (fn. 7), I, 61; Thomas G. Belden, "Indications, Warning, and Crisis Operations," *International Studies Quarterly*, xxi (March 1977), 192-93.

major warning failure has occurred. But the period of testing is as yet too brief to demonstrate that these adaptations are more effective than previous procedures. In the area of operational evaluation, it is clear that there was greater consciousness of the limitations and cost-ineffectiveness of aerial bombardment during the Vietnam War than there had been in Korea, due largely to the assessments made by the offices of Systems Analysis and International Security Affairs in the Pentagon and Secretary of Defense McNamara's utilization of CIA estimates and contract studies by external analytic organizations.[63] Yet this greater consciousness did not prevail until late in the war because it was not a consensus; Air Force and naval assessments of bombing effectiveness contradicted those of the critical civilian analysts. Nor has the elaboration and diversification of analytic resources for strategic estimates clearly reduced the potential for erroneous planning decisions. Determination of the salience and proper weight of conflicting indicators of strategic power and objectives or of the comparative significance of quantitative and qualitative factors is inextricable from the political debate over foreign policy: uncertainties always remain, leaving the individual's visceral fears or hopes as the elements that tilt the balance of judgment.

Although marginal reforms may reduce the probability of error, the unresolvable paradoxes and barriers to analytic and decisional accuracy will make some incidence of failure inevitable. Concern with intelligence failure then coincides with concern about how policy can hedge against the consequences of analytic inadequacy. Covering every hypothetical vulnerability would lead to bankruptcy, and hedging against one threat may aggravate a different one. The problem is thus one of priorities, and hedging against uncertainty is hardly easier than resolving it. Any measures that clarify the cost-benefit trade-offs in policy hedges are measures that mitigate the danger of intelligence failure.

[63] *Pentagon Papers*, IV, 111-12, 115-24, 217-32. CIA critiques of bombing results began even before the Tonkin Gulf crisis. CIA/OCI, Current Intelligence Memorandum, "Effectiveness of T-28 Strikes in Laos," June 26, 1964; CIA/DDI, Intelligence Memorandum, "Communist Reaction to Barrel Roll Missions," December 29, 1964. But ambivalence remained even within the CIA, which occasionally issued more sanguine evaluations—e.g., CIA Memorandum for National Security Council, "The Situation in Vietnam," June 28, 1965 (which McGeorge Bundy called directly to the President's attention), and CIA/OCI, Intelligence Memorandum, "Interdiction of Communist Infiltration Routes in Vietnam," June 24, 1965. (All memoranda are in LBJL/NSF-VNCF, Vol. I, item 5, Vol. III, items 28, 28a, 28b, Vol. VI A, items 4, 5, 8.) See also *Pentagon Papers*, IV, 71-74. See also the opposing assessments of the CIA, the civilian analysts in the Pentagon, and the Joint Chiefs in NSSM-1 (the Nixon Administration's initial review of Vietnam policy), reprinted in the *Congressional Record*, Vol. 118, part 13, 92d Cong., 2d sess., May 10, 1972, pp. 16749-836.

One reasonable rule in principle would be to survey the hypothetical outcomes excluded by strategic premises as improbable but not impossible, identify those that would be disastrous if they *were* to occur, and then pay the price to hedge against them. This is no more practicable, however, than the pure form of worst-case analysis, because it requires willingness to bear and inflict severe costs for dubious reasons. Escalation in Vietnam, after all, was a hedge against allowing China to be tempted to "devour" the rest of Southeast Asia. The interaction of analytic uncertainty and decisional prudence is a vicious circle that makes the segregation of empirical intelligence and normative policy an unattainable Platonic ideal.

In the simplest situation, the intelligence system can avert policy failure by presenting relevant and undisputed facts to non-expert principals who might otherwise make decisions in ignorance. But these simple situations are not those in which major intelligence failures occur. Failures occur when ambiguity aggravates ambivalence. In these more important situations—Acheson and Clausewitz to the contrary— the intelligence officer may perform most usefully by *not* offering the *answers* sought by authorities, but by offering *questions*, acting as a Socratic agnostic, nagging decision makers into awareness of the full range of uncertainty, and making the authorities' calculations harder rather than easier. Sensitive leaders will reluctantly accept and appreciate this function. Most leaders will not; they will make mistakes, and will continue to bear the prime responsibility for "intelligence" failures. Two general values (which sound wistful in the context of the preceding fatalism) remain to guide the choice of marginal reforms: anything that facilitates dissent and access to authorities by intelligence producers, and anything that facilitates skepticism and scrutiny by consumers. The values are synergistically linked; one will not improve the use of intelligence without the other. (A third value, but one nearly impossible to achieve, would be anything that increases the time available to principals for reading and reflection.)

Intelligence failures are not only inevitable, they are natural. Some are even benign (if a success would not have changed policy). Scholars cannot legitimately view intelligence mistakes as bizarre, because they are no more common and no less excusable than academic errors. They are less forgivable only because they are more consequential. Error in scholarship is resolved dialectically, as deceptive data are exposed and regnant theories are challenged, refined, and replaced by new research. If decision makers had but world enough and time, they could rely on this process to solve their intelligence problems. But the press of events precludes the luxury of letting theories sort themselves out over a period of years, as in academia. My survey of the intractability of the inadequacy of intelligence, and its inseparability from mistakes in decision, suggests one final conclusion that is perhaps most outrageously fatalistic of all: tolerance for disaster.

NATIONAL SECURITY ADVICE TO U.S. PRESIDENTS:

Some Lessons from Thirty Years

By I. M. DESTLER*

IN large part, Presidents determine the range and quality of advice that they get. They choose their principal officials. They decide day-by-day, personally or through chosen aides, which of these officials will get into the Oval Office, how often, in what contexts. Their styles and preferences also do much to shape the sorts of advice that will reach them from further down in the government, and from people outside it. Clark Clifford once characterized the executive branch as "like a chameleon," taking its color from "the character and personality of the President";[1] certainly this is true of its senior levels. As Dean Rusk noted, "the real organization of government at higher echelons" is "how confidence flows down from the President."[2]

Yet, notwithstanding their power in shaping it, Presidents are sometimes frustrated by the advice they receive. Kennedy had his Bay of Pigs, of which he noted later—with less than full accuracy—that "the advice of every member of the executive branch brought in to advise was unanimous—and the advice was wrong."[3] Johnson pulled back from the multilateral force, but was moved to denounce his advisers vehemently for the counsel which had nearly won the day.[4] Each President may indeed have determined the advice he got by how he handled the issue and how he handled his advisers, but neither did so with that particular outcome in mind; each was shaken by what his advisory system had wrought. And even when Presidents pronounce themselves satisfied, large numbers of citizens may not be. They may find their President isolated from objective analysis and national sentiment (Cambodia), or caught up in an "inside" set of values and ex-

* An earlier version of this essay was presented at the Princeton University Conference on Presidential Advising, October 31–November 1, 1975. I am grateful to Fred I. Greenstein, Carl Kaysen, Alexander George, and Robert H. Johnson for their helpful critical comments on that draft.

[1] Clifford, "The Presidency As I Have Seen It," in Emmet John Hughes, *The Living Presidency* (New York: Coward, McCann, and Geoghegan 1973), 315.

[2] Quoted in *Life*, January 17, 1969, p. 62B.

[3] Quoted in Theodore Sorensen, *Kennedy* (New York: Harper and Row 1965), 305.

[4] On the MLF decision, see Philip Geyelin, *Lyndon B. Johnson and the World* (New York: Praeger 1966), chap. 7; and John Steinbruner, *The Cybernetic Theory of Decision* (Princeton: Princeton University Press 1974), esp. chap. 9.

pectations that says more about himself and his advisers than it does about the world they seek to shape (Vietnam escalation as seen through the *Pentagon Papers*; Watergate as seen through the Nixon tapes).

How Presidents get what advice, then, is an important if difficult subject for analysis. It is important in all areas of national policy. It is particularly important in the sphere alternatively labelled "national security" or "foreign" policy. Many Americans rightly reject the standard cold war belief that foreign policy *ought* always to have primacy over domestic. But it continues to receive priority attention from Presidents. There are enduring reasons—the President's particular constitutional authority and responsibility in foreign affairs; the absence of some of the domestic political constraints that affect other spheres; the opportunity to build a statesman's reputation among current voters and future historians alike; the fact that foreign policy remains, in Kennedy's oft-quoted words, the sphere where a mistake "can kill us."[5]

Presidents seek foreign policy advice from many sources. Much of it comes from persons outside of the executive branch—Congressional leaders whose judgment Presidents value or whose support they need; outside experts on specialized subjects; establishment "wise men" like the Senior Informal Advisory Group that urged Lyndon Johnson to change course on Vietnam in March 1968. Formal external advisory bodies also exist on such subjects as intelligence, arms control, and information policy. Presidents get reams of unsolicited advice as well—from policy critics motivated by strong substantive convictions and/or partisan political interest; from foreign leaders; from interest groups with particular economic stakes; from newspaper editorials and columnists.

Without denying the impact of advice from other sources, however, this essay will focus largely on advice provided by officials and institutions within the executive branch. It is such inside advice that any President gets the most of, and that responds most directly to particular problems as he must deal with them. It is, by all evidence, what influences Presidents most, most of the time, when they make particular foreign policy decisions. Too great a dependence upon senior administration insiders can cost a President dearly, particularly if these insiders are insensitive to broader national political currents. Yet, as Joseph Kraft noted ten years ago, the size and complexity of modern government have sharply limited the advisory influence of outsiders compared to the "trained intellectual bureaucrat" who is there, inside the govern-

[5] Quoted in Arthur M. Schlesinger, Jr., *A Thousand Days* (Boston: Houghton Mifflin 1965), 426.

ment, to push his objective hour by hour, day by day.[6] In foreign affairs, official secrecy gives further advantages to insiders.

Every postwar President has gotten most of his inside national security advice from the occupants of some or all of a handful of senior line and staff positions: the Secretaries of State, Defense, and the Treasury; the Presidential Assistant (entitled *Special* Assistant until 1969) for National Security Affairs; the Chiefs of Staff of the military services (particularly the Chairman of the J.C.S.); and the Director of Central Intelligence. Important policy advice has also flowed from general White House policy aides like Clark Clifford for Truman, Theodore Sorensen for Kennedy, and Bill Moyers for Johnson, and from trusted political advisers like Attorneys General Robert Kennedy in 1961–1963 and John Mitchell during the early Nixon years. Some Presidents have given a regular hearing to sub-Cabinet officials in the State Department; the Under Secretary (now Deputy Secretary) of State has sometimes been one and, less frequently, so have Assistant Secretaries with briefs of particular Presidential interest. The weightiest advisers, however, have usually been holders of senior official foreign policy and national security positions.

The role of these advisers was the target of the central postwar institutional reform in national security policy making, the creation of the National Security Council in 1947.[7] Since then, the formal "White House machinery for the resolution of major foreign affairs issues has remained remarkably stable," as the Murphy Commission report notes.[8] Yet structural continuity has not prevented considerable variation among Presidents and Administrations in how particular issues are typically treated. And how the N.S.C. has evolved over thirty years tells us much about the broader patterns of foreign policy advice to postwar Presidents—what they have desired, what they have received,

[6] Joseph Kraft, *Profiles in Power* (New York: New American Library 1966), 63–68.
[7] Of course, one may argue that the establishment of the Secretary of Defense was of equal if not greater importance. Indeed, in the immediate postwar years the phrase "national security" was considered a near-synonym of "national defense": James Forrestal, as Secretary of the Navy, originally backed the establishment of the N.S.C. as an alternative to defense unification. When both the Council and the Secretary of Defense were established by the National Security Act of 1947, the latter was described in the Act as the President's principal adviser in the field of "national security." In short order, however, the N.S.C. became heavily involved in State Department and foreign policy business, an involvement reflected in Truman's early order that the Secretary of State chair the Council in his absence. "National security policy" then became a near-synonym of foreign policy, or at least of its "security" or "political-military" components. The latter usage is employed in this article.
[8] *Report of the Commission on the Organization of the Government for the Conduct of Foreign Policy* [hereafter referred to as *Murphy Commission Report*] (Washington: G.P.O. June 1975), 4.

and what choices present themselves for the future. Moreover, the story of the Council offers a sobering object lesson to would-be procedural reformers. Its proponents sought to constrain the President, to bind him more closely to his senior Cabinet advisers. But their creation ended up freeing him and lessening his dependence upon these advisers.

THE NATIONAL SECURITY COUNCIL SINCE 1947: THE EVOLUTION
OF A REFORM[9]

The Council has affected advice to Presidents in three major ways. It has served as an advisory forum of senior officials reviewing foreign policy issues for the President, usually in his presence. It has provided a focal point for the development of formal policy planning and decision processes. It has provided the umbrella for the emergence of a Presidential foreign policy staff. Its founders mainly conceived it as the first; the last is what it has most importantly become.

The N.S.C. as forum. In form and in public imagery, the National Security Council is the most exalted committee in the Federal Government. Its statutory membership is now limited to four—the President, the Vice President, the Secretary of State, and the Secretary of Defense. The Assistant to the President for National Security Affairs is the senior staff official of the N.S.C.; the Chairman of the Joint Chiefs of Staff, the Director of Central Intelligence, and (since 1975) the Director of the Arms Control and Disarmament Agency serve as statutory advisers. Unlike many Cabinet-level committees, moreover, the N.S.C. actually does meet—more than 600 times since its inception. Thus, one way

---

[9] These pages on the N.S.C. draw particularly on the following sources: Stanley L. Falk, "The National Security Council Under Truman, Eisenhower, and Kennedy," *Political Science Quarterly*, Vol. 79 (September 1964), 403–34; David K. Hall, "The Custodian-Manager of the Policymaking Process," in Alexander L. George, "Toward a More Soundly Based Foreign Policy: Making Better Use of Information," Appendix D (Volume 2) to the *Murphy Commission Report*, 100–119; Paul Y. Hammond, "The National Security Council: An Interpretation and Appraisal," *American Political Science Review*, Vol. 54 (December 1960), reprinted in Alan A. Altshuler, *The Politics of the Federal Bureaucracy* (New York: Dodd, Mead 1968), 140–56; Robert H. Johnson, "The National Security Council: The Relevance of Its Past to Its Future," *Orbis*, XIII (Fall 1969), 709–35; the early Jackson Subcommittee hearings and staff reports (U.S. Senate, Committee on Government Operations, Subcommittee on National Policy Machinery, *Organizing for National Security*, Vols. I–III [Washington 1961]); James S. Lay, Jr. and Robert H. Johnson, "Organizational History of the National Security Council," August 1960; published *ibid.*, Vol. II, 411–68; Richard M. Moose, "The White House National-Security Staffs Since 1947," in Keith C. Clark and Laurence J. Legere, eds., *The President and the Management of National Security* (for the Institute of Defense Analyses, New York: Praeger 1969), 55–98; I. M. Destler, *Presidents, Bureaucrats, and Foreign Policy* (Princeton: Princeton University Press 1972 and 1974), esp. chap. 5 and Epilogue.

in which it provides advice to Presidents is through its actual debates and deliberations as a sitting body.

To provide advice to the President through a more orderly, even collegial institution was a major objective of the prime exponent of the N.S.C., James Forrestal. His hopes may have been even greater—that the Council might, in practice, actually make the major U.S. policy decisions. A study which he commissioned in 1945 emphasized that, while the Council "would be formally described as advisory . . . the fact that the President himself heads the Council would for all practical purposes insure that the advice it offered would be accepted."[10] The conscious model was the British War Cabinet; the pattern to avoid was Franklin D. Roosevelt's highly personalized, *ad hoc* decision making during World War II, above and around his principal formal advisers. (The N.S.C. was quickly labelled "Forrestal's revenge.") The President was, to some, a "rogue elephant" who needed fencing in (or perhaps, in Truman's case, a "weak reed" in need of shoring up). Such concerns were widely shared. The report of the Hoover Commission Task Force of January 1949 saw Presidential participation in the conduct of foreign policy as "marked with many pitfalls," and emphasized that "the President should consult his foreign policy advisers in the executive branch before committing the United States to a course of action."[11]

The substantive objective of the N.S.C.—more effective coordination of advice and action in U.S. foreign and military policies—was widely applauded in the forties and has been since. But Forrestal's effort to control Presidential advisory processes, even to collectivize executive decision making, reflected, as Paul Hammond has noted, a "failure to understand the Presidency."[12] It also reflected a failure to understand particular Presidents. Thus, President Truman welcomed the Council as a "badly needed new facility" to bring together "military, diplomatic, and resources problems"[13] but, like all of his successors, firmly established its inability to bind him. One way in which he preserved his autonomy in practice was by attending only 12 of the 57 N.S.C. meetings held prior to the outbreak of war in Korea. Even Eisenhower, who convened the Council approximately as many times as

[10] Study by Myron Gilmore for the *Eberstadt Report*, quoted in Hammond (fn. 9), 141.
[11] Harvey H. Bundy and others, "The Organization of the Government for the Conduct of Foreign Affairs," Appendix H to the *Report of the Commission on Organization of the Executive Branch of the Government* (Washington, D.C., February 1949), 51.
[12] Hammond (fn. 9), 141.
[13] Harry S. Truman, *Years of Trial and Hope* (New York: Doubleday 1956), 59.

all other postwar Presidents combined, and who almost always attended personally when his health permitted, felt moved to note his puzzlement that certain Congressmen couldn't understand that the N.S.C. itself had no powers but simply gave advice that a President could take or ignore as he pleased.[14]

The Council did nevertheless function as a major Presidential advisory forum through the fifties. Once the Korean War began, it met more frequently, and with Truman in attendance, dealing not only with Korean problems but with the more general U.S. political-military response to what was seen as a worldwide Communist challenge. Under President Eisenhower, the N.S.C. reached its peak as a sitting institution. Meetings had averaged two a month under Truman. During the Eisenhower Administration, the Council met on the average almost once a week, with Secretaries John Foster Dulles (State) and George Humphrey (Treasury) the most weighty voices.[15] When Eisenhower had a heart attack in 1955, and an operation for ileitis in 1956, Council meetings chaired by Vice President Nixon provided for useful continuity in national security policy deliberations, both actual and symbolic. Yet even under Eisenhower, the Council itself did not truly dominate Presidential foreign policy advice. One reason was that its major mandate was to review general and relatively long-range policy; Eisenhower had other institutions and individuals for day-to-day crises and the many *ad hoc* decisions that inevitably arose. A second reason was the strong individual role played by his Secretary of State, and the strong direct relationship to the President which Dulles succeeded in establishing through assiduous efforts.

If the N.S.C. as a sitting, deliberative advisory body was of at least moderate importance to Eisenhower, his successor perceived it largely as an encumbrance. President Kennedy came to office influenced by the Jackson subcommittee's criticisms of Eisenhower's national security procedures as cumbersome and sterile; his personal penchant for informality meshed nicely with such criticism. Thus, he noted as early as 1961: "We have averaged three or four meetings a week with the Secretaries of Defense and State, [Special Assistant for National Security Affairs] McGeorge Bundy, the head of the C.I.A. and the Vice Presi-

---

[14] Dwight D. Eisenhower, *Waging Peace* (New York: Doubleday 1965), 246n.
[15] The Secretary of the Treasury has never been a formal member of the N.S.C., but was regularly invited to Council meetings under Eisenhower and most other postwar Presidents. The Murphy Commission proposed that he be added as a statutory member in view of the increased importance of economic relations in foreign policy. Congress passed legislation to this end in December 1975, but President Ford vetoed it, declaring that "adequate arrangements for providing advice to the President on the integration of economic and foreign policy already exist."

dent. But formal meetings of the Security Council which include a much wider group are not as effective."[16] Formal N.S.C. meetings continued to be held—sixteen during the Administration's first six months, and less frequently thereafter. But they were seldom the place where really serious Presidential advice was solicited or conveyed.

The preference for less formal advisory meetings whose format and attendance were more susceptible to Presidential control continued under President Johnson. Bill Moyers noted that L.B.J. found the Council to be "not a live institution, not suited to precise debate for the sake of decision."[17] The Council did experience a modest re-emphasis under Special Assistant for National Security Affairs Walt Rostow, who replaced Bundy in early 1966; meetings were held, in Rostow's words, "primarily for generating and exposing a series of major problems on which decisions would be required of the President, not at the moment but in some foreseeable time period."[18] But the heart of Johnson's foreign policy advisory system was the Vietnam-dominated "Tuesday lunch," where he met informally with a small group of his top aides, including the Secretaries of State and Defense and the Special Assistant.

Nixon came to office in 1969 pledged to "restore the National Security Council to its pre-eminent role in national security planning"; he even made this the theme of a late-October campaign speech.[19] "Catch-as-catch-can talkfests" were to be supplanted by actual use of the Council as the "principal forum for the consideration of policy issues" requiring Presidential decision.[20] For a while in 1969, and more sporadically in 1970, Nixon did so employ it. But like other aspects of Nixon's proclaimed "open Presidency," it had by 1973 lapsed into unprecedented disuse, with advice to the President formulated and conveyed primarily by and through National Security Assistant Henry Kissinger, working with his staff and with interagency N.S.C. subgroups that he dominated.[21] Up to President Nixon's trip to China in

---

[16] Quoted in Sorensen (fn. 3), 284.

[17] "Bill Moyers Talks about LBJ, Poverty, War and the Young," *Atlantic*, Vol. 222 (July 1968), 35.

[18] W. W. Rostow, *The Diffusion of Power* (New York: Macmillan 1972), 361.

[19] Report in the *New York Times*, October 25, 1968.

[20] *Ibid.*, and White House Statement of February 7, 1969.

[21] On the operations of the Nixon-Kissinger system generally, see esp. Chester Crocker, "The Nixon-Kissinger National Security Council System, 1969–1972: A Study in Foreign Policy Management," in National Academy of Public Administration, "Making Organizational Change Effective: Case Studies of Attempted Reforms in Foreign Affairs," Appendix O (Vol. 6) to the *Murphy Commission Report* (fn. 8), 79–99; and Destler, (fn. 9), chap. 5 and Epilogue. For an insider's account of how the system was established, see Morton H. Halperin, "The 1969 NSC System," unpub. paper prepared for the Murphy Commission.

February 1972, his Council had had 73 meetings—half of them in his first year. This twice-a-month average was nearly double that of the Johnson Administration. But when Kissinger stated that the controversial October 1973 military alert during the Yom Kippur War had been decided upon only after "a special meeting of the National Security Council," N.S.C. records did not support him. In fact, they showed only two meetings during the first ten months of 1973.[22]

Under President Ford, use of the N.S.C. as a convening forum has been revived somewhat (as of April 1976, the Council had met 31 times during his Presidency)[23] to a frequency slightly above that of the Johnson and Nixon Administrations. But overall postwar experience provides ample reason to conclude that Presidential use of the National Security Council as a regularized, major advisory forum is the exception rather than the rule. A major reason is that the Council's main virtues to its proponents—formality and regularity of membership and meetings; pre-established, well-disseminated agendas—prove to be drawbacks in practice. N.S.C. meetings tend to attract too many people for serious advice to be conveyed—senior advisers and Presidents are constrained to speak "for the record" notwithstanding the formal secrecy of the proceedings, since their remarks are likely to be passed on by word of mouth to a much wider audience inside the Government. Cabinet members consider themselves judged on how effectively they push their departmental briefs; Presidents must take care lest their tentative suggestions close off discussion or be disseminated after the meetings as clear Presidential preferences. These drawbacks can be reduced by limiting attendance, and all Administrations that took the Council at all seriously have made some efforts in that direction. The Nixon regime was particularly stringent in this regard. But security and frankness can be achieved even more effectively through informal meetings or "one-on-one" sessions, and it is these on which Presidents ultimately tend to rely for serious advice.

The Council as committee can nonetheless serve certain Presidential purposes. By calling them together collegially, a President can impress on officials that they share responsibilities for national security and foreign policy advice which stretch beyond their specific job descriptions. Thus the Council tends to meet most often early in an Administration, when the roles of senior advisors are still fluid and susceptible to being defined. But Presidents can build a sense of a collegial advisory

---

[22] *Washington Post*, November 9, 1973.
[23] Information provided by the N.S.C. staff, covering the period through April 28, 1976.

team in other ways. In fact, well-conducted informal sessions may be more effective in this regard, since they can encourage the "real" debate that the Council itself inhibits. Indeed, the most widely praised example of collegial advisory practice was the informal group of his most important advisers that President Kennedy established to explore options during the Cuban missile crisis.

One way in which the Council has proved useful to all Presidents has been in public relations. Convening the Council in a time of crisis is thought to convey the impression of the most somber and careful high-level deliberation. Such meetings can protect the President from charges that he acts arbitrarily and raise the image of his Administration. Thus, Kissinger's insistence that the military alert of October 1973 had the "unanimous" support of the N.S.C. was aimed at combatting the widespread suspicion that Nixon was trying to divert attention from the domestic crisis brought on by his firing of Special Prosecutor Archibald Cox. Eleven years earlier, Kennedy had dubbed his chosen advisory group during the Cuban missile crisis the "Executive Committee of the National Security Council." And in May 1975, Press Secretary Ronald Nessen had a similar goal when he declared, "The President has met with the National Security Council," in the second sentence of his briefing revealing the seizure of the *Mayaguez*. Indeed, the Council did meet five times during that week.[24]

The N.S.C. as formal process. Most of those who have favored a major role for the National Security Council have sought to establish regular means for bringing important policy issues before it, supported by thorough staff work. Fundamental to the early activities of the Council, therefore, were procedures for interdepartmental reviews and policy papers aimed at putting particular issues into focus, and giving the Council documents on which to act. Under President Truman, a considerable number of policy papers were developed for N.S.C. consideration, dealing mostly with individual countries or regions. One of the most famous of all Council papers, NSC–68, was completed during this time; its call for much-increased defense spending was implemented once the Korean War made this possible domestically. NSC–68, however, was not so much instigated by Truman's N.S.C. system as by Paul Nitze and other State Department officials, who felt that the American military response to the Soviet challenge was seriously inadequate. The N.S.C. framework, however, was useful to these

[24] *New York Times*, May 13, 1975; *The New Republic*, June 7, 1975, p. 8; and information provided by N.S.C. staff.

officials in gaining interdepartmental cooperation at a time when the Secretaries of State and Defense were not on speaking terms.[25]

The Korean War infused the policy studies process of the Truman Council with a greater sense of urgency. And the N.S.C.'s role was formally strengthened in July 1950 by a Presidential directive emphasizing that all major national security policies should be recommended to the President through the Council. Truman had stated this earlier, but his personal participation in Council sessions now gave it new significance. However, after a year of intensive activity, the Truman process, in one participant's words, "gradually drifted into the doldrums along with the rest of the government,"[26] as a lame-duck Administration struggled with a war it could not end.

President Eisenhower built upon procedures already established in the Truman Administration, but made them more structured, formal, and comprehensive. He and his Special Assistant for National Security Affairs, Robert Cutler, believed deeply in orderly deliberations based upon thorough staff work. Under them, the Council "Planning Board" (a committee of departmental assistant secretaries) presided over the development of papers that analyzed virtually every significant U.S. foreign policy problem and proposed, on each, a general "policy" for Council review and Presidential approval. The most comprehensive of these was the annual overview document entitled "Basic National Security Policy."

In the development of its structure and the scope of its ambition, Eisenhower's N.S.C. process was therefore unmatched. The aim was not just to get top officials to consider every issue of consequence; it was to have a set of written general policies approved by the President which would serve as guidance for the overall government. But the process proved to have three very serious limitations.

One of these limitations is endemic to all efforts aimed at statements of general policy: they frequently do not and can not provide clear cues for responses to particular events unknown and unanticipated when the documents were written. The tendency of officials is therefore to deal with such events on their own terms without too much reference to policy statements framed earlier. A second limitation arose from its comprehensiveness: such a large number of papers was being drafted and cleared that the whole operation became, to many participants,

[25] The standard account of this episode is Paul Y. Hammond, "NSC-68: Prologue to Rearmament," in Warner Schilling and others, *Strategy, Politics, and Defense Budgets* (New York: Columbia University Press 1962).

[26] Johnson (fn. 9), 714.

a cumbersome, slow-moving "papermill." The third, perhaps most frequently expressed criticism was that, because the process pressed the different agencies to reach agreement on a paper prior to its submission to the Council, key policy issues and choices were suppressed rather than highlighted. Dean Acheson suggested that the way the system handled disagreements was to "increase the vagueness and generality" of the policies adopted.[27]

Defenders of the Eisenhower system argued that major issues were in fact frequently brought up for Council debate during the process; they pointed to the existence of "splits," or disagreements between agencies reflected by alternative language in the papers the N.S.C. reviewed. Eisenhower's Special Assistants for National Security Affairs seem to have been sensitive to this problem, and labored hard to be sure that fundamental issues were not buried in verbiage meaning different things to different people. Nevertheless, since Eisenhower's concept of interagency staff work was that it should, if possible, produce an agreed recommendation, such efforts seem to have had limited effect.

Finally, the Eisenhower process was limited by the evolution of the President's broader advisory system, above all the foreign policy predominance established by the Secretary of State. John Foster Dulles and his subordinates participated actively in the system, but he valued his own flexibility highly in particular negotiations and decisions, and worked very hard to keep it. He preferred to resolve tough choices by dealing privately with the President or, when necessary, in negotiations with other strong officials like Treasury Secretary George Humphrey. Such procedures limited the ability of the managers of Eisenhower's N.S.C. process to ensure that it was the place where the basic policy questions were really addressed.

President Kennedy's attitude toward this process was even more negative than his attitude toward Council meetings. He dismantled it completely, abolishing both the Planning Board and the Operations Coordinating Board whose role was to oversee implementation of policies developed through the N.S.C. framework. In National Security Assistant McGeorge Bundy's words, the new administration "deliberately rubbed out the distinction between planning and operation which governed the administrative structure of the NSC staff in the last administration."[28] Believing that "policy" was shaped primarily through day-to-day decisions and actions, Kennedy put nothing in the place

---

[27] Acheson, "Thoughts on Thought in High Places," reprinted in Jackson Subcommittee (fn. 9), II, 292.

[28] Bundy's letter to Senator Henry Jackson, in Jackson Subcommittee (fn. 9), I, 1338.

of the Eisenhower process; nor generally did his successor, Lyndon B. Johnson. There were some efforts at developing broad policy guidelines outside the N.S.C. framework, such as the "National Policy Papers" pushed by Rostow while he was State Department Policy Planning Chairman; some efforts were conducted under the auspices of interdepartmental committees (chaired by State Department officials) established by Johnson in March 1966. Also, a general counter-insurgency policy had been adopted in the wake of the Bay of Pigs fiasco. But these were exceptions to the informal, operations-oriented style that prevailed.

As already noted, Presidential candidate Nixon sharply criticized this Kennedy-Johnson informality. He was also, however, critical of the Eisenhower process as fostering illusory "concurrences" that limited active assertion of the President's power to choose. Therefore, the formal process for providing policy advice which he established—the so-called N.S.S.M. (National Security Study Memorandum) system—reflected his desire that policy papers drafted by interagency committees offer not agreed recommendations but real "options" from which the President might select. The focus shifted from establishing broad policy to providing an analytic basis for specific decisions. There was also an effort to avoid duplicating the encyclopedism of the Eisenhower period by being selective in the studies ordered. However, since many issues were in need of review, and since the memoranda were a major vehicle for the Kissinger staff in seizing the initiative, 69 studies were ordered in the system's first six months of operation. That volume was enough to convince some departmental officials (mistakenly, it appears) that the purpose of the system was simply to inundate the bureaucracy with paperwork so that Nixon and Kissinger could do their real business without too much molestation. And the number of completed studies soon did become far greater than the capacity of the Nixon Administration to review them and act seriously on them, especially considering the extreme centralization of power under the President and his White House National Security Assistant.

Ironically, the *de facto* Nixon-Kissinger "system" soon evolved into practically the opposite of the one advocated in 1968 and designed in 1969: the two chief officials tended to disregard or discount much of the advice they received from the broader Government. They not only made their own decisions based on their own analyses (or their own private sifting of other analyses), but often kept the bureaucracy in the dark concerning these decisions. And the Nixon Administration's N.S.C. "system" also demonstrated, rather quickly, another limitation of structuring procedures too much around broad policy studies aimed at a limited number of major decisions. Responses to various crises and to ongoing situations which the United States is seeking to influence require day-to-day operational choices by the President and lesser officials which are not easily managed through formal "options" studies that take weeks to prepare. Thus the most active institution in the Nixon system was frequently the Kissinger-dominated "Washington Special Actions Group," which was not even a part of the original system, but was created in the aftermath of the downing of a U.S. intelligence airplane by North Korea. The Group was designed to coordinate advice and operations on similar fast-moving situations.

Nevertheless, N.S.S.M.'s have continued to be employed; 35 new studies were initiated in Ford's first 21 months. And, notwithstanding how the real Nixon-Kissinger "system" evolved, their N.S.S.M. procedure seems a clear improvement over its predecessors in both its selectivity and its focus on Presidential choice. Its formal goal—that agencies reach agreement on a list of options through objective analysis uncolored by agency interest—is probably unrealistic, and may also be undesirable; Alexander George, for example, has argued that Presidents should nourish rather than suppress "multiple advocacy" founded upon the divergent perspectives and interests of different agencies.[29] But in practice, such advocacy is not eliminated, for agencies have frequently used the system to try to ensure that their own preferred options are presented in reasonably attractive form, so that their chiefs can argue for them effectively at high-level meetings. And as George and others have recognized, multiple advocacy works best when senior officials are acting not as narrow pleaders for their departmental briefs, but as senior governmental officials bound by obligations to their President and their colleagues to explore all possible choices in the most objective and thoroughgoing manner. The N.S.S.M. process is designed to push officialdom in that direction.

The N.S.C. as Presidential staff. The third, and surely most important way in which the creation of the National Security Council has shaped foreign policy advice to Presidents is that it has served as the institutional base for the establishment of a strong Presidential foreign policy staff. Unlike the generally declining use of the Council as a sitting committee and the intermittent use of it as a focal point for formal policy-making procedures, the use of the N.S.C. as staff has grown steadily.

[29] George, "The Case for Multiple Advocacy in Making Foreign Policy," *American Political Science Review*, Vol. 66 (September 1972), esp. 753–56.

All postwar Presidents from Truman to Nixon contributed to this development. Truman established the precedent of treating the Council as his body to be housed in his Executive Office, and adopted its staff as a useful addition to Presidential resources. He considered it, however, a career staff like that of the Bureau of the Budget, which would serve from administration to administration, providing continuity. His two N.S.C. Executive Secretaries, Sidney Souers and James Lay, were appointed with this criterion of "neutral competence" in mind.[30]

Support staffing was strengthened in the N.S.C. reorganization that followed the outbreak of war in Korea. It was both strengthened and enlarged in 1953, when President Eisenhower created the new position of Special Assistant for National Security Affairs.[31] This official was to serve as the President's personal staff aide in charge of managing the N.S.C. process, with the Executive Secretary's role now that of head of the career staff. The Council staff was also enlarged and strengthened in other ways, including an enhanced capability for independent analysis and review of agency positions. It remained, however, predominantly a career staff operating under the expectation that most of its members would (or at least could) stay on from administration to administration. The new Special Assistant, though a stronger, higher-ranking official than Truman's Executive Secretaries, was limited in his leverage over the senior national security officials and agencies by, among other things, his separation from the day-to-day processes of national security operations. In fact, Eisenhower had *two* staff aides with national security responsibilities. The Special Assistant was one; the other was his Staff Secretary, General Andrew Goodpaster, whose duties included providing daily intelligence briefings to the President, coordinating the flow of daily national security business, and acting as liaison in arranging for meetings and the communication of decisions on operational issues.

When President Kennedy assumed office, he preserved the position of Special Assistant for National Security Affairs, but abolished most of the formal policy planning system on which the position's previous occupants had lavished their attention. McGeorge Bundy inherited, however, most of the national security tasks of General Goodpaster, particularly the management of day-to-day Presidential foreign policy business. This gave him a new and very important source of leverage,

---

[30] On the issue of neutral competence in U.S. public administration, see Herbert Kaufman, "Emerging Conflicts in the Doctrines of Public Administration," in Altshuler (fn. 9), 75-77; and Hugh Heclo, "OMB and the Presidency—the Problem of 'Neutral Competence,'" *The Public Interest*, No. 38 (Winter 1975), 80-98.

[31] For a careful, illuminating account of the development of this role, and of conflicts among the Special Assistant's *roles*, see Hall (fn. 9).

particularly since he—unlike Goodpaster—was working for a President who was inclined to make a large number of specific decisions himself rather than delegate them to others. Moreover, Bundy's own instinct for power no doubt contributed to his ability to carve a major advisory and coordinating role for himself out of his position at the center of White House national security action processes. Moreover, the Bay of Pigs fiasco of April 1961 strengthened Kennedy's determination to exert control, with Bundy his principal vehicle.

Bundy recruited a small, aggressive, independent staff of intellectual operators who identified particularly with the current administration. They were inclined to seek out issues, to challenge departmental opinions, to press for surfacing of buried policy choices and for implementation of what they saw as Presidential desires. The staff was strengthened because Bundy was an apt delegator of authority, allowing staff members to operate rather freely as his agents. Another major innovation was direct access to information. The White House Situation Room was established, and equipment was installed enabling the White House to receive departmental cables to and from the State and Defense Departments and the Central Intelligence Agency; previously, Presidents and their White House aides had depended on the agencies to forward such communications.

Working for a President who tended to resist any firm sense of organizational structure and divison of labor, Bundy and his staff met the need for an informal yet wide-ranging effort at central coordination. In so doing, they began increasingly to play one of the roles originally envisaged for the Council—developing and pressing a broad, government-wide "Presidential" view encompassing diplomatic, military, and frequently economic elements in foreign policy.

One indication that this staff reform was filling a real need was that it lasted, in modified form, under a very different type of President. Lyndon Johnson did not duplicate his predecessor's wide-ranging involvement in foreign policy, preferring to limit himself to a few issues (though he dominated these), and to lean predominantly on his chief line officers, the Secretaries of State and Defense. Over time, this reduced the power of the Special Assistant and his staff, as did the fact that Bundy's style did not mesh with Johnson's nearly as well as it had with Kennedy's. Nevertheless, Bundy's successor, Walt Rostow—though he was originally given a reduced mandate—ended up performing essentially the same formal functions: coordinating the flow of information and intelligence to the President; managing the flow of decision papers to the President; monitoring governmental operations to promote coordination and responsiveness to Presidential interests; communicating Presidential decisions and instructions to departments and agencies; acting as liaison with Cabinet officers and other high foreign policy officials; and serving as personal adviser and source of staff analysis for the President.[32]

But it was under Henry Kissinger, of course, that the N.S.C. and its staff became synonyms. And as the President's foreign policy adviser, now renamed *Assistant* for National Security Affairs, Kissinger achieved unparalleled personal dominance. If Kennedy's active involvement and preference for an open decision-making style created a need for coordination which a Bundy could fill, Nixon's combination of a desire to dominate foreign policy personally, and a preference for dealing with and through a very small number of people, gave Kissinger an even greater opportunity. Moreover, Kissinger—unlike Bundy—was to become identified as the architect (and actual builder) of a particular set of policies. Under him, the strength of other senior N.S.C. staff members proved less than it had been under Bundy. His own closed style disinclined him to delegate, and this, plus the President's closed style, limited the direct access of Kissinger's subordinates to the Oval Office. The staff grew to unprecedented size, however—over fifty professionals —giving Kissinger considerable issue coverage and analytic and operational resources when he chose to employ them. Kissinger's strength was further enhanced, during the early months, by his role as director of the policy studies program already described. He thus combined the role of Eisenhower's Special Assistants—directing a structured planning process—with that of Bundy and Rostow—managing the day-to-day Presidential process. Before his first year was out, he was to add a further role which became prominent in 1971 and 1972—that of the President's personal, secret envoy handling those negotiations about which Nixon cared the most.

In September 1973, however, Kissinger became Secretary of State. And although he retained his N.S.C. position until November 1975, he gave priority to the Secretaryship almost immediately in order to play a stronger role of public leadership and to gain a measure of separation from the Watergate-enveloped White House. The Council's staff remained in existence, with its day-to-day operations under Kissinger's N.S.C. deputy, Brent Scowcroft. But, with most of Kissinger's chief aides now in State Department positions, it went into relative eclipse. Its formal neutrality vis-à-vis the departments was re-established in November 1975, when President Ford replaced Kissinger with Scowcroft

[32] On Rostow's functions, see Moose (fn. 9), 85–86.

as National Security Assistant. However, the staff did not return to its former power. The major reason, apparently, was that Ford was not playing the kind of assertive, initiating foreign policy role that most of his predecessors had played. Another important reason was the strong role that Kissinger had established and was loath to relinquish as long as he stayed in office. This waning of the N.S.C. staff has precedents in other election years—1952 and 1968 come to mind. In both cases, it rose to new importance after the Presidential inauguration the following January.

Lessons of the N.S.C. experience. What can be learned from this decidedly mixed experience—the fluctuation and evolution of the N.S.C. as Council, as process, and as staff?

The first lesson is that the N.S.C. has taken a course very different from that envisaged by its original proponents. They sought coordination of policy advice and execution, and the development of a transdepartmental view of national security problems, and these the N.S.C. has, to varying degrees, provided. But James Forrestal would roll over several times in his grave were he to learn that Richard Nixon had been able to use the N.S.C. to shield himself from his advisers, as the institutional base for a Presidency of unexampled isolation and considerable flexibility in decision and action.

Nixon was able to do this, of course, because of what the Council did become. Hence, the second clear lesson: the Council's most consistent value to Presidents has been to provide them with a senior official and staff to coordinate their personal foreign policy business, and serve as a broader coordinator of decision and action processes. The Council itself has increasingly been treated as a bore, if not an encumbrance. Formal planning processes have risen and fallen with particular Presidents— or, as in the case of the N.S.S.M.'s—declined within the tenure of a particular President. But three consecutive, very different Presidents found the National Security Assistant and his staff to be of considerable personal value. A fourth, Gerald Ford, emulated them formally by re-establishing the separation of the positions of Secretary and Assistant, though he did not accompany this action with a systematic effort to use the Assistant to reduce his dependence on his chief Cabinet advisers.

Even the rise of the National Security Assistant has been the result of special circumstances, including the disinclination or inability of two Secretaries of State—Dean Rusk and William Rogers—to exert leadership and achieve predominance as Acheson and Dulles did before them and Kissinger after. The third broad conclusion therefore is that the

N.S.C. in all its manifestations has reflected more than it has shaped the foreign policy making of particular administrations. Not only is the N.S.C. at the mercy of particular Presidents, to be used, reshaped, or ignored as they prefer. The impact of particular processes and the emergence of particular roles depends also on the broader pattern of relationships among top Presidential advisers. Eisenhower's planning process was limited by a Dulles determined to be Secretary of State in the maximum sense and a President quite willing to allow it. Both Bundy and Kissinger built the role of National Security Assistant into something much larger than envisaged because they met Presidential needs no one else was meeting. And when Bundy stayed on to serve a second President, his role came to shrink when Rusk increasingly met *Johnson's* criteria of performance for a Secretary of State.

BROADER PRESIDENTIAL ADVISORY SYSTEMS

The foregoing underscores the need to think in terms of broader systems that shape national security advice to Presidents, systems that include the N.S.C. but many other things besides. The need becomes particularly dramatic in the case of a Nixon and a Kissinger: the "closed" system for foreign policy making and execution which they had developed by 1971 and 1972 was so completely at variance with the structured system built around the Council as forum, relatively open to inputs from other officials, which they had proclaimed with much fanfare in January and February of 1969. Other Presidential "systems" for decision and action on foreign policy may defy such brief characterization. But all administrations do develop recurrent patterns of how issues reach the President, with what range of analysis and advice, whose advice is most valued on which subjects, and what roles senior officials play vis-à-vis the President and one another. When a particular issue arises, the manner of handling it will be shaped, to a considerable degree, by the "system" already in place. This is particularly true of crises perceived as requiring a quick response.

What are some of the variations in broad Presidential policy-making systems that have appeared in the postwar period? What substantive, stylistic, or organizational preferences on the part of Presidents and other senior officials have helped to determine them? At least eight related variables among Presidents and their advisory teams seem important in shaping their broader foreign policy-making systems. No attempt is made here to rank them in importance, or to delineate all of the many relationships among them.

One basic variable is *whether a President has a particularly clear organizational sense*, especially a conception of the appropriate roles for occupants of particular positions, and how much he is prepared to insist on its implementation. Eisenhower had such a sense to an unusual degree—he clearly distinguished between staff and line functions, between planning and operations, and he expected his subordinates to keep to their proper roles. Indeed, he himself deferred frequently to others' roles rather than insisting on command over them, a habit that lent support to the view that he became his system's prisoner. At the other extreme was Kennedy, who seems—perhaps by design—to have differentiated very little among individuals' roles. He dealt with those whom he found congenial and useful, handing them such assignments as he felt they could perform—much in the way some Senators handle their staffs. When a McNamara insisted on control of top Defense Department appointments and of his Department more generally, Kennedy could live with it and even came to welcome it. But such organizational order was not something he would have imposed himself, as evidenced by his choice of at least three other state appointees before he decided on Secretary Rusk. And his disorder had costs also, including confusion about who was responsible for what, about what "the policy" was, and who reflected the President's wishes.

A second, related variable is *how much particular Presidents have favored formality and regularity in the flow of analysis and advice to them*. Here Eisenhower similarly ranks as the most in favor of formal procedures, and Kennedy as the least. Truman inclines to the Eisenhower side, Johnson toward the Kennedy side. Nixon is an odd case. He certainly conceived of himself as preferring orderly procedures, but what he seems to have meant by this in practice was having an orderly, controlled personal environment. He ended up being served by highly informal procedures, though these were combined with very limited and controlled channels of access to his person.

A third important variable is *how much particular Presidents have had—and have wanted—strong leaders in the major line positions*, the Secretary of State above all, but also the Secretary of Defense. That is related, of course, to one of the most-discussed issues of foreign policy organization—whether a system of coordination and central management should be State Department-centered or White House-centered. It is related also to whether a President wishes to make a large number of decisions himself or to preside over a process in which decisions are largely made by others. All of this having been said, one is struck by the fact that most postwar Presidents have not perceived their Cabinet members as "natural enemies."[33] Truman and Eisenhower wanted and supported strong Secretaries of State and deferred to them. Johnson likewise deferred to Rusk. Even Kennedy, who was ambivalent on this point, was enthusiastic about Robert McNamara, the archetypal strong Cabinet member, and frustrated with Rusk. Richard Neustadt noted in 1963 that Kennedy "appears far less inclined than FDR to keep his senior ministers at arms length. . . . On the contrary, with those of his department heads whose work is most bound up with his from day to day—State, Defense, Justice, above all—he has sought a relationship as close and confidential and collegial as with his staff, and he has delegated tasks to them and their associates as though they all were members of his staff."[34] Gerald Ford seems particularly to have welcomed strong voices in his Cabinet—he retained some and appointed more. Only Nixon seems consistently to have preferred weakness in Cabinet positions, though he professed the contrary. His appointment of Kissinger as Secretary of State in 1973 seems attributable not to his stated desire "to get the work out in the departments where it belongs,"[35] but to his need to demonstrate renewed Administration vitality and distract attention from his personal plight in the first year of Watergate.

A fourth important variable, partly subject to a President's control but partly beyond it, is *how his principal advisers work out their own particular roles, jurisdictional boundaries, and relationships with one another.* Bundy, as National Security Assistant, deferred to Cabinet members much more than Kissinger did; Rusk accepted McNamara's primacy on military-strategic questions in a way Kissinger, as Secretary, would never have considered accepting Schlesinger's. Another dimension of the relationships among senior Presidential advisers is how much they are collegial and mutually supportive, and how much they are antagonistic.[36] There are always elements of both competition and

[33] The quote is from the first federal Budget Director, General Charles G. Dawes, who used to brief his successors about the job and end with the following: "Young man, if you retain nothing else that I have told you, remember this: Cabinet members are Vice Presidents in charge of spending, and as such they are the natural enemies of the President. Good day." Quoted by Kermit Gordon, "The Budget Director," in Thomas E. Cronin and Sanford D. Greenberg, eds., *The Presidential Advisory System* (New York: Harper and Row 1969), 61. It should perhaps be noted that Dawes was probably referring mainly to Cabinet members in charge of *domestic* Departments, with strong program interests and supporting constituencies.

[34] Neustadt, "Approaches to Staffing the Presidency: Notes on FDR and JFK" in Altshuler (fn. 9), 119.

[35] Quoted in the *New York Times*, August 23, 1973.

[36] On "competitive," "collegial," and "formalistic" management patterns in general

cooperation, but the mix differs—as do the effects on foreign policy. On balance, considerable collegiality seems desirable, but it can cause officials to avoid the hard questions and the rigorous and perhaps wounding debate necessary to subject difficult policy choices to hard scrutiny. This proved to be a serious flaw in policy making toward the end of the Truman Administration, and also, recurrently, in the Kennedy and Johnson regimes. The generally antagonistic relations among senior advisers during the Nixon Administration were also quite damaging, however, reinforcing the lack of interpersonal trust emanating from the President personally, and reinforcing the closed, two-man character of that system.

A fifth important variable is *how widely Presidents have wished to cast their nets for advice*. By this measure, Nixon stood clearly at one extreme and Kennedy at the other, and their unusually "closed" and "open" systems reflected these conflicting tendencies. Ranking the other three Presidents is harder. Johnson seemed to be seeking a range of advice, but frequently came down hard on proponents of views he wished not to face. Truman was content to receive the bulk of his advice through line channels once he found congenial Secretaries of State; Clark Clifford's main impact seems to have been prior to the Marshall-Acheson regime. Eisenhower welcomed and sometimes sought advice from outside line channels, but would defer in action to his Secretary of State. (This and some of the earlier variables help to determine how many senior officials will have a strong personal relationship with the President, and will be able to act, in Washington and vis-à-vis foreign governments, with the weight that such relationships allow.)

A sixth variable is *how broad a substantive involvement a President seeks personally*. Inevitably, he will deal formally with a very wide range of matters, but over what range does he seek to make a strong personal mark? Here Kennedy with his global interests ranks at the broad end. Johnson, in contrast, took on only a few issues that were not forced upon him. Gerald Ford likewise seems to have dealt chiefly with issues brought before him by ongoing world events and by his Secretary of State.

A seventh important variable relates to the type of advice a President wants: *what is his attitude toward divided counsel and toward interpersonal disputes among his principal advisers?* Does he typically seek alternative views as a means of enhancing his choice and leverage, or

Presidential decision making, see Richard T. Johnson, "Presidential Style," in Aaron Wildavsky, ed., *Perspectives on the Presidency* (Boston: Little, Brown 1975), 262–300.

does he want "agreed recommendations" from his advisers? Of the postwar Presidents, Eisenhower and Johnson explicitly pressed for concurrences—Eisenhower through his formal system, Johnson less formally. Kennedy and Nixon more frequently wanted the differences brought to them for decision, and Nixon was perhaps more willing than any of his postwar predecessors to *act* with divided counsel, though he shielded himself from personal exposure to advisory give-and-take. No President since F.D.R. seems to have welcomed personal rivalries among his chief aides.

An eighth variable is *how much a President seeks operational involvement—pre- and post-decision—as opposed to preferring his impact to come at a regular decision point.* How much is he a persistent intruder in the process, as opposed to a magistrate, seeing his role as deciding issues brought to him and having his wishes executed without further extensive personal effort? By this criterion, Kennedy and Johnson were "intruders," whereas Eisenhower and Nixon were "magistrates." Truman and Ford come closer to the latter role than to the former.

In addition to these variations, there is a whole range of personal Presidential characteristics that affect their systems. Do they prefer advice and information orally or in writing? If the former, do they prefer "one-on-one" or group sessions? How do they react to being confronted, personally, with a challenge to their policies? Can they "turn off" an adviser supporting a course they reject without discouraging him from such advocacy on other issues in the future? Nixon offers an unusual case here: a President almost incapable of delivering a strong no or rebuff to an aide, who—partly for that reason—dealt increasingly through staff aides who could.

PRESCRIPTION—PROBLEMS AND CHOICES

In view of the extensive postwar experience analyzed here, how ought Presidents to organize their advice-getting in the future? What can outside observers recommend to them? Given that the systems that evolve are so heavily dependent upon the personalities of Presidents and their chief aides, can general prescriptions be offered that are not tailored to fit a particular chief executive? The remainder of this article is a discussion of some such prescriptions.[37]

A BASIC DILEMMA: CHOICE VERSUS PERSISTENCE

Most thinking and writing about foreign policy advice to Presidents focuses on ensuring the wisest, most fully informed Presidential *choices,*

[37] The discussion will avoid duplication of the more comprehensive organizational proposals on foreign affairs presented in Destler (fn. 9), chap. 9.

from among the widest range of reasonable policy alternatives. That was the purpose of the most sophisticated formal inside effort to date—Nixon's N.S.S.M. system. It is the purpose also of most of the best academic work, notably that of Alexander George and his colleagues. The model (usually explicit) is the chief executive as magistrate, *the President deciding.*[38]

Yet Presidents need advice and support not just in deciding what they want, but in making their choices effective. They need help in implementation. Since it takes considerable time and effort for most policies to be put across, Presidents need both the fact and the appearance of steadfastness of purpose, of knowing and communicating what they are after, and of being skillful in getting it. Neustadt quoted Truman to the effect that what the powers of the Presidency amounted to was the chance to persuade others to do what they ought to do anyway. The word "ought" implies that the President already knew—as when he mobilized his limited power resources in 1947–1948 to win Congressional support of the Marshall Plan. The model here is a different one —*the President leading.*[39]

Obviously, Presidential advisers and advisory institutions need to support the President in both of these tasks: careful deliberation prior to decision; effective pursuit of the goal chosen in a decision when its attainment depends on more than Presidential action alone. Fortunately, all Presidents do get support toward both of these goals. Unfortunately, the goals are frequently in conflict. For Robert McNamara in 1967, continued escalation in Vietnam was futile and foreclosed other possibilities. What was needed was to reevaluate the situation and consider other, more limited options. His President, however, believed—or dearly wished to believe—that what was needed above all was perseverance to prevail over adversaries at home and abroad. And when McNamara surfaced some of his arguments before the Senate Armed Services Committee, Johnson "drew the analogy of a man trying to sell his house, while one of the sons of the family went to the prospective buyer to point out that there were leaks in the basement."[40]

To use Vietnam as an example today hardly presents the best argument for perseverance. But Richard Nixon behaved similarly in a much more successful case—that of China policy. Once he had set his course, he gave the utmost priority to careful implementation—maintaining

[38] See, for example, George (fns. 29 and 9); Hall (fn. 9); and Irving L. Janis, *Victims of Groupthink* (Boston: Houghton Mifflin 1972).

[39] See above all Richard Neustadt, *Presidential Power* (New York: Wiley & Sons 1960 and 1964).

[40] Quoted in Townsend Hoopes, *The Limits of Intervention* (New York: David McKay 1969), 90.

secrecy until the Kissinger visit (even though this foreclosed any very broad canvassing of alternative approaches), and placing very severe restrictions on intragovernmental consideration of China policy between his surprise announcement of July 15, 1971, and his visit the following February.[41] In both cases, consistency of purpose and execution were given priority; serious policy review was discouraged or prevented. And in both, the conflict between the two goals was real. The need for sending a consistent set of signals to Hanoi or China may have been exaggerated by Johnson or Nixon, but it was a real need and it stood to be threatened by any appearance of reconsideration or irresolution. The tension had other roots as well. Johnson needed unity among his advisers to sell a controversial policy at home; Nixon needed some degree of secrecy in approaching Peking.

The fact that there is a conflict between full consideration of all options (irresolution?) and perseverance in a policy course (tunnel vision?) suggests that Presidential advice must balance and trade off the two; unfortunately, it is hard to develop objective criteria that determine how the trade-off should be made. In practice, people tend to choose one value or the other, according to whether they like the current policy; it is a "conflict between coherence and change."[42] Another way the trade-off has been made in more than one Administration is by emphasizing choice early in the term, and execution thereafter. As Robert H. Johnson has written, "at the beginning of any administration" leaders tend to believe "that existing policy is defective" and that "the international environment is relatively malleable."[43] They are in search of alternatives, of ways to make an impact. Later on, they have a reduced sense of the possible and are hooked to their own choices. This helps explain the evolution of the Nixon-Kissinger system from an open process, oriented toward widening Presidential options, to a very closed implementation system, with the President's Assistant becoming predominantly a "line" officer engaged in making and carrying out decisions on policy execution.

Another basis for making the trade-off is one this author has suggested elsewhere[44]—one's conception of how U.S. foreign policy is made. If one

[41] For one contemporary report, see Rowland Evans and Robert Novak, "Foggy Bottom Faces a Trauma," *Los Angeles Times*, August 30, 1971, cited in John S. Esterline and Robert Black, *Inside Foreign Policy* (Palo Alto, Calif.: Mayfield Publishing Company 1975), 231. It refers to an instruction by Secretary Rogers warning against "written memoranda raising questions about such dramatic policies as Mr. Nixon's approach to mainland China."
[42] Destler (fn. 9), 292.   [43] Johnson (fn. 9), 716.
[44] Destler, "Comment: Multiple Advocacy: Some Limits and Costs," *American Political Science Review*, Vol. 66 (September 1972), esp. pp. 787–89.

sees it as shaped predominantly by a manageable number of Presidential decisions, one advocates a system that spurs the broadest range of pre-decision analysis and advocacy. If one believes that the truly consequential Presidential decisions are exceptional, and that most policy evolves from day-to-day actions at several governmental levels, one emphasizes the advice and support Presidents need in pursuing effective policies over time, as well as the need for the government to act with coherence to achieve consistent impact. One would not favor this degree of emphasis on execution, however, if one felt—either because of a negative view of the Presidency or a skepticism about the prospects of strong policy initiatives in an uncertain world—that strong Presidential leadership were likely to bring more harm than good. In such a case, one might well emphasize care in choice and regularity in reconsideration of choices previously taken, with damage limitation as the goal. This face of the dilemma was highlighted by what Acheson told Neustadt after Johnson torpedoed the multilateral force: "I know your theory. You think Presidents should be warned. You're wrong. Presidents should be given confidence."[45]

Finally, some have argued that it is typically a President's subordinates who favor strong action, while the President's interests are usually served by a deferral of choice—"keeping options open." As Graham Allison has put it: "In policy making then, the issue looking *down* is options: how to preserve my leeway until time clarifies uncertainties . . . the issue looking *upwards* is confidence: how to give the boss confidence in doing what needs to be done."[46] The Neustadt "theory" denounced by Acheson is generally consistent with Allison's proposition—though not with Neustadt's celebration elsewhere of Truman's (and Acheson's) Marshall Plan leadership. In this view, Presidents not only want to have a range of options available, but want to retain them—to avoid choosing as long as possible. By contrast, foreign policy making systems built around options usually assume that a President's interest is often in making a choice; that includes not just the 1969 Nixon system, but George's multiple-advocacy proposal.

But to carry a system of "open options" to its logical conclusion is to forego effectiveness of execution almost entirely. Thomas L. Hughes wrote ten years ago that any prolonged "attempt to keep all options open prevents the persistent pursuit of any one of them. . . . A foreign policy whose chief characteristic is a plethora of unclosed options is

---

[45] Acheson quoted in Steinbruner (fn. 4), 332.
[46] Allison, "Conceptual Models and the Cuban Missile Crisis," *American Political Science Review*, Vol. 63 (September 1969), 711.

not much of a foreign policy at all."[47] Ultimately, a President's influence is not shaped by the choices he defers, though it may be protected by them. It comes from the choices he makes and perseveres in. Admittedly, Presidents do not wish to have subordinates force their hand on decisions. But some, like Truman and Nixon, have placed very positive value on being—to appropriate a phrase recently applied to a Japanese Prime Minister—"men of decision and action." Their historical reputations, for better or worse, will rest on the courses they persisted in following. To quote Dean Acheson again, "Flexibility in maneuver may be highly desirable in certain circumstances, but when it leaves one's own and friendly forces and commanders uncertain of the nature and purpose of the operations or of who has responsibility for what, it can be a handicap. Machiavelli was writing for weak princes."[48]

If one accepts the need to emphasize effectiveness of execution as well as care in decision in foreign policy making systems, and if one accepts further the elusiveness of general rules to establish which value should receive priority when, prescription must fall back upon a need to institutionalize both. This offers a marginally new way of looking at an old question of foreign policy making—whether the President's prime adviser should be the Secretary of State or the National Security Assistant, and what sort of balance should exist between the Secretary and the White House staff.

A STATE- OR WHITE HOUSE-CENTERED SYSTEM: THE NEED TO CHOOSE ONE
AND BALANCE IT WITH THE OTHER

Typically, those who stress policy review and choice focus on staff functions and officials; those who emphasize execution stress line officers. Thus, Alexander George and David Hall concentrate on the actual and potential role of the National Security Assistant, while Dean Acheson's views were clear enough on the other side, notwithstanding his partial eleventh-hour recantation.[49] For the Assistant's chief roles are, or ought to be, "staff functions."[50] And while the Secretary of State also performs, and should perform, important staff duties for the President, his direct "line" responsibilities—representation, negotiation, direction of a major department, advocating policy before the public and the Congress—are very great.

This observer's (relative) emphasis on execution, on the difficulty of

---

[47] Hughes, "Relativity in Foreign Policy," *Foreign Affairs*, xlv (July 1967), 676.
[48] Acheson, *Present at the Creation* (New York: Norton 1969), 734.
[49] Acheson, "The Eclipse of the State Department," *Foreign Affairs*, xlix (July 1971), esp. pp. 603–06.
[50] *Murphy Commission Report* (fn. 8), 4.

actually pursuing coherent, purposive foreign policies, has led him to advocate a system built around a team of "Presidential" officials combining line and staff roles, headed by the Secretary of State and including other senior State Department officials. Such a team seems more likely to be able to combine responsiveness to the President with leadership of the broader government in translating Presidential policy into day-to-day bureaucratic action. But a simple "line solution" of the sort apparently favored by Acheson (and adopted, to some degree, by Truman) does not seem desirable. Such a solution would meet the needs of subordinates at the expense of superiors, who would become overdependent upon them for information and advice as well as action. There is a need for each executive to have a staff strong enough to act as a check and a prod to the executives at the level below, to review policies, and to look for alternatives.

In two respects, the argument for prime reliance on the Secretary of State seems stronger today than when it was advanced in 1971 and 1972.[51] For one thing, the *possibility* has been demonstrated anew— there has been a strong Secretary for the past three years. Second, the strong current immediate impact of domestic politics on foreign policy —the subject of the next section of this essay—increases the importance of having the President's chief foreign policy adviser in an office where he must deal regularly, seriously, and often openly with Congress, press, and public.

This does not, however, mean that the Secretary of State should have the lead on all issues in which some foreign policy interest is involved. This article has concentrated on national security advice, but international economic problems also play a major role in American foreign policy. On these it should not be assumed that foreign policy concerns will or should prevail over domestic ones. When a question on grain sales to Russia, for example, comes to the President for decision, he cannot normally expect from the Secretary of State a balanced weighing of international considerations against the domestic gains or losses in terms of farm income, consumer food prices, and so forth. The impact of even a strong Secretary of State will and should diminish as foreign policy issues overlap with domestic; he will play less the role of leader responsible for balancing *all* Presidential concerns, and more the role of spokesman for just *some* of these concerns.

Even on issues within the sphere of national security, it is not desirable for the Secretary of State to be the National Security Assistant as well.

[51] Destler, "The Nixon NSC: Can One Man Do?" *Foreign Policy*, No. 5 (Winter 1971–72), 28–40; and Destler (fn. 9), chap. 9.

The danger of too much predominance by one adviser is that execution will gain too much priority over policy analysis and review—that this adviser, overly staked to his own actions and enterprises, will be reluctant to consider and bring up options that threaten these actions and enterprises. Ironically, it seems to matter little in this respect whether the official exercising such predominance is National Security Assistant or Secretary of State. The Nixon system of 1971, bent on opening relations with China its own way, could not have been less suitably structured for fully evaluating the damage its particular approach was likely to do to relations with Japan. So, while a predominant Secretary needs to be checked by a White House foreign policy staff outside of his control, a predominant Assistant needs to be limited also. One way that seems desirable is to keep the Assistant out of direct policy implementation and negotiation (though he can and should continue to monitor such activities by others and transmit relevant Presidential orders to them). Such a limitation requires, of course, that the Secretary of State and other key "line" officials be strong enough, with good and visible Presidential relationships, to carry out these functions themselves. In addition, the Assistant should not play the role of public spokesman and defender of policy (and should be cautious and selective in his private advocacy) in order not to limit his capacity for evenhandedness and openness to policy changes. If the way to check a strong Secretary is through alternative staff resources, the way to check a strong Assistant is through limiting his line functions. In both cases, if it is desirable to have one primary adviser for the sake of effective execution, his power should be limited to promote breadth of choice, to encourage fuller presentation of options to the President than extreme power concentration in one subordinate allows. None of this can be done completely or precisely—the roles of high officials tend to overflow particular functional categories. But norms can and do develop about the roles appropriate to particular high positions, and limits of this sort could—if widely supported—influence various Presidential systems.

In a system centered around the Secretary of State, there remain serious questions about how exactly the White House should be staffed. Is a custodial function of the sort that George envisages possible? It seems unlikely that a "Special Assistant" to the President can be effective in the role of managing the process of Presidential choice—of insuring the broadest canvassing of possibilities and the most fruitful analysis and debate of these possibilities—if that is the only role that he has. He needs other staff roles in which he serves the President and can establish his value to the President; he must also have other roles in order to give him a sufficient feel for where the chief executive's mind is on foreign policy, something that is essential to managing an advocacy process before the President. Such roles should be chosen with an eye to reinforcing his Presidential relationship while limiting the danger properly emphasized by George and Hall—that of distorting the "custodian's" role by compromising his objectivity. The most appropriate ones would seem to be those of managing the President's daily foreign policy business and overseeing policy implementation, especially on issues of particular Presidential concern.

The problem then arises as to whether such roles would not, together with day-to-day proximity to the President, give the Assistant too much weight, conflicting with the exercise of a custodial function and leading inevitably to an influence that precludes the pre-eminence of a Secretary of State. Kissinger seems to have accepted a new National Security Assistant with reluctance, notwithstanding Scowcroft's prior service as his subordinate. As Graham Allison has put it in his recent study for the Murphy Commission: won't the "holder of the ring" typically decide to "play the game himself," as did "Bundy on Vietnam" and "Kissinger on everything"?[52]

The major way to resolve this dilemma, if there is a resolution, must be care in choosing the person to fill the position, combined with Presidential attentiveness to the dangers, and determination to avoid them. One possibility, however, might be to reduce, at least marginally, the title and the status of the National Security Assistant so that he would not pose as great a "threat" to Cabinet officials. This might be done as part of a broader reorganization and merger of White House staffs serving the President on major policy issues.[53]

[52] Allison, "Overview of Findings and Recommendations From Defense and Arms Control Cases," Appendix K (Volume 4) to the *Murphy Commission Report* (fn. 8), 38. The language quoted is in reference to a White House staffing proposal put forward by Francis Bator.

[53] Robert H. Johnson, for example, has suggested eliminating the N.S.C. and other parallel bodies, replacing them with less formal Cabinet-level councils appropriate to particular problems under consideration, and supporting them all with a unified "Cabinet staff." One of "perhaps four deputies" would handle "foreign security" issues, another would concentrate on "international interdependence" issues; the other two would cover domestic matters. (See, for example, his "Managing Interdependence: Restructuring the U.S. Government," in John Sewell, ed., *The U.S. and World Development: Agenda for Action 1977* [Overseas Development Council, forthcoming].) Graham T. Allison and Peter L. Szanton have urged that "an executive committee of the Cabinet become the chief forum for high-level review and decision of all major issues combining 'foreign,' 'domestic,' and 'economic' implications." See *Remaking Foreign Policy: The Organizational Connection* (New York: Basic Books 1976), chap. 4. This "ExCab" would be supported by a staff incorporating those of the N.S.C., the Domestic Council, and the Economic Policy Board.

Although the implications of such proposals require analysis beyond the scope of this

The influence of domestic politics in shaping and constraining American foreign policy hardly needs elaboration today. Yet it has long been considered improper, somehow, to take this fully into account. As Morton Halperin puts it, "There is a strong and widely held view in the United States that it is immoral to let domestic political considerations influence decisions which may affect war and peace. . . . This belief is so strongly held that senior officials frequently deny in public, and even apparently to themselves, that they take domestic politics into account."[54] In the late forties, of course, high U.S. officials were very sensitive to the need to sell particular policies to the Congress and to compromise on details if necessary to do so. They remembered Woodrow Wilson and the League of Nations very well. But as the years passed and (except on foreign aid) Congress acceded to the activist foreign policies of successive administrations, the notion of domestic politics being out of place here joined with *de facto* executive primacy to nourish the conviction that foreign policy was overridingly, by right, the affair of the executive branch. One product of these related tendencies has been that Presidents do not normally have at their disposal analyses explicitly relating foreign policy choices to domestic political realities. To relate them *ad hoc* is to some degree the responsibility of all politically appointed leaders. But foreign policy officials seem to perform this task incompletely, reluctantly, and with a sense that such "low politics" ought not to sully the pursuit of high diplomacy.

---

article, they should certainly not be dismissed as lightly as the *Murphy Commission Report* (fn. 8), 36, rejects a similar proposal. Employing the Cabinet in this way would not necessarily prove "cumbersome and inefficient" because the Cabinet would seldom need to meet as a whole—the real business would be done by ExCab, the Staff, or the particular Cabinet subgroups.

A key issue here is whether current governmental organization gives undue prominence to national security concerns and excessive influence to national security institutions. Graham Allison so argues in his Murphy Commission studies. And though the "militarization of American foreign policy" in the fifties and sixties seems to have had causes mainly outside the structure of Presidential advisory institutions, the continuing institutional emphasis on national security policy as a relatively separate and superior sphere is certainly open to question today. Broadening the N.S.C. and staff to encompass general Presidential policy would remedy these limitations. If such reform were to name the highest aide working full time on national security a *Deputy* Assistant to the President, it would certainly make him less likely to eclipse Cabinet members. The question then arises, of course, whether he would have enough leverage at that level to play the staff role strongly and effectively. Certainly he and the other major deputies would need to deal directly with the President.

[54] Morton H. Halperin, *Bureaucratic Politics and Foreign Policy* (Washington, D.C.: Brookings Institution 1974), 63–64.

Many questions can be raised about this attitude. Why should sensitivity to domestic politics elsewhere—a must for effective diplomacy—be legitimate while response to home politics is considered illegitimate? What *should* be the source of American foreign policy priorities if not the domestic political process? The point to be made here is more limited. Misreading of domestic politics—or failure to take it *very* seriously —can be disastrously counterproductive in terms of the goals of foreign policy leaders themselves. There are numerous recent examples, such as the fiasco over arms to Turkey, and the long wrangle over relating most-favored-nation treatment to Soviet policy on Jewish emigration. One will be singled out here: President Ford's request for a $522 million supplemental appropriation for military aid to Vietnam and Cambodia in January 1975. (This request was made before any of the devastating military setbacks that brought a Communist victory by May; the universal prognosis was that a major challenge was at least a year away.) The 93rd Congress had cut the money requested for Vietnam from the Administration's request, and now the much more militant, more anti-Vietnam, more Democratic 94th Congress was being pressed to restore the cut. One might have expected that a foreign policy leadership still bleeding over Turkey and Soviet trade would not go around looking for another rebuff, another issue where its inability to "deliver" the Congress would be dramatized. Yet, Ford and Kissinger plunged ahead and strongly urged the new Congress to reverse the old. As was easily predictable,[55] the request never had a chance, and this Congressional inaction (and the more general criticism of Vietnam military aid which the request was bound to trigger) may have helped to bring President Nguyen Van Thieu to make the disastrous strategic decisions that led to the North Vietnamese victory. It is important to emphasize that this particular request, unlike the emergency request later that spring, was not forced by crisis; rather, it may have helped to precipitate one.

Certainly, in the years to come, American foreign policy is either going to involve creative, constructive Presidential cooperation with a yet-to-emerge Congressional leadership, or a trimming of American sails to the prevailing, rather negative winds. In either case, the effective integration of domestic political advice and foreign policy advice becomes a matter of some urgency. Foreign policy leaders must face, explicitly and systematically, the constraints, interests, and values that have weight in the U.S. domestic process and build their policies upon these interests and values. Alternatively, they must form strong alliances

---

[55] *Congressional Quarterly Weekly Report* of February 15, 1975, for example, indicated that the request had "little support."

with leading political figures to overcome some of the constraints, as Truman did with Senator Arthur Vandenberg.

One useful prescription, implemented (though not for this reason) by President Nixon in 1973, is to make the primary foreign policy adviser the Secretary of State, since this position makes him deal directly and continuously with Congress and the broader public political arena, and since he will suffer badly—as Henry Kissinger sometimes has—from his mistakes in that arena. And domestic political sensitivity should be a major qualification when future Presidents recruit for the secretaryship and other senior foreign policy positions. But such officials' orientation toward foreign relations will necessarily limit such sensitivity, so attention must be given to White House-level staffs and processes as well. Obviously, "inside" advisory reform cannot resolve any President's domestic political problems. Paul Hammond noted sixteen years ago that what may be the National Security Council's policy or the President's policy cannot become *U.S.* policy until "the give and take of the NSC chamber" is "repeated for the interested public in the Congressional-executive dialogue and the other forums of our public life."[56] Still, internal reform can help. One possibility is to assign to a portion of the N.S.C. staff or to the broader White House staff the explicit responsibility of analyzing public and Congressional sentiment and how it affects foreign policy choices.[57] Robert Johnson has recommended a second, more *ad hoc* measure: to provide a combined foreign policy/domestic political staff to whatever official a President chooses to employ as a domestic/political watchdog for his foreign policy.[58]

TOWARD A MID-TERM "SYSTEM REVIEW"?

Finally, one lesson provided by all of the postwar advisory experience is that Presidential systems evolve; the advisory system that a President finds two or three years into his term is not precisely what he or anyone else intended. Perhaps because of our emphasis on the formal, we tend to think of policy-making systems as being set into place at the beginning of a President's tenure, and fully operative thereafter. Public attention, journalistic and academic, focuses on policy-making systems mainly at the beginning of Presidential terms, and when a new President is entering office. And after a system has evolved, there is a

[56] Hammond (fn. 9), 154.
[57] This might prove easier if one of the Cabinet staff proposals noted in footnote 53 was adopted.
[58] Johnson (fn. 53), chap. 5.

tendency to believe that what exists is what the President has wanted all along.

Particular attention to the Presidential advisory system is appropriate at the beginning of a President's tenure, since that is the time when he has the greatest ability to influence it. He is filling all the major positions at once, and the government is waiting to learn what new procedures he will propose or impose. Unfortunately, it is also the time when Presidents know the least about what they are doing—about what being President means in day-to-day practice, and about the individuals and types of individuals they will need in high policy roles. President-elect Kennedy told John Kenneth Galbraith in December 1960: "I must make the appointments now; a year hence I will know who I really want to appoint."[59] Moreover, Presidents come to office with predilections and preferences in style that frequently are internally inconsistent, and even more frequently don't suit their job or their priorities as they come to define them. They make some appointments that mesh with these preferences and predilections, and some that don't. Yet they are unlikely to take a serious, overall second look: they are busy, and they don't want to admit failure in their original efforts.

This suggests the need for a broad mid-term review, conducted for the President, which analyzes how his system is actually working. How well is it providing the President with timely choices, the full range of choices? How well is it facilitating consistent and fruitful action along the general policy lines he prefers? How well is it dealing with and responding to the larger national political community, particularly the Congress? Exactly who would best conduct such a review will vary with the circumstances. Preferably it should be someone responsive directly to Presidential interests and concerns, knowledgeable about high foreign policy making, but not holding a major appointment in the current system. If the system possessed an actor approaching the model of George's "custodian," that official could and should play a role in adapting the system to make it perform more effectively. But, precisely because he would be a central actor of the system to be evaluated, the custodian should probably not conduct the review himself.

No such review could remain above the struggles for power and position which are a part of every administration. The recommendation of the advisory group Ford convened after taking office—that he appoint a National Security Assistant other than Henry Kissinger—was inevitably interpreted as an effort to "get Henry." But a discreetly con-

[59] Galbraith, *Ambassador's Journal* (Boston: Houghton Mifflin 1969), 7.

ducted review that is persuasive in its findings should help convince the President to assume the costs in personal feelings of making immediate personnel changes, in order to gain the greater benefits of improvement in the quality of the advice he gets, and in the advisers and institutions that provide it.

Books Written Under the Auspices of the
CENTER OF INTERNATIONAL STUDIES
PRINCETON UNIVERSITY
1952-79

Gabriel A. Almond, *The Appeals of Communism* (Princeton University Press 1954)

William W. Kaufmann, ed., *Military Policy and National Security* (Princeton University Press 1956)

Klaus Knorr, *The War Potential of Nations* (Princeton University Press 1956)

Lucian W. Pye, *Guerrilla Communism in Malaya* (Princeton University Press 1956)

Charles De Visscher, *Theory and Reality in Public International Law*, trans. by P. E. Corbett (Princeton University Press 1957; rev. ed. 1968)

Bernard C. Cohen, *The Political Process and Foreign Policy: The Making of the Japanese Peace Settlement* (Princeton University Press 1957)

Myron Weiner, *Party Politics in India: The Development of a Multi-Party System* (Princeton University Press 1957)

Percy E. Corbett, *Law in Diplomacy* (Princeton University Press 1959)

Rolf Sannwald and Jacques Stohler, *Economic Integration: Theoretical Assumptions and Consequences of European Unification*, trans. by Herman Karreman (Princeton University Press 1959)

Klaus Knorr, ed., *NATO and American Security* (Princeton University Press 1959)

Gabriel A. Almond and James S. Coleman, eds., *The Politics of the Developing Areas* (Princeton University Press 1960)

Herman Kahn, *On Thermonuclear War* (Princeton University Press 1960)

Sidney Verba, *Small Groups and Political Behavior: A Study of Leadership* (Princeton University Press 1961)

Robert J. C. Butow, *Tojo and the Coming of the War* (Princeton University Press 1961)

Glenn H. Snyder, *Deterrence and Defense: Toward a Theory of National Security* (Princeton University Press 1961)

Klaus Knorr and Sidney Verba, eds., *The International System: Theoretical Essays* (Princeton University Press 1961)

Peter Paret and John W. Shy, *Guerrillas in the 1960's* (Praeger 1962)

George Modelski, *A Theory of Foreign Policy* (Praeger 1962)

Klaus Knorr and Thornton Read, eds., *Limited Strategic War* (Praeger 1963)

Frederick S. Dunn, *Peace-Making and the Settlement with Japan* (Princeton University Press 1963)

Arthur L. Burns and Nina Heathcote, *Peace-Keeping by United Nations Forces* (Praeger 1963)

Richard A. Falk, *Law, Morality, and War in the Contemporary World* (Praeger 1963)

James N. Rosenau, *National Leadership and Foreign Policy: A Case Study in the Mobilization of Public Support* (Princeton University Press 1963)

Gabriel A. Almond and Sidney Verba, *The Civic Culture: Political Attitudes and Democracy in Five Nations* (Princeton University Press 1963)

Bernard C. Cohen, *The Press and Foreign Policy* (Princeton University Press 1963)

Richard L. Sklar, *Nigerian Political Parties: Power in an Emergent African Nation* (Princeton University Press 1963)

Peter Paret, *French Revolutionary Warfare from Indochina to Algeria: The Analysis of a Political and Military Doctrine* (Praeger 1964)

Harry Eckstein, ed., *Internal War: Problems and Approaches* (Free Press 1964)

Cyril E. Black and Thomas P. Thornton, eds., *Communism and Revolution: The Strategic Uses of Political Violence* (Princeton University Press 1964)

Miriam Camps, *Britain and the European Community 1955-1963* (Princeton University Press 1964)

Thomas P. Thornton, ed., *The Third World in Soviet Perspective: Studies by Soviet Writers on the Developing Areas* (Princeton University Press 1964)

James N. Rosenau, ed., *International Aspects of Civil Strife* (Princeton University Press 1964)

Sidney I. Ploss, *Conflict and Decision-Making in Soviet Russia: A Case Study of Agricultural Policy, 1953-1963* (Princeton University Press 1965)

Richard A. Falk and Richard J. Barnet, eds., *Security in Disarmament* (Princeton University Press 1965)

Karl von Vorys, *Political Development in Pakistan* (Princeton University Press 1965)

Harold and Margaret Sprout, *The Ecological Perspective on Human Affairs, With Special Reference to International Politics* (Princeton University Press 1965)

Klaus Knorr, *On the Uses of Military Power in the Nuclear Age* (Princeton University Press 1966)

Harry Eckstein, *Division and Cohesion in Democracy: A Study of Norway* (Princeton University Press 1966)

Cyril E. Black, *The Dynamics of Modernization: A Study in Comparative History* (Harper and Row 1966)

Peter Kunstadter, ed., *Southeast Asian Tribes, Minorities, and Nations* (Princeton University Press 1967)

E. Victor Wolfenstein, *The Revolutionary Personality: Lenin, Trotsky, Gandhi* (Princeton University Press 1967)

Leon Gordenker, *The UN Secretary-General and the Maintenance of Peace* (Columbia University Press 1967)

Oran R. Young, *The Intermediaries: Third Parties in International Crises* (Princeton University Press 1967)

James N. Rosenau, ed., *Domestic Sources of Foreign Policy* (Free Press 1967)

Richard F. Hamilton, *Affluence and the French Worker in the Fourth Republic* (Princeton University Press 1967)

Linda B. Miller, *World Order and Local Disorder: The United Nations and Internal Conflicts* (Princeton University Press 1967)

Henry Bienen, *Tanzania: Party Transformation and Economic Development* (Princeton University Press 1967)

Wolfram F. Hanrieder, *West German Foreign Policy, 1949-1963: International Pressures and Domestic Response* (Stanford University Press 1967)

Richard H. Ullman, *Britain and the Russian Civil War: November 1918-February 1920* (Princeton University Press 1968)

Robert Gilpin, *France in the Age of the Scientific State* (Princeton University Press 1968)

William B. Bader, *The United States and the Spread of Nuclear Weapons* (Pegasus 1968)

Richard A. Falk, *Legal Order in a Violent World* (Princeton University Press 1968)

Cyril E. Black, Richard A. Falk, Klaus Knorr and Oran R. Young, *Neutralization and World Politics* (Princeton University Press 1968)

Oran R. Young, *The Politics of Force: Bargaining During International Crises* (Princeton University Press 1969)

Klaus Knorr and James N. Rosenau, eds., *Contending Approaches to International Politics* (Princeton University Press 1969)

James N. Rosenau, ed., *Linkage Politics: Essays on the Convergence of National and International Systems* (Free Press 1969)

John T. McAlister, Jr., *Viet Nam: The Origins of Revolution* (Knopf 1969)

Jean Edward Smith, *Germany Beyond the Wall: People, Politics and Prosperity* (Little, Brown 1969)

James Barros, *Betrayal from Within: Joseph Avenol, Secretary-General of the League of Nations, 1933-1940* (Yale University Press 1969)

Charles Hermann, *Crises in Foreign Policy: A Simulation Analysis* (Bobbs-Merrill 1969)

Robert C. Tucker, *The Marxian Revolutionary Idea: Essays on Marxist Thought and Its Impact on Radical Movements* (W. W. Norton 1969)

Harvey Waterman, *Political Change in Contemporary France: The Politics of an Industrial Democracy* (Charles E. Merrill 1969)

Cyril E. Black and Richard A. Falk, eds., *The Future of the International Legal Order*. Vol. I: *Trends and Patterns* (Princeton University Press 1969)

Ted Robert Gurr, *Why Men Rebel* (Princeton University Press 1969)

C. Sylvester Whitaker, *The Politics of Tradition: Continuity and Change in Northern Nigeria 1946-1966* (Princeton University Press 1970)

Richard A. Falk, *The Status of Law in International Society* (Princeton University Press 1970)

276

John T. McAlister, Jr. and Paul Mus, *The Vietnamese and Their Revolution* (Harper & Row 1970)

Klaus Knorr, *Military Power and Potential* (D. C. Heath 1970)

Cyril E. Black and Richard A. Falk, eds., *The Future of the International Legal Order*. Vol. II: *Wealth and Resources* (Princeton University Press 1970)

Leon Gordenker, ed., *The United Nations in International Politics* (Princeton University Press 1971)

Cyril E. Black and Richard A. Falk, eds., *The Future of the International Legal Order*. Vol. III: *Conflict Management* (Princeton University Press 1971)

Francine R. Frankel, *India's Green Revolution: Economic Gains and Political Costs* (Princeton University Press 1971)

Harold and Margaret Sprout, *Toward a Politics of the Planet Earth* (Van Nostrand Reinhold Co. 1971)

Cyril E. Black and Richard A. Falk, eds., *The Future of the International Legal Order*. Vol. IV: *The Structure of the International Environment* (Princeton University Press 1972)

Gerald Garvey, *Energy, Ecology, Economy* (W. W. Norton 1972)

Richard H. Ullman, *The Anglo-Soviet Accord* (Princeton University Press 1973)

Klaus Knorr, *Power and Wealth: The Political Economy of International Power* (Basic Books 1973)

Anton Bebler, *Military Rule in Africa: Dahomey, Ghana, Sierra Leone, and Mali* (Praeger Publishers 1973)

Robert C. Tucker, *Stalin as Revolutionary 1879-1929: A Study in History and Personality* (W. W. Norton 1973)

Edward L. Morse, *Foreign Policy and Interdependence in Gaullist France* (Princeton University Press 1973)

Henry Bienen, *Kenya: The Politics of Participation and Control* (Princeton University Press 1974)

Gregory J. Massell, *The Surrogate Proletariat: Moslem Women and Revolutionary Strategies in Soviet Central Asia, 1919-1929* (Princeton University Press 1974)

James N. Rosenau, *Citizenship Between Elections: An Inquiry Into The Mobilizable American* (Free Press 1974)

Ervin Laszlo, *A Strategy for the Future: The Systems Approach to World Order* (George Braziller 1974)

R. J. Vincent, *Nonintervention and International Order* (Princeton University Press 1974)

Jan H. Kalicki, *The Pattern of Sino-American Crises: Political-Military Interactions in the 1950s* (Cambridge University Press 1975)

Klaus Knorr, *The Power of Nations: The Political Economy of International Relations* (Basic Books, Inc. 1975)

James P. Sewell, *UNESCO and World Politics: Engaging in International Relations* (Princeton University Press 1975)

277

Richard A. Falk, *A Global Approach to National Policy* (Harvard University Press 1975)

Harry Eckstein and Ted Robert Gurr, *Patterns of Authority: A Structural Basis for Political Inquiry* (John Wiley & Sons 1975)

Cyril E. Black, Marius B. Jansen, Herbert S. Levine, Marion J. Levy, Jr., Henry Rosovsky, Gilbert Rozman, Henry D. Smith, II, and S. Frederick Starr, *The Modernization of Japan and Russia* (Free Press 1975)

Leon Gordenker, *International Aid and National Decisions: Development Programs in Malawi, Tanzania, and Zambia* (Princeton University Press 1976)

Carl von Clausewitz, *On War*, edited and translated by Michael Howard and Peter Paret (Princeton University Press 1976)

Gerald Garvey and Lou Ann Garvey, *International Resource Flows* (D. C. Heath 1977)

Walter F. Murphy and Joseph Tanenhaus, *Comparative Constitutional Law: Cases and Commentaries* (St. Martin's Press 1977)

Gerald Garvey, *Nuclear Power and Social Planning: The City of the Second Sun* (D. C. Heath 1977)

Richard E. Bissell, *Apartheid and International Organizations* (Westview Press 1977)

David P. Forsythe, *Humanitarian Politics: The International Committee of the Red Cross* (Johns Hopkins University Press 1977)

Paul E. Sigmund, *The Overthrow of Allende and the Politics of Chile, 1964-1976* (University of Pittsburgh Press 1977)

Henry S. Bienen, *Armies and Parties in Africa* (Holmes and Meier 1978)

Harold and Margaret Sprout, *The Context of Environmental Politics: Unfinished Business for America's Third Century* (University Press of Kentucky 1978)

Samuel S. Kim, *China, The United Nations, and World Order* (Princeton University Press 1979)

S. Basheer Ahmed, *Nuclear Fuel and Energy* (D. C. Heath 1979)

Robert C. Johansen, *The National Interest and the Human Interest: An Analysis of U.S. Foreign Policy* (Princeton University Press 1980)

Richard A. Falk and Samuel S. Kim, eds., *The War System: An Interdisciplinary Approach* (Westview Press 1980)

James H. Billington, *Fire in the Minds of Men: Origins of the Revolutionary Faith* (Basic Books 1980)

Bennett Ramberg, *Destruction of Nuclear Energy Facilities in War: The Problem and the Implications* (D. C. Heath 1980)

Gregory T. Kruglak, *The Politics of United States Decision-Making in United Nations Specialized Agencies: The Case of the International Labor Organization* (University Press of America 1980)

W. P. Davison and Leon Gordenker, eds., *Resolving Nationality Conflicts: The Role of Public Opinion Research* (Praeger Publishers 1980)

278

James C. Hsiung and Samuel S. Kim, eds., *China in the Global Community* (Praeger Publishers 1980)

Douglas Kinn'ard, *The Secretary of Defense* (University Press of Kentucky 1980)

Richard Falk, *Human Rights and State Sovereignty* (Holmes & Meier 1981)

James H. Mittelman, *Underdevelopment and the Transition to Socialism: Mozambique and Tanzania* (Academic Press 1981)

Gilbert Rozman, ed., *The Modernization of China* (The Free Press 1981)

Robert C. Tucker, *Politics as Leadership*. The Paul Anthony Brick Lectures. Eleventh Series (University of Missouri Press 1981)

Robert Gilpin, *War and Change in World Politics* (Cambridge University Press 1981)

Nicholas G. Onuf, ed., *Law-Making in the Global Community* (Carolina Academic Press 1982)

Ali E. Hillal Dessouki, ed., *Islamic Resurgence in the Arab World* (Praeger Publishers 1981)